MANAGEMENT, WORK
AND ORGANISATIONS

Series editors:

ONE WEEK LOAN

This series of new textbooks _____ the _____ of _____ and general _____ ____ ____nal behaviour and related business _____ and _____ field. _____ as been specially commiss_____ _____ by leading experts in a clear and accessib__ ___y. ___ books _____ serious and challenging m_____ _____ analytical rather than prescriptive approach and are particularly suitable for use by students with no prior special____ knowledge.

The series is relevant for many business and management courses, including MBA and post-experience cou____, specialist masters and postgraduate diplomas, professional courses and final-year undergraduate courses. These texts have become essential reading at business and management schools worldwide.

Published

Paul Blyton and Peter Turnbull **The Dynamics of Employee Relations (3rd edn)**
Sharon C. Bolton **Emotion Management in the Workplace**
Peter Boxall and John Purcell **Strategy and Human Resource Management**
J. Martin Corbett **Critical Cases in Organisational Behaviour**
Keith Grint **Leadership**
Irena Grugulis **Skills, Training and Human Resource Development**
Damian Hodgson and Svetlana Cicmil **Making Projects Critical**
Marek Korczynski **Human Resource Management in Service Work**
Karen Legge **Human Resource Management: Anniversary Edition**
Helen Rainbird (ed.) **Training in the Workplace**
Jill Rubery and Damian Grimshaw **The Organisation of Employment**
Harry Scarbrough (ed.) **The Management of Expertise**
Hugh Scullion and Margaret Linehan **International Human Resource Management**
Adrian Wilkinson, Mick Marchington, Tom Redman and Ed Snape **Managing with Total Quality Management**
Colin C. Williams **Rethinking the Future of Work**
Diana Winstanley and Jean Woodall (eds) **Ethical Issues in Contemporary Human Resource Management**

For more information on titles in the Series please go to www.palgrave.com/busines/mwo

Invitiation to authors

The Series Editors welcome proposals for new books within the Management, Work and Organisations series. These should be sent to Paul Thompson (p.thompson@strath.ac.uk) at the Dept of HRM, Strathclyde Business School, University of Strathclyde, 50 Richmond St Glasgow G1 1XT

Series Standing Order
If you would like to receive future titles in this series as they are published, you can make use of our standing order facility. To place a standing order please contact your bookseller or, in case of difficulty, write to us at the address below with your name and address and the name of the series. Please state with which title you wish to begin your standing order.
Customer Services Department, Macmillan Distribution Ltd
Houndmills, Basingstoke, Hampshire RG21 6XS, England

Books by the same author

A Commodified World? mapping the limits of capitalism

A Helping Hand: harnessing self-help to combat social exclusion (with J. Windebank).

Alternative Economic Spaces (co-edited with A. Leyshon and R. Lee)

Bridges into Work? an evaluation of Local Exchange and Trading Schemes (LETS) (with T. Aldridge, R. Lee, A. Leyshon, N. Thrift and J. Tooke)

Cash-in-Hand Work: the underground sector and hidden economy of favours.

Community Self-Help (with D. Burns and J. Windebank)

Consumer Services and Economic Development

Corporate City? partnership, participation and partition in urban development in Leeds (co-edited with G. Haughton)

Examining the Nature of Domestic Labour

Informal Employment in the Advanced Economies: implications for work and welfare (with J. Windebank)

Perspectives towards Sustainable Environmental Development (co-edited with G. Haughton)

Poverty and the Third Way (with J. Windebank)

Revitalising Deprived Urban Neighbourhoods: an assisted self-help approach (with J. Windebank)

The Hidden Enterprise Culture: entrepreneurship in the underground economy

Rethinking the future of work

Directions and visions

Colin C. Williams

University of Sheffield

First published 2007 by
PALGRAVE MACMILLAN
Houndmills, Basingstoke, Hampshire RG21 6XS and
175 Fifth Avenue, New York, N.Y. 10010
Companies and representatives throughout the world

PALGRAVE MACMILLAN is the global academic imprint of the Palgrave
Macmillan division of St. Martin's Press, LLC and of Palgrave Macmillan Ltd.
Macmillan® is a registered trademark in the United States, United Kingdom
and other countries. Palgrave is a registered trademark in the European
Union and other countries.

ISBN-13: 978–1–4039–9371–7
ISBN-10: 1–4039–9371–8

This book is printed on paper suitable for recycling and made from fully
managed and sustained forest sources.

A catalogue record for this book is available from the British Library.

Library of Congress Cataloging-in-Publication Data
Williams, Colin C., 1961–
    Rethinking the future of work:directions and visions/Colin C. Williams.
        p.   cm. — (Management, work and organisations)
    Includes bibliographical references and index.
    ISBN-13: 978–1–4039–9371–7 (pbk.)
    ISBN-10: 1–4039–9371–8 (pbk.)
    1. Work—Forecasting. 2. Labor—Forecasting. 3. Employment
    forecasting. I. Title.
    HD4904.W489 2007
    306.3′60112—dc22   2006052767

10   9   8   7   6   5   4   3   2   1
16   15   14   13   12   11   10   09   08   07

Printed and bound in China

This book is dedicated to Jan and Toby

Contents

List of tables

List of figures

List of case studies

Acknowledgements

Many individuals have provided advice and guidance and a number of organizations have funded research projects that directly feed into the writing of this book.

The Joseph Rowntree Foundation funded a study of work practices in the UK deprived urban neighbourhoods, and the Countryside Commission funded a follow-up mirror project on rural areas. Both projects have proven immeasurably useful in understanding the contemporary work practices discussed in Chapter 3. The Economic and Social Research Council (ESRC) grant, 'Evaluating Local Exchange and Trading Schemes as a tool for social cohesion' (R000237208), meanwhile, conducted in collaboration with Theresa Aldridge, Roger Lee, Andrew Leyshon, Nigel Thrift and Jane Tooke, directly fed into the writing of the relevant section in Chapter 12.

Various UK government departments and agencies, furthermore, have funded projects on various aspects of work organization. The Office of the Deputy Prime Minister (ODPM) in the UK supported, in collaboration with Mel Evans and Stephen Syrett, a review of work and worklessness in deprived neighbourhoods. The Small Business Service (SBS) and Small Business Council (SBC) financially supported an investigation of small business working practices and in this regard, I am grateful to both members of the SBC Steering Group, especially Paul Harrod, Monder Ram and Simon Topman for their insights, as well as numerous SBS officials, but particularly Sheena O'Sullivan and Caroline Berry. And finally, the Office of National Statistics (ONS) supported an evaluation of data on informal work and entrepreneurship, and I owe a great deal of debt to my collaborators, namely Rebecca Harding of London Business School (now at Deloitte), Simon King of Hedra PLC and Angela Zvesper of Social Research Associates.

Two European Commission projects, funded under the Targeted Socio-Economic Research (TSER) programme, meanwhile, proved immensely stimulating in helping me think through different visions of the future of work and welfare. First, and in relation to the six-nation 'Inclusion through Participation' (INPART) project, managed by Rik van Berkel, I would like to thank all who participated, particularly my UK colleagues, namely Maurice Roche and Jo Cooke. Second, the 12-nation 'Comparative Social Inclusion

Policy and Citizenship in Europe: Towards a new social model' project, provided a wonderful forum for testing out some of the ideas contained herein. In this regard, I would like to thank the following for their inputs: Claire Ainesley, Rik van Berkel, Soledad Garcia, Henning Hansen, Pedro Hespanha, Iver Hornemann-Møller, Angelika Kofler, Jens Lind, Enzo Mingione, Maurice Roche, David Smith, Ben Valkenburg, Jacques Vilrokx and Enid Wistrich.

With regard to understanding the trajectories of work organization in East-Central Europe discussed in Chapters 3 and 4, I need to thank, first, the ESRC for funding a project entitled 'Surviving Post-socialism: Evaluating the role of the informal sector in Ukraine' (grant no. RES-000-22-0985) and, secondly, the University of Leicester School of Management for supporting an empirical study of work practices in Moscow. Both enabled a much deeper appreciation of the issues than would otherwise have been possible. In relation to both projects, my deep gratitude is expressed to my collaborator, John Round.

There are a multitude of additional academic colleagues who have either discussed some of the issues over the years or read drafts of various chapters, namely Peter Armstrong, Liliana Bàculo, Danny Burns, Angus Cameron, Jenny Cameron, Julie Gibson, Katherine Graham, Graham Haughton, Bill Jordan, Roger Lee, Enrico Marcelli, Sue Marlow, Graham May, Pete North, Martin Parker, Monder Ram, Piet Renooy, Michael Samers and Richard White. As always, however, I owe by far the largest debt to my long-time research collaborator, Jan Windebank, without whom none of this would have been possible.

Last but not least, I would like to thank all of my colleagues in the School of Management at the University of Sheffield. Indeed, this book could not have been completed without a period of study leave provided by the University of Sheffield.

The usual disclaimers of course apply. The ideas conveyed in this book are those of the author and do not necessarily represent the position of any of the above individuals, organizations or institutions.

1

Introduction: rethinking the future of work

There are many visions of the future of work. Indeed, there seem to be as many visions as there are commentators. For some, the future of work is rosy; for others, full of despair. For some, radical changes are about to take place; for others, the future will be much like the present apart from a few changes at the margins. Some visions of the future are portrayed as scientifically rigorous descriptions, others as prescriptions of what ought to be.

With such a cacophony of competing voices and styles of writing, one might think that somebody would have attempted to review the multitude of claims about the future of work, not least so that those new to this subject could gain an overarching appreciation of it. In any other social scientific topic, after all, undertaking a review of the previous literature is the necessary first step taken before putting forward one's own new insight so that it is grounded in what has gone before. When writing on the future of work, however, this process appears to be more the exception rather than the rule. Similarly, in any other subject in the social sciences, re-packaging previous ideas and re-labelling them so that what is being propounded appears 'new' is wholly unacceptable, especially if one fails to acknowledge what has gone before. Yet this approach is far too often the norm when studying the future of work. The outcome is that those reading on this subject are too often left marooned with no compass, swept along without bearings in a torrent of apparently 'original' insights.

The first intention of this book, therefore, is to provide readers interested in the future of work with an understanding of the range of competing perspectives so that they can, on the one hand, locate previous literature when reading yet another supposedly 'new' vision and, on the other hand, escape from travelling round and round the same island reading similar texts and instead venture out across the whole ocean of thought available to them. Although others have indeed attempted to fill this void before by providing sketches of the competing visions of the future of work (Nolan and Wood, 2003; Ransome, 1999; Thompson and Warhurst, 1998; White et al., 2004), on the whole, these have tended to be detailed charts of particular continents of thought. This book, in contrast, seeks to map the whole world and, in so doing, to provide a more comprehensive tour of the multiple perspectives than so far attempted.

In the process of mapping this diverse array of perspectives, my second intention is to make some significant advances in how the future of work is thought about. Until now, as will be shown throughout this book, it has too often been the case that commentators have employed a very similar mode of reasoning when thinking about the future and, in doing so, have produced over-simplistic stories of what is occurring in lived practice. Once one begins to analyse the multifarious visions of the future of work, that is, it becomes apparent that a very similar storyline is commonly adopted across many of these contrasting perspectives. To begin to gain an insight into the nature of this storyline, consider for example the following visions, some of which are more widely believed than others:

- Products and services are increasingly being produced and delivered by people in formal jobs meaning that informal work (e.g., subsistence production, unpaid exchange) is disappearing almost entirely from the economic landscape (i.e., henceforth referred to as the 'formalization' of work thesis).
- Capitalism is spreading its tentacles ever wider and deeper to colonize the few remaining vestiges of the world that remain untouched by its grip (i.e., variously called the 'commodification', 'marketization' or 'commercialization' thesis).
- There is a rapid movement towards an open world economy with businesses increasingly operating in a de-regulated seamless global marketplace (i.e., the 'globalization' thesis) as regulated national-level economies disappear.
- Industrial society is being replaced by post-industrial societies (i.e., the 'post-industrialism' thesis).
- Post-Fordist flexible work practices are increasingly replacing Fordist mass production (i.e., the 'post-Fordism' thesis).
- Post-bureaucratic work organization is steadily replacing bureaucratic work organization (i.e., the 'post-bureaucracy' thesis).

What, therefore, is the common argument or storyline being adopted across all these perspectives? The first step in constructing their story in each and every one of these visions is that they marshal most, if not all, economic life into one side or the other of a dichotomy which is deemed crucial for understanding the future of work (e.g., Fordist and post-Fordist work practices, bureaucratic and post-bureaucratic work organizations, informal and formal work, non-commodified and commodified work). Second, and having squeezed all of economic life into this dualism, the two sides are then ordered into a temporal sequence whereby one side is seen as universally replacing the other. Finally, and to depict this one-dimensional linear trajectory of work, some label is created which usually involves using some '-ation' (e.g., formalization, globalization, commodification), '-ism' (e.g., post-industrialism, informationalism) or 'post-something-or-other' (e.g., post-capitalism, post-Fordism, post-bureaucracy).

This narrative structure is a popular device. It is used not only in most of the best-selling 'pop-futurism' written by seer-like management gurus, but also in much of the serious academic writing presented in a fastidious manner as accurate scientific portrayals of the changes underway. It is also a very powerful device. As evidence of the persuasiveness of such a storytelling technique, one has only to consider how some of these dualistic either/or visions are often taken to be facts or descriptions about the future of work with few doubting the yarns that they spin. Indeed, it is precisely this recognition that some such stories have achieved the status of 'facts' about the future of work (as if such a thing could exist) that this book is being written.

When most dominant visions of the future of work, that is, are based on pinpointing a dichotomy and then ordering the two sides into a temporal sequence in which one immutably, inevitably and universally replaces the other over time, and such narratives achieve the status of facts about the future, then the need for a critical text that cuts through such simplistic visions becomes apparent. Rather than pay homage to tales about a universal linear trajectory towards some '-ation', '-ism' or 'post-something-or-other', as is the case in so many texts that seek to portray the future in instantly understandable terms, I instead wish to show here that these over-simplified narratives need to be transcended.

By evaluating critically each of these narratives in turn, the intention of this book is to unravel how these are not universal but particularistic trends. These one-dimensional 'stairway to heaven' (or hell) views of 'development' and 'progress', so commonly adopted by futurists – whether of the pop-futurist or serious academic variety – will be shown here to result from looking in particular places in particular ways and universalizing the trends identified. The outcome, it will be shown, is that a gross injustice is done to the complex and multiple directions of change that are occurring in lived experience. In consequence, rather than reproduce what Thompson and McHugh (2002: 169) call 'The basic pattern . . . of stereotypical polarization, limited evidence and neglect of diversity, [which] tends to be produced in each new generation of macro arguments', the objective throughout this book will be to display the need for a more kaleidoscopic view (c.f., Tsoukas and Cummings, 1997) in which there are no universal linear logics but instead many fragments moving in different directions in various parts of the picture.

For example, in some particular nations, sectors and occupations, it is possible to identify a shift towards post-bureaucratic management practices, such as in some Western nations, the advertising industry and the higher echelons of management. In other nations, sectors and occupations, however, such a trend is notable by its absence. This is similarly the case with other trends. In some nations, sectors, occupations and places, post-Fordist practices can be identified as taking hold. In others, however, there is the continuing dominance, even resurgence, of Fordist and Taylorist practices, as witnessed in 'burger flipping' service occupations (e.g., Ritzer, 1998). In some places and population groups, similarly, products and services are increasingly produced and delivered through formal employment but in others subsistence work, unpaid exchange and informal employment are growing. And although a commodification of work is occurring in some populations (e.g., amongst Western women), de-commodification is apparent amongst others (e.g., Western men), always assuming of course that all work can be crammed into such dichotomies. Throughout this book, therefore, it will be shown that once one evaluates critically each of the one-dimensional linear visions of the future of work that commentators assert are occurring (e.g., from Fordism to post-Fordism, informal to formal work, non-commodified to commodified practices, bureaucracy to post-bureaucracy), it becomes apparent that divergent trajectories are being pursued in different populations.

The consequent argument developed in this book about the future of work is that there are no universal linear paths being pursued but, rather, multiple and divergent trends depending on where and how you look. Although this might not superficially appear so earth-shattering as the visions conveyed by the best-selling futurologists with their simplistic one-dimensional linear storylines, such a portrayal is perhaps more in keeping with the changes in lived practice being experienced by different people in varying places. With no linear trajectories, no immutable forces, no inevitable tendencies, but instead heterogeneous development paths, numerous questions arise that have so far received little attention and will need to be addressed about the degree to which the future is open. There is a lot of ground to cover, however, before reaching that point.

Structure of the book

To understand the full range of contemporary perspectives towards the future of work, this book is divided into three parts. Part 1 introduces three narratives (often treated as 'facts') concerning the trajectory of work that hold considerable sway over how the future of work is envisaged. These are the stories of a supposedly universal shift towards formal work (formalization), capitalist endeavour (commodification) and an open de-regulated world economy (globalization). Taking each in turn, Part 1 will reveal the complex and multiple directions of change in different populations and places so as to paint a more multi-dimensional picture of the trajectories of work than these dominant narratives convey. Part 2 then turns its attention to some of the major trajectories propounded so far as the future of employment is concerned – namely the shifts from an industrial to information/knowledge economy, Fordism to post-Fordism, and bureaucratic to post-bureaucratic management – while Part 3 explores a range of commentaries on the future of work that have so far received little coverage in management and business studies texts. These are the visions that provide counter-narratives to the dominant formalization, commodification and globalization theses by discussing post-employment, post-capitalist and localist green visions of the future of work respectively.

In Part 1, therefore, the dominant narratives concerning the future of work will be introduced and evaluated critically. Chapter 2 commences this process by introducing three grand narratives that have an over-bearing influence on how the future of work is envisaged at the present juncture in history. To depict how the configuration of economies is changing, commentators commonly differentiate three modes of delivering goods and services, namely the 'market' (private sector), the 'state' (public sector) and the 'informal sector'. Viewed in these terms, this chapter reveals the current widespread consensus that most nations are witnessing a common trajectory of work (where the future is seen as a linear extrapolation of a perceived past trajectory rather than in cyclical or dialectical terms).

First, the future of work is popularly seen to involve an ongoing 'formalization' of work in the sense that goods and services are increasingly produced and delivered through the formal (market and state) sphere under the social relations of formal employment rather than through the informal sphere (termed the 'formalization' thesis). Secondly, this formal production and delivery of goods and services is depicted as increasingly occurring through the market sector (rather than by the state or informal sphere) by capitalist firms for the purpose of profit; in other words, there is what is variously called a 'commodification', 'commercialization' or 'marketization' of economic activity. Finally, this formalization and commodification of work is seen to be increasingly taking place with an open (de-regulated) world economy (i.e., the globalization thesis). Despite all three narratives being widely accepted as accurate accounts of the direction of change, this chapter starts to put question marks against them by revealing that despite (or perhaps because of) their near universal acceptance, evidence is seldom provided to corroborate them.

The next three chapters then evaluate critically each of these supposed descriptions or 'facts' about the direction of work. The widely recited storyline of a linear and universal demise of the informal economy and a concomitant growth of the formal economy (i.e., the 'formalization of work' thesis) is the focus of Chapter 3. Until now, this narrative of 'progress' and view of the trajectory of economic development has exerted a firm grip on how the future of work is envisaged. Indeed, so strong is its hold that the degree of formalization has been taken as a measuring rod and used to define the Third World countries as 'developing' and that of the First World as 'advanced'. In this vision, the persistence of supposedly 'traditional' informal activities is a manifestation of 'backwardness' which it is assumed will disappear and be replaced by formal work with economic 'advancement' and 'modernization'. As such, the future of work is cast in stone; there is a uni-dimensional and linear trajectory so far as the future of work is concerned and it is one in which there is a natural and inevitable process of formalization. In Chapter 3, however, reviewing a wide array of evidence from the Western 'advanced' economies, the transition economies of East-Central Europe and the majority (Third) world, little evidence is found of any universal linear progression towards formalization. Instead, heterogeneous development paths are identified not only across but also within these different regions of the world. There is even evidence within the advanced economies that although some nations have witnessed formalization, others have witnessed an informalization of working life over the past four decades. The outcome will be to raise strong doubts over this meta-narrative until now portrayed as an immutable fact about the trajectory of work and which has closed off the future, not least by its adherents castigating visions of alternative futures as prescriptive utopianism.

Chapter 4 then turns its attention to a second widely held narrative that has similarly curtailed the scope of what is deemed realistic and feasible so far as the future of work is concerned. This is the discourse that there is no alternative to capitalism. In this vision, a universal process of what is variously termed 'commercialization', 'marketization' or 'commodification' is seen to be taking place, whereby capitalism becomes evermore powerful, expansive and totalizing as it penetrates deeper into each and every corner of economic life and stretches its tentacles wider across the globe to colonize those remaining areas previously left untouched by its powerful force. Indeed, for many, this vision of the future has taken on the semblance of an indisputable and irrefutable fact. This is the case not only amongst neo-liberals who extol the virtues of, and celebrate, such a future but also amongst the swelling ranks of those heavily opposed to its encroachment into every crevice of life where a certain fatalistic despondence prevails about its inevitability. This unstoppable transition towards a commodified world is so widely held and felt that it is perhaps difficult today to consider any other future. There really does seem to be 'no alternative to capitalism'. Analysing whether capitalist firms rather than the state and the community increasingly produce goods and services, however, Chapter 4 will reveal not only a much shallower penetration of capitalism than often assumed but also how this is far from a universal trajectory. Again, different trajectories are identified in various areas and amongst different populations, suggesting that the direction of change is rather more heterogeneous and divergent than assumed by adherents to this thesis.

Chapter 5 then evaluates critically the third dominant pillar that has acted to close off how the future of work is envisaged. This is the widely recited story about the advent of an evermore open world economy (i.e., the globalization thesis) and how people, organizations and governments have no choice but to bow to the power of this inevitable force. Reviewing the evidence of the degree of economic, financial, cultural and political globalization, this chapter finds that the imagined economies of globalization are very much a product of a particular way of looking at the world and a result of only looking in particular narrow confined spaces, and that once one interrogates this phenomenon, a very different picture emerges of the shallow and uneven contours of globalization.

Having contested these three dominant grand narratives that have closed off what is considered valid regarding the future of work and displayed the heterogeneous and diverse directions of change occurring in different places, Part 2 then turns its attention to some visions regarding the changes taking place in one type of work, namely employment. Once again, these perspectives delineate a dichotomy of organizational forms and then depict a linear temporal progression from one opposite to the other over time. As Table 1.1 displays, these visions are of three broad types. First of all, there are those that represent the future of work organization primarily in terms of a shift from an industrial society to a post-industrial, information or knowledge economy. Secondly, there are those depicting the future of work in terms of a shift in employment practices from Fordist to post-Fordist practices, and, finally, those portraying the shift in work organization as being from bureaucracy to post-bureaucracy, or what is sometimes

Table 1.1 Dichotomous visions of futures for employment

Nature of change	Old	New
Sector-based	Industrial society	Post-industrial Knowledge economy Information economy
Employment Practices	Fordism	Post-Fordism
Organizational	Bureaucracy Compliance Direct control Hard human resource management	Post-bureaucracy Commitment Indirect control Soft human resource management

referred to as from direct to indirect control, compliance to commitment, hard to soft human resource management, or industrial relations to human resource management. In Part 2, each is evaluated in turn so as to display the very real dangers of conflating present-day differences across space, sectors and occupations into some temporal sequence where one side of the coin (e.g., Fordism, bureaucracy) is viewed as being supplanted by the other side of the coin (e.g., post-Fordism, post-bureaucracy).

In Chapter 6, the various visions that view 'industrial society' as being replaced with a post-industrial/information/knowledge economy are first reviewed through the eyes of both those who view this transition as a positive move and those who view such a transition in more pessimistic terms. Following this, the degree to which this can be viewed as a universal trend is evaluated critically. This will reveal that for all of the talk of the advent of post-industrialism, the knowledge economy or the information society, there is little evidence that it has penetrated either as deeply or as widely as many of the 'exagger' authors associated with this perspective suggest.

Following this, Chapter 7 turns attention to an alternative popular dichotomy used to depict the direction of change in the employment place and which has perhaps had an even wider purchase on how scholars envisage the future of employment. This is the perspective that envisages a transition to be taking place in work practices from a Fordist to a post-Fordist mode of economic organization. Similar to the previous chapter, here, this thesis is again outlined, along with its optimistic and pessimistic variants, followed by a critical evaluation of the degree to which it can be identified as occurring.

Chapter 8 then discusses the idea of a transition from bureaucratic to post-bureaucratic management practices in a similar vein. This again will reveal the limitations of attempting to squeeze the future of work organization into such a dichotomous and one-dimensional linear transition. Although this will be shown to be increasingly recognized, as displayed in recent discussions of the emergence of 'hybrid' managerial practices that display both bureaucratic and post-bureaucratic managerial styles, the argument of this chapter is that these are not new hybrid forms but rather have perhaps always existed and it is simply the case that the dualistic thought of bureaucratic and post-bureaucratic management was incapable of recognizing such hybrids.

Common to all these post-industrial, post-Fordist and post-bureaucracy theses is an implicit acceptance that a process of formalization and commodification is taking place in the nature of work. Indeed, if this were not assumed, they would not focus upon the employment place, and the employment place alone, when considering the changing nature of work, nor would they focus their attention within the sphere of employment on the commodified realm. In Chapter 9, however, a vision of the future of employment that accepts the formalization thesis, but questions the commodification thesis, will be reviewed. This is a perspective towards the future of work that envisages the future of work organization where non-capitalist employment comes to the fore. Until now, due to the dominance of the commodification thesis, this vision has been seldom discussed in business and management texts, and when it has been, it has been portrayed simply as a form of prescriptive utopianism. This chapter, nevertheless, reveals that such a vision is far from being more prescriptive than any other vision so far discussed. First, this chapter introduces those visions that depict a shift from capitalist to non-capitalist employment; secondly, it discusses those which envisage this future of work in a positive light; thirdly, those which view it in a more negative light; and, finally, the extent to which employment practices appear to be moving in this direction is evaluated.

In Part 3, attention moves away from perspectives solely discussing changes in the employment place and towards those visions that reject either descriptively or prescriptively the meta-narratives of formalization, commodification and/or globalization and, in so doing, construct alternative views of the future of work (Table 1.2). Indeed, it is the incorporation of such literature into this book that marks it out as distinct from other business and management texts.

In the opening chapter of Part 3, the 'third way' vision of the direction of change is evaluated. To review this vision of the future of work, this chapter first of all outlines the first way (neo-liberalism) and the second way (socialism) thought so as to reveal how the debates between them were (or are) about the best way of achieving

Table 1.2 Dominant visions and counter-visions of the future of work

Dominant visions	Counter-visions
Formalization	Informalization of welfare: third way visions (Chapter 10) of work: post-employment visions (Chapter 11)
Commodification	De-commodification of employment: non-capitalist visions (Chapter 9) of work: post-capitalist visions of work (Chapter 12)
Globalization	Localization of work and welfare: green visions (Chapter 13)

formalization, commodification and globalization. Following this, attention then turns towards depicting the advent of 'third way' thought and the ways in which this expands out visions for the future of work to incorporate work beyond employment. This will reveal that even though the third way visions recognize work beyond employment, a key, if artificial, distinction is made between its relevance to 'economic' and 'welfare' policy in this approach. The outcome is that it is in the sphere of welfare provision and this realm alone that the third way exponents believe that not only private and public sector provision but also a third prong of the 'third sector' or 'civil society' needs to be harnessed (e.g., Giddens, 2000). In the realm of 'economic' policy, however, its vision of the future of work remains entrenched in an employment-centred ideology. This starkly contrasts with the subsequent approaches that will be outlined in Part 3 , which variously view informal work as becoming a complement or alternative to formal employment (see Chapter 11), non-capitalist economic practices as an alternative to commodified work (see Chapter 12) and locally oriented work beyond employment as a palliative to neo-liberal globalization (see Chapter 13).

Chapter 11, therefore, explores those visions of the future of work that contest the meta-narrative of formalization on descriptive and/or normative grounds. In 'organizing work in a post-employment world', those perspectives that envisage the future of work to lie in the development of informal work as an alternative and/or complement to the formal realm will be reviewed (e.g., Archibugi, 2000; Aznar, 1981; Beck, 2000; Delors, 1979; Gorz, 1999; Greffe, 1981; Lalonde and Simmonet, 1978; Laville, 1995, 1996; Mayo, 1996; Rifkin, 1996; Sachs, 1984) along with their reasons for advocating a reduction in the hegemony of the formal economy, and the initiatives being pursued to implement such an organization of work.

Chapter 12, meanwhile, explores visions of the future of work that have contested the narrative of commodification. In these 'post-capitalist' visions of the future of work, as will be displayed, the argument is that there is a need to cease mapping an evermore commodified world because of the performative effects of such a discourse. In other words, such a mapping is viewed as creating what is then seen, and for these analysts there is a need to recognize, value and create non-capitalist economic practices that are already here and emerging so as to shine a light on the demonstrable construction of alternative possibilities and futures (e.g., Byrne *et al.*, 2001; Community Economies Collective, 2001; Escobar, 1995; Gibson-Graham, 1995, 1996; Gibson-Graham and Ruccio, 2001; Williams, 2005a,b). For these analysts, a discursive analysis of the commodification thesis is advocated, coupled with the articulation of alternative regimes of representation and practice in order to imagine and enact alternative futures for work.

Chapter 13 then explores those visions of the future of work that contest the narrative of globalization by arguing for greater localization in order to foster a future of work which is environmentally sustainable (e.g., Dobson, 1993; Ekins and Max-Neef, 1992; Fodor, 1999; Goldsmith *et al.*, 1995; Henderson, 1978, 1999; Hoogendijk, 1993; Mander and Goldsmith, 1996; McBurney, 1990; Robertson, 1991; Roseland, 1998; Trainer, 1996; Warburton, 1998; Wright, 1997). An important facet of this chapter will be to distinguish between the 'environmental-lite' approaches that foster business-as-usual and the 'deeper green' perspectives that promulgate a radically different future for work grounded in localization and self-reliance.

Finally, Chapter 14 synthesizes the previous chapters to draw together the arguments and evaluate critically the diverse ways in which the future of work has been envisaged. Displaying how common to nearly all visions is some dichotomy that concocts in a temporal manner a linear transformation from some 'old' to 'new' form of work organization, this chapter then summarizes how such single linear trajectories are too simple to capture the diverse trajectories taking place. All these perspectives towards the future of work are the product of looking in particular places at what is taking place and extrapolating from these places wider trends, none of which wholly capture and reflect the heterogeneous directions in which work is moving in the contemporary world. Although in some nations, sectors, occupations or population groups, shifts towards formalization, commodification, globalization, information society, post-Fordism, post-bureaucracy and non-capitalist employment practices can be identified, once the lens is widened and other nations, sectors, occupations or population groups examined, shifts in the opposite direction can be marked out, namely informalization, de-commodification, localization, industrialism, Fordism, bureaucracy and capitalist practices. There are multiple, often contradictory, trajectories being pursued in different places. This concluding chapter then explores the various issues that arise regarding how the future of work is thought about from this more kaleidoscopic view where there are many fragments moving in different directions in various parts of the picture.

part 1

Dominant perspectives on the direction of work

2

The dominant narratives

Introduction

All societies have to produce, distribute and allocate the goods and services required by their citizens. Every society, therefore, has an economy of some type. Economies, however, can be organized in various ways. To depict the configuration of economies, many commentators commonly differentiate three modes of delivering goods and services, namely the 'market' (private sector), the 'state' (public sector) and the 'community' (informal or third sector) (Boswell, 1990; Giddens, 1998; Gough, 2000; Polanyi, 1944; Powell, 1990; Putterman, 1990; Thompson et al., 1991), although different labels are sometimes used, with Polanyi (1944) referring to 'market exchange', 'redistribution' and 'reciprocity', and Giddens (1998) discussing 'private', 'public' and 'civil society'.

Taking these three modes of delivering goods and services as its starting point, this chapter will reveal how a widespread consensus exists on how work will be organized in the future. First, it is believed that goods and services will be increasingly produced and delivered through the formal (market and state) sphere rather than through the community or informal sphere (i.e., henceforth known as the 'formalization' thesis). Secondly, it is held that this formal production and delivery of goods and services will increasingly occur through the market sector (rather than by the state or informal sphere). This will be referred to as the 'commodification' thesis. Finally, this process of commodification is asserted to be increasingly taking place within an open world economy in which businesses operate in a de-regulated seamless global marketplace (i.e., henceforth known as the 'globalization' thesis).

Here, it will be shown that these three meta-narratives about the future of work, namely formalization, commodification and globalization, are widely accepted as truths, even 'facts', about how work will be organized in the future. Yet despite being viewed as descriptions of the future, and visions challenging them denoted as prescriptive utopianism, this chapter uncovers that evidence is seldom sought to corroborate these supposed trajectories of work.

13

The formalization thesis

The formalization thesis asserts that goods and services are increasingly provided through the formal economy (the state and market spheres) and that the informal economy is in demise. Here, the intention is to reveal how this vision of the future of work, often seen as descriptive of what is taking place rather than as prescriptive of what should occur, not only constrains what is considered feasible and valid in the future but also marginalizes those contesting this vision as prescriptive utopian dreamers, despite the lack of evidence to corroborate this thesis.

To know whether goods and services are increasingly provided by the formal economy (the state and market spheres) and the informal economy dwindling, it is necessary to be able to differentiate 'work' from 'leisure' since unless this is done, one cannot know whether there is an ongoing shift in work from the informal to the formal economy. Some might assert that it is whether a task is paid or not that defines whether an activity is work or leisure. This, however, is not the case. Many unpaid tasks are viewed as 'work' so far as those doing these tasks are concerned, including housework, do-it-yourself activity, and caring for children and elderly people. Alternatively, therefore, it might be suggested that work can be distinguished from leisure according to the type of task being conducted. Yet, although tasks such as watching films, cooking or writing can be leisure, they can also be work. Film critics are engaged in work when watching films, chefs when cooking and authors when writing.

The most widely accepted way of distinguishing work from leisure, therefore, is to assess whether the task under consideration could be conducted by a third person (see Reid, 1934). If one is engaged in cooking as a leisure pursuit, for example, a third person could not undertake this task. A third person could undertake the cooking, however, if this task were perceived as work. The third-person criterion, or what can be seen as the possibility of labour substitution, thus distinguishes activities in the fuzzy area between work and non-work. Using this distinction between work and leisure, one can then evaluate whether a formalization of work is taking place. That is, it enables the differentiation of work from leisure so that one can assess whether an increasing amount of the total workload is being conducted through formal employment and a decreasing amount through 'informal' work, an accurate adjective that portrays how the social relations differ from the more 'formal' social relations of official employment.

Evaluating the amount of formal employment is relatively straightforward compared with evaluating the amount of informal work. Data is readily available in many countries, for example, on the numbers in employment, the hours worked and so forth. Determining the amount of informal work and how it is changing over time, however, is less simple and data not so readily available. A common way forward, therefore, is to break down informal work into its component parts for the purpose of estimating its

	Paid	Unpaid
Exchange	Formal employment	Volunteering
	Undeclared work	Reciprocal exchange
Non-exchange	–	Self-provisioning

Figure 2.1 A typology of work

magnitude. As Figure 2.1 identifies, there are at least three distinct categories of informal work. These are as follows.

1. 'Self-provisioning': It is unpaid work undertaken by household members for themselves and each other. This ranges from domestic labour through unpaid caring activities conducted for and by household members to do-it-yourself home maintenance and improvement work.
2. 'Unpaid community work': It is work provided on an unpaid basis by and for the extended family, social or neighbourhood networks and more formal voluntary and community groups, and ranges from kinship exchange, through friendship/neighbourly reciprocal exchanges, to one-way volunteering for voluntary organizations.
3. 'Paid informal exchange': Here legal goods and services are exchanged for money, but these exchanges are unregistered by, or hidden from, the state for tax, social security or labour law purposes. Although some of this work is market-like and conducted for profit, some is also conducted as paid favours for kin, friends and neighbours and more akin to unpaid community work than market-like employment (Williams, 2004a).

Each form of work, to reiterate, is not composed of different tasks. For example, it cannot be asserted that cooking is domestic work and window cleaning is employment. Cooking, for instance, can be conducted as unpaid domestic work (e.g., where one cooks for oneself and/or one's family), unpaid community work (e.g., where one cooks for neighbours or friends on an unpaid basis), paid informal work (e.g., where one cooks in a restaurant on an off-the-books basis for 'informal' payments that are not declared to the government for tax, benefit or labour law purposes) or formal employment (e.g., where one is a formally employed chef either registered, self-employed or paid on a PAYE basis). Therefore, it is not the tasks that differentiate one form of work from another, but the social relations within which the work is embedded (Gershuny, 2000; Morris, 1994; Pahl, 1984; Williams and Windebank, 2003a). In the formalization thesis, the trajectory of work asserted to be taking place is one in which goods and services are increasingly provided through the social relations of formal employment. The shaded segment of Figure 2.1, in other words, is depicted as expanding, and the informal spheres of self-provisioning, unpaid community exchange and paid informal work as contracting.

This narrative of formalization is not only widely held but also at the heart of some of the most popular depictions of the trajectory of economic development. Consider, for example, how the world is conventionally divided up into First, Second and Third worlds. The First World, the supposedly 'advanced' economies of the West, is in major part so defined because it is viewed as having already undergone the transformation from informal to formal modes of production to the greatest extent. Based on the view that formalization is a natural and inevitable trajectory of economic development that all nations will and must follow, these First World nations are thus placed at the front of the queue in this linear and one-dimensional vision of economic development while those nations in the second and third worlds are positioned behind them in the queue due to their slower progression towards formalization. The way in which economies that are more grounded in 'community' or 'subsistence' are labelled 'backward' compared with economic systems that rely more on formal employment, meanwhile, is nowhere better seen than in those countries aggregated together under the banner of the Third World. Labelled 'developing', 'undeveloped' or 'under-developed' countries precisely due to their slowness in moving towards formalization, these name tags denote clearly that there is only one possible trajectory, as well as a singular 'route to progress', and it is towards formalization.

This powerful discourse of formalization, however, does not only describe the direction of change, hierarchically ordering countries in the present and informing them of their trajectory, but also serves to shape thinking about what action is required by supranational institutions, national governments, economic development agencies and individuals themselves. Take, for example, Western governments. Grounded in this grand narrative that details what constitutes 'progress', governments of Western nations have tended to concentrate exclusively on developing the formal economy and viewed informal work as at best playing a supporting role, and at worst deleterious to development and something to be formalized so as to allow this future of work to be implemented. It is similarly the case in the ex-socialist bloc of East-Central Europe where the whole thrust of economic policy has been focused upon how to facilitate the 'transition' to a formal market economy. In the majority (Third) world, it is again the pursuit of formalization that sets the economic policy agenda. One has only to consider the structural adjustment programmes applied to these countries to realize that a strong normative view exists that progress lies in encouraging a successful transformation towards an economic system where the formal economy becomes an increasingly dominant mode of producing and delivering goods and services. Throughout the world, therefore, the narrative of formalization whereby the formal economy replaces the informal sphere is not only a thesis viewed as descriptive of the trajectory of economic development but also a thesis that has shaped what is viewed as 'progress' (i.e., it asserts what should occur).

The formalization thesis, in consequence, is not just a theory that is seeking to reflect the supposed reality but is also being used to shape how work will be organized in the future. As Carrier (1998: 8) puts it, there is a 'conscious attempt to make the real world conform to the virtual image, justified by the claim that the failure of the real to conform to the idea is a consequence not merely of imperfections, but is a failure that itself has undesirable consequences'. In this so-called 'virtualism', the formalization thesis is thus more than merely a theory seeking to portray the trajectory of work. It is a prescriptive discourse 'driven by ideas and idealism [and] the desire to make the world conform to the image' (Carrier, 1998: 5). This is nowhere more finely displayed than in the seminal work of Escobar (1995) who displays how the so-called 'Third World economies' became viewed as a problem due to their lack of 'development' (i.e., formalization), and charts how a whole range of institutions and practices were constructed to help them conform more to the desired image.

The formalization thesis is therefore not so much a theory about the trajectory of work but more a prescription that superimposes onto formal and informal work normative judgements about their desirability. The formal economy in this thesis represents progress, modernity and advancement while the informal economy is indicative of backwardness, under-development and traditionalism. As such, this formalization thesis depicts the formal and the informal economy as what Derrida (1967) calls a 'binary hierarchy'. For him, Western thought is dominated by a hierarchical binary mode of thinking that, first, conceptualizes objects/identities as stable, bounded and constituted via negation and, secondly, reads the resultant binary structures in a hierarchical manner where the first term in any dualistic opposite (the superordinate) is endowed with positivity and the second term, the subordinate (or subservient) 'other' with negativity. Read through this lens, the depiction of the formal and the informal economy in the formalization thesis is one in which the informal economy represents the subordinate 'other' endowed with negativity while the formal economy is read as a superordinate and is attributed with positivity.

Indeed, to see how the informal economy is read in this dominant narrative as a subservient 'other' endowed with negativity, whose meaning is established solely in relation to its superordinate opposite (the formal economy), one needs look no further than the numerous adjectives to denote this sphere. As Latouche (1993: 129) recognizes, 'most of them simply qualify – either directly or indirectly – whatever is meant, in a *negative* way'. Variously referred to as 'non-structured', 'unpaid', 'non-official', 'non-organized', 'a-normal', 'hidden', 'a-legal', 'black', 'submerged', 'non-visible', 'shadow', 'a-typical' or 'irregular', this sphere is thus denoted as 'bereft of its own logic or identity other than can be indicated by this displacement away from, or even effacement of, the "normal"' (Latouche, 1993: 129). It is described by what it is not – what is absent from, or insufficient about, such work – relative to the formal sphere and this absence or insufficiency is always viewed as a negative feature of such work.

It is not simply the adjectives used to denote this sphere, however, that display how the formal/informal economy is represented as a binary hierarchy. The narrative of what constitutes progress in the formalization thesis similarly privileges the superordinate over the subordinate other. The informal sector is read as primitive or traditional, stagnant, marginal, residual, weak and about to be extinguished; a leftover of pre-capitalist formations that the inexorable and inevitable march of formalization will eradicate. Indeed, a universal natural and inevitable shift towards the formalization of goods and services provision is envisaged as societies become more 'advanced'. The persistence of supposedly traditional informal activities, therefore, is taken as a manifestation of 'backwardness' (e.g., Geertz, 1963) and it is assumed that such work will disappear with economic 'progress' (Lewis, 1959). Informal work is read as existing in the interstices, or as scattered and fragmented across the economic landscape. Formal work, by contrast, is represented as systematic, naturally expansive, and coextensive with the national or world economy.

Such a hierarchical and temporal sequencing of formal and informal work in the formalization thesis, therefore, focuses upon the imminent destruction of the informal economy, its proto-capitalist qualities, its weak and determined positions, viewing it either as 'the mere vestige of a disappearing past [or as] transitory or provisional' (Latouche, 1993: 49). Never is the informal sector represented as resilient, ubiquitous, capable of generative growth, or driving economic change in the formalization thesis. Nor is it represented as part of a multitude of different forms of work coexisting in the contemporary world but instead is always positioned in a temporal sequence where the informal sphere is characterized as a remnant of the past and 'backward', whilst the formal sphere is characterized as 'modern' and 'progressive'.

In the formalization thesis, furthermore, the informal sphere is near enough always viewed as possessing wholly negative attributes whilst the 'progressive' formal sphere is assumed to possess positive features. To see this, one needs look no further than how the populist commentator Jeremy Seabrook (2003: 9–10) views those working in the informal economy: 'The Western poor are dead souls ... hustlers and survivors, economic shadows in the shadow economy, the discouraged and despairing who have fallen through the bottom line of accounting systems.' Such a negative depiction of the informal sphere is not confined to populist commentators. Many political economists, recognizing that the informal sector is persistent and growing, have portrayed it as a new form of work emerging in late capitalism as a direct result of the advent of a de-regulated open world economy, which is encouraging a race-to-the-bottom. In this reading, informal workers are viewed as sharing the same characteristics subsumed under the heading of 'downgraded labour': they receive few benefits, low wages and have poor working conditions (e.g., Castells and Portes, 1989; Gallin, 2001; Portes, 1994; Sassen, 1997). In sum, the depiction is of the informal sphere as a pre-modern sector composed of workers engaged in exploitative and oppressive work, and thus a hindrance to 'progress'. Seldom are positive attributes assigned to the informal sphere, such as how this work is autonomous and often rewarding in nature for its participants.

The outcome, and whether the First, Second or Third Worlds are under the spotlight, is that the trajectory of work has become closed. There is only one future of work organization in this story and it is one in which there is a linear development path towards a formal world. Yet despite the widespread acceptance of this thesis along with its normative propositions, little evidence is ever brought to the fore to corroborate that this is indeed the direction of change and that formal work possesses positive attributes and informal work negative features. Instead, it is simply assumed that this is the case. Given that no other idea in the social sciences (with one or two exceptions discussed below) is simply accepted without evidence, there is a dire need for some rigorous investigation of this thesis, especially when it is recognized that it not only seeks to reflect lived practice but also acts as a narrative that is being used to shape how work will be organized in the future.

Imagine just for a moment that such an investigation revealed that economies were not becoming ever more formalized and that the formal sphere was actually receding in many quarters of the globe as a mode of producing and delivering goods and services. Rather than the future being cast in a straitjacket of the ever wider and deeper encroachment of the formal economy, the future would suddenly become much more open and full of endless new possibilities. For those believing in the grand narrative of formalization, this probably comes across at best as a romantic dream of somebody who wishes the future to be a return to some primitive past, and at worst as nonsensical. In Chapter 3, however, this questioning of formalization will be shown to be far from some pipedream. Once this narrative of a linear development path towards formalization is rigorously evaluated rather than merely accepted as 'fact', it becomes quickly apparent that some large question marks are required over this purported trajectory of work and that it is perhaps those assuming the ubiquity of formalization who are romanticizing the future rather than facing the stark reality that economies are moving in heterogeneous directions.

The commodification thesis

It is not only the story of an ongoing formalization of work whereby goods and services are increasingly produced and delivered through the formal (market and state) sphere rather than using informal work (e.g., unpaid self-provisioning, volunteering, reciprocity) that narrows the scope of what is considered feasible, valid and possible regarding the future of work. A further dominant narrative that severely constrains how the future is envisaged is the story that the formal production and delivery of goods and services is increasingly occurring through the market sector (rather than by the state or informal spheres). This is here termed the 'commodification' thesis but might also be termed the 'commercialization' or 'marketization' thesis.

At the present moment in history, the near universal belief is that of the three modes of delivering goods and services, the market is expanding while the other two spheres are contracting (e.g., Lee, 1999, 2000a; Polanyi, 1944; Scott, 2001; Smith, 2000; Watts, 1999).

Few can today imagine a future based on anything other than the further encroachment of capitalism. As Amin *et al.* (2002b: 60) pronounce, 'the pervasive reach of exchange-value society makes it ever more difficult to imagine and legitimate non-market forms of organization and provision'. This belief in the growing dominance of capitalism not only has few doubters but to even question such a belief is near heresy in the current climate. To do so results in one being marked out at best as prescribing some unachievable utopia, and at worst as some idealistic dreamer who is way out of touch with reality.

How, therefore, does the commodification thesis view the trajectory so far as the production and delivery of goods and services is concerned? Breaking this thesis down into its component parts, first, the belief is that goods and services are increasingly produced for exchange; secondly, these exchanges are seen to increasingly take place on a monetized basis; and, finally, this monetized exchange is viewed as increasingly occurring for the purpose of profit.

Given this definition of commodified work (monetized exchange for the purpose of profit), its opposite, non-commodified work, can be divided into three distinctive types of work (Figure 2.2). First, there is non-exchanged work, often referred to as 'self-provisioning', 'self-servicing', 'housework', 'subsistence' or 'domestic work'. Secondly, there is non-monetized exchange where goods and services are exchanged but no money changes hands. Finally, there is monetized exchange where the profit-motive is absent, as found in the public and 'not-for-profit' sectors.

For adherents to the commodification thesis, the shaded area of Figure 2.2, namely monetized for-profit exchange, is seen to be expanding while non-commodified economic practices are contracting. Although few would assert that the process of commodification is complete, the near universal belief is that economies are rapidly shifting towards such a situation. Populist writers such as Rifkin (2000: 3) argue that 'The marketplace is a pervasive force in our lives', political economists such as Ciscel and Heath (2001: 401) argue that capitalism is transforming 'every human interaction into a transient market exchange', while anthropologists such as Gudeman (2001: 144) purport that 'markets are subsuming greater portions of everyday life', and Carruthers

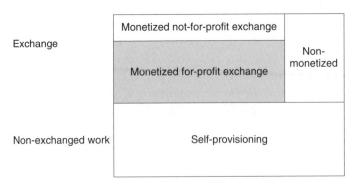

Figure 2.2 Forms of economic activity

and Babb (2000: 4) believe that there has been 'the near-complete penetration of market relations into our modern economic lives'. As Gough (2000: 17) puts it in the context of the changes in East-Central Europe,

> Following decolonization and the collapse of state socialism at the end of the 1980s, few areas of the world remain to resist the logic of capitalist markets and economic enterprises. This in turn is imposing the needs of capital in more and more areas of life and is weakening the resources of states and citizens to fight back.

Castree *et al.* (2004: 16–17) argue, similarly, 'that this is a predominantly capitalist world seems to us indisputable . . . there's scarcely a place on the planet where this mode of production does not have some purchase . . . this system of production arguably now has few, if any, serious economic rivals'. As Dicken (2003: 579–80) puts it,

> More than at any time in the past 50 years, virtually the entire world economy is now a *market economy*. The collapse of the state socialist systems at the end of the 1980s and their headlong rush to embrace the market, together with the more controlled opening-up of the Chinese economy since 1979, has created a very different global system from that which emerged after World War II. Virtually all parts of the world are now, to a greater or lesser extent, connected into an increasingly integrated system in which the parameters of the market dominate.

The outcome, in the eyes of a leading neo-liberal economist is that 'Capitalism stands alone as the only feasible way rationally to organize a modern economy' (De Soto, 2001: 1) and asserts that 'all plausible alternatives to capitalism have now evaporated' (De Soto, 2001: 13). It is not just neo-liberals, however, who view this to be the case. As one of the key intellectuals of the Western left, Perry Anderson, asserts, 'For the first time since the Reformation, there are no longer any significant oppositions – that is, systematic rival outlooks – within the thought-world of the West; and scarcely any on a world scale either, if we discount religious doctrines as largely inoperative archaisms' (Anderson, 2000: 17).

For adherents to the narrative of commodification, in sum, one mode of exchange is replacing all others. The commodified realm is becoming *the* economic institution rather than one mode of producing and delivering goods and services amongst many. This is seldom questioned. The notions that the commodified realm is expanding and the non-commodified sphere shrinking have today taken on the aura of uncontested facts.

The only debate and discussion seems to concern the pace, extent and unevenness of this process. Take, for example, the extent of commodification. For some, the process is rather more complete and the commodity economy more hegemonic than for others. Comeliau (2002: 45), for example, talks of 'its almost *exclusive* use to solve the great majority of economic and social problems', while Thrift (2000: 96) asserts that 'What is certain is that the process of commodification has reached into *every* nook and cranny of modern life'. For others, however, there is still seen to be some distance to travel before the total commodification of working life is absolute (e.g., Gough, 2000; Lee, 1999; Watts, 1999). As Watts (1999: 312) puts it,

> The process by which everything becomes a commodity – and therefore everything comes to acquire a price and a monetary form (commoditization/commodification) – is not complete, even in our own societies where transactions still occur outside of the marketplace. But the reality of capitalism is that ever more of social life is mediated through and by the market.

Amongst such commentators, therefore, there is no questioning of whether a process of commodification is taking place. The only debate is over the extent to which it has so far colonized the non-commodified realm and the distance that needs to be travelled before the process is complete. To assess this, and as can be seen above, commentators seldom offer more than some broad-brush qualitative judgement. None attempt to measure, even in the crudest terms, the extent of its encroachment. Instead, it is more examples that tend to be provided, such as the one shown in Case Study 2.1, as evidence that its tentacles are stretching wider and deeper.

Case Study 2.1 The commodification of communities of interest

To display how the commodified realm is supposedly stretching its tentacles ever wider into previously inviolable sanctuaries, Rifkin (2000) points to how social relationships are becoming commodified. Whereas in the past, communities of interest might have developed organically around hobbies and were firmly anchored in civil society, today, commercial companies for profit-motivated purposes are asserted to manufacture communities of interest with the intention of nurturing longer-term customer–supplier relationships so as to extract 'lifetime value' from the customer.

Cross and Smith (1995) identify four key stages for businesses when developing 'communities of interest'. Stage I is 'awareness bonding', where the customer is made aware of the firm's product or service with the expectation of negotiating a first sale. Stage II is 'identity bonding', where the customer identifies with the firm's product or service and incorporates it into his or her sense of self (e.g., driving a VW beetle becomes a social statement as much as a means of transportation). Stage III is 'relationship bonding', where the firm and customer move from an arm's length relationship to an interactive one, where customer intimacy is developed, such as by sending birthday and anniversary cards. Stage IV is 'community bonding', where the company brings its customers into relationships with one another based on their shared interest in the firm's products or services. This establishes long-term commercial relationships for the company and optimizes the lifetime value of each customer. For the customer, to break this bond means to break social ties.

Rifkin (2000) provides examples of how these communities of interest are created using events, gatherings and other activities to bring customers together to share their common interest in the company's brand. For example, the recreational vehicle (RV) industry has more than 30 manufacturer-sponsored RV clubs that draw members who own the same kind of RV together into a community. The Winnebago-Itasca Travellers Club, for example, has 19,000 members and its 250 chapters hold frequent rallies throughout the US and Canada with members receiving a monthly magazine and perks, including travel route advice, insurance product discounts and even a mail-forwarding service when on the road. The club accounts for more than 20 per cent of the company's annual motor home sales.

That commercial firms nurture long-term 'customer intimacy' and 'community bonding' as a surrogate social sphere within a commercial wrapper displays for adherents to the commodification thesis, such as Rifkin (2000), how the commodified realm is permeating wider and deeper into everyday life.

It is similarly the case that few seek detailed empirical evidence when discussing the pace and unevenness of commodification. On the pace of commodification, it is often simply remarked that it is speeding up. On the issue of the unevenness of its penetration, broad-brush qualitative judgements are again made rather than measured evaluations. As Harvey (2000: 68) posits with regard to what he considers a highly uneven process,

> if there is any real qualitative trend it is towards the reassertion of early nineteenth-century capitalist values coupled with a twenty-first century penchant for pulling everyone (and everything that can be exchanged) into the orbit of capital while rendering large segments of the world's population permanently redundant in relation to the basic dynamics of capital accumulation.

Indeed, this is the consensus. Even if the commodified realm is forever stretching outwards to pull in more spheres of life and colonize areas previously untouched by its hand, this is widely regarded as a highly uneven process. This is clearly seen in discussions and comparisons of the First, Second and Third Worlds. In nearly all analyses, the stark differentials between the penetration of the commodity economy in the First World compared with the Second and the Third Worlds are continuously drawn so as to highlight the unevenness of commodification. Few, however, doubt that the overarching global trajectory is towards commodification.

Neither is there much difference between right- and left-wing political discourses. Both sides of the political spectrum concur that the overarching process is one of commodification, even if their reasons for asserting this and normative views on its consequences vary considerably. As such, besides discussions on the pace, extent and unevenness of the process of commodification, there are also contrasting normative positions about, first, whether it is to be celebrated or not and, second and often inextricably interrelated, whether it is a 'natural' and 'organic' or a 'socially constructed' process.

Commodification: a positive or negative trend?

On whether this turn towards a commodified world is to be celebrated or not, various positions exist. At one end of the spectrum are those neo-liberals for whom commodification is a positive trend that results in liberation, freedom and progress from the irrational constraints of tradition and collective bonds, creating a social order from the market-coordinated actions of free and rational individuals. This advocacy of commodification is often inextricably tied to a view of market-oriented behaviour as the natural basis for all social life. Depicted for instance in Thatcherism, a cultural and political revolution is viewed as required to remove from social life anything that might reduce the centrality of market models as the basis of social order.

As Block (2002) points out, this celebratory view of capitalism in neo-liberal thought has taken on board many of the tenets of what originally was a critical Marxian discourse. On the one hand, the very term 'capitalism', that until the late 1960s was unused in polite company, has now been adopted by neo-liberals in a much more positive sense to convey the type of society being sought. On the other hand, the core Marxist idea that economic organization sets the basic frame for the larger society, previously considered objectionable and rejected as 'vulgar materialism', is now widely accepted by neo-liberals. The result is that today 'capitalism' is the name that the business media uses, and the idea that the structure of the economy determines the wider society has been transformed from 'vulgar materialism' to common sense. Even more importantly, the fundamentally Marxian claim that capitalism as an economic system is global, unified and coherent was embraced by Margaret Thatcher, Ronald Reagan and other apostles of neo-liberal ideology in order to encourage their goals of privatization, deregulation and public sector retrenchment. In an increasingly global capitalist economy, it was asserted that countries had no choice but to follow such a path.

For many on the left of the political spectrum, meanwhile, commodification is again accepted but seen more negatively. For them, the increasing penetration of the market is highlighted so as to display how it leads to an eroding of communal life and has deleterious consequences for social values that might stand above the merely economic measure of price (e.g., Comeliau, 2002; Slater and Tonkiss, 2001). As Comeliau (2002: 45), for example, states,

> wherever market rationality acquires dominance, it transforms *social relations in their entirety*. Resting as it does upon private appropriation and competition, it entails individualist rivalry far more than mutual support as the basis for relations among the members of a society. It thus has a destructive impact upon the 'social fabric' itself.

This highlighting of the deleterious impacts of commodification, of course, is by no means new. Indeed, Beveridge (1948: 322), widely recognized as the founder of the modern welfare state, was seriously concerned about the emergence of what he called the 'business motive'. For him, there was a need to hold onto 'something other than the pursuit of gain as the dominant force in society. The business motive . . . is . . . in continual or repeated conflict with the Philanthropic Motive, and has too often been successful.'

He concludes that 'the business motive is a good servant but a bad master, and a society which gives itself up to the dominance of the business motive is a bad society'. The negative view of commodification thus views the implementation of an implacable logic of quantification and formal rationality as producing inequality, social disorder, loss of substantive values and a destruction of both individual and social relations.

Commodification: a natural and inevitable process?

Interrelated to this debate on the virtues and drawbacks of commodification is a discussion concerning whether such a trajectory of work is 'natural' and 'organic', or 'socially created'. For neo-liberals, commodification is usually seen as a natural or organic process whilst for those critical of the consequences it is more commonly viewed as socially constructed. Before analysing these contrasting positions, however, it is necessary to reiterate the shared 'buying into' the meta-narrative of commodification by both bodies of thought. As Slater and Tonkiss (2001: 3–4) assert, 'recent political and economic orthodoxies treat markets as self-evident, permanent and incontestable'.

In the 'natural' or 'organic' view, this trajectory towards capitalist hegemony is portrayed as inevitable, all-powerful and all-conquering, even a supernatural force that is unstoppable. Indeed, this natural force is even sometimes assigned with human characteristics and emotions. In the business media, for example, markets are often described as buoyant, calm, depressed, expectant, hesitant, nervous and sensitive. Sometimes the pound sterling, euro or US dollar has a good day, at other times it is ailing or sinking fast. Markets seem, therefore, to be ascribed with human attributes beyond the control of mere mortals. They are superhuman figures. This is more than simply a ruse to make them more comprehensible to the public by financial journalists. It is imbuing markets with the force of nature, giving them a divine will. The result of such imagery becomes that 'there is no alternative' but to obey the logic of this all-powerful force. Read through this lens, capitalism is constructed as existing outside of society or even above it. Reflecting the stance of many economists and formal anthropologists, the economy becomes a separate differentiated sphere. Instead of economic life being part of broader social relations, these relations become an epiphenomenon of the market; there is an economization of culture.

For those more critical of its consequences, however, this 'un-embedded' and organic view of capitalism is rejected. For them, this economy is socially constructed and although the momentum is towards an ever more commodified world, this does not mean that it cannot be stopped. Following Polanyi (1944: 140), it has been widely recognized that 'the road to the free market was opened and kept open by an enormous increase in continuous, centrally organized, and controlled interventionism' and, as such, that commodification is a created system rather than an organic one.

One way in which this view of commodification as a created system has come to the fore, albeit implicitly, is in the literature on the 'varieties of capitalism' (e.g., Albert, 1993;

Berger and Dore, 1996; Coates, 2002a,b,c; Crouch and Streek, 1997; Hollingsworth and Bayer, 1997; Orru *et al.*, 1997; Whitley, 2002). The contention that different varieties of capitalism developed in Anglo-Saxon countries, Continental Europe and East Asia, for example, displays that there is no one single variety with one uniform logic but a multiplicity of strains reflecting the different social systems in which they are created. The key problem with this varieties-of-capitalism literature, however, is that it has been largely silent on the critical issue of capitalism as a natural system (Block, 2002). Although implicit is the idea that there is no single unified system that operates like a force of nature, it is seldom explicit. The outcome is the persistence of a view that capitalism is some natural or organic system beyond the control of the societies in which it exists.

Nevertheless, even when depicted as a created rather than organic system, the validity of the commodification thesis is still not widely questioned. A commodification of economic life is still seen to be taking place. Although in principle, social constructionists need not argue this since they recognize that commodification is not inevitable, in practice, few do so. To transcend the commodification thesis, in consequence, it is necessary to investigate much more directly whether there is evidence to support this meta-narrative concerning the direction of work.

Where is the evidence to support the commodification thesis?

Given the widespread belief that a process of commodification is taking place, one might think that there would be mountains of evidence in support of this view of the direction of work. Yet a worrying and disturbing finding, once one starts to investigate the musings of adherents to commodification, is that hardly any evidence is ever brought to the fore either to show that a process of commodification is taking place or even to display the extent, pace or unevenness of its penetration. For example, the above-stated pronouncements by Rifkin (2000: 3) that 'The marketplace is a pervasive force in our lives', Ciscel and Heath (2001: 401) that capitalism is transforming 'every human interaction into a transient market exchange' and Gudeman (2001: 144) that 'markets are subsuming greater portions of everyday life' are offered to the reader with no supporting data of any kind. Similarly, the assertion by Carruthers and Babb (2000: 4) mentioned earlier that there has been 'the near-complete penetration of market relations into our modern economic lives' is justified by nothing more than the statement that 'markets enter our lives today in many ways "too numerous to be mentioned"' and the spurious notion that the spread of commodified 'ways of viewing' particular spheres of life signals how commodification is becoming hegemonic. Watts (1999: 312), in the same vein, supports his belief that although 'commodification is not complete... the reality of capitalism is that ever more of social life is mediated through and by the market' merely by avowing that subsistence economies are increasingly rare.

The thin evidence offered by these authors is by no means exceptional. Few commentators move beyond what Martin and Sunley (2001: 152) in another context term 'vague theory and thin empirics'. Perhaps because it is a widely accepted canon of wisdom, evidence is seldom deemed necessary. If this were some minor inconsequential academic theory, this might not greatly matter. However, commodification is seemingly the principal rationale underpinning the restructuring approach adopted in both 'transition' economies and the 'Third World'. It is also the main concept underpinning the focus upon the market in economic policy in Western nations. It is thus crucial that this key issue is interrogated. Unless this occurs, it will not be known whether the current focus of economic policy upon the commodified realm is built upon firm foundations or not.

Perhaps the process of commodification, akin to formalization, is so obvious to all concerned that there is little need to provide evidence. Perhaps, however, it is not. As mentioned above, no other ideas in the social sciences are accepted without detailed corroboration and there are no grounds for exempting the commodification thesis from a similar process of enquiry. Perhaps the only reason for exempting it is if one believes that it is an irrefutable fact. If so, then interrogating that this is indeed the case should be welcomed, especially given the paucity of evidence so far provided.

Why, therefore, is evidence not sought? One principal reason is that the emergence of commodified 'ways of viewing' each and every aspect of daily life is mistakenly taken to signify a process of commodification. To take just one example, recent years have seen the advent of discussions of a 'marriage market' whereby people seek out and take decisions on partners much like any other profit-orientated investment. Yet just because a sphere of human life can be read in a commodified manner does not mean that this sphere is now commodified. Just because one can read marriage and partnership in a commodified way does not mean that everybody now marries or chooses partners for profit-motivated purposes. The advent of a commodified way of viewing some aspects of life does not delineate that it is now commodified.

Just because the language of commercialism is now colonizing more and more areas of human existence, reaching far into inviolable sanctuaries, such that we can now talk of emotional investments and of the returns on our relationships, does not mean that all human relationships are now commodified. Making such and such a friendship might pay dividends, be profitless, rewarding, cost us dear, we may shop around for new friendships, be in the market for a new relationship, have the assets of our youth, intellect or energy so that we can make capital out of them, there may be pay-offs, bonuses to be had and meagre returns from friendships, and we may all have our price, but this language does not mean that commodification is omnipresent. When Wolff (1989: 76) argues that the logic of the market has increasingly penetrated our most intimate social relations of family and community, and 'in a way unprecedented in the American experience the market has become attractive not only in the economic sphere, but in the moral and social spheres as well', the advent of a way of viewing is being confused with a process of commodification itself.

Despite this imagining of an increasingly commodified world from the development of commodified 'ways of viewing', commentators must know that this is not the case.

They live in societies and understand the social mores that prevail. Those living in Western societies must know that seeking monetary profit in all social transactions is widely deemed unacceptable and inappropriate. Even if one acts in a market-like manner in commercial transactions, the same cannot apply to exchanges between friends and kin where reciprocity, altruism and charity should and must prevail. Different exchange relations are appropriate and acceptable in different social situations. Doing a favour for kin, friends or neighbours is very different to selling a service to a client, and disputes over whether something is a favour or a service is a dispute over whether the relationship is friendship or commerce. Just because an altruistic favour can be read as market-like and profit-motivated does not make it so.

There are thus well-defined socially constructed boundaries that it is unacceptable to cross, or what Block (2002) calls 'blockages to commodification'. Indeed, such blockages or barriers have been the main theme underpinning some 'blockbuster' movies. An example is the 1993 film tellingly entitled *Indecent Proposal*. Starring Robert Redford as a Las Vegas playboy who pays $1 million to spend a night with Woody Harrelson's wife Demi Moore, despite her initial protest, 'The dress is for sale, I'm not', this movie deals with one particular type of 'blocked exchange'. Indeed, the fact that this type of exchange remains 'blocked' well over a decade later is evident from the wide media coverage given to a case in the UK involving a married multi-millionaire who had supposedly offered a husband the sum of £1 million if his wife spent the rest of her life with him. The publicity surrounding the case and the fact that this 'market exchange' reached the High Court reflect the fact that this remains a 'blocked exchange' that crosses the boundaries of what is an acceptable transaction. Another example, provided by Hochschild (2003), concerns the degree to which it is acceptable to buy various intimate services (see Case Study 2.2).

Case Study 2.2 Commodification: the boundaries of acceptability

To display the barriers to the commodification of intimacy, Hochschild (2003: 30) reproduced the following advertisement for her students that apparently appeared on the Internet on 6 March 2001:

(p/t) Beautiful, smart, hostess, good masseuse – $400/week

Hi there.

This is a strange job opening, and I feel silly posting it, but this is San Francisco and I do have a need! This will be a very confidential process.

I'm a mild-mannered millionaire businessman, intelligent, travelled, but shy, who is new to the area, and extremely inundated with invitations to parties, gatherings and social events. I'm looking to find a 'personal assistant', of sorts. The job description would include, but not be limited to:

- being hostess to parties at my home ($40/hour)
- providing me with a soothing and sensual massage ($140/hour)
- Coming to certain social events with me ($40/hour)
- Travelling with me ($300/day + all travel expenses)
- managing some of my home affairs (utilities, bill-paying, etc.) ($30/hour)

You must be between 22 and 32, in-shape, good-looking, articulate, sensual, attentive, bright and able to keep confidences. I don't expect more than 3 to 4 events per month, and up to 10 hours a week on massage, chores and other miscellaneous items, at the most. You must be unmarried, unattached, or have a very understanding partner!

I'm a bright, intelligent 30-year old man, and I'm happy to discuss the reasons for my placing this ad with you on response of your e-mail application. If you can, please include a picture of yourself, or a description of your likes, interests, and your ability to do the job.

NO professional escorts please! NO sex involved!

Thank you

You can e-mail me at . . . '

Hochschild (2003) asked her upper-division students at the University of California their response to this advertisement. Responses were largely negative ranging from anxious refusal ('he can't buy a wife') through condemnation ('he shouldn't buy a wife') to considerations of the emotional and moral flaws that led him to write this advertisement, thus displaying the well-defined blockages to commodification. For Hochschild (2003: 31), therefore, this is evidence that a 'commodity frontier' exists. As women enter the labour force, personal tasks are becoming monetized and impersonalized, but there remain frontiers beyond which it remains unacceptable to pass so far as the commodification of intimacy is concerned.

Many further examples can be provided of how profit-motivated transactions are blocked. Society expects professionals such as doctors, lawyers and architects not simply to maximize their incomes, but to obey a series of ethical injunctions. Of course, professionals might sometimes ignore these ethical considerations: journalists may slant their coverage in exchange for personal favours or gifts; or surgeons may recommend the same lucrative operation to patients whether they need it or not. The point, however, is that the effective functioning of these institutions is compromised if these ethical injunctions are disregarded. If, for example, accountants were simply to charge a little extra to approve a firm's balance sheet no matter how much financial fraud is involved, economic activity would quickly grind to a halt because investors would no longer be able to trust the financial information that they were receiving.

Further evidence that commodification is blocked in contemporary Western society can be seen when considering the flow of money between people. Domains can be identified where, although money may not be completely excluded, its use is often highly constrained or restricted. Take, for example, the exchange of gifts. Although the giving of gifts is a universal trait, its pattern and meaning vary cross-culturally (Bloch and Parry, 1989; Carruthers and Espeland, 2001). In many Western societies, gift exchange tends to be personal and altruistic relative to impersonal and self-interested commodity exchange. As Gregory (1982: 12) states, 'commodity exchange is an exchange of alienable things between transactors who are in a state of reciprocal independence . . . Non-commodity (gift) exchange is an exchange of inalienable things between transactors who are in a state of reciprocal dependence.' Gift exchange establishes and/or maintains a social relationship between the giver and recipient. A gift invokes an obligation – a relationship of indebtedness, status difference or even subordination. As such, the meaning of the gift must be appropriate to the relationship. And in contemporary advanced economies, money is seldom seen as an appropriate gift. As Carruthers and Espeland (2001: 301) state,

> some exchanges are protected from monetarization and commodification because of their inappropriate ethos. Money in our society is so strongly identified with market exchange that its attachment to something brings with it strong 'economic' connotations that may be deemed unsuitable. In many situations, the use of money violates and endangers the spirit of gift-giving. Consequently, money is generally inappropriate as a gift, and even when it is used as such, all kinds of restrictions, framings, markings, and reinterpretations come into play.

Furthermore, one would never offer money to somebody who invited you to dinner as a substitute for returning the favour. The debt is personal and direct and must be repaid in kind. Norms of exchange evolve, however, and are not timeless and unchanging. What is inappropriate at one time period or place can become acceptable later or elsewhere.

Similarly, there persists in some liberal Western middle-class circles a perception that one should not employ 'domestic workers' to undertake one's housework since this is deemed an unacceptable exploitative practice that smacks of domestic servitude. The point quite simply is that blockages are always present. Although these blockages change over time and space, there are always blockages of one form or another. The argument of exponents of commodification, therefore, can be read as contending that the spheres subject to blocked exchanges are dwindling in number over time as the tentacles of commodification stretch ever deeper and wider. Until now, no evidence has been provided of whether this is the case. This will be evaluated in Chapter 4. The strong consensus embedded in the commodification thesis, nevertheless, is that the commodity economy is increasingly totalizing, hegemonic, all encompassing and universal. Indeed, it is this assumption of an increasingly commodified world that underpins the final meta-narrative, which often delimits what is considered valid and feasible to discuss regarding the future of work.

The globalization thesis

> Imagine a manifesto for global capital, written by a guru of globalization. Its object would be to present a picture of the world in which opposition to globalization and to capitalism itself would be futile, a world in which the best we can do is go with the flow, lie back and think of Nike . . . it would probably begin by insisting that the globalization of capital and the integration of the global economy have so transformed the world that the nation-state has become a fiction, as capital flows have far outreached the borders and the powers of the state. The world is now essentially ruled by the impersonal laws of the global market. (Meiksins-Wood, 2003: 61)

The above quotation captures the essence of what is meant by the globalization thesis. It is not simply believed that goods and services are increasingly produced and delivered by capitalist firms for the purpose of profit (i.e., the commodification thesis). In the globalization thesis, these capitalist firms are also increasingly viewed as operating in a borderless and seamless open world economy in which hyper-mobile and homeless capital restlessly roams the globe unrestrained in search of profit-making opportunities.

Globalization, akin to formalization and commodification, is frequently presented as some natural and inevitable process that is unstoppable. Indeed, politicians around the world often hold up their hands and lay the blame for the need for austerity policies, including all manner of reductions in welfare spending, at the door of this seemingly unstoppable force called 'globalization'. Yet it takes only a moment's reflection to realize that this is anything but a natural or organic process. As Faraclas (2001: 67) puts it,

> Corporate globalization is presented to us as inevitable . . . discussed in the media as if it were a natural phenomenon. But can the most massive transfer of wealth in the history of humanity from the poor to the rich sponsored by the World Bank/International Monetary Fund (WB/IMF or 'the Bank') and enforced by the World Trade Organization (WTO) under the agenda of corporate globalization be considered natural? . . .

For many, therefore, the process of globalization is socially constructed. As Held (2005: 8) argues, the ongoing stripping away of national and international regulations is a direct product of what is known as the Washington Consensus or Washington-led neo-liberalism that advocates the following measures:

- Free trade;
- Capital market liberalization;
- Flexible exchange rates;
- Market-determined interest rates;
- The deregulation of markets;

- The transfer of assets from the public to the private sector;
- The tight focus of public expenditure on well-directed social targets;
- Tax reform;
- Secure property rights; and
- The protection of intellectual rights.

The outcome of this Washington-led neo-liberalism is four trends. First, there is asserted to be a process of 'economic globalization' in which free trade occurs in an unrestrained manner and, secondly, a process of 'financial globalization' in which a seamless world of hyper-mobile and homeless capital emerges resulting in the end of geography (O'Brien, 1992) and a 'borderless world' (Ohmae, 1990). This, moreover, is accompanied by a third process of 'political globalization' in which nation states witness a diminution in their ability to regulate either national or international capital as an unregulated global capitalism takes hold resulting in the 'end of sovereignty' (Camilleri and Falk, 1992) and the end of the 'nation state' (Ohmae, 1990). As Kindelberger (1969: 207) puts it, 'the nation state is just about through as an economic unit' since states are increasingly decision-takers and not decision-makers. Finally, running alongside is seen to be a process of 'cultural globalization' in which an homogeneous global culture emerges founded upon what might be called 'Westernized' or 'Americanized' cultural values (e.g., Held, 2005; Held *et al.*, 1999; Reich, 1991).

For globalists, therefore, economic, financial, political and cultural globalization is real and tangible. The impacts can be witnessed everywhere. National finance, cultures, economies and politics are subsumed under networks of global flows. These lessen local and national differences, autonomy and sovereignty, and result in a more homogeneous global culture and a global market for goods and services. Globalization, for many, is thus an unstoppable and inexorable trajectory, with any attempts to resist it doomed to failure. As Reich (1991: 3, 8) puts it,

> We are living through a transformation that will rearrange the politics and economics of the coming century. There will be no national products or technologies, no national corporations, no national industries. There will no longer be national economies, at least as we have come to understand that concept... As almost every factor of production – money, technology, factories, and equipment – moves effortlessly across borders, the very idea of an American economy is becoming meaningless, as are notions of an American corporation, American products, and American technology. A similar transformation is affecting every other nation, some faster and more profoundly than others; witness Europe, hurtling toward economic union.

That we live in a globalized or globalizing world is such a dominant narrative that it today heavily determines what is considered feasible regarding the future of work. Many academics, journalists, commentators and politicians, embracing such a narrative, claim little scope for manoeuvre. To embrace the globalization thesis therefore leads to a disarming and debilitating attitude, diminishing severely the scope of what is considered achievable.

This process of globalization, however, is viewed as having markedly different outcomes. Similar to the commodification thesis, believers in globalization can be divided into those who celebrate its advent and those more pessimistic about its consequences (see, for example, Cochrane and Pain, 2000; Seabrook, 2004).

Positive globalists

'Positive globalists', or optimists, highlight the advantages of globalization and view the outcomes as something to be welcomed. They focus on how the advent of an open world economy and unrestrained capitalism will improve the quality of life, raise the living standards and bring people together. This, in turn, is seen to promote the sharing of cultures and understanding among nations around the world – in a sense making us all world citizens through global communication. Although they sometimes recognize dangers inherent in this opening up of the world economy such as global environmental pollution, optimists believe that these problems can be overcome and that the net effect is a positive one.

Not all positive globalists, however, are the same. Indeed, Cochrane and Pain (2000) break down positive globalists into two camps: those who focus on the progressive possibilities of the 'global village' grounded in the work of Marshall McLuhan in the 1960s and those neo-liberals pointing to the democratic nature of the free market and the benefits of greater choice. An example of the former is Friedman (1999: xvii–xviii), who argues that

> What is new today is the degree and intensity with which the world is being tied together into a single globalized marketplace and village. What is also new is the sheer number of people and countries able to partake of today's globalized economy and information networks, and to be affected by them . . . This new era of globalization . . . is turbocharged.

Far more numerous, however, are the neo-liberals celebrating the advantages of a global free market and unrestrained capitalism who want goods, services and capital to flow without restriction across national boundaries. For them, global 'free market' capitalism is a positive trend that will benefit consumers by increasing the scale and allocative efficiency of markets for both goods and capital. National regulation is held to be futile, and welfare and workers' rights above a low international norm are seen to simply damage national competitiveness. Indeed, these economic liberals have been highly successful in their advocacy of the deregulation of trade, investment and capital movements (see Dawson, 2000). For them, any risk that results is an unavoidable symptom, and resultant uncertainties are viewed as potentially exhilarating and innovative forces that provide opportunities for risk-taking entrepreneurs. Moreover, the volatility and unpredictability in the employment-place resulting from global markets is seen as a driving force for innovation and adaptability of individual workers and firms.

Pessimistic globalists

'Pessimistic globalists' in contrast, although accepting that economic, financial, political and cultural globalization is taking place, view this in a largely negative manner. They accept the apparently inexorable and unstoppable replacement of regulated national and international capitalism by an unregulated global capitalism but condemn it. An example is Altvater and Mahnkopf (1997) for whom the triumph of the global marketplace is intensifying the tendency towards a process of 'global disembedding' in which the market is becoming increasingly separated from its social bonds. For them, as 'commodification envelopes the global system' (Altvater and Mahnkopf, 1997: 451), temporal and spatial co-ordinates become compressed by the growth and speeding up of commodification, resulting in a range of not only negative economic and social impacts but also serious environmental problems as natural resources are used up and not replaced.

For these 'global phobics' – a somewhat derogatory term used by optimists to denigrate pessimists – globalization is to be resisted if at all feasible due to its largely negative impacts on the majority of the world. As Boron (2005: 3–4) explains,

> While a handful of developed capitalist nations increased their capacity to control, at least partially, the productive processes at a global level, the financialization of the international economy and the growing circulation of goods and services, the great majority of countries witnessed the growth of their external dependency and the widening gap that separated them from the centre. Globalization, in short, consolidated the imperialist domination and deepened the submission of peripheral capitalisms, which became more and more incapable of controlling their domestic economic processes even minimally.

For Hardt and Negri (2000), nevertheless, although opposing globalization, a different viewpoint is adopted. For them, there is the gradual disappearance of a territorially located centre that 'organizes' the international structure of domination meaning that the classic distinction between core and periphery, North and South, is vanishing. In its place is the primacy of a global logic of domination. Castells (1998: 70–165), in another vein, argues that globalization creates a global elite with a similar lifestyle in every big city of the world. At the same time, he says, it generates a pool of migrant and local labour that exists at the bottom of the labour market in every world city. He uses the notion of the 'Fourth World' to define these populations excluded from participation in the new global economy. The 'Fourth World' for him is composed of multiple holes of social exclusion that are present in nearly every country and city. A further pessimist is Pettifor (2003a,b), who adopts yet another viewpoint:

> Globalization has not been 'corporate-driven' nor is 'technology' responsible. Instead . . . the origins lie with the United States' need to finance the post Vietnam War-deficit. This led US politicians, backed by the UK government, to lift controls over capital markets – so as to tap their resources to fund the US deficit. Globalization, therefore, was created by politicians and can be reversed by politicians. (Pettifor, 2003a: xxv)

For some of these pessimists, one apparent outcome is a trend towards a global homogenization of cultures that again is seen as having many negative impacts, not least that everywhere is becoming like everywhere else, with standardized global cultural products being created by global corporations. As Norberg-Hodge (2001: 182) puts it, 'people around the world are being bombarded by media and advertising images that present the modern, Western consumer lifestyle as the ideal, while implicitly denigrating indigenous traditions'. A global culture is seen to be emerging, therefore, that is Westernized or Americanized in character.

Globalization: a natural or constructed trajectory?

Amongst adherents to the globalization thesis, there are not only those optimistic and pessimistic about this apparent trajectory but also, as indicated above, those viewing it as a natural tendency and those viewing it as socially constructed. On the whole, positive globalizers, especially of a neo-liberal persuasion, concoct globalization as natural and inevitable. For them, the inexorable rise of an open world economy is part of an organic and immutable tendency towards free markets about which little can be done. As Boron (2005: 14) states, there is a view that 'the irresistible rise of globalization is a natural phenomenon as uncontrollable as the movement of the stars'.

Pessimistic globalizers, in contrast, view globalization as socially constructed (e.g., Castree et al., 2004; Massey, 2000, 2005; Norberg-Hodge, 2001; Seabrook, 2004). For them, globalization is not predestined but chosen. As Norberg-Hodge (2001: 179) puts it, 'Globalization is often portrayed . . . as an inevitable evolutionary trend. But it is far from a natural process: it is occurring because governments are actively promoting it and subsidizing the framework necessary to support it.' Massey (2005: 5) reinforces such a view:

> 'globalization' in its current form is not the result of a law of nature (itself a phenomenon under dispute). It is a project . . . statements . . . such as there is no alternative . . . is not a description of the world [but] . . . an image in which the world is being made.

For some pessimistic globalizers, globalization is thus viewed as a discourse being held up as a benchmark against which 'progress' can be measured and the reality found wanting. It is, in other words, a performative discourse used to shape the world rather than merely to describe it. As Cameron and Palan (2004) argue, globalization is less a real objective process and more a form of storytelling driven by powerful interests. It helps create the realities it purports merely to describe. For them, even if globalization is demonstrated to be no more than a myth as some have claimed (Shipman, 2002), this is still insufficient to invalidate this thesis. What is required is a critical evaluation of this narrative of globalization (see Chapter 5) and a re-reading of the trajectory of development from other viewpoints so as to provide alternative narratives. We will return to this in Part III.

Conclusions

We have allowed ourselves to be boxed in by words, by slogans whose content we have not tried to clarify, and by methods of conceptualization, accounting and analysis which distort social reality. We have let ourselves be trapped – or, to be more precise, 'alienated' – by constraints which, though certainly real and present, have been wrongly taken as divine decrees, or at least as imperatives inherent in the nature of the world and the 'inescapable' laws of economics. For in fact, these constraints are the results (intentional and unintentional) of human decisions that it is possible for us to question, at least partially and on certain conditions. (Comeliau, 2002: 130)

In this chapter, three grand narratives – formalization, commodification and globalization – have been introduced that currently dominate how the future of work is envisaged and close off other possibilities from consideration. All three adopt a similar storyline of a single linear trajectory of work that marshals differences across space into a temporal sequence. Through this temporal convening of spatial difference, they close off not only the notion of difference but also the idea that multiple trajectories are being pursued in different places.

Formalization, commodification and globalization, therefore, can be seen as the grand narratives that at present shape how the future of work is envisaged and what is considered feasible and valid to discuss (e.g., Beck, 2000; Comeliau, 2002; Massey, 2005). All propose futures that are inevitable, inexorable and unstoppable. In this chapter, however, attention has been drawn to the lack of evidence provided to support these theses and the literatures that highlight how these are not only far from natural and inevitable processes but also (per)formative discourses that act to shape the reality rather than merely reflect it. In order to assess whether the future of work is more open than these grand narratives suggest, therefore, each will need to be evaluated critically in turn. This is the subject matter of the next three chapters.

Further reading

Gershuny, J. (2000) *Changing Times: Work and Leisure in Post-industrial Society*, Oxford: Oxford University Press.

This is an excellent detailed review of the shifts in how people spend their time in 21 countries. In highlighting the changing amounts of time spent on paid and unpaid work by various populations, it provides a wealth of evidence with which to question the universality of formalization.

Polanyi, K. (1944) *The Great Transformation*, Boston: Beacon Press.

The ideas in this book are at the heart of much contemporary writing on marketization/commodification and there is no better place to start than this seminal text that offers the reader a balanced portrayal of the transformation towards market society.

Block, F. (2002) 'Rethinking capitalism', in N.W. Biggart (ed.) *Readings in Economic Sociology*, Oxford: Blackwell.

An excellent short introduction to the concept of commodification that covers the major perspectives and issues involved, as well as the evolution of thought on this subject.

Held, D. (2000) (ed.) *A Globalising World? Culture, Economics and Politics*, London: Routledge.

This edited volume provides a good introduction to the concept of globalization, with clearly written and well-structured chapters that review in turn economic, political, cultural and financial globalization.

3

The demise of the informal economy and the growth of the formal economy

Introduction

A popular prejudice about the future of work that is seldom questioned is that goods and services will be increasingly produced and delivered through employment (i.e., the formalization of work thesis). In this view, supposedly 'traditional' informal activities, namely self-provisioning, unpaid exchange and cash-in-hand work, will disappear with economic 'advancement' and 'modernization'. The natural and inevitable future of work, therefore, is away from informal modes of production and towards goods and services being provided through the formal economy. Indeed, so widely accepted is this view of the direction of work that the degree to which economies are formalized is frequently taken as a measuring rod of the extent to which countries are 'modern' and 'developed', with majority ('Third') world countries defined as 'developing' or 'under-developed' due to their lack of formalization and the First World as 'advanced'. For adherents to the formalization thesis, therefore, the future of work is cast in stone; there is a linear trajectory and it is one in which there is a natural and inevitable process of formalization.

In this chapter, the common idea that this is some predestined future of work will be brought into question. Reviewing the evidence, it will display that whether one examines the Western 'advanced' economies, transition economies of East-Central Europe or the majority (Third) world, a linear progression towards formalization is not verified. Instead, diverse development paths are apparent in different countries. While there is formalization in some, in others there is neither formalization nor informalization, and in yet others a process of informalization. Rather than the future being cast in a straitjacket of the deeper encroachment of formal work, therefore, this chapter displays that the trajectories of work are more heterogeneous than so far assumed.

Evaluating the formalization of the advanced economies

In the formalization thesis, there is assumed to be a long-run historical tendency whereby ever more goods and services are produced and distributed through the formal sphere, and fewer by people through self-provisioning, unpaid exchange and cash-in-hand work. Whereas in the past people might have toiled in fields and their homes on a subsistence basis, today it is accepted that people generally earn a formal wage with which they then purchase the goods and services from formal enterprises, and that in this way the formal economy has fed upon itself and expanded.

To evaluate the validity of this view, on the one hand, this can be indirectly assessed using the proxy measure of employment participation rates. If relatively few goods and services were produced, sold and distributed through the formal economy, then few people would be in formal jobs. However, as more goods and services are exchanged in this manner, then a growth in the employment participation rate would be witnessed, culminating in a state of 'full-employment'. On the other hand, and perhaps more accurately, the extent of formalization and how this is changing over time can be directly evaluated by comparing the volume and value of formal and informal work in different time periods using measures of either the inputs into or the outputs of such work. Each measure of formalization is here evaluated in turn.

A proxy measure of formalization: Evaluating the shift towards full(er) employment

Analysing the degree to which citizens in the Western world are immersed in the formal labour market, as stated, is a proxy measure of the degree of formalization. In 2004 in Europe, the employment participation rate of the working-age population in the EU-15 was just 64.7 per cent and for the EU-25 some 63.3 per cent (Eurostat, 2005). Over one in three working-age people in Europe were therefore jobless. To achieve full participation, one new job for every two currently in existence is thus needed (a 50 per cent increase in the number of jobs). Table 3.1 displays the results for various countries. This reveals that even if the 'jobs gap' is narrower in some nations than others, all are far from a state of full-employment. Contrary to the hyperbole and rhetoric of politicians who often assert that full-employment is nearly upon us, even Denmark, the country with the highest employment participation rate in the EU (76 per cent), requires one new job for every three existing jobs in order to achieve full-employment.

Is it the case, nevertheless, that employment participation rates are moving closer to full-employment over time? As Table 3.1 displays, this is not the case. For over four decades, few European nations have managed to close their 'jobs gap'. Indeed, just three nations in this table made any progress at all. Over this 44-year period, Denmark managed to raise employment participation rates from 74 to 76 per cent, the Netherlands from 64 to 73 per cent, and Portugal starting from the low base level

Table 3.1 Labour force participation rates, 1960, 1973, 1999 and 2004

Country	Total participation rate				
	1960	1973	1999	2004	Growth (+) or decline (–) 1960–2004
Sweden	75	75	71	72	–
Denmark	74	75	76	76	+
UK	72	73	71	72	=
France	70	68	60	61	–
Germany	70	69	65	65	–
Ireland	68	64	63	63	–
Greece	66	57	55	61	–
Italy	65	58	53	57	–
Netherlands	64	61	71	73	+
Spain	61	60	52	61	=
Belgium	60	61	59	59	–
Portugal	58	64	67	68	+

Source: ILO (1997: Table 2.2), European Commission (2001a: Annex 1) and Eurostat (2005)

of 58 per cent participation to 68 per cent. In other nations, however, the 'jobs gap' widened. Some falls were quite dramatic. Employment participation rates in France fell from 70 to 61 per cent, in Greece from 66 to 61 per cent and in Italy from 65 to 57 per cent. The view that there is a long-term universal trend towards fuller-employment, therefore, must be treated with considerable caution. It is not borne out by the evidence.

Neither is it any different elsewhere in the Western world. In the US, although the employment participation rate is higher at 73 per cent, one job still needs to be created for every three that currently exist if full participation is to be achieved (European Commission, 2000b). A 37 per cent increase in the number of jobs in the US economy is required. In Japan, similarly, the employment participation rate is 70 per cent, necessitating a 43 per cent growth in the number of jobs to achieve full participation (European Commission, 2000b).

Across Western nations, in sum, a wide gap exists between current employment levels and a situation of full participation, and the trend is not narrowing over time. Indeed, the principal historical lesson is that full-employment was achieved for at most 30 years or so following the Second World War in just a handful of advanced economies (Pahl, 1984). Even then, however, this was only full-employment for men, not women (Gregory and Windebank, 2000). As Beveridge (1944: 18) puts it, full-employment is a state in which there are 'more vacant jobs than unemployed *men* [sic]' and where there are jobs 'at fair wages, of such a kind, and so located that the unemployed *men* [sic] can reasonably be expected to take them' (my emphasis). Although this language reflects the widely accepted sexist prose of the time, Beveridge was correct to refer to the full-employment of men alone. Any talk of a return to some previous 'golden age' of full-employment is illogical if by that is meant an era of full-employment for both men and women. Such an era has never existed so to seek its return is not possible. Even this gloomy portrait of employment participation rates, however, still does not tell the full story. It omits to mention that over time an increasing proportion of those in employment are employed part-time rather than full-time (e.g., European Commission, 2000b; Townsend, 1997), masking the degree to which under-employment is also rising.

Employment participation rates thus provide no evidence of a universal process of formalization in advanced economies over the past four decades. However, this is perhaps a very poor proxy indicator. Analysing employment alone tells us nothing about whether and how the balance is altering between formal and informal work. For example, increased participation in employment is not always accompanied by a decline in informal work. It may be accompanied by a quicker or slower growth in informal work, a decline in informal work or a similar growth rate resulting in no change in the overall balance of formal and informal work. Unless both formal and informal work are analysed, therefore, whether there is a process of formalization will not be known.

Direct measures of formalization: The changing size of the formal and informal economies

To evaluate whether a formalization of work has taken place in advanced economies, in theory, one could evaluate the volume and value of the formal and informal spheres in terms of either their inputs or outputs (Goldschmidt-Clermont, 1982, 1998, 2000; Gregory and Windebank, 2000; Luxton, 1997). In practice, it is only data on the volume and value of the inputs that are readily available in the form of time-budget data (e.g., Gershuny, 2000; Murgatroyd and Neuburger, 1997; Robinson and Godbey, 1997). Here, the participants fill in diaries of what they do, and analysing the data, the time that they spend in formal employment and in other forms of work can be calculated (Gershuny and Jones, 1987; Gershuny et al., 1994; Juster and Stafford, 1991).

Table 3.2 collates the findings of time-budget studies conducted in 20 countries. This reveals that unpaid work occupies 44.7 per cent of all working time, meaning that the tentacles of the formal economy are far shorter than expounded by proponents of formalization. Unpaid work, so long considered a marginal 'other', is only slightly smaller than paid activity, measured in terms of the amount of time spent engaged in it. This, however, should come as no surprise. When Polanyi (1944) depicted over half a century ago 'the great transformation' from a non-market to a market society, he strongly emphasized that this was merely a shift in the balance of economic activity between these spheres. He never suggested it was a total transformation. Even if some have since depicted formalization as rather more all encompassing than Polanyi ever wished to portray (e.g., Harvey, 1982, 1989), this table demonstrates that Polanyi was quite correct not to over-exaggerate the encroachment of the formal economy.

Table 3.2 also displays that it is perhaps presumptuous to talk of a process of formalization. Countries such as Denmark, Finland, France, the UK and the US have

Table 3.2 Unpaid work as a % of total work time, 1960–present

Country	1960–73	1974–84	1985–present	Trend
Canada	56.9	55.4	54.2	Formalization
Denmark	41.4	–	43.3	Informalization
France[a]	52.0	55.5	57.5	Informalization
Netherlands	–	55.9	57.9	Informalization
Norway	57.1	55.4	–	Formalization
UK	52.1	49.7	53.9	Informalization
US[b]	56.9	57.6	58.4	Informalization
Finland	–	51.8	54.5	Informalization
20 Countries	43.4	42.7	44.7	Informalization

Sources: [a] Chadeau and Fouquet (1981), Roy (1991), Dumontier and Pan Ke Shon (1999)
[b] Robinson and Godbey (1997)
Other countries derived from Gershuny (2000: Tables 7.6, 7.12, 7.16)

witnessed a process of informalization, not formalization, over the past four decades. This trend is not due to an absolute growth in the time spent on unpaid work. It is because the time spent in paid work has decreased faster than the time spent in unpaid work (Gershuny, 2000). Different advanced economies are therefore witnessing divergent development paths.

Who engages in informal work?

For some, this process of informalization is because informal work is concentrated amongst populations marginalized or excluded from the formal economy, known as the 'marginality thesis' (e.g., Button, 1984; Rosanvallon, 1980; Sassen, 1989), and is a result of advanced economies off-loading the social reproduction of these populations from the formal welfare sphere onto the informal realm in order to stay competitive, meaning that a large excluded minority now seek to eke out their livelihoods in the informal sphere (Sassen, 1997).

The vast majority of studies conducted throughout the advanced economies, however, negate such an explanation for the growth of informal work. Take, for example, northern Europe. In the Netherlands, Van Geuns *et al.* (1987) find in all six localities studied that the unemployed generally do not participate in informal work to the same extent as the employed. This finding is reinforced by Van Eck and Kazemeir (1985) and Koopmans (1989). It is also echoed in studies carried out in France (Barthe, 1988; Cornuel and Duriez, 1985; Foudi *et al.*, 1982; Tievant, 1982), Germany (Glatzer and Berger, 1988; Hellberger and Schwarze, 1986) and Britain (Economist Intelligence Unit, 1982; Howe, 1990; Morris, 1994; Pahl, 1984; Warde, 1990; Williams, 2004a,e). All display that informal work is greater amongst the formally employed rather than the unemployed. Similar findings are identified in southern Europe in Spain (e.g., Benton, 1990; Lobo, 1990a),

Portugal (Lobo, 1990b) and Italy (Cappechi, 1989; Mingione, 1991; Mingione and Morlicchio, 1993; Warren, 1994). This is also the finding in North America (e.g., Fortin *et al.*, 1996; Jensen *et al.*, 1995; Lemieux *et al.*, 1994; Lozano, 1989).

Similarly, deprived areas are found to conduct less informal work than more affluent areas. In the Netherlands, a study of six localities by Van Geuns *et al.* (1987) asserts that the higher the rate of unemployment in an area, the lower is the level of informal work. In France, meanwhile, studies in both Orly-Choisy (Barthe, 1985) and Lille (Foudi *et al.*, 1982) indicate poverty black spots in which the unemployed cannot escape from their deprivation through informal work. Studies of more affluent new towns and commuter areas in France (Cornuel and Duriez, 1985; Tievant, 1982), in contrast, discover a relatively high amount of informal work. In Italy, similarly, studies show that such activity is more extensive in the relatively affluent northern regions than in the more deprived southern regions (Mattera, 1980; Mingione, 1991). As Mingione and Morlicchio (1993: 424) declare, 'the opportunities of [*sic*] informal work are more numerous, the greater the level of development of the surrounding social and economic context'. Although this finding is by no means universal (see Williams and Windebank, 1998), it is now widely accepted that informal work is not always and necessarily concentrated in marginalized populations, signalling that the growth of informal sphere is not purely due to the abandonment of marginal populations. How, therefore, can the prevalence and even growth of the informal sphere be explained?

Explaining the persistence and growth of informal work: lessons from England

To explain the persistence and growth of informal work, Williams and Windebank (2003a) undertook 861 face-to-face interviews between 1998 and 2002 with households in deprived and affluent urban and rural English localities. They analysed the work practices used by households to complete 44 common domestic tasks and their motives for using each form of work. As Table 3.3 displays, the first important finding of this English Localities Survey is that informal work is widely used, reinforcing the above notion that advanced economies are far from being fully formalized. The second important finding is that it does not appear to be deprived populations who are most heavily engaged in informal work. For many, the assumption is that as households become more affluent, they will externalize to the formal economy a greater proportion of their workload. This study, however, finds that the situation is more complex. Although households in affluent areas are more formalized and monetized in their household work practices, they also undertake more informal work. In consequence, the disparity is not between relatively formalized and informalized populations. Rather, it is between 'fully engaged' (or 'work busy') populations using both formal and informal labour to get work completed and relatively 'disengaged' (or 'work deprived') populations with lower levels of both formal and informal work taking place and a lesser ability to get necessary work completed.

Table 3.3 Economic practices used by English households to undertake 44 domestic services: by geographical area

% of tasks last conducted using	% of 44 tasks completed	Tasks last conducted using								χ^2
		Unpaid domestic work		Unpaid community exchange		Paid informal labour		Formal labour		
		%	No.	%	No.	%	No.	%	No.	
All areas		71.4		5.0		5.5		18.1		
Deprived rural areas	53.4	67.1	15.7	7.2	1.7	5.6	1.3	19.9	4.7	89.76
Deprived areas – Southampton	45.3	74.8	14.9	3.6	0.7	4.4	0.9	17.3	3.4	64.46
Deprived areas – Sheffield	49.0	77.4	16.7	3.9	0.8	5.4	1.1	13.3	2.9	174.19
Affluent suburb – Southampton	53.3	71.3	16.7	1.9	0.4	6.5	1.5	20.3	4.8	29.88
Affluent suburb – Sheffield	57.3	72.8	18.4	1.9	0.5	11.2	2.8	14.1	3.5	29.86
Affluent rural areas	53.9	63.4	15.0	7.5	1.8	4.1	1.0	24.0	5.7	28.88

Note: $\chi^2 > 12.838$ in all cases, leading to a rejection of H_o within a 99.5 per cent confidence interval that there are no spatial variations in the sources of labour used to complete the 44 household services.
Source: Williams (2004c: Table 9)

How, therefore, can engagement in informal work be explained? Amongst households in affluent areas, the work practices used are more likely to be a product of choice than necessity, whilst in deprived areas this is much less the case. Self-provisioning in affluent areas, for example, is more commonly a matter of choice than a product of a lack of choice (Table 3.4).

Table 3.4 Reasons for engaging in self-provisioning in England: by geographical area

Reason (%)	Deprived urban neighbourhoods	Affluent urban neighbourhoods	Deprived rural	Affluent rural
Economic	44	10	46	11
Ease	18	37	24	40
Choice	21	24	18	22
Pleasure	14	32	12	27

Source: Williams (2005a: Table 7.3)

First, it was often felt to be *easier* to do a task oneself than to contract out the work, accounting for 18 and 24 per cent of all self-provisioning in deprived urban and rural neighbourhoods, and 37 and 40 per cent in affluent urban and rural areas. It was often stated, for example, that tradespeople were difficult to contact and even more difficult to persuade to come around to do a job so it was often easier to do the job oneself than rely on them. This was particularly prevalent in rural areas, perhaps due to the lesser accessibility and/or availability of formal firms.

Secondly, the proportion of self-provisioning conducted out of *choice* was 21 and 18 per cent in deprived urban and rural neighbourhoods respectively, and 24 and 22 per cent of cases where it was last used in affluent urban and rural areas. This clearly displays how some populations are using homemaking as a form of identity politics (e.g., Miller, 2001) to enable them to define who and what they are outside of their formal jobs. The use of self-provisioning for this purpose, however, was more frequent in affluent urban and rural areas than deprived localities.

Finally, and related to the above factor, self-provisioning was used due to the *pleasure* people got from such endeavour. Indeed, this reason accounted for some 14 and 12 per cent of cases where self-servicing was last used in deprived urban and rural localities respectively, and 32 and 27 per cent of cases where it was last used in affluent urban and rural areas. On the whole, it was non-routine self-provisioning that was seen to be pleasurable and this is the reason why pleasure was more heavily cited as a reason for engaging in such work in affluent localities where a greater proportion is of the non-routine variety and there is greater financial ability to engage in such activity.

In consequence, this study displays that self-provisioning is not simply the result of the financial inability of households to formalize work. There is also a strong resistance to its transfer to the formal sphere. Households prefer to use self-servicing due to ease, choice or pleasure. Formalization, in consequence, is constrained not only by economic factors but also by 'cultures of resistance'. The relative influence of economic constraints and agency in determining decisions to engage in self-provisioning, however, varies over space as displayed in the differential preference/necessity ratios. In affluent areas, self-provisioning is much less a product of economic constraints than in deprived areas. Indeed, despite being financially able to formalize, they choose only to formalize a narrow spectrum of mostly routine, mundane and repetitive tasks and use some of the time released to engage in more non-routine, creative and rewarding self-servicing activity that they conduct out of preference rather than necessity. In deprived areas, however, where self-provisioning is composed mostly of essential and/or routine tasks, necessity tends to prevail to a greater extent.

Many people in affluent populations thus avoid externalizing activity in order to forge forms of self-identity and worth through this type of endeavour. Self-provisioning thus provides an alternative nexus to formal employment through which people forge and display who and what they are and wish to be. The outcome is that engagement in such work seems to be retained as an act of resistance to the notion of defining who and what one is through employment alone (c.f., Gorz, 1999; Rifkin, 1996). Of course, and just as in the formal economy, the abilities of different populations to use such work in this manner vary and the sizes of the rewards differ. In deprived areas where self-servicing is compelled more by necessity, it is much less about choice and display, and much more about having to manage on one's own. In more affluent localities, however, informal work represents a sphere where needs can be fulfilled, capabilities developed and creative desires expressed, resulting in larger material and psychological benefits.

In sum, although affluent areas are more formalized in their work practices, they also engage in a wider range of informal work much of which is out of choice. Meanwhile, if households in deprived areas are witnessing an off-loading of their social reproduction functions onto the informal realm by a state and market sphere seeking to reduce social costs (e.g., Castells and Portes, 1989), this study displays that it would be erroneous to describe such areas as possessing an extensive and well-developed informal sphere. Instead, the informal sphere appears to be smaller than in affluent areas.

In the advanced economies, in conclusion, the formal economy is less pervasive than popularly assumed and there is no evidence of a universal path towards formalization. Instead, a multiplicity of work practices persists and the difference between affluent and deprived populations is not over the degree of formalization and informalization, but whether they are able to harness the resources of both the formal and the informal economies in pursuing their livelihoods and exercise choice about which to use in any particular circumstance.

Formalization in East-Central Europe

Turning away from those countries perceived to be at the front of the queue in the supposed race towards formalization and towards those viewed as further behind and therefore pre-modern, thwarted, under-developed and/or traditional in their mode of work organization, this section examines the ex-socialist economies of East-Central Europe followed by 'majority' (or 'Third') world nations further below. In both cases, answers to the following questions will be sought: What has been the nature of the transformation in these economies? To what extent have they undergone a transition towards the formal economy? And how far have they progressed, if at all, in this direction?

Until now, the widespread assumption has been that the so-called 'transition' economies of East-Central Europe are uniformly undergoing a process of formalization (and marketization), albeit with some moving at a slower rate than others. To evaluate this, two data sources are analysed here. First, time-budget studies are interrogated so as to provide a measure of the degree to which unpaid work persists in these nations. Secondly, and so as to analyse the direction of change, the New Democracies Barometer (NDB) surveys conducted in the years 1992, 1994, 1996 and 1998 in 11 countries are analysed; the countries being Poland, Czech Republic, Hungary, Slovakia, Slovenia,

Croatia, the former Republic of Yugoslavia, Romania, Bulgaria, Belarus and Ukraine (see Rose and Haerpfer, 1992; Wallace and Haerpfer, 2002; Wallace *et al.*, 2004). In each country, face-to-face interviews were conducted with a random survey of 1000 people in each of these years by established national institutes who regularly undertake nationwide representative surveys.

The penetration of the formal economy in East-Central European countries

To assess the progression of transition nations towards formalization, time-budget studies are used here to evaluate the persistence of unpaid work. As Table 3.5 reveals, across the six transition economies for which data is readily available, some 45.6 per cent of total working time is spent engaged in unpaid work. These transition economies, therefore, are far from a state of being totally formalized. However, just as there are cross-national variations in the degree to which paid work has permeated work schedules in Western economies, the same applies in East-Central Europe. In Hungary and Poland, some 58 per cent of working time is spent on paid work. For nations such as the former East Germany and ex-Yugoslavia, meanwhile, a relatively smaller amount of time is spent in the paid sphere.

Besides these time-budget data on the paid/unpaid work balance which clearly indicate the lack of penetration of paid work in these transition economies, another data set reinforcing this finding is the NDB survey. To analyse the relative importance of different forms of work to people's living standards, the NDB survey asked the following question: 'Which activity on this card is the most important for the standard of living of you and your family?' The categories of response were: growing one's own food; repairing the house; what we get as favours; what we get with help of friends, relatives; getting foreign money; earnings of second job; incidental earnings; earnings of regular job; pension, unemployment benefit; benefits at place of work; and don't know. Respondents were

Table 3.5 The paid/unpaid work balance in East-Central European nations

Country	Paid work (minutes)	Unpaid work (minutes)	% of work time spent on unpaid work
Hungary	345	254	42.4
Poland	332	244	42.4
Bulgaria	285	245	46.2
Czechoslovakia	320	272	45.9
East Germany	298	276	48.1
Ex-Yugoslavia	308	292	48.7
Mean	314	263	45.6

Source: Derived from Gershuny (2000: Table 7.1)

asked to state the sphere on which they most relied and the question was then repeated for the second most important to them for their standard of living.

Responses were then grouped for analytical purposes into four spheres. First, the earnings of a regular job, pension, unemployment benefit and benefits at the place of work were taken to delineate reliance on the 'formal economy' (work or benefits from the public formal economy). Secondly, growing one's own food and repairing the house were taken to signify reliance on 'self-provisioning' (production for household consumption). Thirdly, what we get as favours, and what we get with help of friends or relatives portrayed reliance on 'unpaid community exchange' (favours and help from friends, acquaintances and kin living outside their household), and, finally, getting foreign money, earnings of second job and incidental earnings were taken to delineate reliance on the 'undeclared sector' (paid work hidden from, or unreported to, the state for tax and/or social security purposes). The results are reported below. Table 3.6 reveals the primary sphere households rely on in these 11 transition economies, and Table 3.7 the results of asking households for both the primary and the secondary sources used.

Commencing with the primary sphere used, Table 3.6 displays that only some two-thirds (68 per cent) of households primarily rely on the formal economy for their standard of living. A third of households chiefly use the informal sphere. Such an overall statistic masks considerable cross-national variations. Comparing East-Central European nations in 1998, the proportion of households primarily depending on the informal sphere ranged from 54 per cent in Romania to 15 per cent in the Czech Republic.

Table 3.6 Primary sphere relied on by households in East-Central European countries, 1998

Country	Most important to standard of living (% of households)			
	Formal economy	Cash-in-hand work	Unpaid community exchange	Self-provisioning
Czech	85	2	2	11
Hungary	83	3	1	14
Slovenia	80	7	2	11
Slovakia	70	4	1	25
Poland	70	5	5	21
Croatia	69	10	2	18
Bulgaria	69	4	4	24
FRY	68	14	2	16
Belarus	64	8	4	26
Ukraine	57	8	3	33
Romania	46	5	2	47
Mean	68	6	3	22

Source: Derived from Wallace *et al.* (2004: Tables 5, 6, 7 and 8)

Table 3.7 Primary and secondary spheres relied on by households in East-Central European
countries, 1992–98

Combinations	1992	1994	1996	1998
Household and household	4	5	5	6
Household and social	3	2	3	2
Household and cash	3	3	3	4
Household and formal	11	10	11	11
Social and household	1	1	1	1
Social and social	0.4	1	0.3	0.4
Social and cash	1	1	1	1
Social and formal	1	1	1	1
Cash and household	2	2	1	2
Cash and social	1	1	1	1
Cash and cash	1	2	1	1
Cash and formal	3	3	3	2
Formal and household	36	33	36	32
Formal and social	8	9	11	8
Formal and cash	13	14	13	16
Formal and formal	11	11	10	13
N	10,160	10,709	10,069	11,296

Source: Derived from Wallace and Haerpfer (2002: Table 2)

These data on the principal sphere used, moreover, mask the degree to which households in practice draw upon the resources of both the formal and the informal spheres. As Table 3.7 reveals, when the primary and secondary spheres upon which they rely are analysed, the finding is that just 11 per cent of households across these countries depend on the formal sphere. Some 57 per cent of households draw on both the formal and the informal spheres while 32 per cent state that the formal sphere is neither the primary nor the secondary most important sphere for maintaining their standard of living. For a third of the population of these countries, therefore, the formal sphere plays only a minor role in their coping practices, and for a further half of the population the resources gained from the formal sphere are combined with the informal resources in their coping practices. To refer to these as 'formalized economies' when only one-tenth of households define themselves as reliant on the formal sphere is thus a gross misnomer. Most households in these transition economies draw upon diverse economic practices.

Which informal spheres are relied upon to the greatest extent to maintain living standards? As Table 3.6 reveals, in 1998 over one-fifth (21 per cent) of households relied primarily on self-provisioning, 3.4 per cent on unpaid community exchange and 7 per cent on cash-in-hand work in East-Central Europe. It appears, therefore, that even if subsistence economies are defined narrowly as meaning economies where households are reliant primarily on subsistence production for their livelihoods, such economies are alive and well in these transition economies, contrary to the nostrums of Watts (1999) who sweepingly declares, without any attempt to look at the evidence, that they are dead and gone. One in five households in East-Central Europe relies primarily on such subsistence production.

Even where the formal sector is used as either a primary or a secondary means of livelihood, moreover, it is usually combined with informal work practices. A heterogeneous portfolio of economic practices is the norm rather than the exception, with around 90 per cent of households relying on sources other than the formal sphere as either their most important or second most important source of livelihood. These data thus clearly portray the limited importance of the formal sector. What, however, about the trajectory of work?

East-Central Europe: Towards formalization?

Table 3.8 reveals no evidence of a universal process of formalization across East-Central European nations. Between 1992 and 1998, little overall growth took place in the proportion of households primarily reliant on the formal sphere for their living standards. However, these aggregate data mask considerable variations between nations. Of the ten countries for which longitudinal data is available, the proportion of households primarily reliant on the formal sphere rose in five nations over this six-year period (Czech Republic, Hungary, Slovenia, Bulgaria and Ukraine), remained stable in one country (Croatia) and fell in four nations (Belarus, Romania, Slovakia and Poland).

An alternative reading of these differences is to depict three groups of countries according to their reliance on the formal sphere and trajectories. In the first group (Czech Republic, Hungary and Slovenia), a large proportion of households (more than 80 per cent of households in 1998) depend on the formal economy as their main source of support and these countries are undergoing a process of formalization. In the second group (Slovakia and Poland), although a similar proportion of households previously relied on the formal sphere as their primary source of support as in the first group, these nations are witnessing fluctuations and even informalization over time. In the third group (Bulgaria, Belarus, Croatia, Ukraine and Romania), meanwhile, formalization is relatively low and again fluctuating.

However these countries are grouped together, the overall finding is that there is no universal linear path towards formalization. Instead, there are heterogeneous development paths. If by 'transition' economies are meant those in transition to formalization, therefore, then this term is largely inappropriate and inadequate. Nor can this region be depicted as even relatively dependent on the formal economy. As shown in Table 3.7, just 11 per cent of households in 1992 relied on the formal sphere as both their primary and secondary sources of livelihood. By 1998, this had risen to just 13 per cent. Meanwhile, the proportion of households relying on both the formal and the

Table 3.8 Primary sphere relied on by households in East-Central Europe, 1992–98

Country	Primary sphere relied on	1992	1994	1996	1998
NDB Mean	Formal	68	67	70	68
	Unpaid work	22	22	21	22
	Cash-in-hand	7	7	6	6
Czech Republic	Formal	80	82	88	85
	Unpaid work	17	15	9	11
	Cash-in-hand	7	2	2	2
Hungary	Formal	80	77	80	83
	Unpaid work	16	19	15	14
	Cash-in-hand	2	3	4	3
Slovenia	Formal	71	64	59	80
	Unpaid work	25	33	37	11
	Cash-in-hand	3	3	4	7
Slovakia	Formal	78	80	82	70
	Unpaid work	20	15	14	25
	Cash-in-hand	2	3	3	4
Poland	Formal	82	82	67	70
	Unpaid work	13	12	21	21
	Cash-in-hand	3	4	7	5
Bulgaria	Formal	67	67	63	69
	Unpaid work	24	22	28	24
	Cash-in-hand	7	9	5	4
Belarus	Formal	71	59	78	64
	Unpaid work	14	26	12	26
	Cash-in-hand	11	10	7	6
Ukraine	Formal	26	52	58	57
	Unpaid work	59	30	30	33
	Cash-in-hand	5	10	7	8
Romania	Formal	61	55	59	46
	Unpaid work	26	29	33	47
	Cash-in-hand	10	11	3	5
Croatia	Formal	69	66	71	69
	Unpaid work	7	13	11	18
	Cash-in-hand	21	17	14	10
Former Republic of Yugoslavia	Formal	–	–	–	68
	Unpaid work	–	–	–	16
	Cash-in-hand	–	–	–	14
Total sample		10,160	10,709	10,069	11,296

Source: Derived from Wallace and Haerpfer (2002: Table 1)

informal spheres declined from 57 to 56 per cent between 1992 and 1998, and the share who did not rely on the formal sphere as either their principal or secondary source of support declined from 32 to 31 per cent.

In sum, and as many have previously shown, different regions in post-socialist Europe have pursued different transitions (Boren, 2003; Piirainen, 1997; Rose and Haerpfer, 1992; Wallace and Haerpfer, 2002). Similarly, and on a household level, the diversity of coping practices used appears to show no sign of withering. Who, therefore, relies on these informally orientated coping practices and who relies on more formally oriented practices?

Socio-economic disparities in the penetration of formalization

Until now, as stated above, a popular assertion (known as the marginality thesis) has been that informal work is concentrated amongst marginalized populations who use such activity as a survival strategy. Table 3.9 reveals that although more likely to be relied on as the primary source of livelihood by the poorest sections of the population, the informal sphere is by no means used only by the poorest quartiles of the population. A large proportion of the most affluent quarter of the population also depends upon the informal spheres as their principal source of livelihood. In consequence, participation in the informal sector and reliance on it is not confined to the poorest. Its use as a principal means of livelihood occurs across the spectrum of socio-economic groups.

Whether this reliance on the informal sphere by the more affluent is an active choice is not known. It might be the case, for example, similar to advanced economies, that marginal populations use informal practices more out of economic necessity while for affluent populations such practices are more an active choice and thus a space of hope than despair (see Williams and Windebank, 2003a). Until such time as detailed research is conducted on why households use different work practices in these post-socialist

Table 3.9 Primary sphere relied on by households in East-Central Europe: by socio-economic group, 1998

	Formal	Household	Social	Cash
Household income quartile Cramers $V = .083p < 000$				
First quartile	20	32	27	22
Second quartile	24	25	19	26
Third quartile	26	25	26	26
Fourth quartile	30	18	28	26
N	4996	1968	202	499

Source: Derived from Wallace and Haerpfer (2002: Tables 4 and 5)

societies, however, little more can be said on this matter. All that can be stated is that although reliance on informal practices is more prevalent in the poorest sections of these post-socialist societies, such practices are by no means confined to these sections of the population.

In sum, East-Central European nations have heterogeneous economies and most households draw upon a plurality of economic practices in their daily lives (see Piirainen, 1997; Rose and Haerpfer, 1992; Wallace and Haerpfer, 2002). Neither is there a common trajectory towards formalization. Instead, a multitude of trajectories can be identified at the level of both the nation state and the household. It is therefore erroneous to denote these countries as being on a uniform and linear development path towards formalization. Is this also the case when the majority ('Third') world is analysed?

Formalization in the majority (Third) world

A key source of data on informal work in a majority world context is the International Labour Organization (ILO) that defines this work rather narrowly as all earning activities outside legally regulated enterprises and employment relations and, in doing so, excludes unpaid work and/or production for final use (ILO, 2002b). Despite this rather narrow definition, Table 3.10 identifies a very sizeable informal sphere relative to the formal economy in all regions of the majority world. In some Latin American countries, more workers are in the informal than formal economy (e.g., Peru) and in others one in three of the workforce is employed in this sphere (e.g., Mexico, Brazil). It is similarly the case in Africa. In Mali, some three in four jobs are in the informal economy, two in three in the United Republic of Tanzania and one in two in Ethiopia. Even in those African countries with a relatively small informal economy such as South Africa, one in four jobs is in the informal economy. In Asia, meanwhile, the informal economy is again sizeable with three in four jobs in Nepal in this sphere and nearly one in five in the Philippines.

It is similarly identified as a large sphere when the contribution of paid informal work to GDP is analysed in the majority world (Table 3.11). The average (unweighted) share of the informal sector in GDP ranges from a low of 27 per cent in Northern Africa through 29 per cent in Latin America and 31 per cent in Asia to a high of 41 per cent in sub-Saharan Africa. However, wide variations exist within each region, in part reflecting not only the varying ways in which the informal economy is defined but also actual differences in different nations and regions.

To map the contours of the informal economy in the majority world, the rest of this section charts for each major region the extent and changing size of the informal economy along with case studies of specific nations. The chief intention is to reveal that despite the rhetoric of formalization, little evidence of its widespread and ongoing penetration exists. Similar to the 'First' and 'Second' Worlds, in the 'Third' or majority

Table 3.10 % of persons employed in the informal sector: majority world countries

Country	Year	Number (in thousands)			Women/ 100 men	% of total employment		
		Total	Men	Women		Total	Men	Women
Latin America								
Mexico	1999	9141.6	5693.8	3447.7	61	31.9	32.7	30.7
Barbados	1998	6.9	4.2	2.7	63	5.9	6.8	4.9
Peru	1999	3606.1	1897.8	1708.3	90	53.8	48.9	60.6
Brazil	1997	18113.3	8652.6	9460.6	109	34.6	28.3	43.3
Africa								
Mali	1996	370.6	214.3	156.3	73	71.0	n.a.	n.a.
Benin	1999	275.5	174.8	100.7	58	46.0	50.0	41.4
Botswana	1996	60.5	21.1	39.4	187	19.3	12.3	27.6
South Africa	1999	2705.0	1162.0	1544.0	133	26.1	19.3	35.5
Ethiopia	1999	1149.5	485.6	663.9	137	50.6	38.9	64.8
Kenya	1999	1881.0	1090.4	790.6	73	36.4	43.9	29.5
United rep Tanzania	1995	345.9	221.0	124.9	57	67.0	59.7	85.3
Asia								
India	2000	79710.0	63580.0	16130.0	25	55.7	55.4	57.0
Nepal	1999	1657.0	1052.0	605.0	58	73.3	67.4	86.5
Philippines	1995	539.3	282.8	256.5	91	17.3	15.8	19.4
Turkey	2000	10139.5	1183.0	136.5	12	9.9	10.6	6.2

Source: ILO (2002b: Table 2.1)

world, not only the informal economy persists but the trajectories of work are by no means uniformly towards formalization.

Trajectories of work in Africa

In Africa, informal work represents the 'core' of the economy rather than a marginal superfluous sphere, accounting for almost 80 per cent of non-agricultural employment, over 60 per cent of urban employment and over 90 per cent of new jobs (ILO, 2002b). There is also little, if any, evidence of a uniform process of formalization on this continent. Of 13 sub-Saharan African countries, 5 have witnessed a reduction in the number of formal jobs, and job growth in another 3 countries has been significantly below the growth rate of the labour force. Of the remaining 5 that have seen jobs increase at a faster rate than the available labour force, only 2 (Mauritius and Botswana) have displayed significant growth rates in formal employment (ILO, 2002b). Similar heterogeneous trends are apparent in North Africa (ILO, 1996). This indirect proxy indicator of formalization thus intimates the existence of heterogeneous trajectories of work in different countries. Numerous studies also reveal a similar diversity in

Table 3.11 Contribution of paid informal work to GDP in majority world countries

Country	Informal sector as % of non-agricultural GDP
Northern Africa	*27*
Algeria (1997)	26
Morocco (1986)	31
Tunisia (1995)	23
Sub-Saharan Africa	*41*
Benin (1993)	43
Burkina Faso (1992)	36
Burundi (1996)	44
Cameroon (1995–96)	42
Chad (1993)	45
Cote d'Ivoire (1997)	30
Ghana (1988)	58
Guinea Bissau (1995)	30
Kenya (1999)	25
Mali (1989)	42
Mozambique (1994)	39
Niger (1995)	54
Senegal (1991)	41
Tanzania (1991)	43
Togo (1995)	55
Zambia (1998)	24
Latin America	*29*
Colombia (1992)	25
Mexico (1998)	13
Peru (1979)	49
Asia	*31*
India (1990–91)	45
Indonesia (1998)	31
Philippines (1995)	32
Republic of Korea (1995)	17

Source: ILO (2002b: Table 2.8)

trajectories within countries at the local and regional levels. In Nigeria, for instance, Anheier (1992) compares the cities of Lagos and Ibadan concluding that they have very different trajectories of work.

A case study of South Africa

Under apartheid, most informal selling in urban centres was defined as illegal, even criminal, endeavour. 'Informal', 'illegal' and 'black' were treated as synonyms and such work was discouraged by the apartheid government, but occurred because formal jobs

Table 3.12 Size of the informal economy in South Africa, 2000

	Total	Women	Men
Total employment	11,946,000	5,434,000	6,511,000
Total non-agricultural employment	10,110,000	4,581,000	5,528,000
Total agricultural employment	1,836,000	853,000	983,000
Total informal employment			
Number of persons	4,063,000	2,449,000	1,613,000
% of total employment	34	45	25
Employment in informal enterprises			
Number of persons	3,059,000	1,486,000	1,572,000
% of total employment	26	27	24
% of total informal employment	75	61	97
Non-agricultural employment in informal enterprises			
Number of persons	1,977,000	888,000	1,088,000
% of total employment	17	16	17
% of total non-agricultural employment	20	19	20
% of total informal employment	49	36	67
Agricultural employment in informal enterprises			
Number of persons	1,082,000	598,000	484,000
% of total employment	9	11	7
% of total agricultural employment	59	70	49
% of total informal employment	27	24	30
Employment in paid domestic work			
Number of persons	1,004,000	963,000	41,000
% of total employment	8	18	1
% of total informal employment	25	39	3

Source: ILO (2002b: Table 3.4)

were not obtainable by black people. Since the ending of apartheid, the informal economy has continued to grow. The South African informal economy has been estimated to be 34 per cent of total employment in the year 2000 (Table 3.12). This includes employment in informal enterprises (26 per cent of total employment and three-quarters of all informal employment) and employment in paid domestic work (8 per cent of total employment and a quarter of all informal employment in the country). Individuals working informally in formal firms are not included in these estimates, meaning that this is a conservative estimate.

Some 2.4 million women are employed in this sphere compared with 1.6 million men. Indeed, nearly half of all employed women work in the informal economy compared with a quarter of all employed men. The total number of men and women working in the informal economy, nevertheless, is similar due to the gendered composition of the overall (formal and informal) labour force. There is also a gendered segmentation of the informal labour force in terms of the sectors in which they work: some 39 per cent of women's informal employment, for example, is in domestic services compared with just 3 per cent of men's informal employment.

Over half of all employment in non-urban areas is informal (53 per cent) but only a quarter in urban areas (27 per cent). There are also marked disparities between provinces, reflecting in part both the country's apartheid history and the poverty levels. In the poorest provinces mainly located in the previous 'homeland' areas, Eastern Cape and Northern Province (now renamed Limpopo), informal work accounts for just over half of total employment. Conversely, in Western Cape and Gauteng, the two wealthiest provinces, the informal sector accounts for about one-quarter of all employment. A large part of the informal employment in these poorer provinces is comprised of subsistence agricultural workers (ILO, 2002b).

Analyzing the sectors in which informal work is currently concentrated, some 27 per cent is in the agricultural sector, 25 per cent in domestic services, and of the remainder some 30 per cent is in the construction and trade sectors. Although few clerks, professionals, technical personnel and operators work informally, the majority of farmers, gardeners and other skilled agricultural workers (81 per cent) are in the informal sector as are 36 per cent of unskilled workers, 32 per cent of craft workers and 27 per cent of service and sales workers.

Trajectories of work in Latin America

In Latin America, the informal sector is again a large and dynamic sector that employs around half of the total non-agricultural workforce and is growing in many countries faster than the formal economy. Indeed, during the 1990s in Latin America, the informal sector was the primary jobs generator with informal employment increasing by 3.9 per cent per year while formal employment grew by just 2.1 per cent (ILO, 2005).

Similar to the advanced and transition economies, however, the trajectories of economic development in Latin American countries are by no means uniformly towards formalization. As Table 3.13 depicts, there are heterogeneous trajectories of work across different nations in this region. Some nations have witnessed a formalization of their economies during the 1990s (e.g., Honduras, Panama), albeit at different rates and to varying extents. Others, however, have witnessed informalization (e.g., Paraguay, Chile), again at very different rates and from contrasting base levels. The pattern as such is one of polarized development and this polarization increased in intensity during the 1990s. Of those Latin American nations that are formalizing, that is, the countries doing so at the quickest rate during the 1990s were generally those with already relatively high levels of formalization (e.g., Panama). Similarly, of Latin American nations pursuing informalization, it was again the countries already heavily informalized that were moving

Table 3.13 Share of informal sector in non-agricultural employment, Latin America, 1990 and 1994

Country	1990	1994	Trend 1990–94
Venezuela	38.8	44.8	Informalization
Panama	40.4	40.2	Formalization
Costa Rica	42.3	46.2	Informalization
Argentina	47.5	52.5	Informalization
Chile	49.9	51.0	Informalization
Ecuador	51.6	54.2	Informalization
Peru	51.8	56.0	Informalization
Brazil	52.0	56.4	Informalization
Honduras	54.2	51.9	Formalization
Mexico	55.5	57.0	Informalization
Bolivia	56.9	61.3	Informalization, Rapid
Colombia	59.1	61.6	Informalization
Paraguay	61.4	68.9	Informalization, Rapid

Source: ILO (1996: Table 5.5)

along this development path at the fastest speed (e.g., Paraguay). As such, a divergence in the trajectories of work is taking place in Latin America.

Heterogeneous development paths are apparent not only on a cross-national but also on an intra-national level. A study of six metropolitan areas in northeast Brazil (Rio, Sao Paulo, Belo Horizonte, Recife, Salvador, Fortaleza) finds significant differences in the magnitude, growth and character of informal work (Schuster, cited in Lautier, 1994). In a study of Mexico, in addition, PREALC showed significant differences between Guadalajara, Monterey and Mexico City in terms of both the extent and the nature of informal work which they put down to the rather limited variable of the contrasting industrial structure of the three areas (see Roberts, 1990). Martin (1996), again in Mexico, identifies significant differences in the intensity to which, and how, informal work is employed in household work strategies in urban and rural areas.

A case study of Mexico

In 1998, informal work accounted for 64 per cent of total employment in Mexico, suggesting that the trend towards informalization identified in Table 3.13 accelerated during the late 1990s. Indeed, some two-thirds of total employment was in the informal sector in 2000 and a third of GDP was produced in the informal economy (Table 3.14). The non-agricultural component represented 45 per cent of total informal employment and was equally divided between employment in informal enterprises (23 per cent of total employment) and informal employment outside informal enterprises (22 per cent of total employment). Informal work in agriculture was 19 per cent of total employment.

Table 3.14 Size of the informal economy in Mexico, 2000

	Employment (in thousands)	% of all employment	% of GDP	% of non-agricultural GDP
Informal enterprises	8,858	23.0	13.0	13.4
Informal employment outside informal enterprises	8,480	22.0	14.0	14.8
Non-agricultural informal employment	17,338	45.0	27.0	28.2
Agricultural informal employment	7,334	19.0	5.0	–
Total informal employment	24,673	64.0	32.0	–

Source: ILO (2002b: Table 3.2)

As Table 3.15 reveals, twice as many men as women worked informally in 2000, 16 million men compared with 7.7 million women. Since fewer women than men are in the labour force, the gender gap is narrower in terms of the relative shares of informal employment in total employment: 58 per cent of women workers are in informal employment compared with 64 per cent of men. For both men and women, informal employment is about 55 per cent of non-agricultural employment and almost evenly divided between employment in informal enterprises and informal jobs outside informal enterprises. Across the major industry groups, some 94 per cent of the total agricultural workforce is employed informally, 73 per cent in construction and trade, 63 per cent in transportation, 48 per cent in communal, personal and other services and 22 per cent in financial services, insurance and real estate (ILO, 2002b).

Informal work, however, is not a low-paid exploitative form of employment in Mexico. Per capita income from the informal sector (informal sector GDP divided by employment in informal enterprises) is well above the Mexican minimum wage, and the gap widened between 1995 and 1999. Indeed, per capita informal income was 4.5 times the minimum wage in 1995 and increased to 5.2 times the minimum wage in 1999. For men, the ratio went from 4.9 in 1995 to 5.8 in 1999, while for women it went from 3.8 to 4.2 (ILO, 2002b). However, wages in the informal labour market are as polarized as wages in the formal labour market (see De Pardo *et al.*, 1989; Guisinger and Irfan, 1980; Roberts, 1989, 1990). In consequence, informal work is not always a low-paid form of work conducted by marginalized groups as a last resort. Neither can such paid informal work simply be seen as a way of exploiting cheap labour. As Tokman (1986) finds in Costa Rica, Colombia and Peru, considerable variation in informal wage rates exists and for some categories of informal workers such as shop owners, earnings are higher than for formal workers. Portes *et al.* (1986) discover much the same situation in Montevideo,

Table 3.15 Nature of the informal economy in Mexico, 2000

	Total	Women	Men
Total employment	38,983,855	13,311,213	25,672,642
Total non-agricultural employment	31,923,149	12,349,830	19,573,319
Total agricultural employment	7,060,706	961,383	6,099,323
Total informal employment			
Number of persons	24,075,641	7,699,621	16,376,020
% of total employment	62	58	64
Non-agricultural informal employment			
Number of persons	17,418,280	6,794,849	10,623,431
% of total employment	72	88	65
% of total non-agricultural employment	55	55	54
Agricultural informal employment			
Number of persons	6,657,361	904,772	5,752,589
% of total employment	28	12	35
% of total agricultural employment	94	94	94
Non-agricultural informal employment in informal enterprises			
Number of persons	9,122,222	3,660,584	5,461,638
% of total employment	23	28	21
% of total non-agricultural employment	29	30	28
% of total informal employment	38	48	33
% of non-agricultural informal employment	52	54	51
Non-agricultural informal employment outside informal enterprises			
Number of persons	8,296,058	3,134,265	5,161,793
% of total employment	21	46	20
% of total non-agricultural employment	26	25	26
% of total informal employment	34	41	31
% of non-agricultural informal employment	48	46	49

Source: ILO (2002b: Table 3.3)

Uruguay. Defining informal work as always low paid is to ignore the large number of well-paid informal workers and the considerable number of formal employees earning less than the average informal wage.

Trajectories of work in Asia

In Asia, informal workers constitute from 45 to 85 per cent of non-agricultural employment and from 40 to 60 per cent of all urban employment (ILO, 2002b). In parts of East Asia, namely Japan, the Republic of North Korea, Singapore, Hong Kong and China, the informal economy declined as manufacturing industry expanded and created jobs in the formal economy. Increasing emphasis on education and training enabled the labour force to keep up with the growing demand for more skilled workers. As this demand increased, social protection expanded, wages rose and working conditions improved. A consequence was the need to identify cheaper sources of labour for more repetitive and labour-intensive manufacturing industries. During the 1980s and 1990s, a lot of this type of manufacturing shifted first to Southeast Asia and then also to South Asia, with much of the sourcing done by companies still based in Japan, the Republic of Korea, Hong Kong and China.

East and Southeast Asia are often assumed to be the regions of the world that have undergone a process of formalization due to the new international division of labour (NIDL) that has increasingly dispersed physical production functions, and more recently call centres, into this region whilst retaining the control and command functions in a network of global cities in advanced economies (e.g., Sassen, 1991). During the 1970s and 1980s, the beneficiaries of the NIDL were the middle-income nations such as the Republic of Korea, Hong Kong and Singapore, who have now purportedly joined the ranks of the advanced economies and been replaced by a second-wave of middle income countries including Malaysia, Thailand and Indonesia (Hall, 1996). It appears superficially, therefore, that formalization is a widespread phenomenon in this region of the world. Indeed, the evidence on employment growth seems to support this assertion. Between 1986 and 1993 in East and Southeast Asian nations, with the sole exception of Indonesia, employment rose at more than 3 per cent per annum, well in excess of the rate of increase in the labour force (ILO, 1996).

However, is the process of formalization so clear-cut in these 'tiger' economies? For example, examining Hong Kong, Singapore, South Korea and Taiwan, Cheng and Gereffi (1994) highlight the way in which informal modes of production have played a major role in their recent economic development and growth. In Taiwan, for instance, very weak regulation of the small firms sector enabled the growth of cash-in-hand work that has been a central pillar in the country's success at pursuing export-led development. As Cheng and Gereffi (1994) clearly display in the case of both the Hong Kong and the Taiwanese economies, formal jobs have not replaced informal work. Rather, they have grown in tandem. Caution must be therefore exercised when taking the remarkable growth rate of formal jobs in East and Southeast Asia as an indicator of formalization. Instead, it appears that there are different processes in different nations. For example, whilst in Hong Kong and Taiwan informal work seems to have expanded alongside formal jobs, in the more highly regulated economies of South Korea and Singapore such work appears to be both limited and, if anything, contracting relative to formal employment. Again, therefore, and similar to Latin America but perhaps more marked, there is evidence of heterogeneous development paths being pursued within this region with some countries undergoing a process of rapid formalization whilst others have either maintained their formal/informal balance or undergone a process of informalization.

The case of India

The informal workforce in India is an estimated 370 million workers, nearly 93 per cent of the total workforce (Table 3.16). In this country, therefore, the informal economy is very much the 'mainstream' and the formal economy a minor peripheral 'backwater'. The informal workforce is comprised of three main segments. First, there is informal work in agriculture – comprised of the self-employed in small-scale farm units and of

Table 3.16 Size of the informal economy in India, 2000

	Total	Women	Men
Total employment (in thousands)[a]	397,720	123,270	274,450
Total non-agricultural employment (in thousands)	159,897	31,061	128,836
Total agricultural employment (in thousands)	238,197	92,308	145,889
Total informal employment[b]			
Number of persons (in thousands)	369,755	118,220	251,533
% of total employment	93	96	92
Non-agricultural informal employment[c]			
Number of persons (in thousands)	133,355	26,601	106,751
% of total employment	34	22	39
% of total non-agricultural employment	83	86	83
% of total informal employment	36	23	42
Employment in informal enterprises			
Number of persons (in thousands)	110,034	22,200	87,834
% of total employment	28	18	32
% of total non-agricultural employment	69	71	68
% of total informal employment	30	19	35
% of non-agricultural informal employment	83	83	82
Residual[d]			
Number of persons (in thousands)	23,321	4,401	18,917
% of total employment	6	4	7
% of total non-agricultural employment	15	14	15
% of total informal employment	6	4	8
% of non-agricultural informal employment	17	17	18
Agricultural informal employment			
Number of persons (in thousands)	236,779	91,723	145,056
% of total employment	60	74	53
% of agricultural employment	99	99	99
% of total informal employment	64	78	58

[a] Refers to population age 5 or above
[b] Total informal employment includes both agricultural and non-agricultural informal employment
[c] Non-agricultural informal employment consists of employment in informal enterprise plus 'residual'
[d] The 'residual' equals total non-agricultural informal employment minus employment in the informal sector
Source: ILO (2002b: Table 3.1)

agricultural labour – which represents 60 per cent of total employment and 64 per cent of total informal work. Secondly, there is employment in informal enterprises outside agriculture, which represents another 28 per cent of total employment and 30 per cent of total informal work. Finally, there is informal employment outside informal enterprise and agriculture – an estimated 6 per cent of the total informal workforce (this is the residual category in Table 3.16). Of the total non-agricultural workforce, 133 million workers or 83 per cent are in the informal economy.

Women constitute one-third of all informal workers (118 million) and men thus account for two-thirds (252 million). These women informal workers are mainly concentrated in agriculture, with about three-quarters of all employed women working informally in agriculture. Over half (53 per cent) of all employed men are in informal agricultural work and 32 per cent in informal enterprises (ILO, 2002b). Informal work accounts for virtually all employment in agriculture and in trade (99 per cent for both industries) and the overwhelming share of employment in construction (94 per cent). It also accounts for the majority of workers employed in transport and storage (79 per cent) and in social and personal services as well as financial services (66 per cent in both industries).

The National Accounts Statistics of India estimates the contribution of the formal and informal sectors to Net Domestic Product (NDP), that is, the GDP minus depreciation. In 1997–98, the contribution of the informal sector was 60 per cent of the total NDP. Excluding agriculture, the informal sector contributed 45 per cent of non-agricultural NDP (see ILO, 2002b). These figures are well below the proportions employed because the assumption made is that productivity is much lower in the informal economy. Whether this is the case, however, is by no means clear-cut and it is also perhaps the case that other indicators of performance are required besides productivity when assessing the contribution of these sectors to people's livelihoods.

In sum, this brief tour of the majority world reveals the existence of an informal sector that is often so large, even using a narrow definition that excludes self-provisioning, that it is the mainstream and the formal economy a minor backwater. It also reveals that the trajectory of work throughout the majority world is by no means towards formalization. Instead, diverse trajectories are being pursued throughout the majority world. Whether these trajectories should be temporally convened and those pursuing formalization denoted as 'modernizing' and those pursuing informalization as moving 'backwards', as is the case in the formalization thesis, is a mute point. This, after all, is to overlay onto formalization a set of normative judgements about what ought to be the direction of change and values about the nature of formal and informal work that are far from proven.

Conclusions

This chapter has revealed that even if employment participation rates were found to be increasing, this does not indicate a process of formalization. This is because formal jobs do not everywhere and always replace the informal economy. Sometimes formal and informal work may display a substitutive relationship but they may also possess a strong co-constitutive relationship with the growth of one leading to the growth of the other. In consequence, an increase in employment participation rates might indicate a process of formalization (if formal work is growing faster than informal work), no change in the overall balance of formal and informal work (if formal and informal work grow at the same rate) or informalization (if informal work grows faster than formal work). Employment participation rates alone, therefore, do not indicate whether or not formalization is taking place. Instead, the changing balance between the formal and the informal economies needs to be investigated.

Comparing how the relative volume of formal and informal work is changing across the world, some remarkable findings have been identified here. In Western economies, the degree of formalization is far less than perhaps commonly imagined and there has been no uniform path towards formalization over the past four decades or so. Instead, Western economies appear to be composed of a plurality of economic practices with heterogeneous development paths being pursued. Although some are pursuing formalization, many others are undergoing a process of informalization.

In the so-called 'transition' economies of East-Central Europe, a similar diversity of economic practices and trajectories is witnessed. Plural economic practices are the norm rather than the exception, and diverse trajectories of work can be identified with some nations formalizing, others maintaining a balance between formal and informal work and yet others witnessing informalization. Similarly, the majority ('Third') world in general terms possesses large informal sectors and sometimes very small formal economies that can only be characterized as relatively marginal and peripheral backwaters, and again there is little clear evidence that formalization is the universal trajectory.

Consequently, the notion that all nations can be ordered into a queue according to their degree of formalization, with nations at the back waiting to follow those at the front, is far from the lived experience. Not only are many nations at the front (Western economies) pursuing a path of informalization but also there is little evidence that those in the middle and at the back are edging towards formalization. Conflating current spatial differences into such a temporal sequence fails to capture the complexity and multi-dimensionality of the situation.

Until now, therefore, and based on the assumption that the formalization of working life is a near universal process, business and management studies has confined the study of work organization to the sphere of formal employment grounded in the view that this is becoming the dominant form of work globally. However, this chapter has revealed that defining business and management studies in general, and work organization in particular, as being about the study of formal employment (whether in public, private or third-sector enterprises) misses the vast bulk of work in the world today. Beyond formal employment is a vast territory of economic endeavour that has been largely ignored. Yet if the ways in which work is organized in the present and might be organized in the future are to be more fully understood, then such work that constitutes the majority of economic endeavour cannot be ignored. In the past, it has been assumed that because work was shifting into the formal economy, it was wholly acceptable to focus on the formal sphere and ignore this 'other' realm. This chapter, however, reveals that this is far from the case. The consequences are profound. When studying the current and future organization of work, formal employment alone can no longer be the sole focus. To do so is to study just one rather minor segment of the world of work in a vacuum rather than the organization of work as a totality and how this is changing.

Further reading

Robinson, J. and Godbey, G. (1997) *Time for Life: The Surprising Ways Americans Use Their Time*, Pennsylvania: Pennsylvania State University Press.

Discussing North America, this book provides a detailed analysis of how North Americans use their time and displays the persistence and even growth of unpaid work even in this part of the world where formalization is supposedly near hegemonic.

Wallace, C. and Haerpfer, C. (2002) 'Patterns of participation in the informal economy in East-Central Europe', in R. Neef and M. Stanculescu (eds) *The Social Impact of Informal Economies in Eastern Europe*, Aldershot: Ashgate.

This chapter reports evidence from the NDB surveys conducted in 1992, 1994, 1996 and 1998 in 11 East-Central European countries and reveals the geographical variations in the degree to which a path of formalization has been pursued across these post-socialist societies.

ILO (2002a) *Decent Work and the Informal Economy*, Geneva: International Labour Organization.

This seminal text on the informal economy not only reviews the extent and nature of the informal economy in Third World nations but also explores some of the policy options concerning what should be done about this form of work.

ILO (2002b) *Women and Men in the Informal Economy: A Statistical Picture*, Geneva: International Labour Organization.

This book provides a comprehensive portrait of the variations in the degree to which men and women engage in paid and unpaid work in Third World nations, displaying the significant differences in different countries and the variations in the direction of change.

4

The all-pervasive penetration of the market

Introduction

It is not just the formalization thesis that dominates thought on the future of work. Another pervasive narrative is that the capitalist mode of production is becoming more powerful, expansive and totalizing, penetrating deeper into each and every corner of economic life and stretching its tentacles wider across the globe to colonize those remaining areas left untouched by its powerful force. For many, this is an indisputable and irrefutable fact. Indeed, this unstoppable transition towards a commodified world is so widely believed that it is perhaps difficult today for many to consider any other future. Seemingly, there really is 'no alternative'. The future is cast in stone and it is one in which there will be an ongoing process of what is variously referred to as 'commercialization', 'marketization' or 'commodification'.

In this chapter, this widely held (often fatalistic but sometimes celebrated) acceptance of an ever more commodified world is put under the spotlight. To analyse whether goods and services are increasingly produced for monetized exchange by capitalist firms for the purpose of profit, rather than by the state or community, this chapter investigates the changing nature of work organization in, first, the heartlands of commodification, namely the advanced 'market' economies, secondly, the post-socialist ('second') world of East-Central Europe and, finally, the majority ('Third') world. This will display that commodification is far from a universal process.

The advanced economies: a commodified world?

It is today widely believed that the vast majority of goods and services in advanced 'market' economies are produced and delivered for monetized exchange by profit-seeking capitalist firms and that non-commodified forms of production and delivery have gradually disappeared as commodified practices have encroached deeper into everyday life. To evaluate this, and given that commodified work refers to monetized exchanges for the purpose of profit, first, whether non-exchanged work persists in advanced economies, secondly, whether non-monetized exchanges continue to prevail and, finally, whether there exist monetized exchanges outside the logic of profit will be evaluated here.

Is non-exchanged work in decline?

According to those believing that the world is becoming ever more commodified, few remaining vestiges of non-exchanged (subsistence) work persist in the advanced economies and those remnants that do are little more than leftovers of pre-capitalism existing in the peripheries and rapidly dwindling (e.g., Watts, 1999). Even if others would perhaps not go that far, it is widely believed that the realm of non-exchanged work is steadily declining as the commodified realm takes hold. It is often asserted, for example, that Western populations now engage in fewer activities like do-it-yourself, repairing clothes, preparing their own meals, growing their own food and mending goods. The overwhelming perception is that such subsistence work has been, or is being, replaced by commodified practices. There may be the odd example of either peasant households where subsistence living is practised or of people 'downshifting' to a simpler life, such as the 'back-to-the-landers' in the US (Jacob, 2003), but on the whole, such a mode of work organization is viewed as a minor practice in contemporary commodified societies. Indeed, so obvious is this that many commentators seldom pause long enough to consider whether this is indeed the case.

However, it takes only a little reflection to realize that this view is highly contestable. People and households cannot and should not be classified according to their reliance on one principal form of work. It is much more an understanding of how households combine different modes of production that is important if the nature of work and its direction in advanced economies is to be more fully understood. Of course, if one examines how many today rely solely or primarily on subsistence production, then Western economies have probably witnessed the death of the subsistence economy. As Jacob (2003) displays, even those 'back-to-the-landers' in the US seeking to return to a subsistence economy have found that pursuing a single mode of production is difficult, if not impossible, to achieve. The mistake of these 'back-to-the-landers', however, similar to the commodification theorists, is that they have viewed subsistence production as a separate 'economy' rather than as one of many forms of work that can be used by households.

Once subsistence work is viewed as one of a range of economic practices employed by households, a very different picture of such work emerges. It may be correct that the subsistence 'economy' (i.e., people and households relying on non-exchanged work as their principal mode of production) hardly exists in advanced economies. However, this is not correct so far as subsistence 'work' is concerned (Bennholdt-Thomsen and Mies, 1999; Bennholdt-Thomsen et al., 2001). Even if goods production has moved out of the household, it is not the same with service production. Households still engage in a tremendous range of self-servicing activity from routine housework, cleaning windows, cooking, gardening, childcare and elder-care through to car maintenance along with home maintenance and improvement activity. The move of goods production into the marketplace, therefore, seems to have been only partially followed by a shift of service provision into the market realm (Gershuny, 1978; Williams and Windebank, 2001h).

Measuring the proportion of working time spent on subsistence work

As displayed in the last chapter, nearly half of the total time that people spend working in advanced economies is spent engaged in non-exchanged work (see Table 3.2). In the UK in 2000, for example, a time-budget study conducted by the Office of National Statistics found that on average a person spent 3 hours and 25 minutes each day engaged in formal employment and study, while 3 hours and 6 minutes was spent engaged in subsistence work, 4 minutes in formal volunteering and 8 minutes in giving informal help to others (Ruston, 2003). Non-exchanged work and non-monetized exchange therefore occupies 3 hours and 14 minutes of people's work schedules while formal employment and study occupies only a few minutes more. This means that of total working time, some 49 per cent of time is spent on unpaid work, the bulk of which is spent engaged in subsistence work. This is similarly the case in many other Western nations, as shown in last chapter. The sphere of subsistence work, so long considered the residual and diminishing 'other', is the same size as the paid sphere, measured in terms of the volume of time spent on it. Working life, in consequence, is far from totally commodified.

To put a monetary value on this time, three techniques have been adopted: opportunity costs; housekeeper wage costs and occupational wage costs. In each, monetary values from the market sector are used to impute values to subsistence work or its products (Luxton, 1997). The opportunity-costs model calculates the income the worker would have earned if he or she had been in the paid labour force instead of undertaking subsistence work. The housekeeper wage-costs approach calculates how much a worker in paid employment doing similar work is paid, and the occupational wage-costs approach measures the price of household inputs by calculating market equivalents for the costs of raw materials, production and labour for each product and/or service (e.g., Ironmonger, 1996, 2000, 2002; Luxton, 1997; OECD, 1997, 2002).

In Britain, a 1995 survey using these valuation methods finds that subsistence work was worth anywhere between 56 and 122 per cent of GDP (Murgatroyd and Neuburger, 1997). In France, meanwhile, unpaid work was found to be worth one half of GNP in 1975 according to the opportunity-cost and replacement methods (which on the whole use women's wage rates as a basis of calculation) and two-thirds of GNP on the final method which uses wage rates current for men as well as women (Chadeau and Fouquet, 1981). Far from being some minor vestige of pre-capitalism, therefore, the subsistence sphere is alive and well in advanced economies and reports of its death are at best premature and at worst unwarranted.

It is unwarranted because over the past 40 years by no means all countries have witnessed a shift of work from the unpaid to the paid sphere (see Chapter 3). Working life is not becoming universally more monetized, as propounded by exponents of the commodification thesis who depict a hegemonic, pervasive, victorious, all-powerful and expansive commodity economy, and thus a weak, primitive, traditional, stagnant, marginal, residual or dwindling non-commodified realm. Rather, subsistence (non-exchanged) work is as large as the realm of paid work measured in terms of the time that the populations of the advanced economies spend engaged in this work, and is even growing in some countries relative to the commodified realm. As such, grave doubts must be cast over this dominant discourse that advanced 'capitalist' economies are becoming ever more commodified. Indeed, as Byrne *et al.* (2001: 3–4) state, 'to call a society or economy "capitalist" is an act of categorical violence, one that obliterates from view the economic activity that engages more people for more hours of the day over more years of their lives than any other'. It is not only the persistence of subsistence work, however, that casts doubts over the notion of an increasingly commodified Western world.

Non-monetized exchanges

A second component of the commodification thesis is that whenever goods and services are exchanged, money changes hands. For adherents to the commodification thesis such as Harvey (1982: 373), 'Monetary relations have penetrated every nook and cranny of the world and into almost every aspect of social, even private life.' As such, in the commodification thesis, non-monetized exchange is viewed in one of two ways. On the one hand, it is simply seen as a minor work practice leftover from pre-capitalism, rapidly diminishing and of little importance. As Rifkin (1990: 30) asserts, 'What we have lived through in the rich world has been the accelerating passage of non-monetized activity into the formal economy, its colonization by market transactions.' On the other hand, and for those who recognize that this colonization of non-monetized exchange by the market is not so complete, the ongoing incursion of commodification remains unquestioned. This is because of how they conceptualize such exchange. By siphoning off non-monetized activity into the 'non-economic' or welfare realm separate from the 'economy' proper, its persistence does not challenge their view that work is becoming more commodified (see Chapter 10). To what extent, therefore, does non-monetized exchange prevail in advanced economies?

The changing size of the sphere of non-monetized exchange

A multitude of studies exist of various aspects of non-monetized exchange such as volunteering and unpaid reciprocity (e.g., Berking, 1999; Caplow, 1982; Cheal, 1988; Dekker and van den Broek, 1998; Putnam, 2000; Wuthnow, 1992). Many use participation rates to show that such work is extensively undertaken in the advanced economies. Wuthnow (1992), for example, points out how 80 million US citizens (45 per cent of the population aged over 18) spend five or more hours each week on voluntary services and charitable activity, which adds up to well over US$150 billion per annum.

In the European Union, meanwhile, it has been similarly shown that three out of ten people spend time helping people on a voluntary basis (European Commission, 2001a) and that 6 per cent of citizens provide unpaid informal care to sick or disabled adults and older people in the same household or outside on a daily basis (European Commission, 2000a).

In the UK, for example, the 2001 Home Office Citizenship Survey (HOCS), surveying a sample of 15,475 people aged 16 and over in England and Wales (see Prime et al., 2002) found that in the prior 12 months, 67 per cent of people had helped a neighbour and 39 per cent had done work for a voluntary organization. Given that in the prior 12 months 110.5 hours were spent on formal volunteering, some 1.82 billion hours of formal non-monetized exchange was identified as taking place. Of the 28.3 million engaging in one-to-one unpaid exchange in the last 12 months, meanwhile, the average number of hours was 66.4 hours, meaning that some 1.88 billion hours had been conducted. Comparing the volume of inputs into non-monetized exchange with the volume of inputs into commodified work, the 3.7 billion hours of volunteering in the previous 12 months represents the equivalent of just over 2 million people employed full-time (at 35 hours per week). In short, for every 14 hours worked in formal employment in the UK (assuming 27 million people working on an average of 35 hours), approximately 1 hour is spent working on a non-monetized basis. Non-monetized exchange thus constitutes some 7 per cent of the total time that people spend engaged in formal employment in the UK, meaning that such work is far from a marginal leftover, especially when it is recognized that not all paid exchange, as will be shown below, is commodified work.

Another way of measuring non-monetized exchange relative to the commodity economy is to analyse the value of the outputs. Ironmonger (2002) in South Australia has found that in 1997 unpaid exchange was worth some A$24–31 billion per annum depending on the valuation method used, and South Australian volunteers are estimated to have donated the equivalent of an additional 11.5 per cent of Gross State Product (GSP) in 2000 to other households, both directly and through organizations and groups. These donations are additional to actual donations of money made directly to other households or through charitable organizations. Alternatively, measuring total volunteer time in relation to the total wages earned by South Australian employees, such activity represents an additional 21.7 per cent of the total value of the wages paid to employees in employment in South Australia in 2000.

Whatever technique is used to measure the amount of non-monetized exchange, therefore, the finding is that non-commodified work is not some minor remnant in advanced capitalist societies. It is a significant proportion of the total work that is taking place. But is it growing or diminishing? Although the commodification thesis purports it to be diminishing, the evidence points in the opposite direction. Take, for example, the study of South Australia (Table 4.1). Ironmonger (2002) finds that between 1992 and 2000, the hours per week spent by the average adult on volunteering activity rose by 35 per cent in the first 5-year period (1992–97) and 30 per cent in the second 5-year envelope of time (1995–2000).

Table 4.1   Hours per week per adult spent engaged in formal and informal volunteering
(averaged over all adult population aged 18+), South Australia, 1992–2000

Volunteering	1992	1995	1997	2000	Change 1992–97 (%)	Change 1995–2000 (%)
Organized	0.62	0.91	1.11	1.40	80	54
Unorganized	1.44	1.58	1.68	2.82	17	15
Travel	0.51	0.55	0.58	0.63	15	14
Total	2.56	3.05	3.37	3.86	32	27

Source: Derived from Ironmonger (2002: Table 2)

Table 4.2   Total value of volunteer work in South Australia, 1992–2000

Volunteering	1992	1995	1997	2000	Change 1992–97 (%)	Change 1995–2000 (%)
Organized ($m)	566	948	1272	1810	124	91
Unorganized ($m)	1325	1650	1931	2356	46	43
Travel ($m)	465	575	670	814	44	42
Total value	2357	3174	3873	4980	64	57
Gross State Product ($bn)	30.3	34.6	37.9	43.3	25	25
Compensation of employees ($bn)	14.8	16.9	18.4	20.35	24	20

Source: Derived from Ironmonger (2002: Table 5)

Table 4.2 puts a market value on this work and evaluates how its value is changing over time, finding that as a proportion of GSP, non-monetized work is growing. South Australian volunteers donated an additional 7.8 per cent of GSP in 1992 but an extra 11.5 per cent of GSP in 2000 to other households, both directly and through organizations and groups. Put another way, the total volunteer time was equivalent to an additional 14.1 per cent of the total value of the wages paid to employees in employment in South Australia in 1992 and 21.7 per cent in 2000.

In sum, and contrary to the tenets of the commodification thesis, non-monetized exchange is expanding relative to the commodified realm. Today, non-monetized exchange is conducted by a large proportion of the population, is equal to somewhere around 10–12 per cent of GDP and is growing. When combined with the above data on subsistence work, moreover, it is difficult to accept the view that the commodity economy is universally penetrating deeper and wider across the advanced economies.

Not-for-profit monetized exchanges

The final assumption in the commodification thesis is that as money penetrates more areas of life, this marches hand in hand with the profit motive. So is the monetized sphere everywhere and always composed of transactions conducted for the purpose of economic gain? Or are there realms in which monetary exchanges are conducted for reasons other than profit? If so, are these not-for-profit monetary transactions growing or declining? To answer these questions, three spheres of activity are here analysed: the public sector; the not-for-profit sector and mainstream private sector enterprises.

The demise of the state?

If goods and services were increasingly delivered by the state that by definition is not orientated towards profit, then it could be concluded that monetized exchange is by no means becoming increasingly dominated by the profit motive. However, this is not the case. Trends such as privatization and quasi-privatization of the public sphere, the contracting out of goods and services previously provided by the state directly, and various public–private finance initiatives (e.g., Clark and Root, 1999; Kerr, 1998; Tickell, 2001) all indicate that goods and services are being delivered more by the market than the state, intimating that the relationship between monetized exchange and the profit motive is becoming stronger.

However, two important caveats need to be raised. First, just because the state is now providing fewer goods and services on a direct basis does not necessarily mean that profit-motivated exchange is becoming more dominant. Not all goods and services are being off-loaded onto the private sector. Many are being transferred to not-for-profit organizations (e.g., Amin *et al.*, 2002a; Birchall, 2001a; Lutz, 1999). Even when provided by the private sector, moreover, it is by no means certain that profit is the sole motive in attendance in such businesses (see below).

Secondly, even if the state is receding in importance as a direct provider of goods and services, its role is not diminishing. Indeed, the state remains a vital component in the constitution of capitalism (e.g., Jessop, 2002; O'Neill, 1997; Painter, 2003). State power permeates almost all aspects of work organization and even if direct state provision of goods and services may be in decline, wider goods and services provision is affected by the state in deep-seated and enduring ways (Painter, 2003). Contrary to the rhetoric of neo-liberals, the state has not been 'rolled back' if by that is meant that work organization is beyond the scope of state power. Rather, the exercise of state power appears to have become more intense over time, not less. One has only to consider how the state in Western economies implements policies on an ever-widening range of economic issues. New legislation and regulations are added much more quickly than old ones are repealed. Each year, new aspects of work organization become subject to surveillance, regulation and intervention.

The state, market and civil society, therefore, are not wholly independent entities. They interpenetrate each other. Indeed, many goods and services delivered by the market and civil society are either contracted out by the state sphere or heavily regulated and even controlled by it. As O'Neill (1997: 291) thus asserts, there is a need to reject

the politically charged discourse that markets are capable of a separate, private existence beyond the actions of the state's apparatus. Rather, a qualitative view of the state is preferred. In this view, the state is seen to play an indispensable role in the creation, governance and conduct of markets, including at the international scale.

Drawing upon the work of scholars such as Polanyi (1944) and Block (1994), O'Neill (1997: 294) thus sets out four tenets concerning the role of the state:

First, economy is necessarily a combination of three events: markets, state action and state regulation. A corollary of this constitution is that there is an infinite number of ways in which an economy can be organized. Second, although economic efficiency is dependent on markets, markets are state-constrained and state-regulated and thereby incapable of operating in a laissez-faire environment. Third, neither capital nor the state is capable of achieving its goals simultaneously nor independently. Finally, it should be recognized that any coherence that exists about the idea of economy derives essentially from our cultural beliefs, which (in Anglo cultures at least) have led to constructions of economy being overlain with the dichotomy of planned versus market, which, in turn, has had the effect of denying the existence of multiple forms of economy.

These four tenets are important. They display that even if the production and delivery of goods and services is moving away from the state to the market, this does not mean either that the state is in demise or that there is now a commodified sphere beyond the reach of the state. In short, the demise of the state as a direct provider of goods and services does not spell the increasing dominance of the profit motive. To argue this is to assume that goods and services provided by the state have been transferred to profit-motivated capitalist firms. This is blatantly not the case. Many, as will be now shown, are being transferred to either the unpaid sphere (already discussed) or the not-for-profit organizations (e.g., Amin et al., 2002a; Birchall, 2001a; Lutz, 1999), and the advent of the latter mode of delivery suggests that the relationship between the profit motive and monetized exchange is not becoming stronger.

The not-for-profit sector

This sector covers organizations that are private (not part of the apparatus of government), not profit distributing (do not distribute profits to their managers or owners), self-governing (fundamentally in control of their own affairs) and voluntary in that membership in them is not legally required and they attract some level of voluntary contribution of time or money (Salamon and Anheier, 1999; Salamon et al., 1999). Using this common definition of the not-for-profit sector, a major international piece of research, the John Hopkins Comparative Non-Profit Sector Project, has provided a baseline assessment of its size and nature in 26 countries (Austria, Belgium, Finland, France, Germany, Ireland, Italy, the Netherlands, Norway, Spain, Sweden and the UK in Western Europe; the Czech Republic, Hungary, Poland, Romania and Slovakia in East-Central Europe; Argentina, Brazil, Colombia, Mexico and Peru in Latin America; and Australia, Israel, Japan and the US).

The findings of this cross-national project provide strong evidence that this sector is not some insignificant backwater but is in fact a major 'third prong' in the mixed economies that constitute the Western nations. In the 26 countries studied in the first wave of their project, they identify that the transactions of non-profit organizations represented 4.6 per cent of GDP on average across these nations, and that there were some 31 million full-time equivalent workers (or 6.8 per cent of the non-agricultural workforce) including 19.7 million full-time equivalent paid workers and 11.3 million full-time equivalent volunteer workers. Indeed, if the non-profit sector in the 26 nations surveyed were to be a country, its GDP of US$1.2 trillion would make it the sixth largest economy in the world, ahead of the UK, Brazil, Russia, Canada and Spain. The not-for-profit sector in consequence, cannot be dismissed as of only limited or marginal importance and nor can it be assumed that the transfer of responsibility for delivering goods and services away from the state has resulted in a universal shift to the market.

Indeed, and as the John Hopkins Non-Profit Sector Comparative Project reveals, this sector is growing relative to the wider formal economy over time. Examining the changes in non-profit sector full-time equivalent (FTE) employment in a number of countries relative to overall employment, Table 4.3 reveals that in all eight nations analysed (with the exception of Israel), the pace of job growth in the not-for-profit sector has outstripped total job growth. In the US, for example, although there was an overall increase in FTE employment of 8 per cent between 1990 and 1995, the growth in FTE employment in the not-for-profit sector was 20 per cent. In the four EU nations considered (France, Germany, the UK and the Netherlands), meanwhile, the 24 per cent

Table 4.3 Changes in non-profit sector FTE employment, by country, 1990–95

Country	Non-profit sector 1990–95 change		Total economy* 1990–95 change	
	Net	as % of 1990 level	Net	as % of 1990 level
France	157,202	20	−329,000	−2
Germany	422,906	42	2,163,875	8
Hungary	12,200	37	−25,641	−1
Israel	19,182	15	395,237	33
Japan	450,652	27	7,525,680	14
Netherlands	41,623	7	240,000	5
UK**	119,068	28	−202,058	−1
US	1,360,893	20	8,080,793	8
EU total/average 4 countries	740,800	24	1,872,817	3
Other total/average 4 countries	1,842,927	25	15,976,069	14
Total/average	2,583,727	24	17,848,886	8

* Total non-agricultural employment
** Excluding sport and recreation, unions and parts of education
Source: John Hopkins Comparative Non-Profit Sector Project (www.jhu.edu/~cnp/compdata.html)

growth in overall FTE employment in the not-for-profit sector far outstripped the 3 per cent growth in the economy as a whole, thus accounting for 40 per cent of total employment growth (3.8 million new FTE jobs). In the three other developed countries for which there were employment data (Israel, Japan and the US), the increase averaged 21 per cent, though this accounted for a somewhat smaller 11 per cent of the 16 million new FTE jobs.

The not-for-profit sector is therefore a large and growing sphere of activity, meaning that the relationship between monetized exchange and the profit motive is not as strong as suggested by adherents to the commodification thesis.

It is also the case, as Table 4.4 reveals, that those countries where a relatively greater proportion of total working time is spent engaged in unpaid work are also the countries with a relatively larger share of the workforce employed in not-for-profit organizations. The two countries in which the penetration of paid work is shallowest (the US and the Netherlands) are also those with the largest non-profit sector. The intimation is that the cross-national variations in the penetration of commodification are more marked and polarized than suggested by the time-budget studies discussed above.

However, it is not only the size and growth of the not-for-profit sector that displays how monetized exchanges are not always imbued with the motive of profit.

Monetized exchanges in the private sector

It might be assumed that whenever the private sector partakes in monetary transactions, the motive of profit is always to the fore. In a bid to deconstruct this belief so as to deprive capitalism of its solid and coherent identity, numerous studies have displayed that private sector enterprises are not all, and always, driven by a common imperative of profit. For example, Schoenberger (1998) traces the effects of culture, tradition and affinity upon enterprise behaviour, showing how personal values and relationships within management undermine many of the assumed corporate goals of efficiency and profit maximization. O'Neill and Gibson-Graham (1999), similarly, explore the role of

Table 4.4 Relationship between the prevalence of unpaid work and the non-profit sector: a cross-national comparison

Country	Unpaid work as % of total working time	Non-profit sector as a % of total employment
US	58.4	18.7
Netherlands	57.9	11.9
France	57.5	9.6
Finland	54.5	6.3
UK	53.9	10.6

Sources: Gershuny (2000) and John Hopkins Comparative Non-Profit Sector Project (www.jhu.edu/~cnp/compdata.html)

competing discourses in shaping 'the capitalist firm'. Examining an Australian minerals and steel multinational, they display the multiple logics circulating within and without the corporation, representing the enterprise as an unpredictable and potentially open site, rather than as a set of practices unified by a predictable logic of profit maximization or capital accumulation. No longer tethered to a pre-ordained logic of profit, the enterprise is shown to be an ordinary social institution; one that often fails to enact its will or realize its goals or even fails to come to a coherent conception of what these might be.

Lee (2000b) in a study of the horticultural firms specialized in the production and sale of ornamental hardy nursery stock in the Southeast of England finds that this apparently commercial sector is composed of spaces of production *within* the market but resistant to, and subversive of, capitalist norms. For him, they are spaces of non-capitalist production operating within an apparently hegemonic capitalism. He finds that many of the producers are not so much oriented towards profit or exchange-value but rather do it 'for love'.

A similar finding is uncovered by an examination of the specialist sectors of model railway and canary retailing (see Burns *et al.*, 2004). In both sectors, they identify that those engaged in selling these commodities had directly come into this industry because it was their hobby and from this interest they had then established retail businesses. The vast majority, however, were not driven by profit. For them, it was a way of becoming more 'central' to those sharing their interests and a way of covering the expenses involved in their hobby. Indeed, they shared their knowledge of the industry freely with customers and often engaged in exchanges for reasons that had little or nothing to do with profit.

Moving away from studies of specific market sectors and towards rationales for firms taking particular actions, furthermore, numerous studies exist of the charitable contributions that capitalist firms make to the arts and cultural industries (e.g., Morel, 2003). These reveal that the motives underpinning these donations have little or nothing in most cases to do with profit or economic gain but rather reflect the desire of the directors or owners to display their taste and refinement. Here, therefore, one has actions taken by firms that are seldom, if ever, related to economic gain either directly or indirectly. The commercial sphere of monetized exchange, therefore, so dominantly perceived as the embodiment of the profit motive, is not always tethered to the motive of profit and profit alone, and this appears to apply across a range of formal occupations, sectors and exchanges (see, for example, Zafirovski, 1999).

Work in advanced economies: towards a commodified world?

Having revealed that non-exchanged work takes up nearly a half of people's working time (and is valued at between 50 and 120 per cent of the existing GDP), whilst non-monetized exchange adds another 10–12 per cent to existing GDP, the unpaid sphere in total contributes 60–132 per cent to GDP in the advanced economies. Not all paid work, moreover, is profit-motivated. To estimate the proportion of GDP that is

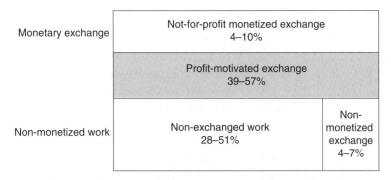

Monetary exchange	Not-for-profit monetized exchange 4–10%	
	Profit-motivated exchange 39–57%	
Non-monetized work	Non-exchanged work 28–51%	Non-monetized exchange 4–7%

Figure 4.1 The anatomy of the 'whole economy' in contemporary Western societies: maximum and minimum contributions of each sphere

profit-motivated monetized exchange, one needs to extract from the current GDP measure those monetized exchanges conducted chiefly for purposes other than profit.

Figure 4.1 provides a graphic representation of the outcome. The range of estimates for each realm have been here achieved by taking both the highest and the lowest estimates of its size and then comparing this with the lowest and the highest estimates respectively for each other realm. This provides an estimate of the *maximum* and *minimum* ranges expected for each sphere in the Western world. It reveals that anywhere between 28 and 51 per cent of total GDP derives from non-exchanged work, 4–7 per cent from non-monetized exchange, 4–10 per cent from not-for-profit monetized exchange and 39–57 per cent from profit-motivated monetized exchange. The commodity economy, in sum, is far from hegemonic. As Zelizer (1994: 215) puts it, 'The vision of society fully transformed into a commodity market is no more than a mirage.' Indeed, to label Western economies as advanced 'market' economies, or as 'capitalist' or 'commodified', is a gross misnomer, for it obliterates from view vast swathes of work in these nations that are non-commodified.

Even if the accuracy of these estimates can and should be questioned, this thumb-nail sketch nevertheless displays how profit-motivated monetized exchange is just one of several economic practices used in Western economies to produce and distribute goods and services. Such an overarching portrait of the anatomy of work in Western economies, however, ignores how the pace and extent of commodification varies across different groups, tasks and places, and it is important to explore these if commodification is to be more fully understood. To see this, just one such difference in trajectories will now be briefly charted.

Towards a commodification of work? men and women compared

Are men's work patterns more commodified than women's and how is this changing over time? Is a process of convergence taking place? Examining purely changes in formal employment, convergence might be assumed. Over the past half-century, the employment participation rates of women and men have steadily converged and are now approaching parity in many Western economies. At the turn of the millennium in the UK, for instance, some 75 per cent of the total population of working age was in employment, but 70 per cent of women of working age compared with 80 per cent of men. Indeed, during the past decade, the particular life-cycle pattern of women's participation in employment that was so evident in the past has disappeared (Gregg and Wadsworth, 1996), even if the pay rates and hours that have long distinguished women's employment remain. Until recently, a graph of women's participation rates by age would have revealed two peaks: amongst young women until their mid-twenties, after which rates declined until they peaked again by about the age of 40. Presently, however, this line is almost flat, paralleling that of men's participation, but about 10 per cent below it. A significant change in women's participation, therefore, and which has been evident since about 1975, is that women in their thirties with dependent children are now near enough as likely to be in the labour force as women of other ages. Although there remain marked gender differences in hours of employment, with women constituting the vast majority of part-time employees and also their pay being lower (e.g., Gardiner, 1997; Himmelweit, 2000; McDowell, 2001), the widespread view is that employment represents a route to their liberation. All that is seen to be required now by some are fairer conditions of employment to match those of men.

For men of working age, meanwhile, the last few decades of the twentieth century saw a decline in overall participation rates in the UK from 91 per cent in 1979 to 84 per cent by the end of the 1990s, an absolute decline of 3.5 million men in waged employment. This fall has been particularly noticeable for men over 50 years of age, whose average participation rates now match those for women of their age. This 'lost generation' of men aged 50–65 is the result of both corporate de-layering and downsizing as well as the continuing decline of male-dominated manufacturing industries, similar to many other advanced economies.

With the immersion of women into formal employment and men's increasing exclusion, is it the case that men and women are also converging in terms of the proportion of time that they spend engaged in non-exchanged work? In other words, has a renegotiation of the gender division of domestic labour taken place? Table 4.5 investigates the changing ways in which men and women spend their working time in 20 countries. This reveals that while women have witnessed a commodification of their work schedules, for men it has been a de-commodification of working time. The share of unpaid work in men's total working time has increased from 19.4 per cent in 1960–73 through 22.0 per cent in the period 1974–84 to 26.4 per cent from 1985 until the present. For women, in contrast, there has been a process of commodification, at least if the period from 1985 to the present is compared with 1960–73. The share of women's total work-time occupied by unpaid domestic work has reduced from 64.6 to 62.7 per cent. Nevertheless, nearly two-thirds of women's total working time is still spent on domestic work whilst for men under a quarter of their total working time is spent on this realm.

Table 4.5 Distribution of working time in 20 countries: by gender

Minutes/day	Mean	1960–73	1974–83	1985–present
Men and women				
Paid work	297	309	285	291
Domestic work	230	237	212	235
% of time spent on domestic work	43.6	43.4	42.7	44.7
Women				
Paid work	196	198	193	196
Domestic work	339	362	310	329
% of time spent on domestic work	63.4	64.6	61.6	62.7
Men				
Paid work	403	424	382	391
Domestic work	115	102	108	140
% of time spent on domestic work	22.2	19.4	22.0	26.4

Source: Derived from Gershuny (2000: Table 7.1)

Importantly, moreover, and contrary to popular myth, the reduction in the proportion of time that women spend on unpaid work is not due to an increase in the time spent in employment. Rather, it is mostly due to the decrease in the time spent on domestic work. Slowly therefore, there appears to be a convergence of men's and women's work patterns, even if there is an extremely long way to go before they fully converge. It is important to highlight, however, that this convergence is taking place within the context of an overarching process of de-commodification, not commodification.

From these data, it is far from evident that 'the commodification of domestic labour . . . has continued to expand' (McDowell, 2001: 457). Merely pointing fingers at the expansion of paid domestic workers, as McDowell does along with others (e.g., Anderson, 2001a,b), provides no clue as to whether or not there is an overall process of commodification. It is only by comparing the amount of unpaid work relative to paid work that this can be understood, and the overwhelming evidence presented in Table 4.5 is of a process of de-commodification.

While the working lives of men in the advanced economies have been shown to be witnessing a process of de-commodification, quite the opposite is revealed to be happening for women. Until now, few commentators writing from the perspective of women's position have read such a trend negatively. It has been widely assumed that the commodification of women's working lives is liberating. Few have stopped to consider whether advocating the greater subjugation of women by capitalist social relations, especially given the low-paid nature of women's employment, is the route to 'gender progress', doubtless because they equate or maybe confuse this with financial independence from men. However, even if women are entering the commodified realm, they remain responsible for much of the non-commodified work, suggesting that perhaps greater attention needs to be placed on resolving the gender disparities in the non-commodified realm by encouraging men to engage more in such activity rather than solely seeking to immerse women into commodified social relations.

In sum, there are distinct differences among social groups, in this case men and women, in terms of the changing nature of their working lives. While some are witnessing commodification (e.g., women), others are witnessing a de-commodification of their working time (e.g., men). It is important, therefore, to look beyond aggregate data when evaluating the process of commodification. Divergent trends are apparent across different social groups across the advanced economies.

Post-socialist societies: in transition to the market?

Ever since the collapse of the socialist bloc, the recurring narrative has been that the post-socialist societies of East-Central Europe are in transition to capitalism, reflecting and reinforcing the broader worldwide process whereby an all-conquering capitalism stretches its wings wider across the globe and penetrates deeper into every crevice of everyday life (see Chapter 2). This process is often treated as indisputable, irrefutable and irreversible (e.g., Ciscel and Heath, 2001; Gough, 2000; Kovel, 2002). It is seemingly the case that there really is no alternative to capitalism in these transition economies (e.g., Comeliau, 2002; Slater and Tonkiss, 2001; Watts, 1999). The demise of the state as a direct provider of goods and services in favour of the formal market economy – even if the state continues to regulate, albeit in poorer ways and with less developed and appropriate legislation than in Western economies (Neef, 2002; Sik, 1993, 1994; Wallace and Haerpfer, 2002) – is often taken as evidence. However, such a trend towards privatization within the formal sphere is insufficient to inform an understanding of whether or not an overall process of commodification is taking place. If, for example, non-commodified work were growing relative to the combined state and market spheres, then commodification would not be occurring.

To question this discourse of market-ism that serves the vested interests of capitalism (by constructing market hegemony as a natural and inevitable future) and closes off discussion about alternative futures for work, the degree to which these East-Central European nations are witnessing the advance of the market is evaluated critically. Indeed, even the nomenclature of 'transition economies', often used to refer to these post-socialist societies, intimates that they are on a pathway to commodification. At first glance, it might seem like a fruitless exercise to raise doubts about the incursion of capitalism into post-socialist societies. Here, however, I wish to show that this is far from the case. Reviewing the data reported in depth in the last chapter, the limited degree to which market practices have penetrated these post-socialist societies will be highlighted along with not only how there is little evidence of any shift towards greater reliance on the formal economy in general and market more particularly in the years immediately following the collapse of the socialist bloc, but also how it is by no means obvious that turning to market practices results in higher household living standards. The outcome will be a call to transcend the 'there is no alternative to capitalism' discourse that closes off the future of work and to more fully consider the possibility of alternative futures than has so far been the case.

De-centring the market in post-socialist societies

Is the formal sphere in general, and commodified realm in particular, now universally the dominant means by which households are securing their livelihoods in East-Central Europe? In the last chapter, the results of the NDB survey were reported. This revealed that just two-thirds (68 per cent) of households in 1998 relied primarily on the formal sphere (which includes not only the market sphere but also the public and not-for-profit sectors) for their standard of living. A third of households, in consequence, rely first and foremost on non-commodified practices for their living standard, with just under a quarter (22 per cent) primarily reliant on non-exchanged work (Table 3.6). Contrary to the speculations of adherents to market-ism, therefore, subsistence economies (in which households primarily rely on non-exchanged work) are far from a vestige of some pre-capitalist past (Watts, 1999).

Even these data, however, perhaps overestimate the central role of the commodified sphere in East-Central Europe. As Table 4.6 displays, when households were asked for the second most important sphere used to secure their livelihoods, just 11 per cent of households cited the formal realm as both the first and the second most important sphere. Instead, 57 per cent cited a combination of both formal and non-market practices and 32 per cent stated that the formal sphere was neither the first nor the second most important sphere contributing to their standard of living. To portray post-socialist societies as marketized is thus a mistake. Only some one in ten households define

Table 4.6 Spheres households rely on for their standard of living in East-Central Europe, 1998

Primary sphere relied on	% of all households	Of which second most important sphere is			
		Non-exchanged work	Non-monetized	Cash-in-hand	Formal
Non-exchanged work	22	6	2	4	11
Non-monetized exchange	3	1	0.4	1	1
Cash-in-hand	6	2	1	1	2
Formal	68	32	8	16	11

Source: Derived from Wallace *et al.* (2004, Table 9)

themselves as reliant on the formal sphere (which to repeat is composed of not only market sphere but also the public and not-for-profit sectors).

For 90 per cent of households, in consequence, sources other than the formal sphere are either most important or second most important to their standard of living and they pursue a heterogeneous portfolio of work practices to secure their livelihoods, as many smaller-scale qualitative studies have previously displayed in rich detail (e.g., Arnstberg and Boren, 2003; Burawoy and Verdery, 1999; Meurs, 2002; Pavlovskaya, 2004; Piirainen, 1997; Smith, 2002a,b). These data thus clearly delineate the limited contribution of the formal sector (where goods and services are provided through paid employment), never mind the commodified realm (where this formal provision is conducted by the private sector firms for profit-motivated purposes rather than the public or not-for-profit sectors). What, however, about the changes over time? Even if these post-socialist societies are nowhere near a situation of market hegemony, is it not the case that they are nevertheless in a process of transition towards market-ism?

Examining the shifts between 1992 and 1998 in the proportion of households citing the formal sphere as the most important contributor to their living standards, there has been no overall shift, remaining static at 68 per cent, although some countries were formalizing and others informalizing. Divergent development paths, therefore, are occurring with no clear linear trajectory towards formalization in general and commodification in particular. This was shown in the last chapter in Table 3.7 that charted how not only nations but also households have pursued divergent development paths and how the heterogeneity of practices used show no signs of withering or conforming to some standard market-oriented type. Who, therefore, primarily relies on these market-oriented practices, and is there any evidence that they provide higher living standards?

Commodified work practices: delivering higher living standards?

To analyse who relies on commodified practices and whether they deliver higher living standards, households can be grouped together by their reliance on particular forms of work. First, those primarily reliant on non-exchanged work and non-monetary exchange can be grouped into a single category of 'community economy'. Secondly, those citing cash-in-hand work as either the first or the second most important contributor to their living standard can be grouped into a 'cash-in-hand' category, and thirdly those primarily or secondarily reliant on 'formal' work.

As Table 4.7 reveals, non-commodified practices are not confined to the poorest sections of the population. A large proportion of those in the most affluent quartile rely on these spheres as their principal source of livelihood. In consequence, reliance on non-commodified work occurs across the household income spectrum. Are those households reliant on the formal and market sphere, however, more adept at getting-by than those more reliant on non-market realms? To assess this, albeit in a relatively limited manner, the NDB survey asked the following question: 'Sometimes people have to do without things that people usually have. In the past year has your household had to do without any

Table 4.7 Relationship between primary sphere relied on and living standards in East-Central Europe: by household income, 1998

	Formal	Community	Cash-in-hand
Household income quartile Cramer's $V = 0.083p > 000$			
First quartile	22	32	18
Second quartile	25	25	22
Third quartile	26	24	27
Fourth quartile	27	19	33
Deprivation scale $(n = 10,642)$ Cramer's $V = 0.094p < 000$			
1 Never deprived	44	36	45
2	10	8	10
3	11	11	11
4	9	12	10
5	7	7	6
6	6	6	5
7	6	9	6
8	3	3	3
9	2	4	2
10 Often deprived	2	4	2
No. of consumer goods possessed $(n = 9732)$ Cramer's $V = 0.127p < 000$			
None	15	24	11
1	31	34	26
2	26	24	26
3	22	15	27
All 4	6	3	10

Source: Derived from Wallace *et al.* (2004: Table 11)

of the following: food; heating and electricity; clothes you really need: often, sometimes, rarely, never?' The deprivation scale in Table 4.7 was constructed by combining these responses. Analyzing the results, it can be seen that formal (including market-oriented) and cash-in-hand-orientated households are less lacking than community-orientated households in terms of this deprivation scale. Nevertheless, it is by no means clear-cut that formal (including market-orientated) oriented households are always less deprived than their counterparts who pursue non-commodified strategies. All households are spread in a broadly similar manner across the deprivation spectrum.

Similar patterns are identified when the number of consumer goods possessed by different household types is examined. Although those dependent upon the community sector have the least number of consumer goods, those dependent on the cash-in-hand sphere acquire on average a larger number than formally (and market-oriented) orientated households. It might be tentatively concluded, in consequence, that cash-in-hand-orientated households are getting by better than their formal-orientated counterparts in East-Central Europe, at least so far as the acquisition of consumer goods is concerned.

It is thus by no means clear-cut that non-commodified work practices are conducted solely by those excluded from the formal and market realm. Many relatively affluent households also heavily rely on such practices. Whether this is an active choice amongst such affluent households is not known. It might be the case, for example, that different populations engage in these practices for different reasons. For marginalized populations, non-commodified practices might be much more an activity conducted out of economic necessity while for affluent populations such practices might be more of an active choice and thus more a space of hope than despair, as identified in Western societies (see Williams and Windebank, 2003a).

East-central Europe: in transition to what?

The recurring belief has been that this ex-socialist bloc is in transition towards a commodified society and economic policy has consequently concentrated near enough entirely on developing the market economy in these societies. Indeed, Kostera (1995) has likened the massive intervention and investment to facilitate market-ism to a religious crusade where management educators and consultants have acted like missionaries transferring the cult of what Parker (2002c) calls 'market managerialism' to the heathen masses. Yet as shown, East-Central European countries have remained steadfastly grounded in a form of work organization based on economic pluralism and there appears to be no sign of this abating over the early years of this transformation.

In common with the above findings in relation to Western economies, therefore, little evidence exists of an ongoing encroachment of the commodified realm in post-socialist societies. Non-commodified economic practices are not some traditional, stagnant, declining, backward, marginal sphere but instead are thriving, even growing. Nor is there evidence that they are always and everywhere worse at raising living standards, measured in terms of securing basic consumer goods. There is perhaps a need, in consequence, for those who have pursued market-led policy prescriptions with missionary zeal, and ignored developing other means of livelihood, to question whether this remains the appropriate way forward and whether all of one's eggs should be put into the basket of developing the commodified realm when considering the future of work in post-socialist societies. This will be returned to in Chapter 12.

The majority world

Are majority world countries witnessing commodification, or is a process of de-commodification taking place? Alternatively, is such an either/or choice too simplistic to capture the diverse experiences of this large portion of the globe? Moreover, is the 'marginality thesis' applicable across the entire majority world? In other words, is participation in non-commodified work merely a response to economic austerity and confined to marginalized groups or is there a ubiquitous and heterogeneous non-commodified sphere? If so, does it mitigate or reinforce the socio-spatial divisions prevalent in the commodified sphere? In asking these questions concerning the magnitude and character of the commodified and non-commodified spheres, the intention here is not necessarily to provide comprehensive answers. Instead, it is merely to explore whether there is a need to question the commodification thesis not only in the advanced and transition economies but also in the majority world.

The commodification thesis asserts that as economies develop and mature, a shift of economic activity takes place from the non-commodified to the commodified sphere. Indeed, much discourse in economic development and development studies is so embedded in this thesis that commodification is often the 'measuring rod' used to define an economy as either 'modern' or 'backward' (e.g., Rostow, 1960). However, there are good reasons for believing this trajectory of work organization to be neither natural nor inevitable.

First, evidence from the advanced economies has already displayed that Western economies are by no means all pursuing a trajectory towards commodification. Instead, there are heterogeneous trajectories in different places. Secondly, and the focus of attention here, there is evidence from the majority world itself. Unlike the advanced economies, and as the International Labour Organization (ILO) (1996) states, it is often the case that national data is not even available to indicate whether formalization is occurring, never mind commodification. In the majority world, therefore, the evidence is even patchier than in the so-called 'advanced economies' but it is still there.

The little evidence available, reviewed in some depth in the last chapter and summarized here, displays that not only is the formal economy in general, and commodified realm more particularly, relatively weak compared with the advanced and transition economies, but the assumption of a progression towards formalization and commodification is by no means universally apparent. Instead, heterogeneous trajectories can be identified throughout the majority world. Although some nations are formalizing (and, doubtless, commodifying), others are either static or witnessing informalization (and de-commodification). Similar to the advanced and transition economies, therefore, there are varying processes in different places in the majority world. Formalization in general and commodification in particular cannot be assumed to be evenly and continuously occurring in a universal manner. Neither, however, can informalization and de-commodification. Rather, heterogeneous development trajectories are being pursued.

Similar to the advanced and transition economies, moreover, the long-standing notion that non-commodified work is the last resort for peripheral populations, who are obliged to perform it as a means of survival (e.g., Lagos, 1995; Lubell, 1991; Maldonado, 1995), has been widely refuted. It is now considered that this depiction gives a misleading homogeneous portrait of un-commodified economic practices (Bromley and Gerry, 1979; Connolly, 1985; Dasgupta, 1992; Lautier, 1994; Meagher, 1995; Peattie, 1980; Portes *et al.*, 1986; Rakowski, 1994; Sharpe, 1988; Tokman, 1978). Throughout the majority world, this is a ubiquitous practice and not confined to the poorest sections of communities and there is also significant diversity in this sphere in terms of the benefits received (Bromley and Gerry, 1979; Peattie, 1980; Tokman, 1978). In this sense, the definition and conceptualization of un-commodified work has taken a similar path in both the minority (Western) and the majority (Third) world. In both regions, its heterogeneity, its interdependent relationship with the commodity economy and its non-traditional nature have been widely recognized (e.g., Castells and Portes, 1989; Rakowski, 1994).

One question that remains unanswered, however, concerns the motivations for engaging in non-commodified work in the majority world. Until now, there has been an assumption that all such workers are purely economically motivated and use such endeavour as a survival practice. In future research, however, this needs to be analysed in greater depth. What makes both formally employed as well as non-employed workers engage in the non-commodified realm and how do their motivations differ? And is this reflected in the types of non-commodified work that they undertake and, if so, how? In the advanced economies, as shown above, economic rationales tend to be a primary rationale amongst more deprived populations, but amongst relatively affluent groups it is more an expression of a culture of resistance to commodification. Do similar motives appear in the majority world? Are there those who engage in such activity not only due to economic motives but also as a way of resisting the shift towards 'modernization' in their countries?

There is now some evidence by commentators that some specific non-commodified practices are developed as a way of opposing the penetration of the commodity economy (e.g., Bennholdt-Thomsen *et al.*, 2001; Escobar, 1995; Esteva, 2001; Hines, 2000; Norberg-Hodge, 2001; Shiva, 2001). However, for the majority of the poor who use non-commodified work, such a rationale is probably far from the case. As Quijano (2001) has shown in Latin America, the non-commodified realm is not some chosen site of resistance but rather an economy into which those no longer needed by capital are subsumed in order to gain their welfare and livelihood. Indeed, he focuses upon paid informal work and argues that to greater or lesser degrees this sector is centred around waged work and groups unequally situated in relation to control of the means of production and thus to production or profits. Their activities are geared to the acquisition of profits and accumulation, and they consequently operate, completely or in part, within the logic of capital. In many cases this amounts to a 'capitalism of the poor' according to Quijano (2001: 160). Referring to the wider non-commodified realm of subsistence work and reciprocity conducted by the poor, moreover, Quijano (2001: 161) argues that 'only with difficulty could we accept that it amounts to an alternative economy' in the sense of an alternative to capitalism. Great care, however, should be taken not to assign such motives to all non-commodified work. There remains little doubt that such activity represents in some circumstances a site of resistance to the forces of capitalism and its associated bedfellow of globalization. To see this, one has only to consider the local currency experiments in Argentina (e.g., Powell, 2002) or the commentaries of Esteva (2001) on Latin America.

In sum, when considering the majority world, there is little evidence of a universal natural and inevitable trajectory towards commodification. This discourse acts not only to define as 'backward' those nations that are less commodified but also to provide a clear prescription of the direction in which they need to develop. The result, as Escobar (1995) has tellingly revealed, is that this discourse closes off the future of work from alternative possibilities.

Conclusions

Until now, the terminology used when discussing all regions of the world has been very much grounded in the commodification thesis. While the West is denoted as 'advanced' due to the supposed extent to which commodification has permeated its organization of work, the terms 'transition economies' and 'developing economies' construct other parts of the world as becoming commodified. As shown throughout this chapter, however, this is by no means the case. Instead, what has been revealed are the diverse configurations of economies and how not all economies are following the same development path.

The intention, in so doing, has been to contest the myth that commodification is an inevitable and natural process and that no other options exist regarding the future of work. On the issue of the inevitability of commodification, this chapter has made it very clear that a future of work where capitalism becomes hegemonic is not cast in stone. Indeed, to assert that commodification is unavoidable is to fly in the face of the macro-level changes occurring globally. On the issue of whether commodification is a natural process, meanwhile, this chapter has shown that the market sphere is not an autonomous sector that grows with little or no help. Rather, it has been energetically facilitated and sustained by a barrage of state intervention. Bearing this in mind, one has to quite wonder how widely and deeply the market would have penetrated without such massive state intervention and encouragement. If the market has only captured such a minor share of all economic activities even when governments have so actively intervened to encourage its growth, then one does quite wonder how expansive the commodified realm would have been if left to its own devices. Given this continuous and ongoing nurturing and support by government, it is thus obvious that commodification is not an organic process. Once recognized, then the future of work becomes more open. Seeking to develop the commodified sphere through controlled interventionism and paying little heed to the development of the non-commodified sphere becomes clearly recognized as just one option available regarding the future of work.

Further reading

Gibson-Graham, J.K. (1996) *The End of Capitalism as We Knew It?: A Feminist Critique of Political Economy*, Oxford: Blackwell.

This book provides a critical account of the depth and extent to which capitalism has penetrated and reconfigures the economic so as to demonstrate alternative futures for work beyond the market paradigm.

Rifkin, J. (1996) *The End of Work: The Decline of the Global Labor Force and the Dawn of a Post-market Era*, New York: G.P. Putnam.

This populist book, packed full of examples and case studies, demonstrates how the advanced economies might be moving into a post-market era in which non-market modes of production emerge to replace market production.

Ertman, M.M. and Williams, J.C. (2005) (eds) *Re-thinking Commodification*, New York: New York University Press.

This edited collection provides case studies of the debates concerning whether to commodify or not and then asks whether this is the appropriate question to ask. It moves the debate beyond whether commodification is good or bad by discussing the quality of the social relationships involved in each form of work in different contexts, including slavery, organ transplants and sex work.

Williams, C.C. (2005) *A Commodified World? Mapping the Limits of Capitalism*, London: Zed.

This book charts the degree to which non-commodified work persists across the world and displays the significant geographical and social variations in the dominance of the capitalist mode of production.

5

The advent of a globalized world

Introduction

The final dominant narrative concerning the future of work extends the belief that capitalist firms now produce the vast majority of goods and services produced in the world (i.e., the commodification thesis) by arguing that this process of commodification is increasingly taking place within an open world economy in which firms operate in a de-regulated and seamless global marketplace. In this globalization thesis, it is a specific type of commodified economy that is becoming hegemonic and stretching its tentacles wider and deeper across the globe, namely 'unregulated' or 'free market' capitalism. Regulated national and international capitalism are increasingly being replaced by unregulated global capitalism composed of hyper-mobile and homeless capital operating in a borderless world.

To evaluate critically whether this is the case, this chapter first reviews the degree to which a process of economic globalization is occurring, secondly, the extent to which political globalization is taking place, thirdly, the degree to which a process of financial globalization can be identified and, finally, whether there is evidence of cultural globalization. To commence, however, some of the schools of thought that have provided a critique of the globalization thesis are briefly introduced.

Beyond globalists: Alternative perspectives towards globalization

As highlighted in Chapter 2, adherents to the globalization thesis, or what Held (2000) calls 'globalists', argue that we live in an increasingly global age. With the recent and rapid intensification of international trade and investment ('economic globalization') and the emergence of hyper-mobile and homeless capital ('financial globalization'), a seamless and borderless world is resulting in which there is a diminution of the sovereignty of nation states, and their ability to regulate either national or international capital ('political globalization') as an unregulated global capitalism takes hold. This is resulting in a homogeneous global culture founded upon what might be called 'Westernized' or 'Americanized' cultural values ('cultural globalization'). Critiques of this globalization thesis derive from two major schools of thought, namely what Held (2000) calls 'traditionalists' and 'transformationalists'.

Traditionalist views of globalization

'Traditionalists' are deeply sceptical about this claim of the globalists that a fundamental or systemic shift is taking place and assert that they are exaggerating both its advent and the extent to which it is a distinctively new phenomenon. Emphasizing the continuities between the past and the present, traditionalists argue that even if there has been an increase in the global flows of trade and money around the world, these are not substantially different to the past. Indeed, they point to how even in the nineteenth century, open trading and liberal economic relations were the norm worldwide and, akin to today, globally powerful economic and political interests were not hard to find. As Wheen (2004) highlights, the East India Company collected more than £3.5 million in taxes at a time when the total expenditure of the British government was just £7 million, and its omnipotence was beyond the dreams of companies today. A series of royal charters in the seventeenth century, for example, granted it the right to mint its own coins, raise armies, declare war and exercise jurisdiction over millions of subjects in India. For traditionalists, therefore, the present is simply a continuation of the past and the degree of globalization should not be exaggerated. Indeed, traditionalists see the majority of economic activity as still being essentially regional rather than global in scale, with the European Union being cited as an example of the increased importance of regionalization rather than globalization.

Unlike globalists, moreover, traditionalists assert that nations (as relatively autonomous entities) remain able to shape their economic and political priorities and to defend the post-Second World War welfare states from neo-liberalism. For these traditionalists, the argument of globalists that interventionism is not possible in the new open world economy is seen as little more than part of an ideological crusade by those of a neo-liberal persuasion wishing to impose their ideology and big business reluctant to pay taxes and adequate wages.

Transformationalist views of globalization

Transformationalists not only agree with traditionalists that globalists exaggerate their case and that militarily, economically and politically nation states remain powerful, but also believe it erroneous to dismiss the process of globalization or to underestimate its impacts. For them, globalization is transforming the powers of the nation state and the context in which it operates and they assert that politics can be no longer based on nation states. Solutions are therefore sought in new and progressive structures for democratic accountability and a global system of governance. In this system, global institutions would be democratized and empowered, but nation states would also retain a key role as territorially specific, legitimate and accountable frameworks for policy. From this perspective, therefore, the consequences of contemporary globalization are diverse, uneven and unpredictable, and largely seen as negative, but are not seen as inevitable and are certainly viewed as reversible.

Although Held (2000) only contrasts 'globalists' with these traditionalist and transformationalist perspectives, it is important to state that these are not the only perspectives contesting the globalization thesis. As will be seen in Chapters 12 and 13, besides these perspectives that seek to either reinforce nation states or regulate the world economy at the global level, other commentaries seek to replace rather than reform global capitalism (the 'anti-globalization' movement) and/or to envisage and enact a more localized future of work organization so that sustainable development can be achieved (the green movement). For the moment, however, these additional counter-narratives to globalization are left aside. The focus in this chapter is on evaluating critically the globalist depiction of the emergence of an open world economy where firms operate in a de-regulated seamless global marketplace, the sovereignty of nation states diminishes and a global culture comes into existence. The intention in so doing is to show that this meta-narrative is less a reflection of emerging lived practice and more an ideological discourse that is seeking to shape reality, in order that globalization can be recognized as a normative discourse, and other futures of work beyond a neo-liberal de-regulated open world economy no longer viewed as utopian dreams of the future beyond the bounds of possibility.

A critical evaluation of economic globalization

For *globalists*, the rapid and recent intensification of international trade and investment is at such a level that distinct national economies are dissolving into a singular global economy. For optimistic globalists, who are primarily of a neo-liberal persuasion, this is to be celebrated. Indeed, they advocate a continuing deregulation of trade, investment and capital movements (e.g., Dawson, 2000). Swimming with the supposed tide of globalization is a positive move that will benefit consumers by increasing the scale and allocative efficiency of markets for both goods and capital. National regulation is held to be futile, and welfare and workers' rights above a low international norm will simply damage national competitiveness and result in a loss of international movement. For pessimistic globalists, meanwhile, although accepting the shift towards an open world economy, this is condemned outright, viewing it as just another attempt by international capital to extend and secure power and exploitation at the global level.

For *traditionalists*, however, the international economy is not as global as inferred by these globalists. Their argument is that it has not altered to the extent posited and that national economies remain. They accept that a degree of international economic interdependency and integration has occurred (Himmelweit and Simonetti, 2000), reflected in the growth of international trade and the activities of Multinational companies (MNCs), but argue that this has not undermined the importance and relevance of national economic management, or the ability of nations through co-operation to govern the international economic system.

Transformationalists, meanwhile, not only view national economies managed in the interests of domestic objectives as no longer viable, but also reject the ubiquity of market forces as a viable alternative. Instead, they view the present era as one of international enmeshment and marginalization of economic actors, resulting in a very uneven and complex relationship between territorial boundaries and transnational forms of business activity. For them, new forms of intense interdependence and integration are sweeping the international economic system, which place constraints on the conduct of national policy-making and make it very difficult for international public policy to govern and manage the system. It sees the present era as one step in a long evolutionary trajectory in which closed local and national economies disintegrate into more mixed, interdependent and integrated economies.

To evaluate the degree and nature of economic globalization, so as to determine whether the globalist view of an open, seamless and de-regulated world economy is valid, a starting point is to analyse the growth of international trade and the degree to which companies invest overseas to duplicate their capacity. As the World Trade Organization (1995) reports, between 1950 and 1994, world merchandize trade increased almost 20-fold whilst world merchandize production increased just over 6-fold, indicating the growing interconnectedness of the global economy. However, just because there is a growth of merchandize trade it does not mean that this is a linear and continuous trend, nor a universal one. Indeed, and as Table 5.1 displays, the experience between the two World Wars shows that the continuous growth of international trade is not inevitable. During this period, the open world economy that had come into being in the period

Table 5.1 Ratio of merchandise export trade to GDP, 1913, 1950, 1973 and 1995, at current prices

	1913	1950	1973	1995
France	17.7	10.6	14.5	17.8
Germany	17.6	10.0	17.6	28.5
Japan	15.7	8.5	9.1	9.1
Netherlands	51.8	35.1	40.0	42.6
UK	22.3	18.0	19.7	18.0
US	5.6	3.5	5.2	7.6

Source: Derived from Thompson (2000: Table 3.2)

between 1870 and 1913 was largely reversed by nation states pursuing protectionist policies, and it took a long time to return to a similar degree of openness.

Such trade data, however, do not take into account companies investing overseas. This also needs to be considered if the extent of economic globalization is to be assessed. Foreign direct investment (FDI) arises when a company decides to set up economic activity abroad under its direct control. Multinational companies are companies with at least some of their productive capacity located abroad but retaining a clear national base and national management style and personnel, and are regulated and policed by a national authority where they have their home base and from where they operate. Transnational corporations (TNCs), in contrast, are disembodied from any nation with no clear home base. They source, produce and market internationally and roam the globe for the cheap but efficient production locations and have an internationalized management style and personnel. To evaluate whether companies now operate in seamless, borderless and open world economy, as contended by globalists, a useful barometer is therefore to measure the advent and growth of TNCs (the 'global corporation' thesis).

The 'global corporation' thesis

For globalists, large corporations are abandoning their ties to their country of origin and are now transnational, placeless and boundaryless organizations operating in a worldwide space freed from the old national hurdles and restrictions. To evaluate this 'global corporation' thesis, Table 5.2 explores whether the majority of the world's largest TNCs have the overwhelming majority of their assets and employment outside their home country. To do this, a 'transnationality index' (TNI) of the world's 100 largest TNCs is calculated using each TNC's foreign assets to total assets, foreign sales to total sales and foreign employment to total employment, and then the average calculated. The two right-hand columns show the percentage of each firm's assets and employment that are located outside the firm's home country.

The results display the limited extent of economic globalization even amongst TNCs. The average TNI is only 52.6. Indeed, only 57 of the 100 companies have an index of greater than 50, and just 16 TNCs have an index greater than 75. Significantly, the 14 most transnational firms (in terms of the TNI) originate from small countries (Switzerland, the UK, Netherlands, Belgium and Canada). Conversely, the biggest TNCs in terms of total foreign assets all have relatively low TNI scores. For example, the largest TNC (in terms of foreign assets), General Electric, ranks 75th on the TNI; GM (4th in terms of foreign assets) ranks 83rd; IBM ranks 50th, VW ranks 45th, Toyota, the 6th ranking TNC in foreign assets ranks 82nd on the TNI. On this measure, therefore, there is little evidence of TNCs having the share of their activities outside their home countries that might be expected if they were truly global corporations.

Examining the top 200 global and transnational companies, meanwhile, Boron (2005) identifies that some 96 per cent have their headquarters in only 8 countries. Less than

Table 5.2 How 'global' are the world's top 100 transnational corporations (TNCs)?

TNI Rank	Index	Company	Country	Assets (%)	Employment (%)
				Foreign share of	
1.	95.4	Thomson Corp.	Canada	98.6	92.5
2.	95.2	Nestlé	Switzerland	89.9	97.2
3.	94.1	ABB	Switzerland	88.2	96.3
4.	93.2	Electrolux	Sweden	92.9	90.4
5.	91.8	Holcim	Switzerland	91.9	93.4
6.	91.5	Roche Group	Switzerland	90.4	85.6
7.	90.7	BAT	UK	84.0	96.8
8.	89.3	Unilever	UK/Netherlands	90.4	90.5
9.	88.6	Seagram Company	Canada	73.1	–
10.	82.6	Akzo Nobel	Netherlands	85.0	81.0
11.	82.4	Nippon Oil Co.	Japan	88.7	74.5
12.	81.9	Cadbury-Schweppes	UK	88.8	79.7
13.	79.4	Diageo	UK	69.3	82.6
14.	78.3	News Corporation	Australia	61.2	72.5
15.	76.9	L'Air Liquide Group	France	–	–
16.	76.6	Glaxo Wellcome	UK	70.2	74.1
17.	73.8	Michelin	France	–	–
18.	73.7	BP	UK	74.7	77.3
19.	72.5	Stora Enso OYS	Finland	–	–
20.	71.6	AstraZeneca	UK/Sweden	37.3	83.3
21.	70.3	TotalFina	France	–	67.9
22.	68.0	Exxon/Mobil	US	68.8	63.6
23.	67.8	Danon Group	France	62.9	–
24.	67.1	McDonald's Corporation	US	57.6	82.8
25.	65.6	Alcatel	France	52.1	74.1
26.	65.2	Coca-Cola	US	83.3	–
27.	64.7	Honda	Japan	58.4	–
28.	63.8	Compart Spa	Italy	–	68.2
29.	62.2	Montedison Group	Italy	–	71.7
30.	61.4	Volvo	Sweden	–	53.4
31.	60.9	Ericsson	Sweden	44.5	57.4
32.	60.9	BMW	Germany	69.1	40.1
33.	60.2	Bayer	Germany	58.0	53.2
34.	60.2	RTZ	Australia/UK	61.2	62.5
35.	59.9	Philips	Netherlands	76.2	–
36.	59.2	BASF	Germany	57.0	44.4
37.	58.9	Bridgestone	Japan	44.6	69.0
38.	58.2	Renault	France	–	–
39.	57.5	Crown Cork and Seal	US	62.6	–
40.	57.1	Canon	Japan	48.4	52.8
41.	56.8	Siemens	Germany	–	56.7

42.	56.7	Sony	Japan	–	61.0
43.	56.3	Royal Dutch Shell	Netherlands/UK	60.3	57.8
44.	56.2	Motorola	US	58.0	55.3
45.	55.7	Volkswagen Group	Germany	–	48.3
46.	55.3	Robert Bosch	Germany	–	49.8
47.	54.6	Cemex	Mexico	58.8	–
48.	54.2	Johnson & Johnson	US	67.1	50.7
49.	54.0	Aventis	France	–	–
50.	53.7	IBM	US	51.1	52.6
51.	53.7	Daimler-Chrysler	Germany	31.7	48.3
52.	53.1	Hewlett-Packard	US	–	49.1
53.	52.7	Royal Ahold	Netherlands	69.9	19.2
54.	51.7	Elf Aquitaine	France	43.5	–
55.	51.6	Repsol	Spain	70.3	–
56.	51.2	Texaco	US	–	–
57.	51.2	Mitsubishi Motors	Japan	27.6	–
58.	49.1	Suez Lyonnaise des Eaux	France	–	68.2
59.	48.9	Mannesman	Germany	–	44.9
60.	46.2	Dow Chemical	US	39.7	42.8
61.	45.5	AES Corporation	US	48.8	–
62.	44.7	Peugeot	France	39.2	30.3
63.	43.5	Usinor	France	47.4	24.9
64.	43.3	Viag	Germany	–	51.0
65.	42.4	Veba Group	Germany	27.1	37.7
66.	41.3	Du Pont	US	36.3	38.3
67.	40.9	ENI Group	Italy	47.2	–
68.	40.7	Nissan	Japan	–	–
69.	40.4	Texas Utilities Co.	US	42.5	39.2
70.	40.3	Proctor & Gamble	US	33.3	–
71.	39.3	Matsushita	Japan	19.2	49.5
72.	38.4	Fujitsu	Japan	36.2	38.6
73.	38.0	Telefonica	Spain	37.8	–
74.	38.0	Hutchison Whampoa	Hong Kong	–	50.9
75.	36.7	General Electric	US	34.8	46.1
76.	36.4	Metro	Germany	37.7	32.4–
77.	36.1	Ford	US	–	52.5
78.	34.7	Carrefour	France	36.5	–
79.	34.2	Chevron	US	49.4	25.8
80.	34.0	Vivendi	France	–	–
81.	33.4	Fiat	Italy	18.9	44.6
82.	30.9	Toyota	Japan	36.3	6.3
83.	30.7	General Motors	US	24.9	40.8
84.	29.8	Petroleos de Venezuela	Venezuela	16.9	–
85.	29.7	Mitsubishi Corp.	Japan	31.3	45.5
86.	29.1	Mitsui and Co.	Japan	30.6	–
87.	28.4	Merck & Co.	US	25.6	38.2
88.	26.0	Marubeni Corpn	Japan	19.9	–
89.	25.9	Lucent Technologies	US	22.4	23.5

90.	25.8	Wal-Mart Stores	US	60.4	–
91.	24.3	Edison International	US	23.1	–
92.	23.3	Toshiba	Japan	13.2	24.4
93.	23.3	Atlantic Richfield	US	–	–
94.	22.9	RWE Group	Germany	19.0	–
95.	19.8	Southern Company	US	25.0	21.0
96.	17.9	Hitachi	Japan	16.0	–
97.	16.1	Sumitomo Corpn	Japan	31.5	–
98.	15.8	Nissho Iwai	Japan	23.6	–
99.	13.7	Itochu	Japan	22.2	–
100.	12.9	SBC Communications	US	–	–

Transnationality index (TNI): represents the average of foreign assets to total assets, foreign sales to total sales and foreign employment to total employment. Calculated from UCTAD 2001, Table III.1
Source: Dicken (2003: Table 7.2)

2 per cent of their board of directors' members, moreover, are non-nationals, while more than 85 per cent of all their technological developments have originated within their 'national frontiers'. As Boron (2005: 15) thus concludes, 'Even in the case of modern corporate leviathans – a small proportion of the total number of companies in the world – whose scale of operations is clearly planetary, ownership and control always have a national base.' For Thompson (2000: 122), in consequence, 'The imagery of a disembodied productive capital roaming the globe for the lowest wage cost, lowest risk and most profitable site to locate would seem to be an exaggerated one.'

Globalization or regionalization of trade?

It is also perhaps the case that the globalist idea of a globalization of trade is a misnomer. As Thompson (2000) argues, and as displayed in Table 5.3 it is more accurate to discuss a trilateral regionalization rather than a globalization of trade. For example, Western Europe exports the equivalent of 16.9 per cent of its output (GDP) to other Western European nations, just 1.9 per cent to North America, 0.6 per cent to Japan and 1.2 per cent to East Asian traders. This displays not only how its trade patterns are regional but also, importantly, how only a small proportion of total output is exported. Japan, similarly, only exports 2.4 per cent of its output to North America and 0.6 per cent to Western Europe, but 3 per cent to its East Asian trading partners, displaying once again both the regional pattern of trade with a 'close to home' tendency as well as the limited proportion of total output that is exported, negating the notion of economic globalization.

Given this regionalism in trade flows, Thompson (2000) seeks to understand the degree to which these Triad economies can be viewed as internationalized. Table 5.4

Table 5.3 Merchandise trade flows as % of originating Triad bloc country GDP, 1996

To From	North America	Western Europe	Japan	East Asian traders	Japan and East Asian traders
North America	3.5	1.9	0.9	1.4	2.3
Western Europe	1.9	16.9	0.6	1.2	1.8
Japan	2.4	0.6	–	3.0	3.0
East Asian traders	1.4	1.3	2.0	n.a.	–
Japan and East Asian traders	3.8	1.9	2.0	–	–

East Asian trade partners: China, Hong Kong, Taiwan, Korea, Malaysia, Thailand and Singapore
Source: Thompson (2000: Table 3.4)

Table 5.4 Measures of the internationalization of economic activity of the Triad economies

	US	EU12	Japan
1. Trade to GDP ratio (imports and exports) divided by 2 (1995)	12.2	8.6	8.7
2. Inward FDI stock as % of GDP (1995)	7.7	13.4	0.3
3. Gross product of foreign affiliates as % of GDP (1994)	5.2	7.7	n.a.
4. Share of inward FDI in gross domestic fixed capital formation (1995)	5.9	6.8	0.0
	US	Germany	Japan
5. Foreign assets as % of total commercial bank assets	2.6	16.0	13.8
6. % of international assets (bonds and equities) held by pension funds (1993)	7.0	3.0	14.0
7. Proportion of outstanding corporate equity owned by foreign investors (end 1996)	5.0	9.0	11.0
8. % of foreign financial assets held by households (end 1996)	11.0	7.5	4.5

Source: Thompson (2000: Table 3.5)

reviews the results. The first row displays the total trade to GDP ratio in 1995 (not just merchandize trade). This is divided by two to display the extent of either imports or exports separately, and is a measure of interdependency. Such a ratio was about 10 per cent for the US, EU and Japan, meaning that only one-tenth of the output was exported, the implication being that 90 per cent of the output was consumed domestically. This displays the limited extent of globalization, even in these Triad economies.

Row 2 examines foreign direct investment (FDI) as a measure of international integration and a similar measure is given in row 3, examining the amount of output produced by foreign-owned affiliates of MNCs or TNCs in the US, EU and Japan. This is the output foreign-owned investment produces as a share of total home output and is another indicator of integration. Row 4, meanwhile, assesses the share of foreign investment in total capital investment (gross domestic fixed capital investment being a measure of total new investment in an economy in any year). Rows 5–8, finally, all measure the extent of financial globalization (see below).

The finding is that just 10 per cent of output in each bloc of the Triad was exported in 1995, so the blocs remain surprisingly economically isolated. This is also true in terms of investment: FDI and MNC/TNC affiliate activity was generally well below 10 per cent of Triad's member's GDP. There was also relatively thin evidence of financial globalization despite these Triad economies having the most open and liberal financial systems. Despite all the rhetoric concerning economic globalization, therefore, economic activity remains largely a domestic affair. As Hirst and Thompson (1992: 394) thus conclude, 'We do not have a fully globalized economy. We do have an international economy and national policy responses to it.' Or as Glyn and Sutcliffe (1992: 91) put it,

> the system has . . . become more integrated or globalised in many respects . . . Nonetheless what has resulted is still very far from a globally integrated economy . . . In short, the world economy is considerably more globalised than 50 years ago; but much less so than is theoretically possible. In many ways it is less globalised than 100 years ago. The widespread view that the present degree of globalization is in some way new and unprecedented is, therefore, false.

Evaluating financial globalization

It is in the realm of finance that globalization is most widely viewed as all pervasive. Optimistic globalists view this as generating major economic benefits enabling capital to flow to where its productivity is highest and providing countries with the opportunity to benefit from their comparative advantages (see Stulz, 1999, 2005). For pessimists, meanwhile, financial globalization is seen to lead to gross inequalities and uneven development. To evaluate the degree of financial globalization, two broad approaches can be adopted. On the one hand, the degree to which there has been a reduction in formal barriers to trade in financial assets can be evaluated. On the other hand, the degree to which financial assets (as reflected in portfolio choice, savings and investment) are now global in orientation can be assessed.

Evaluating financial globalization through the lens of whether formal barriers to trade in finance have been dismantled, there is little doubt looking at the various indices available that significant changes have taken place. For example, using the IMF data published annually since 1950 on restrictions regarding financial transactions,

Quinn (1997) constructs an index of openness where a value of 12 for a country indicates that it is completely open and a value of 0 completely closed. He reveals that the average index for developed countries increased from 4.16 in 1950 to 11.6 in 1999. For 68 developing countries, the index was 5.6 in 1973 reaching 8.34 in 1997. The trend, therefore, is towards a reduction in formal barriers to trade in financial assets.

Another index of trade barriers in financial assets by Kaminsky and Schmuckler (2002) classifies countries into three groups: fully liberalized, partially liberalized and repressed. A value of 1 indicates that the sector is repressed and a value of 3 that it is fully liberalized. Analysing 28 countries in 1973, the cross-country average was 1.43 and no country was fully liberalized. By October 2002, the average was 2.82 and only 3 of the 28 were not fully liberalized, namely Argentina, Malaysia and the Philippines. Edison and Warnock (2003), meanwhile, measure the fraction of a country's equity capitalization represented by shares that foreign investors are not allowed to acquire. Starting in 1989 and examining only less developed countries, 33 per cent of the market capitalization was available to foreign investors for the 14 countries studied. By 2000, this fraction now measured across 28 countries had risen to 76 per cent. Reviewing the results of these indices, Stulz (2005: 1598) therefore concludes that 'If financial globalization means a reduction in formal barriers to trade in financial assets then the process has been dramatic.'

Evaluating financial globalization in terms of the degree to which financial assets are actually traded internationally, however, a rather different picture emerges. In a detailed evaluation of the internationalization of portfolio choice, savings and investment, Stulz (2005: 1601) concludes that 'countries remain very important' despite the barriers to international investment having fallen sharply over the past half century. Below, and to display the limited extent of financial globalization in practice, a case study is presented of a financial services industry often asserted to exemplify the advent of financial globalization, namely the mutual funds sector.

Mutual funds: an exemplar of a borderless world of hyper-mobile homeless capital?

With an ever greater share of the equity market in funds managed by large financial institutions such as pension funds, life assurance, hedge funds and open- and closed-ended mutual funds, 'fund-manager capitalism' has transformed the landscape of money and finance (e.g., Blommestein, 1999; Clark, 2000; Corbridge et al., 1996; Graves, 1998; Leyshon, 1995, 1997, 1998; Leyshon and Thrift, 1997; Martin, 1999a; Porteous, 1995; Singh, 2000; Warburton, 1999). Of all shares listed on the UK stock market, for example, institutional investors owned 36 per cent in 1969 but 62 per cent by 1993 (Martin, 1999b). In the US, the proportion owned by these institutions rose from 6 per cent in 1950, through 34 per cent by 1980, to 48 per cent by 1997 (Singh, 2000).

For globalists, this emergence of fund-manager capitalism is seen to have resulted in three separate but interlocking processes: time compression whereby capital becomes more 'hyper-mobile' (e.g., Appadurai, 1990; Castells, 2000; Warf, 1999); space compression where this hyper-mobile capital roams an increasingly 'borderless' or 'seamless' world in search of investment opportunities (e.g., O'Brien, 1992; Ohmae, 1990, 1995a,b; Singh, 2000; Warf, 1999); and the emergence of 'homeless' or 'stateless' monies (Castells, 1989, 1996; Kobrin, 1997; O'Brien, 1992; Ohmae, 1990, 1995a,b). For influential commentators such as Castells (2000: 374), what is thus being witnessed is

> the annihilation of space and time by electronic means. Its technological and informational ability relentlessly to scan the entire planet for investment opportunities, and to move from one option to another in a matter of seconds, brings capital into constant movement, merging in this movement capital from all origins, *as in mutual funds*. [my emphasis]

The aim here is to evaluate critically whether this is indeed the case. Is financial capital now composed of homeless money that is hyper-mobile and roaming a borderless world in search of investment opportunities?

To evaluate this, first, the degree to which mutual funds work with hyper-mobile money; secondly, the extent to which they operate in a seamless world; and, finally, whether these assets can be characterized as homeless or stateless are investigated. The principal evidence drawn upon is the data produced by Standard and Poor's Micropal database on the nature of the mutual fund industries of nine developed market economies, namely Belgium, France, Germany, Hong Kong, Japan, Spain, Singapore, the US and the UK (Williams, 2004d). This will reveal that although there is evidence of some funds being globally orientated, rapid-fire trading, faster fund switching and the disembedding of capital ownership from place and individuals, the mutual fund industry cannot be described as operating in a seamless world with hyper-mobile and homeless capital. The vast majority of mutual fund assets are geographically 'ring-fenced', money is not and cannot be speedily moved around the world in a hyper-mobile manner and the capital concretely belongs to individuals.

Before commencing, however, it is important to outline how mutual funds operate. Pooling together the money of individuals who wish to invest relatively small amounts in the stock market, mutual funds spread their capital across a wide range of investments so as to allow diversification of risk, professional management and reduced transaction costs. Each investor is allocated a number of units in the fund according to how much they initially invest. Every day, the price of the investments (e.g., the share price of the companies) held in that mutual fund is priced and the unit ('offer') price recalculated. Any new investors then pay that 'offer' price. The job of the fund managers is to pick successful stocks and/or correctly forecast the movement of the market (Bangassa, 1999). For this expertise, actively managed unit trusts charge both an annual management fee of up to 2 per cent of the value of the fund and a 'one-off' entry fee that can be as high as 6 per cent in some countries (see Chordia, 1996).

Do mutual funds operate in a borderless world?

For globalists, financial globalization is resulting in 'the end of geography' in the sense that 'geographical location no longer matters, or matters less than hitherto' (O'Brien, 1992: 1). To evaluate whether mutual funds are indeed operating in a 'borderless' or 'seamless' world (e.g., Appadurai, 1990; Castells, 2000; Ohmae, 1990, 1995a,b; Warf, 1999), Table 5.5 analyses the proportion of all mutual fund assets in nine advanced economies invested in global funds and the proportions invested in particular regions and/or specific nations. Only a small proportion of all mutual fund assets are found to be in 'global' funds, whichever country is investigated. While Singapore has the highest share of all its mutual fund assets in global-orientated funds (37 per cent), investors in all other countries have less than a quarter of their assets in funds with a global reach. As such, there is little evidence that the mutual fund industries of these nine countries are operating in a 'borderless' or 'seamless' world.

In all these countries, the vast majority of capital in mutual funds is geographically 'ring-fenced', with a high proportion invested in domestic markets (85.2 per cent in Japan and 84 per cent in the US), reflecting the widely identified 'close to home' bias in asset allocation (Ahearne *et al.*, 2004; Karolyi and Stulz, 2003; Lewis, 1999; Obstfeld and Rogoff, 2000). Nevertheless, Table 5.5 might be underestimating the extent to which funds flow around the globe. In the US mutual fund market during the 1960s and 1970s, the average time that units were held was 12.5 years; a turnover rate of 8 per cent per annum. By the late 1990s, this 'churning' was equivalent to 31 per cent per annum of all units, indicating that typical investors held their units for barely 3 years (Bogle, 1999).

Table 5.5 A cross-national comparison of the geographical allocation of mutual fund assets: by region of the world, December 2000

% of all assets	Global	Europe		Far East and Pacific		North America	Emerging markets		Home market
		General	Single country	General	Single country		General	Single country	
Singapore	37.0	5.5	0.0	21.8	29.3	1.2	0.7	0.0	(15.2)
Belgium	24.1	31.0	17.5	3.9	6.8	10.8	5.6	0.3	(8.0)
Spain	23.3	24.1	39.4	2.7	1.1	7.9	1.5	0.0	(25.4)
Germany	19.7	26.3	21.4	3.0	15.7	11.0	1.9	1.0	(18.2)
US	14.7	0.6	0.0	0.2	0.1	84.0	0.4	0.0	(84.0)
UK	13.2	16.6	53.4	4.1	4.7	7.0	1.0	0.0	(53.5)
Hong Kong	10.8	38.1	21.3	6.1	12.7	7.4	2.1	0.6	(0.4)
France	9.4	16.9	53.0	3.6	6.3	10.1	0.6	0.1	(53.4)
Japan	<0.1	1.2	0.0	1.8	96.7	0.2	<0.1	<0.1	(85.2)

Source: Derived from Standard and Poor's Micropal, December 2000 (www.sp-funds.com)

If this churning is due to investors increasingly treating the globe as their market and switching money from one region to another as sentiment changes, then investors may be actively managing their funds in a more global manner than indicated by Table 5.5. At present, however, there is no evidence that this is the case.

Further evidence that Table 5.5 might be underestimating the extent of global financial flows derives from the notion that capital is increasingly mobile and global in orientation. As one UK mutual fund manager puts it, 'With almost half the earnings of UK companies now coming from overseas, the UK equity market is increasingly exposed to most regions of the world. This trend has accelerated' (Maxwell, 2000: 3). Even capital invested in single country funds, therefore, is increasingly money invested on a global level. Consequently, if funds themselves are not global in their investment remit, this is certainly the case for the companies in which the money is invested.

As such, even if the level of investment in global-orientated funds is relatively low, the dual trends of faster fund switching by investors and the increasingly global orientation of companies signify that mutual funds operate with capital that is more global than suggested in Table 5.5. Nevertheless, the mutual fund industry does not operate in a 'seamless' or 'borderless' world. Most fund managers still work with money that is geographically 'ring-fenced'.

Do mutual funds work with hyper-mobile capital?

If mutual funds are not operating in a borderless world, is it nevertheless the case that they are operating with hyper-mobile capital? Do mutual fund assets pass 'through national turnstiles at blinding speed' (Appadurai, 1990: 8) as they engage in what Warf (1999: 230) terms 'a syncopated electronic dance around the world's neural networks'? The evidence from the mutual fund industry is that capital is becoming more mobile. Fund managers are holding stocks in their funds for shorter periods. From the 1940s through to the mid-1960s, the annual stock turnover of the average equity fund was 17 per cent, indicating that the average stock was held in a fund for nearly 6 years. By the late 1990s, this annual turnover was 85 per cent. In other words, stocks were on average held for just over 1 year (Bogle, 1999). This speeding up of the turnover of holdings is strong evidence of how capital in these funds is becoming more mobile as it is being switched from one investment to another at an ever-increasing pace.

Indeed, this trend towards 'rapid-fire trading' is reflected in the swift demise of long-term value investors (epitomized by fund management houses such as Templeton and individuals such as Warren Buffet) and the emergence of more fluid investment styles based on holding stocks only for short periods. These include 'momentum' investors (who invest in stocks whose price is rising quicker than its peers and then exit as soon as the momentum decreases), 'aggressive growth' investors (who invest in quickly growing new companies and sell when they plateau) and 'deep value' investors (who seek stocks with low valuations and exit when the market revalues the stock). This shift in style from long-term investment to short-term speculation both reflects and reinforces the increasing 'mobility of money' thesis.

Again, however, although the combined trends towards rapid-fire trading by fund managers, faster fund switching by investors and the increasingly global orientation of companies point to capital becoming more mobile, they do not signify the advent of hyper-mobile capital passing at 'blinding speed' through the world's 'neural networks'. First, most capital is geographically ring-fenced in that investors put it in funds that are only allowed to invest the money in specific geographical areas and are not allowed to put the money elsewhere in the world. Secondly, investors in many countries still contact fund managers in writing if they wish to switch funds and this can often take several weeks (especially if it is a transfer to another fund management group). And finally, companies still cannot easily move fixed capital in many industries. The mutual fund industry, therefore, displays that although capital is becoming more mobile, the notion that there is globally roaming hyper-mobile money (e.g., Appadurai, 1990; O'Brien, 1992; Warf, 1999) is an exaggeration of the lived practice.

Are mutual funds operating with homeless monies?

Finally, there is the issue of whether there is the advent of 'homeless' and 'stateless' money (Castells 1989, 1996, 2000; O'Brien, 1992; Ohmae, 1990, 1995a,b; Kobrin, 1997). At first glance this appears to be the case. Over the long wave of history there has been a disembedding of capital ownership from place and individuals. Owner management and family capitalism have been gradually replaced by private shareholders and large financial institutions (see Martin, 1999b; Singh, 2000). However, this is not the same as asserting that capital has become 'stateless' or 'homeless'. At least in the mutual fund industry, all assets belong to specific individuals. Conceptualizing the capital of mutual funds as homeless and stateless is thus not only a misnomer but also deleterious. It concretely belongs to individuals, and even if the management of that money is delegated to fund managers, it ultimately remains within the control of individuals (and is their responsibility) as to how it is used.

In sum, although there has been a disembedding of capital ownership from place and individuals with the growth of mutual funds, this does not mean it has become homeless or stateless. Indeed, unless such a perception is tackled, the individuals who own mutual funds (and those belonging to pension funds that invest in mutual funds) will continue to abstain from taking responsibility for their investment decisions.

Towards financial globalization? Lessons from mutual funds

Contrary to those globalists asserting that fund-manager capitalism has led to hyper-mobile and homeless capital circulating a borderless globe in search of investment (e.g., Appadurai, 1990; O'Brien, 1992; Ohmae, 1995a,b; Warf, 1999), this evaluation of the mutual fund industry in nine nations reveals that financial globalization should not be over-exaggerated. Despite some funds being globally orientated as well as evidence of greater rapid-fire trading, faster fund switching and the disembedding of capital ownership from place and individuals, the mutual fund industry is not operating in a seamless world with hyper-mobile and homeless capital. Most mutual fund assets are geographically ring-fenced, assets are not and cannot be speedily moved around the world and this money concretely belongs to specific individuals living in particular places. There is thus little evidence that the apogee of financial globalization – a seamless world of hyper-mobile and homeless capital – has been achieved.

Contesting political globalization

For globalists, it is not just a process of economic and financial globalization that is occurring. They also believe that national governments are increasingly powerless and irrelevant. While they are too small to deal with the global problems that affect their citizens, such as global warming and the illegal drugs trade, they are too big to deal with local matters such as refuse recycling. Traditionalists, however, maintain that the capacity of national governments to regulate the lives of their citizens and to manage global affairs has never been more extensive. Rather than the end of the nation state, they argue that globalization is reaffirming the centrality of national government. Transformationalists, meanwhile, take issue with both accounts arguing that, in the global village created by the forces of globalization, national governments are adapting their roles and functions. The result is a reconfiguration in the power, jurisdiction, authority and legitimacy of states.

Exploring these contrasting perspectives on political globalization, there seems little doubt that the characterization presented by the globalists is an exaggeration and more a prescription than description of the situation. As Harvey (2000: 13) so eloquently puts it,

'Globalization'... helped make the diminution in state powers to regulate capital flows seem inevitable and became an extraordinarily powerful political tool in the disempowerment of national and local working-class movements and trade union power... It helped make it seem as if we were entering upon a new era (with a touch of teleological inevitability thrown in) and thereby became part of that package of concepts that distinguished between then and now in terms of political possibilities. The more the left adopted this discourse as a description of the state of the world (even if it was a state to be criticised and rebelled against), the more it circumscribed its own political possibilities.

Mitchell *et al.* (2004: 15) similarly contest the globalist thesis that the powers of the modern state have been so diminished that they may even disappear because the modern state is organized around a bounded territory, and because globalization is creating new transnational economic space, meaning that the nation state is increasingly unable to respond to the needs of the new global economy. Instead, their position is 'that contemporary capitalism is very much dependent upon individual nation states to support, protect, and extend its global reach'. As Dicken (2003: 122) concurs, 'A dominant myth in much of the globalization literature is that we now live in a borderless world where states no longer matter.' For him, this is neither a novel nor a politically neutral view. It has long existed and been propounded by neo-liberalism. As he explains,

> While some of the state's capabilities are, indeed, being reduced, and while there may well be a process of 'hollowing out' of the state, the process is not a simple one of uniform decline on all fronts. The state remains a most significant force in shaping the world economy... All governments intervene to varying degrees in the operation of the market and therefore, help to shape different parts of the global economic map. (Dicken, 2003: 122)

As Porter (1990: 19) puts it, while 'globalization of competition might appear to make the nation less important, instead it seems to make it more so'. It appears, therefore, that the death of the national economy has been greatly exaggerated (e.g., Wade, 1996). It is not only the demise of the nation state, however, that globalists overstate.

Challenging the advent of a global culture

According to some globalists, we live in a world where there is the homogenization of cultures and these cultures are satisfied through the provision of standardized global products created by global corporations. For yet others, much of what now passes for this global culture – Coca-Cola, McDonalds, Levi's, Disney, MTV or Hollywood – emanates from the US. As Cochrane and Pain (2000: 61) argue, ' "global culture" is not something which draws in any even or uniform way on the vast diversity of cultures in the world, balancing or synthesizing these, but, rather, consists of the global dissemination of US or Western culture – the complete opposite of diversity'. As McEwan (2001: 158) puts it,

> contemporary globalization is distinctive in extent, form, rapidity of change, intensity and impact. Today, the idea of a global culture is in the process of becoming as meaningful as the idea of national or local cultures. This is a clear break with the past...

Seabrook (2004), for example, argues that in a bid to construct a global capitalist culture, there has been a colonizing of hearts and minds to create a global monoculture. In his view, there is an export of cultural traits and products from advanced economies and their worldwide adoption ('Westernization', 'Americanization', 'modernization'); in other words, Western culture is globalized alongside Western capitalism. The outcome is that people are viewed as becoming increasingly similar across the world in terms of consumption, lifestyle, behaviour and aspirations. This can be perceived positively by optimistic globalizers as 'modernization' or 'development' or more negatively by pessimistic globalizers as 'cultural imperialism' where 'we' assume that others in the world wish to be like 'us'.

For traditionalists, however, such claims regarding cultural globalization are excessive and ignore how many cultural forms remain deeply national, regional and even local. Cultural imperialism is viewed as overstating external structural forces and undervaluing internal local dynamics and human agency or, to put it another way, overstating change and relegating continuities. Transformationalists, meanwhile, critique the cultural imperialism thesis as a Euro- or US-centric story. It focuses on portraying a one-way dissemination of culture, ignoring international cultural flows and, in particular, countervailing flows (e.g., world music). Implicit in this cultural imperialism thesis, moreover, is a 'cultural swamping' idea of a pre-existing cultural purity being overrun, with authentic culture being replaced by an inauthentic imposed culture. For transformationalists, however, there is no unitary national culture to be protected but rather, already existing 'cultural hybridity' (Hannerz, 1990). For Shurmar-Smith and Hannam (1994: 76), for example, the advent of global culture is not a one-way Westernization or Americanization of culture but is more the mixing or hybridization of cultures through greater interconnections and time–space compression, leading to new universal cultural practices, manifested in the nature of music, restaurants and street fashions in the West that flow from around the world into Western culture (e.g., Feng Shui).

For some, both these explanations are flawed. As McEwan (2001: 160–1) comments, 'If a global culture exists, it is far from a product of unidirectional "westernization". However, alternative ideas about cultures mixing to produce a universal global culture are also problematic. Cultures are mixing, but this does not necessarily mean we are all becoming the same.' As she continues,

> the image of rampant cultural imperialism by the West, and especially the US, is problematic since apparent cultural sameness is rather limited in scope, limited only to the consumption of products and media images. The possibilities of this eroding centuries of local histories, languages, traditions and religions are perhaps rather far-fetched besides, we have a very limited knowledge of how people in different parts of the world respond to these images and products, and they are always translated locally. (McEwan, 2001: 161–2)

However, despite her protestations that there is limited knowledge of how different populations respond to these images and products, evidence does exist of the degree to which an Americanization of culture is favoured in different parts of the world.

Worldwide attitudes towards Americanization

To evaluate the degree to which an Americanization of culture is favoured throughout the world, the 2002 Global Attitudes Project asked respondents for their attitudes towards American values and culture. Table 5.6 displays the proportion of respondents in each country favouring American values and culture, as gauged by four questions:

1. Which of the following phrases comes closer to your view? It's good that American ideas and customs are spreading or it's bad that American ideas and customs are spreading here;
2. And which of these comes closer to your view? I like American ideas about democracy or I dislike American ideas about democracy;

3. Which comes closer to describing your view? I like American ways of doing business or I dislike American ways of doing business; and
4. Which is closest to describing you? I like American music, movies and television or I dislike American music, movies and television.

Table 5.6 The global acceptability of Americanization

% of respondents favouring	American ideas	American democracy	American business style	American cultural products
East Asia and Pacific				
Low income				
Indonesia	20	52	54	59
Vietnam	33	68	45	45
Middle income				
China	0	0	36	55
Philippines	58	69	73	70
High income				
Japan	49	62	40	74
Korea, rep.	30	58	59	53
Europe and Central Asia				
Low income				
Uzbekistan	33	65	76	51
Middle income				
Bulgaria	36	50	50	64
Czech Republic	34	64	44	59
Poland	31	51	46	70
Russia	16	28	41	42
Slovakia	34	54	52	58
Turkey	11	33	27	44
Ukraine	35	53	58	55
High income				
France	25	42	23	66
Germany	28	47	32	66
Italy	29	45	39	63
UK	39	43	37	76
Latin America and Caribbean				
Middle income				
Argentina	16	29	29	52
Bolivia	22	27	32	39
Brazil	30	35	34	69
Guatemala	40	59	63	70
Honduras	44	58	67	71

Mexico	22	41	44	60
Peru	37	47	47	46
Venezuela	44	67	64	78

Middle East and North Africa

Middle income

Egypt	6	0	34	33
Jordan	13	29	44	30
Lebanon	26	49	65	65

North America

Canada	37	50	34	77
US	79	70	63	48

South Asia

Low income

Bangladesh	14	31	21	20
India	24	36	50	24
Pakistan	2	9	14	4

Sub-Saharan Africa

Low income

Angola	33	51	41	81
Ghana	47	80	70	59
Cote d'Ivoire	69	78	76	84
Kenya	40	87	78	50
Mali	35	55	48	56
Nigeria	64	86	85	76
Senegal	34	65	49	63
Tanzania	18	43	47	41
Uganda	50	67	66	57

Middle income

South Africa	43	53	60	71
Low income	34	58	55	51
Middle income	28	43	48	57
Low and middle income	31	49	51	55
East Asia and Pacific	28	47	52	57
Europe and Central Asia	29	50	49	55
Latin America and Caribbean	32	45	48	61
Middle East and North Africa	15	26	48	43
South Asia	13	25	28	16
Sub-Saharan Africa	43	67	62	64
High income	40	52	41	65
World	33	50	49	57

Source: Pew Research Center, Pew Global Attitudes Project 2002. What the world thinks in 2002: (www.People-press.org/reports/display.php3?ReportID=165)

Analysing the results, low-income countries in general, and particularly sub-Saharan African nations, most highly favoured American values and culture. High-income countries generally were more in favour of American values and culture, with the exception of the American business style. Leaving aside such disparities, however, American culture was favoured by less than the majority of the global population, signifying that Americanization can be hardly described as hegemonic. If by cultural globalization is meant an Americanization of global culture as in the cultural imperialism thesis, therefore, then these data display that Americanization is far from hegemonic and that in many parts of the world, there are varying degrees of resistance to its encroachment.

Rather than consider cultural globalization as meaning Americanization, Featherstone (1995: 114), reflecting the ideas of transformationalists, views global culture as a 'third culture'. Instead of imagining global culture as replacing local and national cultures, he sees it as a third culture developing alongside. This, however, is not a universal global culture: 'there is no singular global culture, but a number of different global cultures' (McEwan, 2001: 165). Similar ideas are expounded by Lazreg (2002: 139), who asserts that 'All cultures (including those of industrial nations) are hybrids in one sense or another: they have borrowed from one another and continue to do so.' If correct, this has important consequences because third cultures make all other cultures local. But to billions, their culture is central to their identity. At a stroke, in consequence, this emergent discourse of third cultures diminishes and marginalizes all other ways of life.

The transformative effect of globalization discourses

Above, it has been shown that the globalist depiction of economic, financial, political and cultural globalization is not taking place to the degree they assert. Instead, the rhetoric of globalization has somewhat run ahead of the lived practice. This, as Chapter 2 argued, is perhaps not surprising. The neo-liberal discourse of globalization does not seek just to reflect reality. It seeks to construct reality rather than simply offering a description of current lived material practice.

For those critical of this narrative of de-regulated globalization, a two-pronged approach is seen to be required. First, the powerful influence that globalization has on shaping work organization needs to be tackled by displaying how the lived experience does not match up to the rhetoric but, second and more importantly, counter-narratives that tell different stories about the processes currently underway are required (e.g., Cameron and Palan, 2004). One prominent commentator engaged in the latter project is Massey (2005). As she puts it, under-developed nations

> are assumed to be following the same ('our') path of development . . . they are dragooned
> into line behind those who designed the queue. Moreover, not only is their future thus

supposedly foretold but . . . this turning it into a story of 'catching up', occludes present-day relations and practices and their relentless production, within current rounds of capitalist globalization, of increasing inequality. It occludes the power-geometries within the contemporaneity of today's form of globalization. (Massey, 2005: 82)

So far as under-developed nations are concerned, therefore,

> We are not to imagine them as having their own trajectories, their own particular histories, and the potential for their own, perhaps different, futures. They are not recognised as coeval others. They are merely at an earlier stage in the one and only narrative it is possible to tell . . . It reduces simultaneous coexistence to place in the historical queue. (Massey, 2005: 5)

For her, there is thus a need to abandon this singular universal story. Rather than a single (vertical) history, the many (horizontal) histories of different places are needed. As Massey (2005: 11) puts it, 'the imagination of globalization as a historical queue does not recognize the simultaneous coexistence of other histories with characteristics that are distinct . . . and futures which potentially may be so too'. The re-reading required for her is one in which we do not conflate differences in space into a temporal sequence but instead, recognize the multiplicity of current trajectories. This, therefore, is a shift from what might be seen as a vertical to a horizontal view of difference.

By retelling the story of globalization in this manner, her intention is to open up the future of work organization to alternative possibilities. Although neo-liberal globalization with its portrait of an open world economy ('the world is your oyster' mentality) intimates an open space of new possibilities, the actual practice for her is to close off possibilities because it names the future and renders alternative readings as either 'anti-globalization', nostalgia for the past or taboo. Yet this chapter has hopefully shown that naming the future as a de-regulated open world economy is not a description of what is occurring but ultimately a portrayal of the neo-liberal view of what ought to be occurring.

It is also a very partial story of globalization highly selective in terms of the stories it tells. As many have noted, although neo-liberal globalists tell stories of globalization that support their desire for goods and services to flow freely across the world and campaign endlessly to this end, few of them also campaign for the free migration of people (Boron, 2005; Massey, 2005; Seabrook, 2004; Wheen, 2004). As Daly (2003: 127) asserts,

> the same economic logic of global gains from trade that is used to justify free movement of goods, services and capital applies with equal force to free movement of labour (or human capital). Yet I have seen no advocacy of free migration by the WTO, the IBRD, or the IMF. Why should people not enjoy the same rights and privileges that are extended to goods, services and capital?

This identification of the contradiction in the neo-liberal advocacy of the free migration of capital, goods and services, but not people, however, does not lead those critical of neo-liberal globalization discourse to advocate the same for labour. As Daly (2003: 128) asserts,

If globalization advocates refuse to follow their own logic to embrace free migration, maybe they should question whether their misgivings about the free flow of people might also apply to the free flow of things that are vital to people, namely goods, services, and capital. Markets hate boundaries, but public policy, in the interest of community, requires them.

For these commentators, therefore, regulated trade is required rather than 'free' (i.e., de-regulated) trade. Indeed, this is the argument continuously propounded by transformationalists and traditionalists who criticize neo-liberal globalization. As will be seen later in this book, however, this advocacy of regulated capitalism is not the sole counter-narrative to globalization. Other visions of the future of work organization exist that seek to replace the neo-liberal vision of a de-regulated global economy, not with reforms to create regulated national and global economic systems, but with more far-reaching views of the future of work grounded in post-capitalist and localist green visions that seek to replace capitalism and/or pursue localization (see Chapters 12 and 13).

Conclusions

The discourse of globalization suggests that nations have no choice but to respond to the advent of an open de-regulated world economy. In this chapter, this dominant discourse has been shown to be much less a description of processes that are occurring and more a formative discourse that acts to close off the future to anything other than a neo-liberal de-regulated future of work organization. Here, this imagined world of globalization has been unravelled along with the powerful influence it has had on action and thought. Unpacking the trends, it has been revealed that globalization is very much the product of a particular (neo-liberal) way of looking at the world and a result of only looking, in particular, narrow confined spaces. To show how globalization is not so cut and dried as the globalists purport, each facet of this globalization discourse has been evaluated critically in turn so as to deconstruct this purportedly natural and inevitable future concerning the way in which work is organized.

This has revealed that the actual degree of economic, financial, cultural and political globalization all lag behind the hyperbole by a considerable margin and that globalization is much more a discourse which is seeking to shape the future of work rather than reflect the world as well as negate as unrealistic and invalid visions of alternative futures of work. Both this refutation of globalization and the recognition that it is a neo-liberal prescription have important consequences for how the future of work is envisaged. Today, the rhetoric of globalization is used as a means of legitimizing all sorts of new management thinking such as total quality management, downsizing, flattening, flexibility, outsourcing and so forth. To compete in an open global world, so the rhetoric goes, one needs to adopt these work practices in order to survive. By showing that this notion of a de-regulated open world economy is far from the reality, however, a principal rationale underpinning the adoption of these management methods can be questioned. No longer, in other words, is it necessary to bow down in front of the inevitable logic of globalization and react to the supposed divine will of an open world economy. Other futures for work are wholly feasible and possible since it is neither inevitable nor natural. Similar to formalization and commodification in previous chapters, this chapter has revealed that the future of work is not so hemmed in by globalization as neo-liberal globalists purport or even those critical of this supposed globalization process. The future is much more open than so far considered by those who recite the mantra of globalization.

Further reading

Held, D. (2000) (ed.) *A Globalising World? Culture, Economics and Politics*, London: Routledge.

This edited volume is an excellent introduction to the concept of globalization, with clearly written and well-structured chapters that review in turn economic, political, cultural and financial globalization.

McEwan, C. (2001) 'Geography, culture and global change', in P. Daniels, M. Bradshaw, D. Shaw and J. Sidaway (eds) *Human Geography: Issues for the 21st Century*, London: Prentice Hall.

This chapter reviews the concept of cultural globalization and critically evaluates the diverse array of approaches that have been promulgated.

Stulz, R.M. (2005) 'The limits of financial globalization', *Journal of Finance* LX, 4: 1595–638.

This paper provides a review of the different ways of measuring the degree of financial globalization, displaying how some methods display a process of near total globalization and others quite the inverse.

Massey, D. (2005) *For Space*, London: Sage.

This seminal text retells the story of globalization in a way that opens up the future of work to alternative possibilities.

Cameron, A. and Palan, R. (2004) *The Imagined Economies of Globalization*, London: Sage.

This book discusses globalization as a powerful narrative device and proposes counter-narratives that tell different stories about the processes currently underway so as to open up different futures other than a de-regulated global economy.

part 2

Futures for employment

The rise of the
information/knowledge society

Introduction

Many commentators who discuss how work will be organized in the future believe that Western economies are moving towards a qualitatively different mode of work organization than that associated with modern industrialism, and this is variously characterized as a 'post-industrial', 'knowledge' or 'information' economy. Originating in the late 1960s in the US, an optimistic belief emerged in the inevitability of, and opportunities provided by, rising levels of affluence linked to the emergence of new more efficient labour-saving technology. Popularized by commentators such as Drucker (1969), Toffler (1970) and Bell (1973), this post-industrial thesis had at its core a view of the future of work that is driven by the impact of new information and communication technologies.

Many of the major themes that emerged as part and parcel of this thesis – and, in particular, the post-industrial occupation with the centrality of knowledge, its production and dissemination – are today still apparent in that they are being reproduced in visions that discuss the advent of what is now labelled a 'knowledge' or 'information' economy/society. Here, therefore, the diverse commentators are reviewed who have adopted to differing extents, and with varying degrees of optimism and scepticism about its consequences, a vision of the future of work organization where there is the advent of a knowledge/information society (e.g., Bell, 1973, 1976, 1980; Castells, 2000; Drucker, 1969; Dumazedier, 1967; Kerr et al., 1973; Naisbitt, 1984; Stonier, 1983; Toffler, 1970).

To explore this perspective towards the future of work, and similar to all other chapters in Part 2, first, the arguments of those asserting that there has been a shift from an industrial to a post-industrial/knowledge/information economy will be introduced. Secondly, the optimistic visions, thirdly, the more pessimistic accounts regarding the advent of this knowledge economy will be outlined and, finally, the degree to which such a knowledge economy has permeated contemporary work organization will be evaluated. Conclusions will be then drawn about the degree to which such a vision of the future of work reflects the changes in material practice. This will reveal that for all of the talk of the advent of a post-industrial, knowledge or information economy, there is little evidence that it has penetrated either as deeply or as widely as suggested by many of the 'exagger' authors associated with this perspective.

Towards a post-industrial/knowledge economy

Many have identified transformations that they denote as significant enough to mark the arrival of a new order. One such transformation is the shift from an industrial to a 'post-industrial' mode of economic and social organization where the key resource is knowledge, and in which service work largely replaces manufacturing employment, with knowledge-based occupations playing a privileged role.

Despite being just one of a multitude of views regarding the future of work organization, this perspective has been often discussed as though it were the only vision of the future of work, totally ignoring other perspectives. For example, Thompson and Warhurst (1998: 1), in their introduction to the edited volume entitled *Workplaces of the Future*, contend that

> there is a considerable amount of common ground among popular business and academic commentators about what the trends in work and workplace are. That commonality starts from a re-labelling of the big picture. We are now living in a post-industrial, information or knowledge economy.

Barley (1996: xvii) similarly asserts that 'Future prosperity is likely to hinge on the use of scientific and technical knowledge, the management of information and the provision of services. The future will depend more on brains than brawn.' Such a myopic disregard for other perspectives towards the future of work is by no means confined to these commentators. There seems a widespread tendency to put on blinkers and confine discussions regarding the future of work to some single dualism, which in this case is the shift from an industrial to a post-industrial/knowledge/information society.

Emerging originally in the US during the late 1960s, the post-industrial thesis asserted that a qualitative revolution in the social and economic organization of Western economies was taking place (Bell, 1973; Drucker 1969; Stonier, 1983; Toffler, 1970). This new and emerging post-industrial society was seen to be significantly different from industrial society in terms of its economy, technology and societal structure. The economy was shifting from large-scale industrial plants to both small-scale, research-driven high-technology industries as well as services such as education, health and leisure. In the realm of technology, meanwhile, the new science-based industries were viewed as becoming central, and in the social structure the rise of new technical elites and a new principle of stratification were identified where white-collar outnumber blue-collar workers and in which the professional scientific and technical occupations become predominant. In turn, this would cause a change in the social relations of work itself, which would shift towards being grounded in interaction between people, rather than between people and nature as, Bell (1973) argued, was the case in more traditional industrial organizations.

Post-industrialism, therefore, was seen to be composed of a number of unidirectional trends: from manufacturing to services; from blue collar to white collar; from machine to information technology; from industrialists to technocrats; and from large-scale firms to more flexible organizational structures. A key aspect was the rapidly increasing importance of the accumulation, processing and transmission of codified knowledge. Thus, commentators came to talk of post-industrial society as the 'information society' (Bell, 1973; Webster, 1995), the 'informational city' (Castells, 1989) and the 'information age' (Castells, 1998).

A principal focus in this vision of the future of work is the emergence of new information and communication technologies and their impacts on social and economic organization. These technologies are viewed as having profound impacts by some 'exagger' authors propagating this account of the future. Toffler (1970: 12), for instance, considered the new computer-led revolution to be more significant than the shift from pre-industrial or industrial societies 200 years earlier, arguing,

> what is occurring now, is in all likelihood, bigger, deeper, and more important than the industrial revolution . . . the present movement represents nothing less than the second great divide in human history, comparable in magnitude only with that first great break in historic continuity, the shift from barbarism to civilization.

For Bell (1973), meanwhile, although slightly less euphoric in writing style, the shift from industrial to post-industrial society represented a shift in the axis of the Western world; the movement from a social structure based on industrial production to one based on the primacy of 'theoretical knowledge'. For him, this rise of 'theoretical knowledge' as a commodity was both a result of, and driving force behind, the above-stated major changes in the social and economic relations of modern societies. As Bell (1980: 531) puts it, 'Knowledge and information are becoming the strategic resource and transforming agent of the post-industrial society . . . just as the combination of energy, resources and machine technology were the transformational agencies of industrial society.' So, just as in the transition from traditional to industrial society, the agricultural sector contracted as industry and services expanded, so today a leap was viewed as occurring from the industrial and service society to the knowledge and information society. Knowledge, not work, is seen to become the source of social wealth; and 'knowledge workers' who have the capacity to translate specialized knowledge into profit-producing innovations (products, technological and organizational innovations) are viewed as becoming the privileged group.

Indeed, it was Peter Drucker who in the 1960s coined the idea of the 'knowledge worker'. For him, the shift to knowledge work (typically, work done by professionals) and to competition on the basis of knowledge is the most important change to have taken place in the world of work (Drucker, 1969, 1993, 1998, 2002), heralding a post-industrial age. In the industrial age, businesses competed through their ownership of products, plant and equipment. In the post-industrial age, competition is based on knowledge that is led by key employees who can walk away with it at any time. As Drucker (1998: 17) puts it, 'the productivity of knowledge and knowledge workers will not be the only competitive factor in the world economy. It is, however, likely to become the decisive factor, at least for most industries in the developed countries.' For him, therefore,

> the basic economic resource – the 'means of production' to use the economist's term – is no longer capital, nor natural resources . . . nor 'labour'. It is and will be knowledge. The central wealth-creating activities will be neither the allocation of capital to productive uses nor 'labour' – . . . Value is now created by 'productivity' and 'innovation', both applications of knowledge to work. The leading social groups of the knowledge society will be 'knowledge workers' – knowledge executives who know how to allocate knowledge to productive use; knowledge professionals; knowledge employees . . . the economic challenge of the post-capitalist society will therefore be the productivity of knowledge work and knowledge worker. (Drucker, 1993: 7)

Following in the wake of these agenda-setting commentators has been a very large body of both popular and scholarly literature on the 'knowledge economy' which builds upon this notion that knowledge has become increasingly significant as an economic resource and that the ability of firms, regions and nations, to produce, circulate and apply knowledge is fundamental to economic growth and competitiveness (e.g., Bryson *et al.*, 2001; Castells, 1996; Cooke, 2002; De Geus, 1999; Florida, 2002; Gertler, 2003; Stewart, 2003). The evidence that distinctive 'knowledge economies' are emerging frequently turns on the rise of knowledge-intensive sectors, the reshuffling of the division of labour to create a class of knowledge workers, and measures of the relative shift in the significance of knowledge vis-à-vis materials, capital or labour as a factor of production (Cortada, 1998; Drucker, 1993). The resulting belief, as Nonaka (1991: 96) asserts, is that

> In an economy where the only certainty is uncertainty, the one sole source of lasting competitive advantage is knowledge. When markets shift, technologies proliferate, competitors multiply, and products become obsolete almost overnight, successful companies are those that consistently create new knowledge, disseminate it widely throughout the organization, and quickly embody it in new technologies and products.

Of course, a considerable debate exists on how to define knowledge work and knowledge workers. Almost all jobs involve using knowledge in some form, as seen in the example of taxi drivers who although neither the inputs (driving) or outputs (delivering passengers) would be described by most people as knowledge work, the work process itself involves drivers applying their knowledge of the location, best route, local traffic and so forth. Indeed, London taxi drivers even refer to their training to get a licence as 'doing the knowledge'.

A broad definition of knowledge is thus perhaps too inclusive – everybody is a knowledge worker because everyone's work involves knowledge in some form. For some, therefore, the concept of knowledge work is meaningless (Collins, 1997; Kumar, 1995; Warhurst and Thompson, 1998). For others, however, what is required is a tighter definition. Winslow and Bramer (1994), for example, view knowledge work as interpreting and applying information in order to add value to the organization through creating solutions to problems and making informed recommendations to management. Others, alternatively, consider the type of knowledge being used. Blackler (1995) distinguishes five forms of knowledge:

1. Embrained knowledge – the abstract, conceptual and theoretical information that we have in our heads. It can be applied to solve problems and think about issues in creative ways;
2. Embodied knowledge – practical and applied ways of doing things learned from experience;
3. Encultured knowledge – shared understanding about how things are done around here;
4. Embedded knowledge – systematic routines that mean a person can perform a task or activity without thinking; the task becomes second nature to the person to an extent that the knowledge, learning and skill behind it is submerged; and
5. Encoded knowledge – information conveyed by signs and symbols.

For Blackler (1995), therefore, all organizations have knowledge workers but he suggests that the shift taking place is from embodied and embedded to embrained, encultured and encoded knowledge. Frenkel *et al.* (1995: 780), using different terminology, similarly argue that there is a change in the nature of work from contextual knowledge to theoretical or abstract knowledge, arguing that 'Knowledge workers rely predominantly on theoretical knowledge, and their work requires a high level of creativity for which they mainly use intellectual skills.'

Scharmer (2001: 71) offers a further heuristic framework of forms of knowledge when he identifies three types: codified, tacit and 'self-transcending (and not yet embodied)'. The first two forms refer to knowledges that have been translated into disembodied symbolic forms and those that remain embodied. The third type refers to the 'thought conditions that allow processes and tacit knowledge to evolve in the first place'. For Nonaka *et al.* (2001: 28–30), meanwhile, there are four types of knowledge assets of firms that build upon the distinction and relations between codified and tacit knowledge: experiential, conceptual, systemic and routine. Experiential assets are grounded in shared tacit knowledge. Conceptual assets are codified knowledge 'articulated via images, symbols and language'. Systemic assets refer to those that are codified, systematized and packaged (e.g., handbooks). Routine assets result from tacit knowledge that is 'routinized and embedded in the actions and practices of the organization' (Nonaka *et al.*, 2001: 30).

Reed (1996), in contrast, adopts a narrower more occupational-orientated definition of knowledge work viewing it as 'expert work' performed by specialists whom he labels 'entrepreneurial professionals', such as business and financial consultants, project engineers, computer analysts and media consultants. These knowledge workers have three characteristics: task-specific highly specialized, cognitive and technical skills; a combination of embrained, embodied and embedded knowledge, and aggressively market themselves as purveyors of specialist expertise that can solve complex organizational problems. Knowledge workers, therefore, are distinct from liberal independent professionals (e.g., architects, doctors, lawyers) who have an occupation-specific knowledge-base and rely on embrained and encoded knowledge, and organizational professionals (e.g., managers, administrators and technicians) who have an organization-specific knowledge-base and rely on embedded and encultured knowledge. Karoly and Panis (2004: xiv), examining the US, similarly argue that 'the growing importance of knowledge-based work also favor strong non-routine cognitive skills, such as abstract reasoning, problem-solving, communication and collaboration'.

In sum, this particular vision of the future of work can be seen to be characterized by an evolution of thought that started with the post-industrial society thesis of commentators such as Bell (1973) and then moved through the knowledge society thesis (e.g., Castells, 1998, 2000; Despres and Hiltrop, 1995; Hamel and Prahalad, 1996) to a contemporary discussion that seeks to extend the ideas of 'tacit knowledge' (e.g., Nonaka, 1991; Nonaka *et al.*, 2001), originally expressed in the work of Polanyi (1967), 'embodied knowledge' as displayed in the work of Law (1999, 2001) and Latour (1993, 1995) and the forms of knowing found in 'communities of practice' (Wenger, 1998; Wenger *et al.*, 2002). Common to all is the idea that the shift from industrial to a post-industrial/information/knowledge economy is the major fault-line along which change is occurring. Two very different groups of commentators, however, can be identified depending on how they view the implications of this shift.

Positive visions of the knowledge economy

Whatever label is used to depict these changes (post-industrialism, information society, the knowledge economy or cultural economies), for optimists, there is an implicit belief that the shifts taking place will reap significant benefits for society. In the early visions of the post-industrial society, these optimists argued that the technological developments underway would result in fewer working hours and greater access to leisure, bringing considerable social, psychological, cultural and health benefits (e.g., Bell, 1973; Dumazedier, 1967; Kerr *et al.*, 1973; Naisbitt, 1984; Stonier, 1983; Toffler, 1981).

Indeed, commentators such as Alvin Toffler predicted that the twenty-first century would be an age of leisure due to automation and technological development, and such predictions even led policy-makers and politicians to be concerned about how we could usefully fill our leisure time (Toffler, 1981). Humanity was on the path to a world that was 'more sane, more sensible, and more sustainable, more decent and more democratic than any we have ever known' (Toffler, 1981: 2–3). Information and its free flow across the globe was the path to human salvation, producing a world free of want, war and suffering (Stonier, 1983). It was assumed that workers would welcome being unchained from repetitive, psychologically and socially unrewarding work, and that protests at job losses would be insignificant because welfare support would alleviate distress, and leisure would be recognized as a compelling social benefit. Kerr *et al.* (1973) predicted the emergence of a 'pluralistic industrialism' in which a post-work stratum immerse themselves in enriching cultural and aesthetic activities, and the cultural and social stock of society appreciates in value. The argument was that 'the leisure society' was a viable alternative to capitalism, in which the free and full development of the individual in harmonistic mutual relationship with civil society becomes the central life interest, the basis for this being a socially guaranteed income (see Chapter 11).

Handy (1984, 1989) adopts a similar positive tone regarding the advent of the knowledge economy. He argues that as a substitute for fixed jobs and standard careers, knowledge workers will develop ever-shifting portfolios of self-employed project work, much of it in fluid teams and co-operative networks or partnerships. Knowledge workers will have no fixed workplace but will be mobile, many of them in home-based operations. While their working lives will become more risky, it will also be more varied and creative. The large hierarchical organization will dissolve into looser confederate relationships. As Karoly and Panis (2004: xxxii–xxxiii) put it, there will be

> the disintegration of firms to the individual level in the form of numerous IT-enabled, networked, self-employed individuals or 'e-lancers'. In this new business model, individuals may compete in a global market for project opportunities and may work on multiple projects at any given time. Project teams continually dissolve as old projects are completed and form as new projects begin.

Knowledge work thus moves with the worker, and with the growth of knowledge work, portfolio workers emerge who work either simultaneously or sequentially for a number of employers. In this view, short-term contacts do not have a negative connotation, but reflect the rapidly changing business environment with its emphasis on projects and teams (Handy, 1995; Karoly and Panis, 2004; Leadbeater, 1999). The outcomes are the now familiar themes that networks will replace hierarchies, and flatter organizations with collaboration and collegiality will replace those based on command and control (Barley, 1996; Blackler, 1995; Despres and Hiltrop, 1995; Hamel and Prahalad, 1996; Thurow, 2000).

A further optimistic reading regarding the advent of a knowledge economy is that it will result in a more educated, better-trained workforce due to their need to cope with the increasing complexity of work tasks (Blauner, 1964; Kerr *et al.*, 1973). This is known as the upskilling thesis. Noon and Blyton (2002), however, offer five critiques of this upskilling thesis: it oversimplifies the link with technical change; it overstates the extent to which advanced technology requires higher skill levels on the shop floor (Buchanan and Boddy, 1983; Sorge *et al.*, 1983); it assumes that the growth in the service sector will create skilled jobs; it overstates the extent of change; and it also needs to be put in global perspective.

For some, therefore, this structural shift towards a post-industrial/knowledge/information economy is a trend to be welcomed and ushered into reality as quickly as possible. A picture is painted of a world of work in which the future is much rosier than the past.

Negative visions of the knowledge economy

For others, however, much more emphasis needs to be given to the 'dark side' and negative consequences of such a shift in work organization. Take, for example, the post-industrial thesis. For more pessimistic commentators, the problem with this thesis is that it underplayed the possibility of mass unemployment, civil unrest and schisms between the technocratic elite and the rest (Beck, 2000). Based on rational choice theory, it assumed that the universal benefits of a shorter working life outweighed the cost to particular groups. For these critics, however, this thesis is fundamentally flawed since it fails to identify the new power struggles over wealth, time and status that would result in the wake of mass automation. In particular, they attacked post-industrial society theorists for being too woolly about the allocative mechanisms, and the rights, responsibilities and obligations of citizenship under the leisure society (Touraine, 1974). In subsequent decades, many additional negative by-products of this emergent knowledge economy have been sketched.

Post-work thesis

For some pessimistic about work organization in a post-industrial society, the new technology, and especially ICT, has been depicted as leading to mass unemployment, leaving in its wake a society ravaged by insecurity, where only the smartest and most powerful can prosper (Aronowitz and Cutler, 1998; Beck, 2000; Rifkin, 1996). In this account, technological innovation is viewed as drastically reducing the need for human labour. For Rifkin (1996), for example, we are entering a new phase in history characterized by the steady and inevitable decline in jobs due to the advent of sophisticated computers, robotics, telecommunications and other information age technologies which are replacing human beings in virtually every sector of the economy and every industry. Aronowitz and Cutler (1998) in the US, similar to Gorz (1999) in Europe, assert that we are thus entering a 'post-work' society because in this 'cybernated economy', automation is leading to the shedding of labour. As more and more workers compete for fewer jobs, the longer-term consequences are seen to be social unrest and political tension. Aronowitz and Cutler (1998) and Beck (2000) thus argue that the cybernation of work requires the rethinking of the work ethic. Modern industrialism equated rights and status with paid employment. Given that the technological development and organizational forms associated with post-industrial society reduce the requirement for, and possibility of, full-employment, some alternative is now required. They propose the introduction of a guaranteed income and civil labour.

The 'digital divide'

It is not just the spectre of mass unemployment that is seen as a problematic output of a shift towards post-industrialism. It is also the resultant inequalities, not least the 'digital divide' (Castells, 1996; Rice and Katz, 2003). Castells (1996) stresses the potentially polarizing effects of the information age. In particular, he distinguishes between those people who become a strategic and integral part of the networks of capitalism and those who remain outside, although still needed by capital: whether one is 'out' or 'in' hinges on the informational capacity of labour, and he uses two terms for these primary and secondary groups, namely 'self-programmable' labour (those who are retainable and adaptive) and 'generic' labour (who are exchangeable and disposable). For him, therefore, although the information age produces some individuals more in control of their destinies, it also discards a whole segment of the population leaving them devalued and dispossessed. The downside of the information age is this discarding of human potential. For Castells (1989, 1996), therefore, even if there are apparent benefits in terms of increased levels of material wealth and living standards, the undeniable consequences of such a shift potentially outweigh the benefits. In *The Rise of the Network Society* (Castells, 1996), his argument is that no matter how impressive are the technical developments in the field of IT, the main problem facing the world is the degree to which developing countries are threatened with exclusion from the 'global' community, incapable of matching the technological capabilities of the West.

Indeed, the ILO (2001) identifies the size of the digital divide between developed and developing nations. In October 1997, there were 23 Internet hosts (a computer connected to the Internet that can both access and be accessed) per 1000 inhabitants in OECD nations compared with 0.21 per 1000 inhabitants outside the OECD area. By October 2000, the first figure had jumped to 82 in the OECD area compared with 0.85 per 1000 in the non-OECD countries. The digital divide is more pronounced in access to personal computers and Internet use, owing to the higher costs than in access to telephones, which is a prerequisite for access to the Internet. High-income countries have 22 times as many telephone lines per 100 inhabitants as low-income countries, but 96 times as many computers and 102 times as many Internet users. Indeed, barely 6 per cent of the world's population have ever logged onto the Internet and half the world's population have yet to make a phone call (ILO, 2001). These data depict not only the digital divide but perhaps importantly, and as will be returned to below, the limited degree to which the information age that many commentators discuss as an all-pervasive trend has actually penetrated societies in a global context.

Quality of jobs

A further negative consequence of this emerging knowledge economy, highlighted by more pessimistic commentators, relates to the quality of jobs being created. For these pessimists, optimists have focused far too much on its impacts on highly skilled professional knowledge workers. For pessimists such as Reich (1993: 23), however, 'The foot soldiers of the information economy are the hordes of data processors stationed in back offices with computer terminals linked to worldwide information banks.' As such, a parallel is drawn with the shift from manufacturing to services. Here, the vast bulk of job growth was at the predominantly low-pay and poor job quality end in serving, guarding, cleaning, waiting and helping in the private health and care services, as well as retail and hospitality industries (Crouch, 1999), often in jobs in which the majority required no qualifications (Brown and Keep, 1999). It is similarly the case they assert in the knowledge economy. As Henwood (1996) argues, in the US, symbolic analysts, those who in some way manipulate symbols and ideas, comprise only 7 per cent of the current labour force. Much of the rapidly growing work is low-paid 'donkey work' of serving, guarding, cleaning, waiting and helping.

Surveillance

For pessimists, there is little doubt that information technologies have had a significant impact on the structuring of work organization and its relationship to other aspects of life. Advanced computer and communication systems have changed how organizations communicate both internally and externally, resulting in new problems of organizational control and co-ordination, such as managing across distanciated relations of time and space, challenging managers and management educators to change their way of thinking about traditional models of worker control. Yet technology has also provided certain solutions to the problem of management in terms of increasingly sophisticated modes of electronic surveillance and control (Dandeker, 1990; Lyon, 1993; Sewell and Wilkinson, 1992; Zuboff, 1988). Such surveillance takes not only the form of direct visual observation such as video and CCTV, but also more indirect forms of control such as computerized stock controls, machine switch-on times and so on, which enable employers to track employee movements and time spent actually working. It is the development of such technologies, designed primarily to exert control over activities of the individual, which have raised questions about the supposedly liberating benefits of the information age for the pessimists, and raised fears about the increasingly panoptic nature of the workplace and society at large.

Central to Foucault's writing on power and subjectivity and its incorporation into organizational analysis, that is, is the concept of panoptic surveillance and discipline (Foucault, 1991). Developed from the architectural design for a panoptic prison popularized by Jeremy Bentham, panoptic surveillance is premised upon the idea of a continuous state of maximum visibility. Referring to Bentham's original design, Foucault notes how the underlying principle of the panopticon was to

> Induce in the inmate a state of conscious and permanent visibility that assures the automatic functioning of power. So to arrange things that the surveillance is permanent in its effects, even if it is discontinuous in its action; that the perfection of power should tend to render its actual exercise unnecessary; that this architectural apparatus should be a machine for creating and sustaining a power relation independent of the person who exercises it; in short, that the inmates should be caught up in a power situation of which they themselves are the bearers. (Foucault, 1977: 201)

The design of the panopticon, the central tower, functioned as an omnipresent reminder that the inmate could be under surveillance but, with no means of verification, save committing an action which could lead to punishment, the inmates had to assume that they were under constant observation. The concept of the panoptic power is based therefore on the premise that this assumption is internalized and transformed into a mode of self-control which Foucault terms 'discipline'. In Foucault's work, the physical design of the panopticon thus becomes a metaphorical device, one that describes the principles underlying modern technologies of surveillance and their disciplinary effects.

Zuboff (1988) has applied the concept of panoptic surveillance to her account of the emergence of new information technologies which, while promising to democratize various modes of organizational communication, also produce a far more effective means by which techniques of panoptic surveillance can be designed and administered. As she notes,

> Information subsystems that translate, record and display human behaviour can provide the computer age version of universal transparency with a degree of illumination that would have exceeded even Bentham's most outlandish fantasies. Such systems can become information panopticon that, freed from the constraints of space and time, do not depend upon the physical arrangement of buildings or the laborious record keeping of industrial administration. (Zuboff, 1988: 322)

Information systems viewed from this perspective allow a regime of employee transparency in accordance with the principles of panoptic surveillance. They record not only what is said and done but also the time spent at a workstation by an employee and the rate of output achieved, and so on. This knowledge can then serve to both reinforce asymmetrical relations of managerial power and strengthen the subjective ties which bind employees to the organizational ethos.

Case studies of high-tech manufacturing make much of this enhanced capacity of management to collect, display and attribute performance data through electronic surveillance. With stockpiles of labour and parts eliminated through total quality management (TQM) and just-in-time (JIT) systems (see Chapter 7), production arrangements are highly visible. The information is generated from and fed back through teams of employees that appear to have autonomy, but in practice the teams internalize production norms and discipline themselves through systems such as Nissan's Neighbourhood Watch (Garrahan and Stewart, 1992). Such information is unobtrusive and perceived to be objective, therefore accentuating its legitimacy. Teams may also produce self-surveillance independently of any information-driven process. Delegated responsibilities, whether for routine production decisions or, more exceptionally, induction and evaluation of team members, mean that employees develop their own disciplinary rules, thus collaborating with management to identify and reward the 'good workers' (Barker, 1993; McKinlay and Taylor, 1996).

In consequence, these analyses intimate the possible emergence of an era in which every dimension of daily life is monitored, directed and regulated. While IT may alter facets of the organization of work, for these pessimists it does not seem to have altered the underlying economic and political principles according to which contemporary societies function. As Kumar (1995: 154) argues,

> the imperatives of profit, power and control seem as predominant now as they have ever been in the history of capitalist industrialism. The difference lies in the greater range and intensity of their applications made possible by the communications revolution, not in any change in the principles themselves.

Evaluating the penetration of the post-industrial/knowledge economy

To read this vast and rapidly expanding literature on the post-industrial, information or knowledge age, and its consequences, it might be assumed that the move from an industrial to a post-industrial/knowledge/information age is near enough complete. In this section, however, the degree to which such a dichotomy accurately portrays the direction of work and the extent to which this knowledge/information society has already penetrated is evaluated. This will reveal that for all of the talk of the advent of a post-industrial, knowledge or information economy, there still seems to be some way to travel before it can be depicted as all-pervasive.

Evaluating the encroachment of IT

Is it the case that information technologies have penetrated the employment place as deeply as these particular futurists purport? Steijn (2004: 34), for example, has questioned whether the knowledge revolution is more evolution than revolution, arguing that 'technological developments have been more evolutionary than revolutionary in nature'. There is little doubt, nevertheless, and notwithstanding the digital divide, that ICT has penetrated widely and deeply, and at a much faster pace than normal technological diffusion processes.

In the UK in 1986, two-fifths (40.3 per cent) of employees reported using computer equipment in the course of their daily activities. By 1992 the proportion had risen to over half (56 per cent), and by 2001 it was almost three-quarters (73.7 per cent) (Felstead et al., 2005). In a national survey of 2000 British workplaces in the second half of 2002, the Change in Employer Practices Survey (CEPS-02), White et al. (2004) find that already at one in three workplaces there is a complete penetration of ICT in every job, or something very close. These fully wired workplaces are evenly spread across small, medium and large firms. Equally important is that few workplaces are without ICT: only 1 in 209 overall, and just 1 per cent in larger workplaces. The proportion of workers who use modern technology in their jobs is therefore undergoing significant change. The use of computers and other forms of information technology at work advanced significantly

Table 6.1 Users of new technology in 2000, Britain

% of employees	Internet	E-mail	Pager/mobile	PC at home
Higher management/professional	69	83	53	80
Lower management/professional	52	55	49	70
Administrative	29	51	26	51
Routine non-manual	20	17	23	61
Technicians and supervisors	18	33	52	50
Skilled manual	14	10	33	46
Semi and unskilled manual	15	8	27	41

Source: Taylor (2002a: Table 7)

during the 1990s. However, it is highly uneven and there is a widening 'digital divide' between occupational groupings (Table 6.1).

If solely the penetration of ICT is evaluated in such advanced economies, therefore, then the advent of a knowledge/information society appears to be progressing well. However, it is important not to over-exaggerate this shift. It depends on where one looks. As stated above, the ILO (2001) identify that barely 6 per cent of the world's population have ever logged onto the Internet and half the world's population have yet to make a phone call. It is a curiously Western perspective, therefore, to envisage a future of work in which ICT penetrates ever wider and deeper and to assume that the rest of the world will pursue the same linear pathway and catch up with 'us' at the front in the race towards technological modernity.

Evaluating the penetration of knowledge work/ers

It is similarly the case when it comes to knowledge work/ers. For all of the talk of the new knowledge economy, this applies to but a small segment of the workforce in the minority world, that is, the advanced market economies. This, therefore, is very much a thesis about the future of work in the West. Even in the Western world, however, this shift towards knowledge work is by no means clear-cut. As Nolan and Slater (2003) display, amongst the fastest growing occupations in the 1990s in Britain were software engineers and management or business consultants, but their growth was outstripped by other occupations. Closer scrutiny at the three-digit classification level of occupations displays that growth in the professions, scientific and technical grades has been driven by the expansion of the established professions (education, law and medicine) which account for two in five of the total increase in higher-status employees. In other groups, the most significant growth has been in three areas: hairdressers, sales assistants, data input clerks and storekeepers; state-dominated education and health services; and care assistants, welfare and community workers and nursery nurses. Employment growth, in consequence, is concentrated in occupations that are normally not seen as associated with the new knowledge economy.

Of course, whether there is the advent of a knowledge economy and the depth of its penetration depends on how it is defined. For Reich (2002), some 25 per cent of the US workforce already consists of what he calls 'creative workers', even after excluding public sector jobs, many of which require high levels of qualification. Only 7 per cent of the fastest growing occupations in the US – the imputed model of economic transformation – can be classified as 'knowledge workers' who manipulate symbols and ideas (Harwood, 1996). But as Warhurst and Thompson (1998) note, all workers are knowledgeable about their work and always have been. Owner managers at the turn of the twentieth century were keenly aware of the knowledge, workers possessed and how important it was to the development of their companies. As Jacques (1996) has revealed in his account of the history of management knowledge, it has been the job of management to make capital out of the originality of what labour knows and does. The knowledgeable worker is thus not a product of post-industrial capitalism but rather an integral part of industrial capitalism. What is perhaps new is that management is now keen to introduce organizational structures and practices which facilitate initiative in the form of creativity and learning (see Chapter 8). As Thompson and Warhurst (1998: 7) thus conclude, 'it might be useful to jettison the overly broad notion of knowledge workers in favour of a more realistic appreciation of the growth of knowledgeability in work'.

Similarly, White *et al.* (2004: 170) argue that 'the idea of knowledge work needs to be modified. Organizations are developing wider strategies to meet their needs for know-how, which extend beyond the technical and professional domains and beyond the new technology.' As they continue,

> The picture of the knowledge worker presented in a great deal of recent management writing is of a highly mobile professional who carts technical knowledge from one organization to the next. For this to be possible, the knowledge must itself be equally valid, and valuable, across organizational boundaries. Portable knowledge breaks down the walls of the organization, or renders them futile: no longer can talent be guarded within, since the job market prevails inside as well as outside. If this is generally the situation, then in-house training and career development become wasteful activities. (White *et al.*, 2004: 171)

If one moves beyond the occupational counting of knowledge workers, therefore, then knowledge work is perhaps more pervasive. White *et al.* (2004) refer to functional flexibility as 'intelligent flexibility' whereby employees are made more flexible or adaptable through training, varied tasks and jobs, multi-skilling and team-working, and call it 'intelligent flexibility' because it relies on the intelligence and flexibility of the individual.

Yet for some, the more things change, the more they stay the same. Even if the means of capital accumulation are changing, the nature of economic life itself is not. As Steijn (2004: 35) asserts, 'the current information society is, after all, also an industrial-capitalistic society'.

Conclusions

This post-industrial/knowledge/information vision of how work will be organized in the future starts off by focusing upon the emergence of a particular type of work, mostly in Western societies, and extrapolates from its advent a view of the future of work in which this becomes the dominant type of working pattern. As Nolan and Wood (2003: 173) assert, however,

> the dangers of developing a stylized account of the changing world of work by appealing to simple dualisms, such as the old (industrial) and new (knowledge-intensive) economies, are transparent. Complexity, unevenness and the enduring features in the structure and relations of employment are crowded out by visions of universal paradigm shifts.

This vision, in other words, attempts to squeeze change into an either/or dualism, often by making very fuzzy the boundaries of each side of the dualism by extending the boundaries of what is included within each side, and imbuing the 'old' with negative attributes and the 'new' side with positive attributes (at least in optimistic accounts). In reality, however, it is once again conflating spatial differences into a temporal sequence (e.g., knowledge work in the West is new and 'non-knowledge work' in the majority world is old and backward). Yet this shift from industrial to post-industrial society, non-knowledge to knowledge economies and non-information to information age is far from as clear-cut as is sometimes intimated by exponents. Knowledge work and information (however defined) have always existed and, far from being a temporal streamlined evolution from one to the other, what is actually being described are existing forms of work that are being neatly divided into two types, one of which is privileged over the other, so as to advocate a particular vision of the future.

Further reading

Aronowitz, S. and Cutler, J. (1998) (eds) *Post-Work: The Wages of Cybernation*, London: Routledge.

This book offers a more negative portrayal of the consequences of this vision of the future of work.

Bell, D. (1973) *The Coming of Post-Industrial Society*, New York: Basic Books.

One of the first texts to introduce many of the ideas that still today remain at the heart of this perspective towards the future of work.

Blackler, F. (1995) 'Knowledge, knowledge work and organizations: An overview and interpretation', *Organisation Studies*, 16, 6: 1021–46.

This paper offers a useful review of the diverse meanings of knowledge and knowledge work.

Castells, M. (1996) *The Rise of the Network Society*, Oxford: Blackwell.

This book is a core text on the knowledge economy that takes the reader through a comprehensive and balanced review of this vision of the future of work.

White, M., Hill, S., Mills, C. and Smeaton, D. (2004) *Managing to Change? British Workplaces and the Future of Work*, Basingstoke: Palgrave Macmillan.

This book, focused on the UK context, provides an empirical evaluation of the degree to which the knowledge/information economy has permeated workplaces.

7

New forms of flexible work organization

Introduction

During the 1980s, an account of the direction of employment change began to emerge that had a profound impact upon how many scholars envisaged the future of employment. A range of new conceptual terms – neo-Fordism, after-Fordism, flexible specialization and post-Fordism – appeared that marked the advent of a new dichotomy to conceptualize the shifts taking place in the direction and organization of work.

In this vision, a shift was taking place away from Fordism, a period stretching from the end of the Second World War until the mid-1970s, when there was the widespread mass production of standardized goods using inflexible, dedicated machinery, exploitation of internal scale economies, a Taylorist fragmentation and de-skilling of work, and relatively narrow and rigidly defined job descriptions. A key element of the success of this regime had been that it distributed sufficient income to workers in order to support the mass consumption of industrial products. For adherents to this vision, however, a new post-Fordist era was emerging from the 1970s onwards characterized by the application of production methods considered to be more flexible than those of the Fordist era. These include more versatile programmable machines, labour that is more flexibly deployed (in terms of both the quantity used and the tasks performed), the vertical disintegration of large corporations, greater use of inter-firm alliances (e.g., subcontracting, strategic alliances, just-in-time production) and a closer integration of product development, marketing and production, resulting in a small batch production tailored to specific niche markets.

To evaluate this perspective towards the future of work, therefore, this chapter will outline, first, how the apparent shift from Fordism to post-Fordism is seen to have resulted in significant changes in work practices, secondly, the positive and negative readings of this shift in how work is organized and, finally, the degree to which post-Fordism can be judged to have penetrated the economic landscape will be evaluated. In doing so, the intention will be to reveal that this squeezing of all work practices into a Fordism/post-Fordism dichotomy that is then temporally sequenced, with post-Fordist practices viewed as coming to the fore and Fordist practices receding, grossly oversimplifies and obfuscates the heterogeneous nature of work organization and diverse trajectories taking place in the contemporary world.

From Fordism to post-Fordism

For those adhering to the enlightenment project, the future of work was to be grounded in a rational organization of production. During the twentieth century, this became expressed in the classical management theories associated with the likes of Frederick Taylor (1911a,b) and Henri Fayol (1916). This rational approach to the labour process sought to harness the principles and methods of the natural sciences to uncover the single most objective mode of organization, the 'one best way' to carry out tasks, so as to maximize productive efficiency. Once discovered, it was then to be enshrined in formalized written rules and procedures enforced by an educated managerial stratum who would have full control of the labour force. The motivation of employees to engage in such regimented labour was argued to be relatively high levels of remuneration. This strategy was founded upon the assumption of the rational economic person who would exchange a degree of individual autonomy for higher income levels and an improved material lifestyle. In this vision, in consequence, the irrational and emotional dimension was removed from organizational life, replacing it with universally applicable principles and formal rationalistic structures that would achieve maximum efficiency and minimal conflict (e.g., Fayol, 1916; Gulick and Urwick, 1937; Mooney and Riley, 1931).

Whilst many classical administrative writers advocated what amounts to a set of basic bureaucratic principles for work organizations as a whole, Taylor concentrated on putting forward principles for job and workshop design which would apply to the 'lower parts' of these organizations (Taylor, 1911a,b). Exemplifying this was his experiment to find the one best way to shovel pig iron (see Case Study 7.1).

Case Study 7.1   Shovelling pig iron

In one experiment, Taylor sought to develop a science of shovelling. A first-class shoveller was found to do his biggest day's work with a shovel load of about 21 lbs. Eight to ten different kinds of shovel were thus provided at the Bethlehem steel company, one for each type of material depending on the weight of that material (e.g., a small one for ore which is heavy and a large one for ashes that are light). Providing these different sized shovels prevented the shoveller, who previously owned his own shovel, from shovelling to less than maximum effect. Everyday the

---

shoveller would be given and would implement the instructions for doing each new job. Clerks planned their work. The outcome was that the work of 400 and 600 yard labourers was reduced to the work of 140 (see Wilson, 1999).

The outcome was that Taylor developed a set of universal principles about what scientific management involved:

- The scientific analysis by management of all the tasks which need to be done in order to make the workshop as efficient as possible;
- The design of jobs by managers to achieve the maximum technical division of labour through job fragmentation;
- The separation of the planning and execution of work;
- Reduced skill requirements and job-learning times;
- Minimizing materials-handling by operators and separating indirect or preparatory tasks from direct or productive ones;
- Using tools such as time-study and monitoring systems to coordinate the fragmented components and the work of de-skilled workers;
- Using incentive payments to stabilize and intensify worker effort; and
- Arm's length manager–worker relationships.

This rational approach to the labour process found form in the mechanized assembly line techniques of Henry Ford. Ford adopted the principles of Taylorism for his car plants, having seen the system of mass disassembly in the Chicago meat packing plants before the First World War (Burrell, 1997). Ford appreciated that the process of disassembly of animal carcasses in principle could be applied in reverse to the construction of cars. He found that it took 20 minutes for a man to produce an electrical alternator. When the process was spread over 29 operations, however, assembly time was decreased to 13 minutes, raising the height of the assembly line by 8 inches reduced this to 7 minutes, while further rationalization cut it to 5 minutes. At his car manufacturing plant in Michigan, therefore, Ford adopted Taylor's prescription – high levels of financial remuneration, the separation of conception from execution and the organization of the division of labour according to scientifically grounded observations – with the technology of the moving assembly line, to achieve unprecedented levels of manufacturing output.

'Fordism', as this system of organization was termed, which combined Taylor's principles of scientific management with an assembly-line mode of production, aimed to maximize output with the human worker conforming to the role of little more than a rationalized factor of production in a factory geared to the mass production of standardized products. Since its introduction, the term 'Fordist' has come to be extensively used to describe the combination of linear work sequencing, the interdependence of tasks, a moving assembly line, the use and refinement of dedicated machinery and specialized machine tools. A result was that Fordism, based on Taylorist principles, has been associated with a tendency towards the deskilling and degradation of labour (see Case Study 7.2).

Case Study 7.2   The deskilling thesis

Taylor believed that his system embodied an impersonal fairness: the fairness of a fair day's wage for a fair day's work. Braverman (1974), however, argued that for Taylor a fair day's work meant the maximum amount of work a person could physically do without collapsing, and a fair day's pay meant the minimum amount that could be paid to induce the worker to give this level of effort. From Braverman's perspective, the application of such scientific management strategies over the twentieth century resulted in a deskilling and degradation of labour as managers sought to control the labour process by reducing the discretion exercised by the workforce through the separation of conception and execution of work (organizational de-skilling) and automation which transfers discretion from the shop floor to the office (technological de-skilling).

Fordism, however, was not purely a way of organizing production. Ford himself had understood that the mass production of goods would, if over-production was going to be averted, require a mass consumption culture. Hence, integral to Fordism was a nurturing of mass consumption in which working people would be encouraged and enabled to consume goods provided by the mass production system. Fordism thus developed well beyond the confines of the work organization into a relatively coherent socio-economic system that linked production, consumption and cultural expectations through a process of socio-economic rationalization. As Amin *et al.* (2002a: 2) summarize,

> Fordism is the term that describes the model of capitalist accumulation and regulation from the mid 1950s to the late 1970s. In its heartland in North America and parts of Europe, during its golden age, it provided full employment, consumer and welfare security, and a social pact around national mass political institutions and universalistic beliefs. Its economic logic lay in the employment of large workforces to mass produce goods for a mass consumer market sustained by growing wages, state demand management policies and state welfare provision. A distinctive combination of state and market – centred around the economics of mass production/consumption and Keynesian regulation – catered for economic and social needs across the social spectrum.

To engender such mass consumption, in 1914, Ford reduced the daily hours in his plant from 9 to 8. In 1926, he announced that his factories would be closed all Saturdays. His rationale was that an increase in leisure time would support an increase in consumer spending, not least on automobile travel and automobiles. This was a prescient view for the weekend did become associated with outings and leisure trips and led to a mass production/mass consumption society.

Fordism as a model, however, soon reached a crisis point due to two main developments which meant that its organizational features were no longer appropriate in the face of changing socio-economic conditions. First, the apparent inability of the working class in advanced economies to consume at the rate and in the quantity required failed to ensure the feasibility of Fordist economies of scale, an inability that was largely due to the incapacity of the economy, despite state intervention, to redistribute sufficient levels of income away from capital and towards the labour force. Secondly, the Fordist labour process was unable to extract levels of surplus value necessary to counteract declining rates of profit. For Fordism to survive, therefore, it needed to evolve beyond the limitations placed on it by the organizational principles inherited from Taylorism.

During the 1970s, it began to be asserted that a *neo-Fordist* era was emerging in which new strategies were being adopted to ensure that Fordism could adapt to the changed social and economic circumstances (e.g., Aglietta, 1979). These new strategies were of two kinds. On the one hand, a new international division of labour was identified which extended the Taylorist principle of separating conception and execution to a global level. It was asserted that a strategy of transferring production to lower-cost parts of the world economy, such as East Asia, while centralizing research and management functions in the advanced industrialized nations was being adopted. On the other hand, a strategy of developing more flexible patterns of production and labour organization was identified, which was being applied to reduce costs in areas where the manufacturing process could not be relocated.

To encapsulate this latter strategy, a new concept emerged, namely *flexible specialization*. Originally developed in the work of Piore and Sabel (1984) and Sabel (1982), the argument was that the crisis of Fordism was in major part due to the inability of the mass production system to meet the needs and demands of an increasingly differentiated global marketplace. While Japan was obtaining an internationally competitive edge through the production of high-quality products and more importantly through product diversification, Western manufacturers were argued to be unprepared and ill-equipped to respond to this challenge. The only solution seemed to be for traditional Fordist-based producers to adopt a similar system of 'flexible specialization'. This, as Piore and Sabel (1984: 17) define it, is

> a strategy of permanent innovation, accommodation to ceaseless change, rather than effort to control it. This strategy is based on flexible – multi-use – equipment; skilled workers; and the creation, through politics, of an industrial community that restricts the forms of competition to those favouring innovation.

Introducing such flexible specialization, nevertheless, necessitated a full-scale reversal of the tendency in Fordism to reduce the de-skilled employee to little more than an appendage to the machine and a 'revival of craft forms' of labour (Piore and Sabel, 1984: 17). At first, Sabel (1982) argued that such changes were most appropriately realized through small 'high technology' industries, such as those cooperating through a network system. Later, however, he argued that the same process was not only appropriate to, but also starting to take hold in, more traditional Western mass production industries (Sabel, 1994).

By the late 1980s, however, the ideas of neo-Fordism and flexible specialization had become largely subsumed under the more general heading of *post-Fordism*. While neo-Fordism had intimated that the changes were an attempt to modify Fordist practices and flexible specialization was intimating a return to some previous era, the term 'post-Fordism' was signifying that these changes marked a break with the past Fordist modes of economic and social organization (see Hall and Jacques, 1989). Post-Fordism, that is, marks the advent of more flexible programmable machines; labour that is more flexibly deployed in terms of both the quantity used (numerical flexibility) and the tasks performed (functional flexibility); the vertical disintegration of large corporations; greater use of inter-firm alliances (e.g., subcontracting, strategic alliances, just-in-time production), and a closer integration of product development, marketing and production, resulting in a small batch production tailored to specific niche markets.

In the UK, for example, the retail industry was identified as one arena in which these more flexible post-Fordist work practices were apparent. With the growth of computing systems, producers and retailers were able to carefully match stock to consumer demand and thus overcome, at the point of purchase at least, the problem of Fordist overproduction. In turn, this allowed the retailer to identify and service 'niche markets'. By utilizing computerized information technology (e.g., electronic point of sale), in conjunction with increasingly sophisticated market-research strategies, retailers were able to analyse consumption patterns in depth and meet increasingly differentiated markets with differentiated products. Such niche marketing could only operate effectively, however, if the manufacturing process also fostered the same degree of flexibility. Toyota, the Japanese car manufacturing giant, was particularly singled out as a pioneer in this respect, much as Ford had been 80 years earlier, with two key components of the Toyota post-Fordist strategy being given special attention.

On the one hand, the use of a 'just-in-time' (Hutchins, 1988) system of component supply was given particular attention. Here, aiming to eliminate wasted time and output, the traditional practice of maintaining large in-house stocks of component parts of 'just-in-case' systems is abandoned in favour of a system whereby, through the utilization of computer stock control mechanisms and ordering systems, components are ordered from suppliers on the basis of daily production plans (Table 7.1).

On the other hand, attention was paid to the innovative methods of flexible labour control and organization being used by Toyota. Indeed, studies by the Institute of Manpower Studies in the 1980s (Atkinson, 1985, 1987) suggested that a new employment model of the flexible firm was emerging which had

- A core group of permanently employed primary labour market staff of skilled workers, managers, designers, technical sales staff and so on who in return for their relatively advantageous work, reward and career conditions are flexible in the work they do, and are willing to retrain and shift their careers within an internal labour market as required. They are functionally flexible;
- A first peripheral group of a secondary labour market type also consisting of full-time employees, but with less security and career potential. They do clerical,

Table 7.1 Just-in-case versus just-in-time systems

'Just-in-case' systems	'Just-in-time' systems
Components delivered in large but infrequent batches	Components delivered in small, very frequent, batches
Very large buffer stocks held to protect against disruption in supply or discovery of faulty batches	Minimal stocks held – only sufficient to meet the immediate need
Quality control based on sample check after supplies received	Quality control 'built in' at all stages
Large warehousing spaces and staff required to hold and administer stocks	Minimal warehousing space and staff required
Use of large number of suppliers selected primarily on the basis of price	Use of small number of preferred suppliers within tiered supply system
Remote relationships between customer and supplier	Very close relationships between customer and suppliers
No incentive for suppliers to locate close to customers	Strong incentive for suppliers to locate close to customers

Source: Dicken (2003: Table 4.3)

assembly, supervisory or testing jobs which can more easily be filled from external labour markets;

- A second peripheral group of part-timers, public-subsidy trainees and people on short-term contracts or job-sharing arrangements; and
- A supply of 'outsourced' labour whereby a range of specialized tasks like systems analysis and tasks like cleaning are supplied by agency temporary staff, sub-contractors and teleworkers.

In this flexible firm model, therefore, this division of the workforce allows the adoption of flexibility for adaptability (direct managerial approaches) to be applied to the peripheral groups and flexibility for predictability (indirect management) to the former core groups (see next chapter).

Under post-Fordism, however, it is not just production that changes, but also consumption. Rather than the mass consumption characteristic of Fordism, post-Fordism is asserted to involve the use of advanced production technologies enabling small-batch production so that consumers can be offered a fairly wide range of bespoke and individualized products and services (e.g., Sabel, 1982) heralding in a new era of customized products and services.

This purported shift from a Fordist to a post-Fordist era has been interpreted in two starkly contrasting ways. For optimists it is seen as heralding a new brighter era while for others it is seen as a largely negative phenomenon. Here, each school of thought is briefly considered in turn.

Positive visions of the future of flexible work

For those viewing the advent of post-Fordism as a positive trend, it is usually the case that some aspect of this new mode of work organization is viewed as creating a better world for workers and/or citizens. An example of this is the work of Piore and Sabel (1984), who view this 'second industrial divide' as potentially liberating blue-collar workers from the shackles of scientific management thinking that resulted in their de-skilling and turned them into degraded labour. In its place, new craft forms of work are seen to arise and industrial structures transformed into a small firm-based economy where skilled artisan workers predominate and the quality of work for workers will be greatly improved.

A further example of how this new post-Fordist era is seen as a positive move relates to the resultant vertical disintegration of firms. For Handy (2002), one outcome will be the emergence of the 'federal organization'. Federalism implies a variety of individual groups allied together under a common flag with some shared identity, seeking to make it big by keeping it small, or at least independent, by combining autonomy with cooperation. This is not the same as decentralization where the centre delegates certain tasks to the outlying bits while the centre remains in overall control. In federalism, the centre's powers are given to it by the outlying groups, in a sort of reverse delegation. The centre does not direct or control but coordinates, advises, influences and suggests. They are 'tight–loose' organizations. The centre holds some decisions very tight such as the choice of how to spend new money and where and when to place new people. This gives them the means to shape long-term strategy and to influence its execution through the key executives, leaving the implementation to the parts. But the centre acts on behalf of the parts. Its decisions have to be in consultation with, and on behalf of, them. Federal organizations work on the basis of subsidiarity: it does not keep functions which can be performed better by smaller and lower bodies.

It is not just the organizational changes that are viewed as being positive. So too are the changes in the way in which labour is organized. The shift towards more flexible work is seen as a very positive trend for workers. Peters (1994) argues that workers will come to look upon their work-life as a series of gigs or projects rather than a career while Handy (1995) celebrates the emergence of 'portfolio people' whose working lives are mobile and portable, rather than fixed to a corporation.

Others celebrate the emergence of particular forms of labour resulting from the new flexible firm model and see the advent of such flexible ways of working as marking a significant step forward and advancement in the conditions of work. Many, for example, commonly herald new peripheral forms of work such as part-time employment, fixed-term contracts, temporary employment and term-time working as very positive trends, not least in terms of the establishment of family-friendly working practices (e.g., enabling parents to combine work and family) but also in terms of enabling people to achieve a better work-life balance (Taylor, 2002b).

Other forms of flexible working, such as teleworking, are seen in a similarly positive light. It is often asserted, for example, that with the advent of IT greater numbers of people are working from home and that this is a way of reconciling the work-life balance as well as enabling family-friendly working policies. In other words, it is often painted as a flexible work practice that is in the interests of the labour force (e.g., Becker and Steele, 1995; DEGW and BRE, 1996; Duffy, 1997; Horgen *et al.*, 1999; Laing *et al.*, 1998; Law, 1999, 2001; Myreson and Ross, 1999; Raymond and Cunliffe, 1997; Smith and Kearney, 1994; Turner and Myerson, 1998; Worthington, 1997; Zelinsky 1997, 2002). Indeed, the image often portrayed is that since employers gain from telework practices (Felstead *et al.*, 2005; Ford and McLaughlin, 1995; Weiss, 1994), as do employees (e.g., Baruch 2000; Burch 1991; Olsen and Primps, 1984), the advent of teleworking as a work arrangement is a win–win situation.

In sum, for those optimistic about the advent of post-Fordism, there is a general sense that the emergence of more flexible work patterns and flexible organizations is marshalling in an era in which not only does work becomes more fulfilling but family-friendly work patterns and work-life balance are achieved, something long sought after but until now rarely obtainable, especially under Fordism. If some view the advent of post-Fordist work practices in a positive light, however, they are in a minority. The majority of commentators who explicitly or implicitly overlay a normative judgement onto the advent of post-Fordism view its emergence as a largely negative trend.

Negative visions of the future of flexible work

For pessimists, there are a large number of negative features associated with the rise of post-Fordism, ranging from the negative impacts of flexible working, the off-loading of those no longer required by capitalism, the social polarization that results from post-Fordism, the resultant nature of consumption society and the fact that whatever changes have occurred this remains essentially a capitalist mode of production that puts profit before people.

A common argument of pessimists, for example, is that the advent of post-Fordism has punctured the expectation of a full-employment/comprehensive welfare state scenario that existed under Fordism and guaranteed welfare for all (e.g., Amin *et al.*, 2002a; Gorz, 1982; Rifkin, 1995). Post-Fordism is thus seen to mark the end of full-employment and the rise of under-employment as firms seek to reduce labour costs and rewrite the social contract with labour, leading to growing job insecurity, and the demise of the welfare state.

This vision of the future of work under post-Fordism is exemplified by the 'Brazilianization of the West' thesis of Beck (2000). In semi-industrialized Brazil, the economically active population in full-time employment constitutes only a minority of the working population. The majority are migratory workers involved in low wage, multi-activity. Until now, this form of working has been a feature of mainly female work patterns in the West, but in post-Fordism this is asserted to become a significant feature of the overall labour market. Although labour market flexibility is attractive to the state because it redistributes risks away from the public purse and transfers them to the individual, it comes with great social costs, notably insecurity, low pay, intermittent work experience and social dislocation. Beck's Brazilianization thesis thus argues that society is moving into an indefensible polarization between an economically active minority, with full-time employment, carrying good pay and occupational benefits, and a majority driven to the poverty line by the absence of full-time remunerative work.

For him, three impacts make this trend indefensible. First, the economically active minority are beset by an acute time-famine which prevents them from gaining satisfaction from the fruits of their labour. As many have shown, these workers often complain that they are slaves to their work and do not know how to enjoy time off (Bunting, 2004; Hochschild, 1998; Pahl, 1995). Second, the majority become economically and politically marginalized, lacking the citizenship rights that come with full-time regular employment (Gorz, 1999) and forced into the informal economy to gain their livelihoods. Finally, the ethical foundations of redistributive justice are threatened in post-Fordism by this polarization resulting in a burden upon the minority to sustain the welfare delivery to the majority.

These negative traits of post-Fordist work organization are repeated and expanded in many other commentaries. Take, for example, the reported tendency that in post-Fordism a process of social polarization occurs, not least due to different groups of worker being treated differently by employers. Hutton (1995) encapsulates this in his description of the '40–30–30' society with the top 40 per cent in relatively privileged (full-time secure jobs or unionized jobs as well as the long-term self-employed), the middle 30 per cent being marginalized and insecure, including part-timers and causal workers, low-paid people and those in short-term self-employment, and the bottom 30 per cent being disadvantaged and largely excluded from the labour market, including those on government make-work schemes.

Yet others, moreover, focus upon the negative impacts under post-Fordism of sub-contracting. With the rise in sub-contracting under post-Fordism, it is often highlighted how, in a bid to reduce costs, formal businesses increasingly sub-contract stages of the production process to off-the-books employers who employ workers under degrading, low-paid and exploitative 'sweatshop-like' conditions (e.g., Barlett and Steele, 2000; Bender, 2004; Castree et al., 2004; Espenshade, 2004; Hapke, 2004; A. Ross, 2004; R. Ross, 2004), especially in the garment manufacturing sector (e.g., Bender, 2004; Espenshade, 2004; Hapke, 2004; Ram et al., 2002; R. Ross, 2004). The outcome is that there is a polarization of working conditions not only within firms but also along the supply chain with those at the end of the chain in flexible sub-contracting arrangements being subjected to highly exploitative low-paid informal forms of working (e.g., Barrientos and Ware Barrientos, 2003; Doane et al., 2003; Lund, 2003).

A further way in which post-Fordism is seen as having negative impacts relates to the way in which the responsibility for social reproduction of those no longer required by capitalism is being off-loaded by the state onto the informal realm. In this view, therefore, post-Fordism is further promoting informalization due to the way in which it has led to a demise of the notion of comprehensive formal welfare provision and cast marginalized populations into the informal sphere to eke out their livelihoods (Amin *et al.*, 2002a; Castells and Portes, 1989).

For yet others, trends such as tele-working and home-working identified by the optimists as a positive trend are configured in a very different light. Whilst optimists, as shown above, read such a trend as leading to family-friendly working practices and work-life balance, more pessimistic commentators point to the more negative consequences. Rather than focus upon the core workers who are adopting tele-working and home-working practices, those adopting a negative stance swing the lens around to another group, home-workers working for low pay under exploitative conditions (e.g., Allen and Wolkowitz, 1987; Christensen, 1989; Galpin and Sims, 1999; Huws *et al.*, 1990, 1999; Olson, 1989). As Stanworth (1997) asserts, it is necessary to distinguish between mobile teleworkers who work from (but not always at) home and tend to be male, work full-time and to be higher skilled, and home-based (tele)workers who are mostly female, work part-time and undertaking lower-skilled jobs. For them, such flexible working is not the liberating trend that the more optimistic commentators assert when discussing mostly professional knowledge workers. Indeed, for those more pessimistic about the consequences of post-Fordism, flexible forms of work organization, such as tele-working and home-working, that are part of the trend towards stretching the workplace beyond the office door are much more about intensifying work than offering employees greater freedom and control over their working time (see Case Study 7.3).

Case Study 7.3   Stretching the workplace beyond the office door

In contrast to those management gurus discussed above who argue that tele-working and home-working mark the advent of more autonomous and family-friendly ways of working, other more pessimistic commentators contend that the principal drivers behind such moves towards spatial flexibility in work organization are, first, a desire to reap cost savings in the provision of office space and, secondly, a desire to engender work intensification by reducing non-working time.

For these commentators, it is not simply that a transition is being witnessed from working in offices to working at home. Rather, a wide range of diverse sites and spaces are becoming places where people work. Homes are one important site but only one place among many. The shift is actually from single to plural workplaces. The landscape of work that is resulting is one in which the spaces and times of employment are becoming less clearly separated, with work-time colonizing spaces and times previously set aside for non-work. Mobile phones, video conferencing, text messaging, e-mail, laptops and the Internet mean that increasingly one can work at any time and in any place. The notion that some spaces or times are ring-fenced for work and others for non-work is being swept away. Today, workplaces can include not only office blocks and factories, but also railway trains, domestic homes, motorway service stations, car interiors, airport lounges and hotel rooms. The result is that places of work are no longer singular but multiple, working hours are no longer fixed but stretch throughout the day, week and year, and the boundaries between work and non-work are becoming increasingly undifferentiated.

However, this is not resulting in non-work colonizing the spaces and times of work. Rather, the trend is in the opposite direction. As Felstead *et al.* (2005: 176) argue, 'the times and spaces of work are seeping into and wrapping themselves around those that were once the preserve of non-work activities, such as leisure, family and "down" times. Work has broken out of the constraints of specialized locations and fixed hours.' The outcome is that now that the boundaries between employment and life outside employment have been broken down, there is little to stop the continuing incursion of employment into every nook and cranny of life.

A further perceived problem under post-Fordism, and one which will be returned to in greater detail in the next chapter, concerns the trend towards organizational commitment. As Gorz (1999: 37) states,

> There is a clear regression here by comparison with Fordism: Toyotism replaces modern social relations with pre-modern ones. Fordism was in fact modern in so far as it recognized the specificity of, and antagonism between, the respective interests of living labour and capital. The relationship between the company and the workers was in essence a conflictual one and required of the parties concerned *negotiated compromises* which are continually undergoing review. Workers did not *belong* to the company. They owed it only the work clearly laid down in their contracts of employment, at set hours and on specified terms and conditions. They owed it to the company to *lend themselves* to the accomplishment of tasks which could be affected without their committing themselves to the particular ends concerned. . . . They retained a substantial part of their energies for themselves, that part being effectively withdrawn from productive instrumentalization - from exploitation. . . . It is this dynamic which was at first halted, then reversed, in post-Fordism.

Post-Fordism, however, requested and nurtured unconditional commitment from the worker to the company's goals. For commentators such as Gorz (1999), the outcome is a neo-feudalism where employees enter into vassalage with their employers. As Hancock and Tyler (2001: 60) rather differently put it,

> Do modes of organizing based on the values of flexibility, multi-skilling, employee-friendly work cultures and the like, represent anything other than redefined instrumental technologies designed to extract greater levels of labour from employees than the

modern or Fordist practices they are supposed to have supplanted? While apparently premised upon new concerns with issues of empowerment, involvement and the deconstruction of rigid attitudes towards methods of production and organizational hierarchy, is the criticism that, on closer inspection, they represent merely attempts to colonize employee subjectivity and other 'previously unrationalized aspects of the work organization'. . .

It is not just the mode of production that has been subject to criticism by those adopting a more pessimistic view of the advent of post-Fordism. It is also the mode of consumption emerging under post-Fordism to replace to mass consumption. Although optimists view this as heralding bespoke and individualized products and services, a very different view of the mode of consumption is adopted by more pessimistic commentators. For some analysts, such as Bryman (2004), post-Fordist consumption is captured by what he terms the 'Disneyization thesis' (see Case Study 7.4).

Case Study 7.4   Post-Fordist consumption: the Disneyization thesis

For Bryman (2004: 1), the 'Disneyization thesis' refers to 'the process by which the principles of the Disney theme parks are coming to dominate more and more sectors of American society as well as the rest of the world'. As Bryman (2004: 159) explains, 'Disneyization is a mode of delivery in the sense of the *staging* of goods and services for consumption. It provides a framework for increasing the allure of goods and services. Disneyization seeks to increase the appeal of goods and services that might otherwise appear mundane and uninteresting' by providing an ambience of choice, difference and frequently the spectacular so as to encourage consumers to spend more. Bryman (2004: vii) highlights four aspects of this Disneyization of consumption – theming, hybrid consumption, merchandizing and performative labour.

Theming. When institutions or objects are themed, they are clothed in a narrative largely unrelated to the institution or object to which it is applied, such as a restaurant with a Wild West theme. By infusing objects with meaning through theming, they are deemed more attractive and interesting than would otherwise be the case. Gottdiener (2001) has identified nine prominent themes in the US: status; tropical paradise; Wild West; classical civilization; nostalgia; Arabian fantasy; urban motif; fortress architecture and surveillance; and modernism and progress. Bryman (2004) adds three others, namely music and in particular rock music; sport; and Hollywood and the movies more generally, as well as one other: the company and its logo, which is a form of 'reflexive theming' whereby the theme and the brand and its expression become coterminous.

Hybrid consumption. Hybrid consumption is where the forms of consumption associated with different institutional spheres become interlocked with each other and increasingly difficult to distinguish. The outcome is de-differentiated forms of consumption in which conventional distinctions between these forms become increasingly blurred to the point that they almost collapse. The master principle is to get people to *stay longer* by fusing more consumption items. This is again seen in hotels, theme parks, shopping malls, restaurants, sports stadiums, zoos, airport terminals, cruise ships.

Merchandizing. Merchandizing refers to the promotion and sale of goods in the form of or bearing copyright images and/or logos, including such products made under licence. Disney is perhaps an exemplar of this but it is also seen with feature films (e.g., Jurassic Park, Star Wars, The Lion King), television series (e.g., Thomas the Tank Engine, Tweenies, Teletubbies), theme parks, zoos, sport and even universities.

Performative labour. This refers to the tendency for frontline service work to be viewed as a performance, especially one in which the deliberate display of a certain mood is seen as part of the labour involved in service work. Here, therefore, emotions effectively become the property of the employer. Such emotional labour, which involves the commodification of human feelings (Hochschild, 1979, 1983, 1993, 1998, 2003), has diffused to airline cabin crews, shop workers, call centre workers, restaurants, hotels, zoos. Of course, such emotional labour is often met by resistance from the employees involved, as has been shown to be the case in Disney theme parks (Van Maanen, 1991; Van Maanen and Kunda, 1989). Other analysts even discuss the advent of 'post-emotional society' (Městrović, 1997) where emotional labour creates a world full of emotions yet devoid of any 'real' emotional content as emotions become mechanized, rationalized and commodified in a society characterized by synthetic quasi-emotions.

For Bryman (2004), these four dimensions constitute principles that are pervading many spheres of consumption under post-Fordism, with Disney providing a template for the rest of the service sector.

Ultimately, however, the major critique of those pessimistic about post-Fordism is the notion that although post-Fordism is heralded as bringing in a new era of work organization, in actual fact very little has changed. Such a mode of work organization remains essentially capitalist in orientation and seeks to expropriate profit from the workforce, albeit in new ways. Indeed, it is for ultimately this reason that so many commentators view post-Fordism in such a negative light. Whatever positive aspects are identified by others, these analysts ultimately view such trends as always being in the interests of capital that is seeking to expropriate profit from the workforce or consumer (e.g., Amin *et al.*, 2002a; Harvey, 1989, 2000; Hudson, 2005; Ransome, 2005).

Evaluating the penetration of post-Fordism

This vision of the future of work conflates all types of work organization that exist in the present into two types, namely Fordism and post-Fordism, and then proceeds to place these into a temporal sequence whereby Fordism is characterized as the old and receding mode of production and post-Fordism as the new and emergent form. In this section, however, this vision of the future of work is evaluated critically. Is it indeed the case that Fordism is an old and receding mode of production? Is a shift towards post-Fordism everywhere apparent? To what extent has post-Fordism penetrated production and consumption? And is it so simple that production and consumption can be disaggregated into Fordist and post-Fordist varieties?

The death of Fordism?

Despite the post-Fordism thesis forcing all modes of production and consumption into either Fordist or post-Fordist forms of work organization and then conflating these presently existing types into a temporal sequence whereby post-Fordist practices replace Fordist practices, much evidence exists that Fordist modes of production and consumption persist in contemporary society and are far from minor remnants persisting in a few minor vestiges of the capitalist world. As Hudson (2005: 120) asserts,

> Despite claims about the demise of mass production, Taylorism is far from dead. Firstly, Taylorism has been extended into agriculture and mining, . . . by industrializing and Taylorizing production. Secondly, Taylorist principles have been introduced in many routine sales and service activities, creating 'downgraded services' as work is reorganized to cut costs and tighten managerial control of the labour process. Thirdly, the principles of Taylorization have been further extended with the expansion of 'downgraded manufacturing' (Sassen, 1991). Fourthly, mass production remains prominent, not least in technologically dynamic 'high tech' computing and electronics sectors in which scale economies are crucial. . . . Fifthly, the growth of corporations enabled them to split up production processes, functionally, and spatially [with Taylorist manufacturing preserved in new intra- and inter-national divisions of labour].

Perhaps the most developed example of the persistence of Taylorist and Fordist production methods in the contemporary world, however, is the work of Ritzer (1993, 1995, 1998) and his McDonaldization thesis which displays that such Taylorist practices have now shifted from the management science of shovelling pig iron (see Case Study 7.1 earlier) to the management science of shovelling chips and much more (see Case Study 7.5).

Case Study 7.5   The McDonaldization thesis: from shovelling pig iron to shovelling chips

One of the clearest arguments that the death of Taylorism and Fordism is perhaps premature is the McDonaldization thesis of Ritzer (1993, 1995, 1998). Starting with the example of the fast food restaurant chain, McDonalds, he displays how labour in such restaurants is highly rationalized, and the goal is the discovery of the best, the most efficient, way of grilling a hamburger, frying chicken or serving a meal. Here, managerial control of the work is maximized and it is broken down into its constituent tasks. Although about three-quarters of outlets are owned by franchises rather than the corporation, the company requires that production methods and products meet McDonald's specifications. This covers food preparation, book-keeping, purchasing, dealing with workers and customers and virtually every aspect of the business. A 'bible', an operations and training manual, demonstrates proper placement of ketchup, mustard and pickle slices on each type of hamburger available. Lights and buzzers tell the crew when to take French fries out of the fat, the French fry scoops specify the size of portion and allow the workers to fill a bag and set it down in one continuous motion, specially designed ketchup dispensers squirt the correct portion of ketchup. Crew are also told in what sequence the products of the customers order are to be gathered, what arm motion is to be used in salting the batch of fries, and to double-fold each bag before presenting it to the customer. Only minor variations are allowed.

The key to the success of McDonalds is therefore its uniformity and predictability. Customers know exactly what they will get wherever they are; they will be served quickly, with a smile, courteously. It promises fast service, hot food and clean restaurants. There is centralized planning, centrally designed training programmes, approved and supervised suppliers, automated machinery, meticulous specifications and systematic inspections. Performance is rated and each worker is awarded stars (worn on a badge) which are linked to pay and promotion prospects. McDonald's training centre near Chicago is called Hamburger University and is on a campus, the director is called the dean and the trainers are professors. The trainers work from scripts prepared for them. They try to produce managers with 'ketchup in their veins'. Crew, managers and franchises learn that there is a 'McDonalds way' of doing business and that any diversion from this is wrong. The full training programme requires between 600 and 1000 hours of work and is required by all those wishing to own a McDonald's outlet.

Although Ritzer (1993) argues that fast food restaurants like McDonalds exemplify the persistence of scientific management in the contemporary era, he does not confine his McDonalidzation thesis to this sector. For Ritzer (1993), the basic dimensions of McDonaldization – efficiency, calculability, predictability, increased control through technology – are manifest not only in the fast food industry but in a wide and growing range of settings. For example, they are evident in factory farming (Ritzer 1993: 103). Indeed, Burrell (1997: 138) takes this further when he asserts that McDonald's is an organization dependent on the profitable death of cattle and chickens in profusion. Without automated death, the cost of the Big Mac would be higher. These principles are also present in the credit card industry where computerization means that credit records can now be checked and applications approved or rejected rapidly, reducing unpredictability (Ritzer, 1995), call centres (Taylor and Bain, 1998), banking, retailing, and other services (Beynon, 1992), as well as education, health care, politics and travel (see Smart, 1999).

Yet as Ritzer (1999) points out, in response to Smart's (1999) criticisms of his McDonaldization thesis, these tendencies towards 'McDonalds standardization' are not the sole tendency in the world of work. They are occurring in the world at the same time as post-Fordist moves towards greater flexibility are occurring in other sectors.

Rather than write the obituary of Fordism, therefore, it is perhaps necessary to re-read it as no longer the hegemonic mode of production and consumption (if it ever was) but as one mode of production co-existing alongside others in the present-day. Indeed, the contemporary presence of Fordism, as the McDonaldization thesis exemplifies, is not difficult to identify. In the service industries, and leaving aside McDonalds and other fast food restaurants, the supermarket sector in general and check-outs in particular, epitomize the Fordist approach. Customers pass items along the conveyor belt which are swept across the bar-code reader by an operator performing a monotonous series of repetitive actions. The flow-line, dedicated machinery and the segmented work tasks are exemplary of Fordist principles of work organization.

Similarly, others assert that the myopic view of the advent of post-Fordist work practices is very much a Western view that obscures and glosses over the continued existence and even export of Fordist practices to third world nations in the new international division of labour. As Gamble et al. (2004) display for example, mass production is alive and well in East Asia. Examining MNCs from developed economies and newly industrialized economies in East Asia (Japan, Korea, Taiwan and Hong Kong), they find that Taylorist forms of work organization and low-trust/low-investment Human Resource Management (HRM) policies are an inherent part of their corporate strategies.

It is not just the persistence of Fordist work practices, however, that lead many to be less than convinced by the claims of those who champion the emergence of flexible post-Fordist modes of organization and the death of Fordism (Pollert, 1988a,b; Rustin, 1989; Whitaker, 1992). There is also scepticism as to whether Fordism ever dominated production to the extent suggested by exponents of post-Fordism. Most plants in modern economies have never contained assembly lines (K. Williams *et al.*, 1992a,b, 1997; Jones, 1997). As Kumar (1995) puts it, the charge in this respect is one of mythologization. Put another way, the practice of Taylorism was never as widespread as often assumed, not least due to collective resistance from trade unions (Edwards, 1979; Palmer, 1979).

There is also the issue that many workplaces display, as they probably always have done, modes of work organization that do not entirely reflect the 'pure' pictures of Fordism and post-Fordism often portrayed in the literature. Williams *et al.* (1992b) for example, reveal a picture of greater flexibility at Ford's Highland Park (1909–19) than often considered in the portrayal of Fordism and less standardization of the product. Many other examples exist where the principles and practices of both Fordism and post-Fordism apply (e.g., Clark, 1990; Tomaney, 1990, 1994), leading some such as Williams *et al.* (1997) to argue that the conceptual polarity between Fordism and post-Fordism is misleading. This does not mean, however, that new 'hybrid' forms of work organization are emerging that combine Fordist and post-Fordist principles. Rather, it is much more likely that this reflects how squeezing all work practices into either Fordist or post-Fordist modes of work organization obfuscates the fuzzy boundaries and ways in which work practices tend to combine, and have always combined, elements of both modes of work organization in practice.

This is in major part reflected in discussions of whether there is a process of de-skilling associated with Fordist practices or upskilling associated for some with post-Fordism. As Gallie (1991) identifies, it is neither one nor the other alone that is occurring in workplaces. Rather, there is a process of skill polarization with de-skilling in some parts of the organization and upskilling in other parts. Milkman (1997), similarly, in a case study of General Motors plant in Linden, New Jersey, uncovers skill polarization in that already skilled workers were given opportunities to acquire new skills and retrain while their semi-skilled counterparts on the production line were denied such opportunities. The consequence was upskilling for one group and de-skilling for another, hence a polarization effect.

In another study, De Witte and Steijn (2000) analysed 1,022 Dutch employees on the extent of their autonomy in their work, the complexity of their job (both measures being used to assess the skill level of their job) and the extent of automation, They reveal a general trend in upskilling associated with increasing automation, professional and white-collar workers experiencing the most upskilling while blue-collar workers are least likely to witness upskilling and often witness de-skilling. What earlier were seen as skills strategies separately pursued by Fordist and post-Fordist firms, therefore, have been identified as co-present in individual firms. Of course, if one wished to support the Fordist/post-Fordist dualism, it could well be argued that post-Fordist firms actually apply different skills strategies to different sections of their workforce. Even if this is argued, however, it still displays that within apparently post-Fordist firms what were seen as Fordist practices of de-skilling are retained, even if only applied to a section of the workforce. It appears, therefore, that the neat Fordist/post-Fordist dualism that squeezes all businesses into one or other side of the dualism fails to capture the complexity of what is going on in workplaces in the present and the past. What is certain, moreover, is that the reported death of Fordist work practices is premature.

The penetration of flexible work practices

To evaluate the degree to which post-Fordist work practices have penetrated the business world, one starting point is to analyse the degree to which the conventional model of employment remains valid where a person is in a full-time job of indefinite duration at a facility owned or rented by an employer. In the US, according to Karoly and Panis (2004), just one in every four US workers is now in non-traditional employment implying that the vast majority of workers are not on the flexible working practices associated with post-Fordism. In the UK, meanwhile, the Economic and Social Research Council (ESRC) Future of Work Research programme identified that in both 1992 and 2000 the overwhelming majority at work were not in flexible jobs. As many as 92 per cent of workers held *permanent employment* contracts in 2000 compared with 88 per cent in 1992. By contrast, a mere 5.5 per cent said they were working on a *temporary work* contract of less than 12 months in 2000 compared with 7.2 per cent in 1992. There was also a significant decline in the proportion of employees working on fixed-term contracts (defined as lasting for between 1 and 3 years) with an actual drop from 5 to 2.8 per cent when 2000 is compared with 1992. Such startling figures do not suggest Britain is rapidly developing a more flexible labour market. Indeed, quite the opposite appears to be the case. The permanent job remains very much the overwhelming norm across every occupational category (Taylor 2002a: 12) and, if anything, flexible jobs are becoming less rather than more numerous.

Job tenure rates (the time an individual is employed in one organization), moreover, increased on average from 6 years and 2 months to 7 years and 4 months between 1992 and 2000 (Nolan and Woods, 2003). The widely assumed picture of the flexible labour market with a growing number of foot-loose employees moving from job to job is thus far from the reality. There is more stability than assumed. Nor do employees feel ever more insecure in their jobs in Britain. Only 1.5 per cent of those surveyed said that they expected to lose their job over the next 12 months as a result of the closure of their workplace. This compared with 2 per cent who believed this in 1992. Only 2.2 per cent thought they would lose their job over the same period of time because of being made redundant. This compared with 3.4 per cent ten years earlier (Taylor 2002a). Nor is there much evidence of greater self-determination over work hours. Although the proportion saying that they work flexible hours rose from 16.8 per cent in 1992 to 22 per cent in 2000, roughly the same proportion asserted that they determined their own hours of work in 1992 and 2000 (10.3 per cent compared with 10.7 per cent).

Another test of whether flexible employment patterns are more prevalent is to look at the proportions of workers in self-employment, working from home and holding multiple jobs. Between 1979 and 1984, self-employment grew rapidly from 5 to 11 per cent, and stands now in the UK at about 7 per cent, so no clear evidence of flexibility in this regard is apparent (Nolan and Woods, 2003). Nor is there any significant increase in the number of employees working from home. Only 3 per cent of employees said they worked partly at home in 2000 and a further 1.1 per cent solely at home. This contrasts with 2.2 per cent working partly at home ten years earlier and a further 1.4 per cent working solely or mainly at home (Taylor, 2002a: 12). Such data do not suggest that we are moving into an era of home- or tele-working for the vast majority of employees. Turning to multiple job-holding, meanwhile, around 5 per cent of the workforce holds more than one job and little change is occurring over time. Most of these, moreover, are poorly paid, and located in catering, cleaning and personal services, contradicting the 'portfolio worker' thesis of Handy (1995) that depicts them as people choosing to work in such a manner and living relatively affluent lifestyles.

The emergence of workers engaged in flexible working practices, therefore, taken as a signifier of the advent of a post-Fordist mode of work organization has been exaggerated, at least so far as the UK is concerned.

Conclusions

In sum, this chapter has evaluated the vision of the future of work that first of all crams all forms of production and consumption into a specific either/or dualism, namely Fordist/post-Fordism, and then temporally sequences them by designating Fordism as the 'old' and post-Fordism as the 'new'. In the more optimistic post-Fordist accounts, a normative judgement is then laid over this dichotomy with the 'new' post-Fordism seen as possessing positive attributes and the 'old' Fordist modes of production and consumption many negative attributes. In practice, however, this dichotomy is once again conflating present-day and spatial differences into a temporal sequence. Yet this shift from Fordism to post-Fordism is far from as clear-cut as is sometimes intimated by exponents. Not only was Fordism less universal in the past than often expounded but post-Fordism is also less all-embracing in the present than frequently intimated. Indeed, far from being a temporal streamlined evolution from one to the other, what is actually being described are existing forms of work that are being neatly divided into two types one of which is privileged over the other. Yet the reality is that many organizations include elements of both Fordist and post-Fordist practices, and the boundaries between the two are much fuzzier than often suggested.

For some this might be taken as evidence that 'hybrid' forms of organization are emerging that display both Fordist and post-Fordist principles of organization. What is much more likely, however, is that the strict dichotomy between Fordism and post-Fordism was never able to delineate the complexity of organizational practices and that many businesses have always displayed elements of both Fordist and post-Fordist work practices. As Amin and Thrift (2004: xvii) state, economic readings have ... powerful cultural effects. One has only to think of the work of Marx and Engels to see the way in which such readings are able to reinscribe how cultures see themselves as a single functioning economic system, which, in turn, is returned to these cultures as an established economic and cultural fact. This is exactly how Marx and Engels were able to project nineteenth century English capitalism – despite all its particularities – as a world economic standard and its class culture as the only culture. Exactly the same can be said of the pioneer experiments by F.W. Taylor and Henry Ford in the US early in the twentieth century with principle of mass production and mass consumption, which not only served as a model of accumulation for the rest of the world to copy or measure up to, but also as a way of life pivoted around the individual as specialized worker and as fulfilled consumer.

In other words, this projection of the mode of economic production and consumption is then taken on board as an irrefutable fact of how the economy and the society are structured whilst the reality is far more multifarious and diverse. It is not only this dichotomy, however, that has acted in such a transformative manner. Attention now turns to another dichotomy that perhaps has and is providing an even more important signifier to work organizations of what they should work towards.

Further reading

Felstead, A., Jewson, N. and Walters, S. (2005) *Changing Places of Work*, Basingstoke: Palgrave Macmillan.

This book explores how the trends towards tele-working and home-working are part of a wider shift from single to multiple workspaces, displaying how the spaces and times of employment are now less clearly separate, with work-time colonizing spaces and times previously set aside for non-work.

Gorz, A. (1999) *Reclaiming Work: beyond the wage-based society*, Cambridge: Polity.

This text highlights the negative consequences of post-Fordism by an author writing from a post-employment perspective (see Chapter 11).

Piore, M. and Sabel, C. (1984) *The Second Industrial Divide: possibilities for prosperity*, New York: Basic Books.

This book popularized the notion of 'flexible specialization' and opened up this vision of the future of work and organization to a wide audience.

Ritzer, G. (1998) *The McDonaldization thesis: explorations and extensions*, London: Sage.

This follow-up to his 1993 book which displayed the persistence of a Fordist mode of production opens up and extends the notion of the persistence of Fordism across a range of sectors and industries.

White, M., Hill, S., Mills, C. and Smeaton, D. (2004) *Managing to Change? British workplaces and the future of work*, Basingstoke: Palgrave Macmillan.

This book focused on the UK situation provides a lucid guide to the extent and nature of the penetration of flexible working practices across the UK labour force, dispelling many myths about the degree and character of flexibility.

8

Post-bureaucratic management

Introduction

In the post-Fordist vision of the future of employment, as the last chapter revealed, the desire for functional flexibility within the core workforce has necessitated the emergence of highly motivated and flexible workers. These workers must be motivated so that quality control can be largely delegated to them and sufficiently flexible so that they can take on various roles and tasks that might previously have fallen outside their expertise. These developments have in turn led to a reappraisal of the appropriateness of classical management theory and practice. Addressing issues such as the dismantling of bureaucratic control methods, engendering a commitment to quality, and the cultural climate of, or within, the organization, the necessity for, and desirability of, a transition from bureaucratic to post-bureaucratic management has been widely discussed (Armenakis and Bedeian, 1999; Child and McGrath, 2001; Handy, 1995; Kalleberg, 2001; Kanter, 1989; Peters, 1992). Often presented in the guise of totalizing solutions to the competitive ills of contemporary work organizations such as HRM, TQM and exhortations to 'excellence' from the management gurus, there has been a widespread prescriptive call for managers to marry the subjective and emotional aspirations of their employees with the strategic goals of the organization, through ensuring that employment itself is experienced as meaningful and personally rewarding activity. Dispensing with the Taylorist idea that people work harder with the promise of financial remuneration, there has been what Ciulla (2000) calls a shift away from not only the attempts of scientific management to capture the body but also the humanistic imperatives of the Human Relations Movement to capture the heart. As will be revealed, these post-bureaucrats now want to tap into the soul of the worker.

To depict this vision of the future of work, and similar to the structure of previous chapters, first, the way in which all forms of organizing work are crammed into an either/or dualism, in this case a bureaucratic/post-bureaucratic management dichotomy will be outlined along with how a transition from bureaucratic to post-bureaucratic management is seen to be taking place. Secondly, the resultant visions that view this transition in a largely positive manner are reviewed followed, thirdly, by an analysis of those adopting a rather more critical reading of these post-bureaucratic visions of the future of employment (e.g., Du Gay, 2000, 2005; Parker, 1993, 2002a,b,c; Reed, 1992, 2005; Thompson, 1993). The final section then evaluates critically the degree to which post-bureaucratic management can be seen to have penetrated the organizational landscape. For all of the emphasis in business and management studies on the transition from bureaucratic to post-bureaucratic management, this will reveal that there is ultimately little evidence of a linear replacement of bureaucracy with post-bureaucracy, a good deal of vagueness about what is meant by each term and plenty of signals that the direction of employment is far more complex and multi-faceted than can be captured by this dichotomy. Indeed, and as will be seen, this is perhaps reflected in the post-bureaucratic literature with some now arguing that what is emerging are hybrid forms. This chapter, however, questions whether it is indeed the case that new hybrids are emerging or whether it is more the case that the ideal types of bureaucracy and post-bureaucracy created by management academics and gurus were ever descriptive of organizations in lived practice. What are now being identified as 'hybrids' of bureaucracy and post-bureaucracy may well have been there all the time but uncaptured by this over-simplistic dichotomy. The resulting suggestion, therefore, is that this linear vision of the trajectory of work from bureaucratic to post-bureaucratic work organization is again too simple to capture the multiple and divergent trajectories taking place in the world of work, and that the future is far more open than projected by those depicting the advent of a post-bureaucratic future of work.

From bureaucratic to post-bureaucratic management

All visions of the future have some 'straw person' or measuring rod to contrast their own vision against. For those pointing towards a post-bureaucratic future of work organization, this measuring rod is a past characterized by bureaucratic management. For anybody approaching the discipline of management and business studies for the first time, it will probably come as a surprise to find not only that a lot of thought in this large and important subject revolves around the notion of bureaucracy developed by Max Weber but also that despite many management theorists advocating the need to unshackle management from the 'iron cage' of bureaucracy, they are unable to escape its firm grip when re-imagining the future of work. Always, their visions of the future of work are seemingly either supportive of or defined in opposition to bureaucracy. As Thompson and Alvesson (2005: 91) recognize, 'Most influential social theories of the last two decades from post-Fordism, through to post-modernism and the knowledge economy, have invoked a break with bureaucracy as cause or consequence of change.'

What is meant, therefore, by bureaucratic management and its successor, namely post-bureaucratic management? Weber, in *Wirtschaft und Gesellschaft*, published after his death in 1921, presents a model of what a bureaucracy would look like in its ideal form. This ideal-type is as follows:

- All operating rules and procedures are formally recorded.
- Tasks are divided up and allocated to people with formally certified expertise to carry them out.
- Activities are controlled and coordinated by officials organized in a hierarchy of authority.
- Communications and commands pass up or down the hierarchy without missing out steps.
- Posts are filled and promotions achieved by the best-qualified people.
- Office-holder posts constitute their only employment.
- Posts cannot become the property or private territory of the office-holder, the officer's authority derives from their appointed office and not from their person.
- All decision and judgements are made impersonally and neutrally, without emotion, personal preference or prejudice.

In bureaucracies, therefore, business is discharged 'without regard for person' (Weber 1978: 226) according to purely objective criteria. All love, hatred and purely irrational and emotional sentiments are excluded. With rationalization comes the use of calculative devices and techniques, formal rules, formally rational means, the division of labour, sets of rules, accounting methods, money, technology and other means for increasing that rationality. For Weber, however, this ideal-type bureaucracy was not something that he wanted to see implemented. As Grey (2005: 23) points out,

> Weber was by no means a partisan for the emergence of rational-legal or bureaucratic organizations. On the contrary, he seems to have been alarmed by their rapid spread through the state, business and institutions to the point where he feared that the world was becoming enclosed in an 'iron cage' of rationalization. But why were they becoming dominant? Because, says Weber, they represent the most technically efficient and rational form of organization.

The usual story, therefore, is that this bureaucratic organization of society reached its apogee in the post-1945 period (Bell, 1960; Kerr *et al.*, 1973; Prethus, 1962). Private and public organizations brought in a new era where politics, ideology and conflict were replaced by rational scientific decision-making guided by the administrative elite. Standardized mass production and consumption went hand in hand with this managerial form. The vehicle was 'organization man' (Whyte, 1956). As Biggart (1989: 4) asserts, Whyte was describing 'a generation of organizational workers ... moulded by the needs of the corporation ... conservative, impassive little grey men. Their lives in the organization were routine and largely unemotional.' As Thompson and McHugh (2002: 5) thus state of this period,

> It was pointless to desire significantly different arrangements, as all industrial societies were destined to converge into a single, similar type. The hierarchical and bureaucratic

large-scale organization, with its particular form of technology, was placed at the centre of mature industrial society. In retrospect this kind of perspective is more of an ideology masquerading as science than an accurate description of social trends.

Human relations movement

By the mid-twentieth century, however, many of the assumptions underpinning this bureaucratic model of organizational efficiency were coming under critical scrutiny. Arising out of the Hawthorne studies conducted in the 1920s and 1930s at the Hawthorne works of the Western Electric Company near Chicago in the US (Mayo, 1933; Roethlisberger and Dickson, 1939), a Human Relations Movement emerged that began to emphasize the social character of work and the importance of interpersonal dynamics in the maintenance of motivation and productivity (Blau and Scott, 1963; Etzioni, 1961; Merton, 1949). Although many debates exist within the management literature regarding these Hawthorne studies, the standard account is that through a series of experiments and interviews, the Hawthorne researchers and most notably Elton Mayo identified the importance of the human factor in organizations. Workers were recognized as having social needs and interests. Like Taylor, Mayo wanted to develop an effective scientifically informed management elite. For him, if management could ensure that employees' social needs were met at work by giving them the satisfaction of working together, by making workers feel important in the organization and by showing interest in their personal problems, both social breakdown and industrial unrest could be avoided (see Grey, 2005).

In these terms, two elements of the Hawthorne studies stand out as important: the 'illumination experiment' and the 'bank wiring room experiment'. In the former, lighting levels were varied up and down with an experimental group of workers, whilst they were left unchanged with a control group. Almost all of the lighting changes led to an increase in productivity and productivity also increased within the control group. Apparently, this was because something unusual was happening and the workers felt that they were part of it and that what they were doing was of interest and importance to the researchers. This caused the increase in productivity and demonstrated that workers could not be regarded as parts in a machine, thus giving birth to what is known as the 'Hawthorne effect'.

In the bank wiring room, a small group of male workers were engaged in producing electrical components. It emerged that the group set informal norms around production levels so that rather than produce their maximum output (which would earn them a bonus), they performed sub-optimally. These norms were enforced by a mixture of peer pressure (including physical sanction) and an unofficial 'gang leader'. This suggested that workers were not solely motivated by economic considerations and moreover that the 'informal side of organizations' was as important, if not more so, than the formal side (i.e., rules and official hierarchy).

The discovery of the human factor, so the standard story goes, ushered in a new era in which workers' needs had to be acknowledged and met. For Grey (2005) the flaw in this argument is threefold. First, such an interest can be found well before Hawthorne, including amongst nineteenth-century industrialists such as Quakers who sought to meet the moral needs of workers in towns like Port Sunlight and Bourneville in the UK. It was of course the new science of psychology rather than religious motives that informed the Human Relations Movement but they shared a similar humanizing imperative.

The second issue is that the original impetus of the Hawthorne studies was firmly located in the tradition of scientific management, well established by the 1920s. The desire to ascertain the effect of lighting levels on productivity was informed by the idea that management was about the control of physical variables, and in fact there were many other experiments designed to explore a whole array of such variables. Finally, and crucially, it is wrong to think that Taylor had been unaware of, or was uninterested in, the informal side of organization. On the contrary, the heart of his project was to overcome its effects. The output restrictions observed in the Bank Wiring Room were nothing other than an instance of what Taylor identified as the systematic soldiering of the workforce. Whereas Taylor sought to eradicate the informal side of the organization, the Human Relations message was to acknowledge its irrepressibility and to find ways of managing it into an alignment with the formal parts and purposes of the organization.

In this sense, the Human Relations Movement can be seen as a response to the failure, or at least limitations, of scientific management as a means of organizational control. 'But it is a response which in many ways offers not an alternative to, but an extension of, scientific management... human relations theory bears the same footprint of formal or instrumental rationality as that which is to be found in scientific management' (Grey 2005: 45). Control of the workforce is achieved in scientific management by avoiding human relations and in the latter through human relations. These are major differences since they create different workplaces but they both are instrumentally rational versions of organization. As Alvesson and Willmott (1996: 111) put it, while scientific management sought to eradicate what they saw as the disruptive irrationalities, such as tradition and sentiment from the organization arena, these later approaches viewed 'sentiment... as an untapped resource for securing improved levels of commitment and productivity'. These apparently humanistic developments within the management and structuring of organizational life, associated with Human Relations Theory and Industrial Psychology, have since been interpreted as further attempts to rationalize labour through social engineering (Braverman, 1974) and to extend the rationalization process into the very 'soul' of the worker (Rose, 1990), processes far from incompatible with the logic of bureaucratic organization. As Pringle (1989: 87) notes,

> while human-relations theorists added an informal dimension, they did not challenge the theorizing of the formal bureaucratic structures. In some ways they reinforced the idea of managerial rationality: while workers might be controlled by sentiment and emotion, managers were supposed to be rational, logical and able to control their emotions. The division between reason and emotion was tightened in a way that marked off managers from the rest.

The emergence of post-bureaucratic management

If scientific management sought to capture the body and human relations sought to capture the heart, then post-bureaucratic management, to repeat, seeks to unlock the soul of the worker (Ciulla, 2000) by creating what Bunting (2004) negatively calls 'willing slaves' or what Zohar and Marshall (2001, 2005) more positively view as creating 'spiritual intelligence' or 'spiritual capital'. To achieve this, indirect control methods that engender their commitment to the organization are used rather than direct control methods that seek compliance with the rules. Put another way, a shift from external to internal control takes place.

For those management visionaries and gurus proposing ways of achieving this end (e.g., Heckscher, 1995; Heckscher and Donnellon, 1994; Kanter 1989; Kochan *et al.*, 1986; Peters, 1987), it is envisaged that the future of work will be very different from the past. Table 8.1 contrasts and compares the features of 'old' bureaucratic and 'new' post-bureaucratic organizations. While bureaucratic organizations were large, formal, centralized and hierarchical, and based on planning, rationality, and control and command, post-modern organizations are informal, decentralized and networked, based on spontaneity, empowerment and participation (see, for example, Clegg and Hardy, 1996; Nohria, 1992). As Nohria (1992: 2) puts it, 'If the old model of organization was the large hierarchical firm, the model of organization that is considered characteristic of the New Competition is a network, of lateral and horizontal inter-linkages within and among firms.'

While conventional bureaucratic work organizations focus upon direct control or compliance via close supervision and monitoring, tight rules, prescribed procedures and centralized structures within the context of a low commitment, low trust and adversarial culture, post-bureaucratic organizations emphasize the use of indirect control methods through loose rules, flexible procedures and decentralized structures in the context of a high commitment, high trust culture of mutual interest (see Table 8.2). Similar typologies

Table 8.1 Bureaucratic and post-bureaucratic organizations

Old	New
Stability	Disorganization/chaos
Rationality	Charisma, values
Planning	Spontaneity
Control	Empowerment
Command	Participation
Centralization	Decentralization/disaggregation
Hierarchy	Network
Formal	Informal/flexible
Large	Downsized/delayered

Source: Thompson and McHugh (2002: Table 11.2)

Table 8.2 Direct and indirect approaches in the pursuit of management control in work
organizational design

Direct control approaches	Indirect control approaches
Close supervision and monitoring of activities	Empowerment and discretion applied to activities
Tight rules	Loose rules
Highly prescribed procedures	Flexible procedures
Centralized structures	Decentralized structures
Low commitment culture	High commitment culture
Low trust culture	High trust culture
Adversarial culture	Culture of mutual interest
A tightly bureaucratic structure and culture	A loosely bureaucratic structure and culture

Source: Watson (2003: Table 5.2)

and trajectories regarding work organization are proposed by many other commentators (e.g., Crook *et al.*, 1992; Heydebrand, 1989; Malone, 2004). As Malone (2004: 5), to take just one example, states, post-bureaucratic work organization is 'self-organizing, self-managed, empowered, emergent, democratic, participative, people-centred, swarming and peer-to-peer' or what he sums up as 'decentralized' meaning 'the participation of people in making decisions that matter to them'.

Table 8.3, meanwhile, highlights how these approaches differ in relation to job design. While bureaucratic organizations tend to be composed of de-skilled fragmented jobs where conception and execution are separated, repetitive tasks are undertaken and the worker has little control over his/her work, post-bureaucratic organizations are

Table 8.3 Direct and indirect job design principles

Direct control job design principles	Indirect control job design principles
Deskilled fragmented jobs	Whole, skilled, 'rich' jobs
'Doing' split from 'thinking'	'Doing and thinking' is combined in the job
Worker has a single skill	Worker has a range of skills
Worker does the same task most of the time	Worker does different tasks at different times
Worker has little choice over pace or order of task completion	Worker has choice over the pace and order of task completion
Worker is closely supervised	Workers supervise themselves
Quality of work checked by an inspector	Workers are responsible for their own quality
If there is a group dimension to the work, the supervisor allocates the roles and monitors the work groups performance	If there is a group dimension to the work, workers operate as a team with members allocating roles and monitoring team performance

Source: Watson (2003: Table 5.3)

viewed as composed of more skilled holistic jobs, where conception and execution are combined, a variety of tasks are conducted by the worker and the worker has greater autonomy over the pace and nature of the work, as well as quality control. As Clegg (1990: 181) states, 'Where the modernist organization was rigid, post-modern organization is flexible. . . . Where modernist organization and jobs were highly differentiated, demarcated and de-skilled, postmodernist organization and jobs are highly de-differentiated, de-demarcated and multi-skilled.'

Whether this trajectory in work organization is labelled a shift from bureaucratic to post-bureaucratic management, 'hard' to 'soft' human resource management (e.g., Legge, 1995), industrial relations to HRM (Kochan and Osterman, 1998), a 'low-road' to a 'high-road' strategy (Appelbaum and Batt, 1994) or 'modern' to 'post-modern' management (Clegg, 1990), the emphasis is near enough always on the transition from external to internal control (i.e., from compliance to commitment). For all such commentators, moreover, the emergence of post-bureaucracy marks the emergence of what Rose (1990) calls 'governing the soul' or Thrift (2005: 113) terms 'conviction capitalism' where organizations seek to win the 'hearts and minds' of workers (Willmott, 1993: 516).

For some, this supposed post-bureaucratic future of work organization is taken to be a positive step while for others such a transition is seen in a rather more negative manner. Each group is now considered in turn.

Positive visions of post-bureaucratic management

Latching onto the idea of seeking commitment rather than compliance from the workforce, a whole raft of prescriptive 'how to' textbooks and pop-management best-sellers that provide celebratory odes to post-bureaucracy have saturated the book market (e.g., Peters and Waterman, 1982; Semler, 2003; Simpson, 1999; Zohar and Marshall, 2001, 2005). Indeed, most change programmes that have become fashionable have quite deliberately configured themselves as an integral part of this post-bureaucracy agenda, including TQM and business process re-engineering (BPR), both of which present themselves as flattening structures and reducing hierarchy as employees take increased responsibility, conception and execution are re-integrated, and more complex jobs created.

Why, therefore, is this post-bureaucratic approach so widely advocated? For near enough all adherents, the primary rationale is straightforward. As Isles (2004: 6–7) states, '. . . engaged and motivated workforces drive up productivity and profitability'. Engendering employee commitment is thus primarily about competitiveness and making profit. It is viewed as a better way of doing productivism than bureaucracy. As Harris (1996: 18) puts it, 'without an actively engaged heart, excellence is impossible'.

Yet for many commentators there also seems to be something else underlying their desire to advocate a post-bureaucratic future of work that sometimes bubbles to the surface in their accounts. This is the idea that by pursuing such a mode of work organization, they might be able to create more humanized employment-places that improve the experience of work for those employed in them by giving them greater freedom and empowerment in defining more flexible and fulfilling career paths. As Simpson (1999) argues in her book tellingly sub-titled 'a practical guide to loving what you do for a living', developing 'heart work' is all about creating a culture shaped by 'energy, passion and fun' where each individual feels able to bring his or her heart and soul to the workplace. It is similarly the case in the New Age management literature, with its emphasis on personal growth via techniques like dancing, medicine wheels and the use of I Ching (Heelas, 1991a,b, 1992, 1996; Huczynski, 1993; Rupert, 1992) so as to develop 'soft skills' like leadership, intuition and vision. With their more holistic approach to the person, all seem to view a post-bureaucratic approach as a positive (and let us not forget, profitable) step to take.

For adherents to post-bureaucracy, therefore, and whether one is considering those seeking to nurture organizational culture, learning organizations, commitment, heart, soul or spirit, all such post-bureaucratic initiatives are ultimately seen as potentially humanizing influences on the workplace. Beneath the hard-nosed personae of many post-bureaucratic management gurus who are always sure to emphasize the benefits of post-bureaucratic programmes for competitiveness and profit, in consequence, appears to lurk an optimist who believes that by advocating such programmes, the side-effect will be a more humanized capitalism that adopts a caring, humane and responsible approach towards its workforce.

Consider one of the seminal management guru texts, namely *The Fifth Discipline* (Senge, 1999). Here, utopia is envisaged as the 'learning organization' where 'people continually expand their capacity to create the results they truly desire, where new and expansive patterns of thinking are nurtured, where collective aspirations are set free and where people are continually learning how to learn together' (Senge, 1999: 3). The emergence of the learning organization is thus seen to lead to the emergence of workplaces 'that are more consistent with man's higher aspirations' (Senge, 1999: 5).

It is similarly the case when *team-working* is advocated. Working in a team has existed for as long as people have worked together cooperatively to complete tasks and is a concept that has what Buchanen (1994) calls 'plasticity' in that, as Procter and Mueller (2000) assert, teamwork is intrinsically indefinable. Although team-working can be a bureaucratic management practice such as in Japanese 'quality circles' or 'problem-solving teams' (Buchanen, 1994; Cole, 1989; Heller *et al.*, 1998) or lean production where there is direct management control, repetitive task routines and heightened labour discipline (Danford, 1998), this is by no means always the case. Other forms of team-working that empower workers and give them freedom to act can be seen as very much embedded in post-bureaucratic thought (e.g., Drucker, 1988; Peters, 1987), such as TQM and BPR which enrich jobs and engender self-management (Buchanen, 1993; Carr, 1994; Watson, 2003). In such teams, workers can be multi-skilled, routinely rotate tasks, organize their own work and assume responsibility for both product output and quality. When implemented, inflexible, dehumanizing work methods are replaced with more humanistic methods, as in the Swedish model of autonomous work groups where employees enjoy sufficient freedom to influence matters such as goal formation, performance monitoring, production methods, labour allocations and choice of group leaders (Ramsay, 1992).

For those adopting a positive view of post-bureaucratic management, therefore, some of the popular management fads such as total quality management (see Case Study 8.1) and business process re-engineering (see Case Study 8.2) represent a significant humanizing advance on traditional bureaucratic management methods in that they empower workers and give them more freedom leading to a greater sense of fulfilment with their work.

Case Study 8.1   Total quality management

Total quality management is 'the generation of structures and a culture of quality to pervade all aspects of the organization' (Legge, 1995: 219). Customer satisfaction is the over-riding goal and employees at all levels use statistical and other techniques to monitor their work and seek continuous improvement in the processes used and the quality of what is produced (Howcroft, 1998). Within service delivery, two types of quality in terms of worker–customer interaction can be discerned: 'technical' (Groonroos, 1984, Lewis, 1988) or 'hard' (Hill, 1991) quality that covers product knowledge and knowledge of operational systems; and 'functional' or 'soft' quality that comprises staff behaviour, attitude and appearance during interaction with customers. The aim of TQM is to enhance both. On the latter, there is a difference between 'genuine' quality service (deep acting) and 'feigned' quality service (surface acting). Organizations thus seek deep acting and for this to occur, commitment is necessary.

Although TQM began by focusing on the 'hard' elements, it gradually shifted towards a 'softer' orientation to employee commitment and appropriate cultures (Wilkinson, 1992). Successful implementation of TQM is thus heavily dependent on a shift towards a 'high commitment' style of human resource strategy. TQM emphasizes the following:

1. Quality is defined as conformance to the requirement of the customer. This involves effectiveness (fitness for use) as well as efficiency (conformance to specification – the product must do what it is designed to do).
2. The concept of customer is defined broadly to include internal as well as external customers.
3. Appropriate quantitative performance measures are used routinely to assess the quality of design and conformance, and to initiate corrective action as soon as performance begins to deviate from specification.

4. TQM requires involvement of all.
5. The philosophy underpinning it is a belief in 'kaizen' or continuous improvement for the common good of internal and external customers alike.

In practice, however, it is argued that the fulfilment of espoused TQM values of autonomy, participation, responsibility and trust are precluded by being introduced within an employment context often characterized by job insecurity, hierarchical power relations, management attempts to secure control, reduce costs and enhance short-term profitability (Knights and McCabe, 1998; Wilkinson and Wilmot, 1995).

Case Study 8.2   Business process re-engineering

Business process re-engineering is the restructuring of an organization to focus on business processes rather than on business functions. Advanced management control information technologies are used together with team-working and employee empowerment. All employees are encouraged to focus upon processes such as designing, manufacturing and selling a product rather than business functions whereby, say, a design function focuses on design, a manufacturing function on production and so forth. Advanced information technologies are used to ensure a clear and integrated flow of processes, and employees are empowered and given new degrees of freedom to manage themselves in teams, because organizational members are no longer working in separate silos (Hammer and Champy, 1993; Peppard and Rowland, 1995). BPR can be seen as a post-bureaucratic management technique due to the flatter organizations, empowerment and teamwork that result. While for some, it offers a radical future of change (McCabe *et al.*, 1994); examples of effective implementation are rare (Willcocks and Grint, 1997) and the claims and promises of BPR have been challenged (e.g., Grey and Mitev, 1995; Willcocks and Grint, 1997).

This positive reading that winning the hearts and minds of workers not only facilitates competitiveness but also humanizes the employment-place and improves the experience of work for employees is found whatever post-bureaucratic change programme is considered. Take, for example, corporate culture initiatives. Although less prominent now as a management fad, not least due to the emergence of BPR, the development of 'strong' organizational cultures (e.g., Deal and Kennedy, 1982; Peters and Waterman, 1982), so as to develop a sense of belonging and common purpose within organizations

(Barnard, 1938), is viewed by optimists as an important way in which the conditions can be created to allow people's individualism to flourish by finding meaning as members of a corporate community. Besides mobilizing values, language, rituals and myths so as to unlock the commitment and enthusiasm of employees in order to ensure competitiveness and profit, adherents to post-bureaucracy also see the development of corporate culture as a means of creating a more enjoyable workplace for people employed in such organizations (Guest, 1987; Legge, 1989, 1995; Thompson and Findlay, 1999).

This is similarly the case when discussing the development of 'communities of practice' (CoP) (see Case Study 8.3). Again, the formation of such 'informal' associations so as to nurture learning organizations (Senge, 1999) is generally seen in a very positive manner by those optimistic about the advent of post-bureaucratic organizations in that CoPs are seen to facilitate a shift from technocratic and formal approaches to learning to a more informal and situated understanding of learning as a social process. In doing so, it is asserted that this empowers individuals and makes the workplace a more enjoyable and satisfying environment in which to work.

Case Study 8.3   Communities of practice

In communities of practice, members are brought together by joining in common activities and by sharing what they have learned through their mutual engagement in these activities (Lave and Wenger, 1991; Wenger 1998; Wenger *et al.*, 2002). Some CoPs have names, some do not. Some are formal, some fluid and informal. A CoP is not a community of interest or a geographical community. A CoP differs because it involves a shared practice. According to Wenger (1998), a CoP defines itself along three dimensions: what it is about (its joint enterprise is understood and continually renegotiated by its members); how it functions (mutual engagement that binds members together as a social entity), and what capability it has produced (the shared repertoires of communal resources – routines, sensibilities, artefacts, vocabulary, styles, etc., that members have developed over time). As Smith (2003: 3) puts it,

> For a community of practice to function it needs to generate and appropriate a shared repertoire of ideas, commitments and memories. It also needs to develop various resources such as tools, documents, routines, vocabulary, and symbols that in some way carry the accumulated knowledge of the community. In other words it involves practice: ways of doing and approaching things that are shared to some significant extent among members.

Here, therefore, learning is not seen purely as the acquisition of certain forms of knowledge, but instead as 'a more encompassing process of being active participants in the practices of social communities and constructing identities in relation to these communities' (Wenger, 1998: 4).

For organizational theory, CoPs provide a useful addition to the notion of informal networks or groupings that emerged with the growing interest in 'learning organizations' during the 1990s. CoPs appeared a useful way to share knowledge as well as a way of developing organizational memory (Lesser and Storck, 2001; Vann and Bowker, 2004). The outcome was a shift towards a social learning approach by ensuring that employees feel that they are members of a community (to manage their identity). CoPs have been deliberately created within organizations to encourage them to represent their interests so that performance measures can be imposed on them to measure their value.

For pessimists, this might be seen as an insidious harnessing of the notion of 'community' for value-added purposes. Indeed, emergent forms of resistance to 'community' in the employment-place can be identified. First, there is a refusal to work in ways that constitute a CoP, such as knowledge hoarding. Secondly, there is resistance by reinterpreting things as the same old hierarchy and, third, there are anti-vocational communities.

Until now, those adopting a positive view of the consequences of post-bureaucratic management have envisioned change programmes such as TQM, BPR and CoP as very much embedded in a post-bureaucratic paradigm and branded them as a radical break with the past, even revolutionary. However, it is also wholly possible to read many of these supposedly 'new' post-bureaucratic methods as displaying far greater continuity with the 'old' bureaucratic management than these commentators care to mention. Although some have viewed modern team-working innovations such as TQM and BPR in an optimistic manner pointing to how workers benefit from becoming empowered team workers with greater freedom to define more flexible and fulfilling career paths, those viewing them in a more negative light, as will be discussed below, draw attention to some of the continuities with bureaucratic management practices (e.g., Geary and Dobbins, 2001; Thackray, 1993; Thompson and McHugh, 2002; Wilkinson and Willmott, 1994). Indeed, and as Geary and Dobbins (2001) note, although optimists might believe that they lay the ground for the empowerment of workers and a more humanized workplace, the more pessimistic critical accounts point to the fact that the motive underpinning them is to intensify workers' efforts and improve competitiveness and profitability. In support of the optimists, it can be shown that even if intensification is the result, workers actually welcome the new pressures placed upon them, as shown in a study of TQM by Collinson et al. (1997) where workers appreciated the experience of working harder, given that it was occurring within a context of a welcome sense of order and direction in the workplace. Rather than view such change programmes as either work enhancing or work controlling (Babson, 1995; Waddington and Whitston, 1996), therefore, they can also optimistically be seen as a new form of employee representation (Pils and Macduffie, 1997), a novel way of organizing the production and organization process

(Mueller, 1994) and as directly constituting a new form of employee autonomy (Adler, 1997, 1998).

Yet, even if this optimistic reading of post-bureaucratic programmes exists, there remain those highlighting the worker-control aspect of such initiatives. Whether one adopts a positive approach viewing such initiatives as primarily improving the employment experience or a negative perspective viewing them as a means of controlling people in the workplace and making profit perhaps depends upon whether one views there to be an alternative to profit-seeking capitalism. Those who see no future of work other than a capitalist world predominantly seek to humanize employment through such methods. Those believing that there is an alternative to capitalism, however, highlight the negative consequences of such programmes. It is to these more negative views of post-bureaucracy that attention now turns.

Negative visions of post-bureaucratic management

Those adopting a more critical stance towards post-bureaucratic management do so for at least five principal reasons. First, such practices are seen as a cynical and sinister attempt by organizations to control workers by co-opting their hearts and minds for the purpose of profit. Secondly, it is asserted that as the employment-place becomes the site for the acquisition of meaning, fulfilment and purpose, other realms that previously provided these functions diminish in importance, reducing the scope for other futures for work and sociality. Thirdly, although managers are being asked to create such high commitment workforces, it is seen to be managers themselves to whom this high commitment strategy is directed, meaning that in enacting this discourse, managers themselves are being asked to take it on board. Fourthly, concerns are expressed about the new methods of workforce surveillance that are arising with post-bureaucratic management and, finally, there is for some a rejection of the demonizing of bureaucracy inherent in much of post-bureaucratic management literature.

The ultimate purpose of post-bureaucratic management is competitiveness and profitability

One of the principal reasons many are critical of post-bureaucratic management is that such practices are seen as a sinister attempt by organizations to control workers by co-opting their 'hearts and minds' for the purpose of profit (Boron, 2005; Gorz, 1999; Parker, 2000). Post-bureaucratic management is thus read as a bid to capture subjectivity and trap labour in totalizing institutions with new oppressive forms of regulation using instruments such as team-working, TQM and corporate culture (e.g., Casey, 1995; Delbridge et al., 1992; Gorz, 1999; Willmott, 1993). As McKinlay and Taylor (1997: 3) assert with specific reference to soft HRM practices, critics 'have inverted the euphoric rhetoric of HRM to produce gloomy analyses of emerging factory regimes in which workers lose even the awareness of their own exploitation'. In BPR, moreover, a range of Marxist, Weberian and Foucauldian commentators focus on the ideology, rationalization and self-surveillance inherent in this instrument and view it as a form of internalized coercion (Du Gay, 1991; Hancock, 1997; Kunda, 1992; Miller and Rose, 1990; Silver 1987; Thompson and Findlay, 1998; Willmott, 1993).

Unlike the champions of post-bureaucracy, viewing such instruments as producing a less hierarchical, pluralistic and potentially free society, these pessimistic commentators therefore question whether the employment-place can ever be humanized (e.g., Boron, 2005; Bunting, 2004; Parker, 2000). For Castillo (1999), the pastoral odes and serenades to work commitment of management gurus in institutions such as 'MIT Productions Inc.' play down the plurality of interests that exist in employment-places and ignore the issues of power, conflict and autonomy (see also Parker, 2000; Watson, 2003). As Boron (2005: 48–9) argues,

> If we were to accept . . . the points of view of the business school gurus – the whole debate around the despotism of capital within the corporation loses its meaning . . . the structural tyranny of capital vanishes when wage-labourers go to work not to earn a living but to entertain themselves in an agreeable climate that allows them to express their desires without restriction. This portrait hardly squares with the stories reported . . . about the extension of the work day in the global corporation, the devastating impact of labour flexibility, the degradation of work and of the workplace, the growing frequency with which people are laid off, the precariousness of employment, the trend towards an aggressive concentration of salaries within the company, not to mention the horror stories such as the exploitation of children by many global corporations.

As Wilson (1999: 2) therefore asserts,

> Workplaces are not peopled by high performing, highly committed individuals bound together in a common cause by a corporate mission enshrined within a strong organizational culture . . . Workplaces are sites of inequalities, divided by class, levels of education, race and gender. We need then a critical approach, taking a critical or radical view of contemporary behaviour in organizations, an approach which considers exploitation, repression, unfairness and asymmetrical power relations.

For many, therefore, post-bureaucracy is about one thing alone; seeking commitment to increase profit. To view such a development as a new form of humanized capitalism is a mistake. Indeed, for Gorz (1999: 7), this development of commitment is a return to 'pre-capitalist – and, indeed, almost feudal – relations of vassalage and allegiance'. In seeking to encourage workers to commit to the company, it is advocating 'the worker becoming the "proud vassal" of a company whose interests he/she is enjoined to identify totally with his/her own' (Gorz, 1999: 31).

The growing hegemony of the workplace as the source of meaning, fulfilment and purpose

It is not just that commitment is being co-opted in post-bureaucratic management for the purpose of profit. It is also the case that the employment-place might be steadily becoming the sole or principal site for the acquisition of meaning, fulfilment and purpose. As Parker (1997: 77) comments, '... it is as if we are being asked to weaken or relinquish wider (and increasingly contested) affiliations of nation, gender, occupation, ethnicity, profession, region and so on in favour of (putatively uncontested) organizational membership'. For Gorz (1999: 36) in consequence,

> In a disintegrating society, in which the quest for identity and the pursuit of social integration are continually being frustrated, the 'corporate culture' and 'corporate loyalty' inculcated by the firm offer . . . a substitute for membership of the wider society, a refuge from the sense of insecurity. The firm offers them the kind of security monastic orders, sects and work communities provide. It asks them to give up everything – to give up any other form of allegiance, their personal interests and even their personal life – in order to *give themselves*, body and soul, to the company which, in exchange, will provide them with an identity, place, a personality and a job they can be proud of.

In this view, therefore, the demise of community, political parties, faith institutions, family and so forth, and its replacement with the employment-place as the provider of social identity, status, social contact, collective effort and purpose, time structure and regular activity, is a dynamic process. Rather than the post-bureaucratic employment-place substituting for declining alternative institutions, the employment-place is itself acting as a catalyst for the demise of these other institutions which are unable to compete with its allure. The more companies take on such a role, the more other social institutions decline, closing off alternative avenues through which success, fulfilment, self-actualization and spirituality can be achieved, funnelling such desires into employment and employment alone.

As Bunting (2004: 117) thus states, 'Work is taking on the roles once played by other institutions in our lives, and the potential for abuse is clear'. Increasingly, people focus on employment to the exclusiveness of all else. The outcome is that a self-reinforcing cycle of dependency on the employment-place occurs. The end result is the commodification of human beings, the whole person, to their work organization (Perrow, 1992).

The transformative effects on managers of advocating high commitment

Although managers in post-bureaucratic organizations often view their role to be to engender the commitment of their workforce, it is perhaps managers themselves who are the target. For them, remuneration is seen to be insufficient to enhance productivity and other ways are thus sought of engendering their full engagement. By encouraging them to disseminate and espouse commitment from others, therefore, the organization is in fact enabling managers to internalize the message. Indeed, this may well be the whole point. These managers cannot be incentivized by pay but can be if they believe that they are involved in something meaningful. Bunting (2004: 159–60) explains this as follows,

> At the top you don't need more money, and education can make you less interested in consumer status symbols; so how do you ensure those employees keep working hard? In the mid seventies there were growing fears that the hedonism of consumer culture would erode the Protestant work ethic, the underpinning of capitalism. But the work ethic was reformulated . . . as the route to personal fulfilment, identity and happiness. This ensured that those least motivated by consumerism – either because of wealth or because of education – would still work just as hard, if not harder.

For critics of post-bureaucracy, in consequence, the advocacy by managers of high commitment from the workforce is a performative discourse that results in managers themselves accepting the values of the organization, and this for them is perhaps the whole point of encouraging the dissemination of the ideology of commitment. It is to reinforce in the core workforce, not the peripheries, the value of commitment so as to provide them with an incentive to enhance their performance.

Surveillance and control in post-bureaucracy

For those advocating post-bureaucratic management practices, the implementation of internal controls means that workers need no longer be subject to external surveillance in order to raise productivity and is a positive step. For critics, however, surveillance by no means disappears in high-commitment organizations. Rather, it takes on a different more sinister form.

Take, for example, teamwork. While advocates of post-bureaucracy view teamwork to be about empowering workers, devolving responsibility and reversing workplace control structures; for critics, it is much more about intensifying surveillance through intense peer pressure to conform to group norms (Barker, 1993). Indeed, the recognition of the coercive and potentially totalitarian features of 'devotional' team culture and ideology (e.g., Barley and Kunda, 1992) has resulted in a growing appreciation of its negative consequences for workers (Babson, 1995; Lewchuck and Robertson, 1996; McKinlay and Taylor, 1996; Pollert, 1996; Stephenson, 1996).

Self-discipline, similarly, is read as ultimately enhancing self-exploitation and profitability more than spirituality through false freedom (Rose, 1999). For capital to hand over the management of labour to people for whom such self-management is increasingly understood as constituting 'pleasure in work', and the development of the self, is to achieve unprecedented and sophisticated levels of regulation of labour and the labour process (Donzelot, 1991). 'As such, the practices of soft capitalism take processes of self-regulation of work to new heights, suggesting that for labour, at least, these would be better characterized as "hard" not "soft" capitalism' (Hudson 2005: 124).

Indeed, a large amount of the more negative literature on surveillance in post-bureaucracy draws upon the notion of panoptic surveillance and discipline (Foucault,

1977, 1991) discussed in Chapter 6 and views the emergence of the new forms of surveillance within post-bureaucracy in a negative light (e.g., Sewell, 1998; Steingard and Fitzgibbon, 1993; Townley, 1993, 1994). Sewell (1998) argues that the interaction of 'vertical' electronic surveillance with the 'horizontal' peer group scrutiny discussed above produces a new model of control, countering the optimistic gloss of empowerment in post-bureaucratic literatures. The implication of Sewell's argument is that such a combination solves the direct control/responsible autonomy dilemma that historically troubled generations of managers, to say nothing of management theorists.

The demonizing of bureaucracy

The final critique of the post-bureaucracy literature that leads its vision of the future of work to be cast in a negative light concerns the way in which it envisages the straw person against which it compares itself, namely bureaucracy. For adherents to post-bureaucracy, while post-bureaucracy is seen as possessing positive attributes, bureaucracy is viewed as possessing negative attributes such as inefficiency, dehumanization and ritualism (see Thompson and Alvesson, 2005), akin to a Derridean binary hierarchy discussed in Chapter 2.

In recent years, however, questions have been raised about whether this is wholly appropriate. It has been asked, for example, whether bureaucracy is always wholly a negative phenomenon or whether the more positive attributes need to be brought to the fore. Du Gay (2005), for example, argues how the fairness and justice inherent in bureaucracy is a key attribute that needs to be foregrounded. As Grey (2005) asserts, however, he is only right about the ideal-type bureaucracies. As Kanter (1977) and many other bureaucratic dysfunctionalists display, managers in bureaucracies like to appoint those who share their own background, gender and education. Indeed, the notion that there is a gap between the formal rules of a bureaucracy and what actually happens is clearly shown by Blau (1955) in his discussion of trade unions using the idea of 'working to rule' as an industrial act of disruption. The very fact that following the rules is disruptive clearly displays that there is a gap between the rules and what people actually do. There is a disjuncture between the formal and the informal organization. The formal organization of rules, procedures, what is meant to happen, is not the same as the organization itself.

Evaluating the shift from bureaucratic to post-bureaucratic management

For adherents to a post-bureaucratic vision of the future of employment, the shift from bureaucratic to post-bureaucratic management is sweeping through the business world, leaving no organization untouched by its powerful force. The future of work, therefore, will be one in which the last remnants of bureaucratic management will die out and be replaced by post-bureaucracy. This is asserted not only by those who celebrate such a shift as emancipating workers and humanizing the employment-place but also by many who decry such a future. Here, in consequence, the extent to which such a shift can be detected in the economic landscape is evaluated critically. To do this, first, the degree to which bureaucracy persists, secondly, the extent to which post-bureaucratic instruments are being used in workplaces, thirdly, the depth to which post-bureaucracy has penetrated in terms of worker commitment and, finally, whether hybrid organizational forms can be identified as emerging will be investigated.

Bureaucracy: persistent or diminishing?

Although bureaucratic and post-bureaucratic management practices co-exist in the same moment in time, this post-bureaucratic vision of the future of work places these two types into a temporal sequence where bureaucracy is the 'old' and post-bureaucracy the 'new'. The former, invested with many negative attributes as shown above, is thus seen as in demise, while the latter, invested with largely positive attributes, is connoted as in the ascendancy. The first issue that needs to be dealt with, therefore, is whether this is indeed the case.

Although many have claimed that the end of bureaucracy is just around the corner (Castells, 2000; Giddens, 1998; Heckscher and Donnellon, 1994; Leadbeater, 1999; Peters, 1987), there remain plenty of reasons to be cautious. Thompson and McHugh (2002: 40) say with regard to scientific management and bureaucratic work rules that 'There is little doubt that any burials have been premature.' As Du Gay (2005: 1) puts it, 'bureaucracy, both as an organizational ideal and as a diversely formatted organizational device, has proven remarkably resilient. Reports of its death have turned out to be somewhat premature'. Indeed, he argues that 'bureaucracy, contrary to the views of many of its detractors, is alive, well, proliferating and hybridizing, rather than simply disappearing or decaying.'(Du Gay, 2005: 3). As Thompson and McHugh (2002: 189) assert, there remains a massive gap between the rhetorical claims about the end of bureaucracy and the realities of organizational life: 'Bureaucratic forms are certainly not confined to a few residual institutional niches such as the public sector and where change has taken place it is often in the direction of more rules, hierarchy and centralization.'

Milkman (1998), for example, gathers together a variety of evidence from studies to demonstrate that most US companies remain traditionally managed, wedded to a low-trust, low-skill, authoritarian route to competitiveness, providing a robust critique of the advent of post-bureaucracy. As shown in the last chapter, moreover, a wealth of evidence exists of the bureaucratization of the service sector as exemplified by Ritzer's (1993) 'McDonaldization' thesis. For him, the fast food chain is just the tip of the iceberg and bureaucratic employment-places can be seen across a range of service industries including call centres, credit card companies and hotel chains (Poynter, 2002; Taylor and Bain, 1998). It is not just the persistence of bureaucracy, however, that signifies that the transition from bureaucracy to post-bureaucracy is not as complete as those both celebrating and decrying this transformation assume.

Slow dispersal of post-bureaucracy

There is also little evidence that post-bureaucratic practices are becoming all-pervasive. Similar to the critiques of post-Fordism, many of the criticisms directed at the post-bureaucracy thesis point to the somewhat unconvincing evidence deployed to support what is after all a thesis about empirical change (Parker, 1993; Reed, 1992; Thompson, 1993). Parker (1993: 206) is particularly unimpressed that what he considers to be little more than a 'new phrase to capture the imagination of the jaded reader appears to have little empirical foundation . . . '.

One fascinating investigation of the degree to which such post-bureaucratic organizations have penetrated the organizational landscape is offered by Steijn (2004) who reports a study of Dutch employees who were posed the same question in 2000 and 2002 regarding what decisions that they could (or could not) make on the job. Based on their responses, four production models were distinguished:

1. The 'Taylorist' production model, which is characterized by a large degree of division of labour and little autonomy for workers;
2. The 'professional' production model, which is characterized by a great deal of autonomy for workers;
3. The 'team-oriented' production model, in which employees work in teams, but the amount and scope of autonomous decisions that the team can make is relatively small (as in 'lean production' and BPR teams); and
4. A 'socio-technical' production model, which is based on all manner of working in teams, but in this case the team can make many, and far-reaching, decisions independently.

Table 8.4 presents the percentage of workers who, according to the surveys in 2000 and 2002, are engaged in each model of production. The first two columns display the portion for the population in general. Columns 3 and 4 show the proportions for only the workers who participated in the study in both years and, moreover, who indicated in 2002 that they held the same job as two years earlier. These data show that although a significant portion of employees worked in a Taylorist setting, the proportion fell quite

Table 8.4 Production models in 2000 and 2002 (% of employees)

Production model	Total		Stayed in same job and surveyed in both years	
	2000	2002	2000	2002
Taylorism	27.2	19.1	27.8	20.6
Professional	31.3	46.2	31.4	45.7
Team	28.5	25.1	30.0	23.8
Socio-technical team	13.0	9.6	10.8	9.9

Source: Steijn (2004: Table 2.1)

sharply over the two-year period. The same is true for those engaged in team work. The winner over this two-year period, rising from 31 to 46 per cent, is the professional production model, an organizational design in which workers can make a relatively large number of decisions independently regarding work processes.

These data are interesting, nevertheless, not because of the trends but because they display the shallow penetration of post-bureaucracy. Taylorism persists alongside post-bureaucratic management in the contemporary business world with some one-fifth of workers employed in such an organization setting. Breaking down the models by the type of worker, moreover, Table 8.5 displays that the Taylorist approach is near enough the dominant managerial model applied to manual workers and also to skilled and unskilled service workers and the clerical workforce. Indeed, it is only amongst the managers, professionals and semi-professionals along with sales personnel that Taylorist methods are not common. For all of the talk of the death of Taylorism, therefore, it is indeed correct that it is far too soon to write its obituary (Du Gay, 2005; Thompson and McHugh, 2002). It remains alive and well, at least in Dutch workforce.

The second section of Table 8.5 also explores the implementation of a systematic HRM policy according to these occupational groupings. A systematic personnel policy is defined here as one in which, first, performance assessment interviews are regularly held in the company in which the employee works and, secondly, the outcome of these interviews is translated into agreements related to further training or schooling for the employee. In sum, workers in higher-ranking occupations are more likely to engage in non-Taylorist working practices and to work under a personnel policy that is based on HRM principles than are workers in lower-ranking job categories.

Table 8.5 Production model and use of HRM instruments: by occupational group of worker

Occupation	Production model				Use of HRM instruments		
	Taylorism	Professional	Team	Socio-technical team	No	Limited	Yes
Managers	6	57	26	12	6	31	64
Professionals	15	45	31	9	9	37	53
Semi-professionals	16	18	48	18	15	58	27
Clerical staff	31	30	27	12	20	30	50
Sales personnel	16	40	34	10	26	34	40
Skilled service	42	16	33	9	9	60	31
Unskilled service	32	19	32	17	31	57	12
Skilled manual	37	23	29	11	33	43	24
Unskilled manual	59	18	20	4	38	36	26
Cramers V	$0.24, p < 0.01, N = 765$				$0.25, p < 0.01, N = 825$		

Source: Steijn (2004: Table 2.2)

In another study by Bacon *et al.* (1998) in a survey of 560 organizations, this time in Leicestershire in the UK, it is found that a large proportion have experimented with new approaches such as culture change, devolved management, team-working, flexibility and quality task forces. Asked about initiatives launched in the last five-year period, the results display a significant movement in managerial practices towards what some deem post-bureaucratic management methods (see Tables 8.6 and 8.7). Yet these data

Table 8.6 Implementation of new management agenda in Leicestershire organizations employing 15–24 employees

	Initiative employed (%)	Initiative sustained (%)	'Considerable contribution' to objectives (%)
A culture change programme	23.2	54.5	40.9
Devolved management	56.8	81.5	61.1
Teamworking	74.7	83.1	69.0
Performance appraisals	44.2	71.4	61.9
A mission statement	14.7	100.0	92.9
Team briefing	61.1	82.8	67.2
Quality circles	20.0	78.9	57.9
Harmonized terms and conditions	33.7	96.9	65.6
Psychometric tests	3.2	0.0	0.0
De-layering	8.4	50.0	37.5
Increased flexibility between jobs	73.7	82.9	64.3

Source: Bacon *et al.* (1998: Table 16.2)

Table 8.7 Implementation of new management agenda in Leicestershire organizations employing 25–199 employees

	Initiative employed (%)	Initiative sustained (%)	'Considerable contribution' to objectives (%)
A culture change programme	18.7	80.0	72.0
Devolved management	54.5	75.3	61.6
Teamworking	76.9	89.3	70.9
Performance appraisals	46.3	75.8	59.7
A mission statement	26.9	77.8	58.3
Team briefing	63.4	84.7	69.4
Quality circles	31.3	76.2	66.7
Harmonized terms and conditions	40.3	92.6	63.0
Psychometric tests	5.2	14.3	0.0
De-layering	14.2	68.4	68.4
Increased flexibility between jobs	74.6	89.0	79.0

Source: Bacon *et al.* (1998: Table 16.3)

also display the large number of organizations not moving in this direction across both larger and smaller organizations.

As such, one can only agree with Gordon (1996: 91) who in a US context states that

the extent of adoption of truly "high performance workplaces" is narrower and more superficial than often advertised; we have not yet witnessed a "revolution" in US labor relations. And, at the same time that some employers are abandoning the Stick strategy, at least as many, probably more, are adopting, consolidating and deepening it.

Depth of penetration of post-bureaucracy

Even when post-bureaucracy is introduced, does it manage to capture the soul of the workers, as is so commonly intimated? Although many critical of post-bureaucracy have argued that to do so is to enter deep and dangerous waters (Parker, 2000; Watson, 2001; Willmott, 1995), the evidence is patchy about whether or not post-bureaucratic organizations are successful in their attempts to engender commitment and capture the soul.

Kunda (1992) conducts an ethnographic study of an organization attempting to 'mould' its culture and its employees, exploring the processes of 'normative control' through which attempts were made to win the deep commitment of technical workers to corporate goals and values. He displays strong concern about what he reads as managerial attempts to channel people's feelings, thoughts and ways of seeing the world. Yet he shows how individuals tend to balance an absorbing of some of this with a degree of personal distancing from the corporate embrace. Casey (1995), meanwhile, studies another American company which she calls Hephaestus, one which promoted an 'official discourse' defining an 'ideal Hephaestus person' who worked with 'values of diligence, dedication, loyalty, commitment and the ability to be a good team player, to be adaptive and flexible, and to a good, somewhat conservative, citizen'. Despite limited evidence of resistance and 'defence of self' among employees, Casey notes a homogeneity of views and values and a conformity of self-presentation as the language practices and values become everyday parlance and as employees act out the desired characteristics, most come to own these practices and roles of the ideal Hephaestus employee.

The British evidence, however, suggests more scepticism about the success of commitment initiatives. Warhurst and Thompson (1998) question whether the principles of post-bureaucratic management such as HRM are as able to change employees' subjectively held values and belief systems as some proponents claim. Even where compliance occurs, the question remains of whether this is little more than either a surface act, or indeed the outcome of other more instrumentally driven motivations. Collinson et al. (1998) find that the workers in one British company taken over by an American organization dismissed the new management's corporate culture campaign as 'Yankee bullshit' and 'propaganda', whilst Watson (2001) identifies that employees of ZTC were cautious about, although not universally dismissive of, the management's 'winning culture' and displayed local forms of resistance to the perceived brain-washing associated with corporate culture programmes.

Employees, after all, are not passive objects; they possess agency. They may accept, reject, deny, react, shape, rethink, acquiesce, rebel or conform and create themselves within constraints imposed on them. As Parker (2002c: 54) puts it, 'employees are not always dupes who simply absorb and echo the charters produced by their public relations and personnel departments. If they do echo them, it is likely to be with a degree of subversive irony that almost entirely undermines their intent.'

Besides such qualitative evaluations, there are also a number of more extensive quantitative measures of whether organizations win hearts and minds. One example is the ESRC Future of Work survey that measures workers' attitudes towards their organization in the UK (see Table 8.8). This provides little evidence that workers display any widespread sense of obligation to the organizations employing them and in many respects there has been striking evidence of an actual retreat in the existence of organizational commitment among employees during the 1990s.

Therefore, there is a very real sense of little advance in organizational commitment, at least in the UK. Isles (2004) identifies the same in a separate UK study (see Table 8.9). For example, if the workplace is taking over from the home, as some critics of post-bureaucracy assert, as a source of identity, meaning and expression (e.g., Hochschild, 1998), then the respondents in this sample do not think so. Just 8.4 per cent asserted that they preferred work to home and well over two-thirds agreed that work fits in with other things. If as Hochschild (1998) for instance argues, many find in work they receive recognition for hard work and achievement, whereas at home there is a lot of work to be done, and, usually little recognition forthcoming, few seem to have fallen in love with the employment-place and prefer to be there than at home.

Table 8.8 Extent of organizational commitment

% of employees	1992		2000	
	Strongly Agree	Agree	Strongly Agree	Agree
I would work harder than I have to in order to help this organization succeed	21	60	16	59
I would take almost any job to stay with this organization	5	20	2	19
I am proud to be working for this organization	15	61	11	65
I would turn down a job with better pay to stay with this organization	6	22	4	19

Source: Taylor (2002a: Table 3)

Table 8.9 Expressions of organizational commitment

	Disagree with statement	Agree with statement	Neutral
I couldn't stay in my job if I got no satisfaction from it	22.6	53.6	23.8
My most important relationships are at work	27.9	42.2	42.9
I prefer work to home	80.9	8.4	10.7
Work is just a means to obtaining an income	36.9	38.7	24.4
My work fits in with other things	15.6	69.8	14.5

Source: Isles (2004: Table 14)

Those 8.4 per cent of 'workophiles' that do prefer work are largely in higher income brackets.

In sum, the evidence presented above means that one can only agree with sentiments of Thompson and Alvesson (2005: 103) when they assert,

> many people seem to view the widespread existence and rapid expansion of post-bureaucratic organization as a self-evident fact. But it is easy to identify a wealth of powerful counter-trends. To sum up, empirical studies of changes reveal relatively modest changes in structural terms, and where change has taken place in some spheres it is in the direction of more rules, hierarchy and centralization (Warhurst and Thompson, 1998; Hill *et al.*, 2000). Nor, contrary to some arguments . . . are bureaucratic forms confined to a few residual institutional niches such as the public sector.

Towards hybrid organizational forms?

For some, however, the above evidence might not so much suggest a shallow penetration of post-bureaucracy as the emergence of hybrid organizational forms (e.g., Thompson and Alvesson, 2005). If this is correct, then it suggests a need to transcend the linear story of the evolution of management practices that treats bureaucracy and post-bureaucracy as discrete and separate organizational forms and to recognize how these different organizational forms are interpenetrating each other and resulting in hybrids. Indeed, these 'hybrid' organizations are captured in the emergence of contemporary vocabularies such as 'customer-oriented bureaucracies' (Frenkel *et al.*, 1995), 'social Taylorism' (Webster and Robbins, 1993) and 'soft bureaucracy' in which decentralized responsibilities are combined with centralized decision-making (Courpasson, 2000). For such commentators (e.g., Hudson, 2005; Thompson and Alvasson, 2005), therefore, contemporary organizational changes are not in the main 'post-bureaucratic', but rather tend towards a re-configuration or 'hybridization' of bureaucratic forms.

Indeed, there is a growing rejection of the bureaucracy/post-bureaucracy dichotomy as it becomes more widely argued that contemporary organizational forms are hybrids that combine elements of both. This is seen as a new emerging organizational form (Reed, 2005) which combines elements of markets, hierarchies, networks and communities. In this view, the conventional ideal types of bureaucracy and post-bureaucracy are breaking down and new hybrids are emerging.

Conclusions

In sum, this chapter has evaluated critically the vision of the future of work that depicts a shift from bureaucracy to post-bureaucracy. Although the conventional story is that there has been a linear shift from bureaucracies operated without hatred or passion, according to a legislative rulebook, through human relations to a new kind of post-modern, post-bureaucratic, commitment-based organization, it is now increasingly accepted that in lived practice each organizational form is not discrete and the trajectory fuzzier and less linear than previously suggested (e.g., Grey, 2005; Littler, 1982; Parker, 2002a,b).

In recent years, in consequence, there has emerged an argument that the shift from bureaucratic to post-bureaucratic management does not capture the complexity of the changes taking place in the employment-place. The simple linear trajectory of work organizations from some previous historical era when organizations were supposedly bureaucratic to a contemporary and future era when they are, or are becoming, post-bureaucratic fails to capture the complex, often contradictory, trends taking place in the contemporary workplace. Not only is it sometimes asserted that this is over-simplified as a description of the direction of change but also that as a prescription it is found wanting in many respects. Indeed, it has recently become much more popular to discuss the emergence of hybrid organizational forms. Whether it is indeed the case that new hybrids are emerging or whether it is more the case that the ideal-types of bureaucracy and post-bureaucracy created by management academics and gurus were ever descriptive of organizations in lived practice needs to be questioned. What is now being identified as 'hybrids' of bureaucracy and post-bureaucracy may well have always existed but not been captured by this over-simplistic dichotomy. This, however, is not an argument that there is far greater continuity than so far supposed by the post-bureaucratic literature. Rather, it is an argument that this linear vision of the trajectory of work from bureaucratic to post-bureaucratic work organization is again too simple to capture the multiple and divergent trajectories that are taking place in the world of work, and that the future is therefore far more open than projected by those depicting the advent of a post-bureaucratic future of work.

Indeed, in the following chapters, some of the cosy assumptions shared by many involved in these post-bureaucratic debates will start to be unpacked. Whether bureaucratic or post-bureaucratic forms of work organization are coming to the fore is, for others. A difference that makes no difference. Both forms of organizational culture are ultimately different ways of pursuing greater productivity and profit and there is a need to consider visions of the future which consider forms of employment that do not pursue such ends. Furthermore, and as will be revealed in Part III, these debates over bureaucracy versus post-bureaucracy fail to escape the core assumptions of work-based society, namely that employment is the sole source of work, that employment should remain seen as the dominant form of work and that there is no need to challenge the employment-centred view of work and the obfuscation of other forms of economic endeavour.

Further reading

Bunting, M. (2004) *Willing Slaves: How the Overwork Culture is Ruling Our Lives*, London: Harper Collins.

This is a populist account of the attempts by organizations to capture the souls of workers by turning them into 'willing slaves' and displays the negative features of post-bureaucratic management.

Du Gay, P. (2005) (ed.) *The Values of Bureaucracy*, Oxford: Oxford University Press.

This edited book counters the advocacy of post-bureaucratic work organization with a more celebratory vision of bureaucracy than is often encountered in contemporary management literature. It provides a welcome antidote to the dominant celebratory odes to post-bureaucracy.

Grey, C. (2005) *A Very Short, Fairly Interesting and Reasonably Cheap Book About Studying Organizations*, London: Sage.

As the title suggests, this book provides a light-hearted but comprehensive and concise critical overview of the purported transition from bureaucracy to post-bureaucracy.

Parker, M. (2002c) *Against Management*, Cambridge: Polity.

A critical overview of the advent of post-bureaucracy that asks searching questions about this vision of the future of work.

9

Non-capitalist visions of employment

Introduction

In this chapter, commentators who have sought to expound non-capitalist futures for employment are explored. This vision of the future of work often receives little attention in the mainstream business and management studies literature. At best, non-capitalist employment practices are usually viewed as a relatively superfluous and minor tributary of work organization that has little chance of moving centre-stage in an increasingly commodified world and, at worst, a type of pre-capitalist work that is slowly and surely being subsumed by capitalism. For various scholars, however, these non-capitalist practices have taken on some importance in recent years as beacons of hope. As Fournier (2005: 203–4) comments in this regard,

> Much economic and management knowledge is based on the image of homo economicus: people competing for scarce resources to maximize their self-interests, and mainly their economic gains. Of course, the idea of co-operation has surfaced under various guises (e.g., as teamwork, commitment, partnership . . .) but only to be subsumed to the ineluctable rule of competition; cooperation is reduced to a competitive strategy. But what if (some of our) economic activities and relations were driven by mutual aid, solidarity, cooperation, as indeed has been the case in the cooperative movement? What if decisions about production, work remuneration, were not driven by the need to compete on global markets, but by the desire to support the local economy, as has been the case in the Mondragon cooperative? What if the distribution of surplus was not driven by 'shareholder value' but solidarity to those in need? . . . Yet so far these questions have been remarkably absent from Business Schools who have been more concerned to legitimize neo-liberal policies than to engage in debates about possible alternatives.

To analyse such a vision of the future of work, this chapter will employ the same structure as previous ones. First, it introduces those visions that depict a shift from capitalist to non-capitalist employment, secondly, discusses those who envisage this future of work in a positive light, thirdly, those who view it in a more negative light and, finally, evaluates the extent to which employment practices appear to be moving in this direction.

From capitalist to non-capitalist futures for employment

As stated in Chapter 2, three modes of delivering goods and services are often differentiated in order to highlight the configuration of economies. These are the 'market' (private sector), the 'state' (public sector) and the 'informal or community' sector (Boswell, 1990; Giddens, 1998; Gough, 2000; Polanyi, 1944; Powell, 1990; Putterman 1990; Thompson *et al.*, 1991). In Part 1 of this book, it has been already highlighted that the commodification thesis, which asserts that goods and services are increasingly occurring through the market sector (rather than by the state or civil society), is far from a universal process. In this chapter, therefore, some of the alternative theses that have been put forward as both descriptions and prescriptions regarding the future of work are considered. These are, first, the idea that the public sector is/should be a more prominent vehicle through which goods and services are delivered (the public sector led thesis or what might be called the nationalization thesis) and, secondly, the notion that civil society is/should be a more prominent vehicle through which goods and services are delivered.

In the contemporary period, very few visions of the future of employment advocate that the public sector is or should be a more important vehicle for the delivery of goods and services. In major part, this can be seen as a temporary phenomenon resulting from the recent (in historical terms) collapse of the 'socialist bloc'. Whether correct or not, there is a dominant perception that whilst the West pursued productivism primarily through the private sector, the competing socialist bloc attempted to pursue productivism through the state sector and this was found wanting. Today, so the story goes, the West has won this ideological private versus public sector battle concerning the best way of achieving productivity gains and it is thus no longer relevant to consider a future of employment where the means of production are owned and controlled by the state. Whether this will remain the case in the future, of course, remains to be seen. At present, however, little, if any, attention is given to futures for employment where the state takes responsibility for directly producing and delivering goods and services and few today deem it even worthy of discussion. Although this in itself is not a reason to reject further discussion of such a vision, it is more the fact that few, if any, commentators currently engage with such a vision that it is not considered here in any more depth.

Instead, attention in this chapter focuses on the idea that civil society is/should be a more prominent vehicle through which goods and services are delivered. At first glance, it might not appear that many perspectives towards the future of employment advocate such an approach. However, this is far from the case. If one considers how many visions of the future of employment are embedded in what is variously termed a 'civil society', 'third sector', 'social economy', 'not-for-profit employment', 'mutualism' or 'cooperative' perspective, then it starts to become apparent that the vision of a future of employment that is non-capitalist is far from being some minor strand in thought on the future of work.

Two starkly contrasting views exist, however, regarding a future of work based on such non-capitalist employment practices. On the one hand, there are those who depict such a future of work in a positive light and, on the other hand, those interpreting it as a negative phenomenon. As will become apparent, the vast majority of literature written on non-capitalist futures for employment view it in the former manner, perhaps because the majority of those opposed to such a possibility view it as so unlikely to happen that they seldom deem it worthy of discussion or attention.

Positive visions of non-capitalist employment

For those who imagine that a non-capitalist future for employment is a possibility and view it as a positive move, this future is sometimes explained as a growing inevitability, akin to many of the perspectives towards the future of work already discussed. The reasons why it is seen as inevitable lie in their vision of the contemporary business environment (see, for example, Birchall, 2001a). As post-bureaucratic management takes hold, expectations of employees in general and managers in particular are rising with regard to what they seek from the employment-place. Not least, they are seeking identity, meaning and enjoyment from their formal employment. Business Schools, moreover, are raising expectations amongst their students about what can be expected from the employment-place. Many workers on entering employment, however, are now finding that the reality of the work organization as it is presently constituted does not live up to their expectations. Such workers soon realize that the reason that greater portions of their personality, emotions and identity are being implicated in production is for the sake of profit. With the resultant disgruntlement, these commentators are now seeing an opportunity as arising. These workers have had their expectations raised of what the employment-place should be delivering and find that profit-making organizations are not delivering what is expected of them. With this widespread disgruntlement, there is seen to be a growing demand from these employees for alternative forms of work organization to which they can turn to receive the identity, self-esteem and rewards that they find missing in what might be called the 'soft-centred for-profit zone' of post-bureaucratic organizations. The outcome, they believe, may well be a growing clamour for non-capitalist employment, where the worker can find identity, meaning and emotions in the workplace for purposes other than profit.

For these commentators, therefore, post-bureaucratic management approaches have until now been implemented with an instrumental logic that puts profit first but does so in apparently people-friendly ways because if it is more profitable to be more sociable then being sociable is a good thing. This differs from genuine attempts to put people first. There is thus a major difference between the customer or employee loyalty of high-commitment workplaces that are now considered central to the efficient functioning of profit-making organizations and the more 'human' foundations of 'alternative' economic systems. As long as profit is the goal of economic action, the talk of putting people back at the centre is mere rhetoric. As workers recognize this, and their expectations rise, it is asserted to be inevitable that they will seek out forms of non-capitalist employment in order to satisfy their emotional and identity needs. As Thrift (2005: 49) puts it,

> Managers who are taught to be reflexive about themselves, who are increasingly schooled in the ethics of corporate responsibility, and who are expected to work extraordinarily long hours in order to maintain an organization's culture . . . , can and do become reluctant, sceptical and even disillusioned. . . . Thus, amongst such managers, there is an increasing move to values 'involving empathy, connectedness, emotion, ease and green concerns' (Pahl, 1995: 180) which in turn, are helping to provide new models of economic practice.

As Thrift (2005: 50) continues, 'they are about bringing soft capitalism back on itself by using its procedures and vocabulary, but to different ends'. The reason for their rise is because those who were taught the vocabulary of soft capitalism are finding that they lack fulfilment in their organizational lives due to the structure of the organization for which they work, so they are increasingly turning to other forms of organizational structure in which they can live out what they have received from soft capitalism.

In the past, therefore, many discussions of alternatives to capitalism were based on seeking out alternative meta-theories or ideologies such as socialism or communism. Today, alternatives are being sought in a 'bottom–up' manner through specific initiatives to produce new forms of economic institution that are both immediately feasible and radically democratic. As Thrift (2005: 49) again tellingly reveals, 'Significantly, these institutions have often included quite substantial inputs from business managers looking for new values, and they also often utilize the vocabulary of the new managerial discourses.' The future of the employment-place in this non-capitalist vision, therefore, no longer lies in identifying some new ideology that will replace capitalism but in a multiplicity of often local-level economic experiments with non-capitalist employment practices that seek to enact non-capitalism. For most adherents to this perspective towards the future of work, therefore, the way in which this vision of the future is discussed is by charting the advent of a whole host of alternative economic institutions that open up the possibility of different futures and allow one to re-imagine the future of work as something other than a capitalist world.

Here, therefore, just a few of the non-capitalist employment initiatives and experiments currently in operation are reviewed. To do this, a spectrum of such practices is here envisaged starting from individual-level initiatives, moving through practising non-capitalism at the organizational level (worker and community cooperatives, and alternative financial initiatives) and at the community-level (e.g., intentional communities) to global-level non-capitalist initiatives (e.g., the Focolare movement).

Social entrepreneurship

Commencing at the individual-level, many disgruntled with employment in the private sector might decide to start up not-for-profit businesses. For some, this might be a way of 'downshifting' where they are 'lifestyle' businesses (Leadbeater, 1997). For others, the intention might be to seek out the humanized workplace that they did not find in their former jobs. Analysing the evidence, this seems to be a fairly significant trend in the contemporary business environment. In the UK, the Global Entrepreneurship Monitor (Harding and Cowell, 2004) indicates that almost 7 per cent of the population are engaged in owning, running or managing a social enterprise. A further UK survey of social enterprises, moreover, identifies around 15,000 social enterprises with a turnover of £18 billion and employing around 800,000 staff (Small Business Service, 2005). Similar trends seem to be occurring in many other nations. One recent qualitative study by Johanisova (2005) examining social entrepreneurs in the UK and Czech Republic finds that the interviewees demonstrated an enthusiasm for their work that was in stark contrast to those alienated in the profit zone.

Until now, however, the evidence gathered is rather thin on the ground about the extent to which social enterprises are the product of individuals disgruntled with mainstream private sector employment and seeking the meaning, identity and satisfaction from their employment offered by post-bureaucracy but not fulfilled by it in practice. If future research displayed this was indeed the case, then the above intimation that non-capitalist employment practices are emerging due to the expectations raised by post-bureaucratic management practices could start to be answered more fully than has been the case until now.

Cooperative organizations

Besides the individual-level pursuit of non-capitalist employment, there is a long-standing quest for non-capitalist employment at the collective organizational level in the form of cooperatives. These are associations or groups of associations where ownership and control rests with its members rather than outside owners. According to the International Cooperative Alliance (ICA), a cooperative is an autonomous association of persons united voluntarily to meet their common economic, social and cultural needs and aspirations through a jointly owned and democratically controlled enterprise (www.ica.co-op/ica/ica/index.html). Three types of cooperatives can be distinguished, namely consumer, worker and financial cooperatives. Each is here considered in turn.

Consumer cooperatives

Birchall (2001b) defines a 'mutual' or consumer cooperative as a type of business that is owned and controlled by its customer members rather than by investors. Instead of reading such institutions as a remnant that has outlived its usefulness, as is the case in the commodification thesis that assumes the growing hegemony of capitalism, he argues that such cooperatives should be viewed as an alternative to global capitalism. In other words, he transcends the temporal sequencing of such institutions as 'backward' and instead views them as one of a variety of organizational forms existing in the present. Such mutuals include building societies (Drake and Llewellyn, 2001), credit unions (McCarthy *et al.*, 2001), housing co-ops (Rodgers, 2001), consumer co-ops (Birchall, 2001b), mutual insurance (Mabbett, 2001) and farmer co-ops (Nilsson, 2001). All, moreover, attempt to re-build local economies that counteract the drift towards globalization.

As intimated above, for some analysts, the current post-bureaucratic tendencies in investor-owned businesses to gain an emotional attachment from their customers displays that such companies are attempting to replicate the mutuals. As Birchall (2001a: 3) puts it,

> Investor-owned businesses, openly envious of the advantages that having a membership base might bring, have been trying to capture these advantages by inviting their customers to join a club. Airlines and retail chains in particular have been developing memberships that reinforce brand identities, reward customers' repeat business with discounts and special services, and attempt to engender a feeling of loyalty; all without giving away any ownership or control rights.

Despite this, however, when consumer cooperatives have been evaluated against their commercial counterparts, it has often been the case that they are found wanting, identified as less productive, efficient, profitable and so forth. For Birchall (2001a), this is because evaluations typically use inappropriate (or what is better termed 'market-centred') criteria biased towards market-orientated firms (e.g., levels of profitability). Boxall and Gallagher (1997: 2), for example, analyse mutuality by electing to use the model of the profit-maximizing firm as the 'obvious standard of comparison for an economist'. Comparing them against profit-making organizations using their criteria of success (rather than the objectives of cooperatives) obviously results in consumer cooperatives being marked out as poor performers and lesser organizations. If different criteria such as their social contribution were used, then very different outcomes would result with for-profit enterprises shown to be lesser mortals than their social enterprise counterparts. Yet this is seldom done. At present, therefore, consumer cooperatives are rarely deemed to be viable alternatives to capitalist organizations.

Worker cooperatives

A worker cooperative is a business that is wholly or substantially owned and controlled by those who work in it; it is run for their mutual benefit. Control is exercised on the basis of one person, one vote; membership is open as far as possible to all workers.

Throughout history, the size of the worker cooperative sector has tended to fluctuate quite markedly (Cornforth *et al.*, 1988; Davis, 2004; Earle, 1986; Ehrenreich and Edelstein, 1983; Lichtenstein, 1986; Mellor *et al.*, 1988). One estimate is that some 500,000 people are employed by producer cooperatives in Western Europe (Heller *et al.*, 1998). In a qualitative study of 16 British cooperatives, Cornforth *et al.* (1988) finds that cooperative working is intense and involving, with workers feeling a heightened emotional involvement with their work, just as post-bureaucratic management is seeking to achieve in the private sector today (see Davis, 2004). While instrumental benefits like job security were important, it was also felt to be a welcome luxury to work with people who were congenial, both politically and personally. Working in a cooperative manner was seen as a way in which self-esteem and self-identity needs can be met within a work environment. Many joined because they felt attracted to the radical products or services and egalitarian work practices. Workers were also more able to achieve control over the organization and management of work on the shop floor than is usual. The cooperatives achievements included less supervision, more flexible working arrangements, greater variety of work, lower wage differentials and less direct control over how workers carry out their tasks.

Whenever worker cooperatives are discussed as an alternative future of work, there is always one cooperative in particular that is brought to attention to signify that not all worker co-ops are necessarily small-scale bootstrap enterprises. This is the Mondragon Cooperative Corporation (MCC) on which a great deal has been written (e.g., Azurmendi, 1991; Castree *et al.*, 2004; MacLeod, 1997; Malone, 2004; Mathews, 1999, 2001; Parry, 1994; Shuman, 1998) and is discussed in Case Study 9.1.

Case Study 9.1   The Mondragon Cooperative Corporation

In 1956, a committed social Catholic, the priest Don Jose Maria Arizmendiarrieta, encouraged workers in the Basque region of Spain to take over a redundant factory in order to 'provide Basque workers with good stable employment and to contribute to the growth of the Basque economy' (Clamp, 2000: 559). In Jose Maria's own words, 'We [the Basques] lost the Civil War, and became an occupied region' (cited in Whyte and Whyte, 1991: 242). Unhappy with the close relations between large corporations and the then Spanish government, he set up the Mondragon cooperative to establish a degree of economic and political independence for the region.

The MCC's founding principles were worker sovereignty; worker participation in the management of the cooperatives; and cooperation between cooperatives. Work was to be organized along the following non-capitalist lines: profits were pooled between the different cooperatives; surplus workers were offered employment at other cooperatives; flexible calendars were introduced to accommodate flexible workloads; and loans were given to individuals and cooperatives at discounted rates. This then spawned other worker cooperatives, a bank and a number of educational institutions.

Today, the MCC is a major conglomerate with the number of employees rising from 17,022 in 1978 through 42,129 in 1998 to 68,260 in 2003 with total assets of €16.3 billion (see Table 9.1). Indeed, the MCC is now the largest business group in the Basque region, the seventh largest business group in Spain and a major player in European and global markets. What began as a handful of workers in a disused factory using hand tools to make oil-fired heaters and cookers has become a large conglomerate of some 160 manufacturing, retail, financial, service and support cooperatives.

Table 9.1 The size and growth of Mondragon Cooperative Corporation, 2001–03
(in € million)

	2001	2002	2003
Total sales	8106	9232	9655
International sales	2165	2455	2551
Resources under administration	7891	8474	9247
Equity	2688	3102	3281
Investment	872	683	847
Results	335	370	410
Personnel	60,200	66,558	68,260

Source: MCC 2003, Annual Report: p. 5

The MCC now employs about 3 per cent of the Basque region's one million workers. It is also now Spain's largest exporter of machine tools and largest manufacturer of white goods such as refrigerators, cookers, washing machines and dishwashers, as well as the third largest supplier of automotive components in Europe, and was designated by General Motors in 1992 as 'European Component Supplier of the Year' (Mathews, 2001).

The 'primary' cooperatives are linked through groups. Originally these groups had a geographical basis. However, in 1991, they were reconstituted along functional lines. There is an Industrial Group (employing 48 per cent of the workforce in 2003), the Distribution Group (employing 47 per cent), the Financial Group (4 per cent) and Corporate activities (1 per cent of total employment), with further sub-groups within some of these Groups. The objective is for the cooperatives within each group to engage in continuous and strategic planning to identify and exploit economies of scale and business synergies, and to operate within an agreed overall strategy.

Cooperatives include not only companies operating in various manufacturing industries – automobile parts, household goods, industrial equipment and machine tools – but also a bank, supermarket chain and a management consultancy firm (see www.mondragon.mcc.es). Indeed, whole factories are designed and fabricated to order in Mondragon for buyers overseas. Subsidiaries, moreover, are operated by the MCC in conjunction with overseas partners that manufacture, for instance, semi-conductors in Thailand, white good components in Mexico, refrigerators in Morocco and luxury motor coach bodies in China. MCC construction cooperatives have carried out major civil engineering and building projects at home and abroad, including the building of key facilities for events such as the Barcelona Olympic games, and the steel structure for the Guggenheim Museum in Bilbao was fabricated by a Mondragon cooperative. The MCC also includes Spain's fastest growing retail chain – Eroski – which in 1998 operated 37 Eroski and maxi hypermarkets,

211 Consum supermarkets, 419 self-service and franchise stores, and 333 travel agency branches. The MCC financial cooperatives – the Caja Laboral Popular (CLP) credit union and the Lagun-Aro social insurance cooperative – are among Spain's larger financial intermediaries. The basic building blocks of the MCC are its manufacturing, retail, financial and service cooperatives, otherwise known as its primary cooperatives. The primary cooperatives embody and exemplify its values and principles. Many of the cooperatives employ non-members and by their own constitution and by-laws, no cooperative may employ more than 10 per cent of non-members.

A further level of linkage is afforded by the MCC Congress, the General Council and Standing Committee. The key role of Congress is to set the overall policy and direction of the cooperatives, the General Council is responsible for drawing up and applying overall corporate strategies and coordinating the activities of the cooperatives and cooperative groups. The Standing Committee monitors the performance of the committee and the groups, and sees that the decisions of congress are implemented. Independent of the Assembly and its offshoots, workplace groups within the cooperative elect a Social Council, which has a quasi trade union function, with responsibility for areas such as job evaluation and industrial health and safety. Recent years have seen an increasing emphasis on industrial democracy – on participation and consultation at the shop floor level within many of the cooperatives.

In this bottom–up structure, the overall corporation does not own its 'subsidiary' companies. The opposite is the case. The individual cooperatives own the corporation. The job of the centre is to provide services to the individual cooperatives. The member companies are in effect its customers. Any cooperative can leave the MCC if it decides that it is not receiving adequate value from the corporate managers.

The difficulty of obtaining funding and the need to provide social and welfare services led to the establishment of 'secondary cooperatives' of which the most important is the Caja Laboral Popular, a savings bank. The Caja lays down a democratic governing structure and a code of practice for each cooperative (Mellor et al., 1988) and provides about 60 per cent of the funding for new cooperatives. Workers though must make an investment; this provides an incentive for the workers to seek the success of the cooperative. The primary cooperatives are thus serviced on a mutual basis by a unique system of secondary support cooperatives. Arizmendiarrieta was aware at an early stage of the cooperatives development that they needed to be self-sufficient, so the support cooperatives were his answer. Other secondary cooperatives include the Lagun-Aro social insurance cooperative, R&D services from the Ikelran and Ideko R&D cooperatives, and technical skilling from the University of Technology cooperative. The structure of the support cooperatives differs from that of the primary cooperatives in that they are owned and governed jointly by their workers, together with their primary cooperative clients. Profits distributed to workers in the secondary support cooperatives are linked to those of the primary cooperatives.

The CLP credit union has been more than simply a source of capital for expanding existing cooperatives and creating new ones. What was the Entrepreneurship Division of the CLP offered a comprehensive service for incubating cooperatives. Groups seeking to establish cooperatives were initially assigned a mentor to work with them in the preparation of their application for a loan. Once the loans were secured, the mentors remained with the fledgling cooperatives in order to assist them in the setting up of their business and enabling them to operate profitably. As a condition of their loan, a new business entered into a Contract of Association with the CLP that specified, among other things, the mutual structure and processes it should adopt. Regular and comprehensive reporting of financial data to the CLP means that an early warning is received where cooperatives experience difficulties, and specialist support is provided through an Intervention Group within its Entrepreneurship Division.

Today, however, Mondragon's ongoing expansion is now much less through establishing new cooperatives and more through strategic acquisition and alliances. Analysing the geographical distribution of employment in the MCC, some 49 per cent of employees in 2003 were based in the Basque region, with a further 39 per cent in the rest of Spain and 12 per cent abroad. By 2003, just over half of the current staff was a cooperative member. Non-members are mainly concentrated in the distribution sector outside the Basque country and in industrial plants both outside the Basque country and abroad. In the Basque region, meanwhile, the number of new jobs has risen sharply so that in 2003, 80 per cent of the workforce in this region was a cooperative member. However, many non-members are only temporary non-members since the majority become members within a period of 2–3 years. Within the Basque region itself, therefore, much of the non-membership of the cooperative amongst the workforce was due to the rapid growth in employment.

However, outside the Basque country, jobs have been created in accordance with the non-cooperative system. This is due to the lack of adequate cooperative laws in the areas into which they have expanded; the fact that many new companies have been established as part of a joint venture with other partners; and mostly because the creation of cooperatives requires the existence of cooperative members who understand and are committed to the cooperative culture, something which is impossible to obtain over a short time period and in such a wide variety of locations.

Indeed, this has been recognized as a problem that needs to be at least partially resolved. At the May 2003 Cooperative Congress (General Assembly of all MCC cooperatives), a resolution was approved regarding membership expansion which urged the organizations responsible for this area to study and develop formulas which would enable non-member employees to participate in the ownership and management of their companies, similar to that which occurs in cooperatives. One precedent is the project commencing in 1998 in the Eroski distribution group which, through the company Gespa, offered non-member employees the opportunity of participation in the management of the workplace.

Why, therefore, has the MCC been so successful? Each permanent worker is an equal co-owner of the cooperative in which he/she is employed, with an equal say (one vote, one member) in its governance and an equal proportionate share in its profits (or losses). Each worker has an individual capital account that is credited annually with his/her share of the cooperative's profits and enables him/her to maintain an ongoing appraisal of the performance of the cooperative and its management and his/her fellow workers. Each of the companies in the Mondragon group is itself a worker-owned cooperative. Almost all employees who have been with one of these cooperatives for more than a few years are 'members' of the cooperative. As part owners, the employees of each company are the ultimate decision-makers. It is thus bottom–up. As in most democratic government, however, the members usually exercise their authority through elected representatives.

To become a member of a cooperative, an employee must make an initial capital contribution, equal to about half an average annual salary. Typically, a cooperative loans an employee some or all of this amount. The employee capital account grows over time in two ways. First, interest accrues on the capital contribution. Secondly, the employee gets a share (proportional to his or her salary) of the company's profits each year. The money in a capital account cannot actually be used, however, until the employee retires or quits. Instead, it is used as a reserve fund and a source of investment capital by the company. In years when the cooperative makes a loss, the capital accounts decrease. The cooperatives additionally have rules requiring them to allocate certain proportions of their profits before any distribution to employees. These funds are allocated to build up their own reserve funds, to share with other cooperatives and the overall corporation, and to support social and educational activities.

The most important of these representatives are the members of the governing councils of the different cooperatives. The councils, which are typically made up of seven to ten employees elected for rotating four-year terms, act as a kind of board of directors for each cooperative. The council hires and fires the cooperative's managing director (equivalent to the Chief Executive Officer), approves the distribution of profits and votes on other major policy decisions. In addition to electing representatives to the governing council, employees are also entitled to attend twice-yearly general assemblies in which major issues facing the company are discussed and sometimes voted on.

Another goal is to promote the creation of an egalitarian cooperative community. Unlike many large companies, which pay their CEOs as much as 500 times more than their lowest-paid worker, MCC limits the ratio of salary of the highest to the lowest-paid to no more than six. In general, this means that lower-level workers are paid more than what they would receive in comparable jobs in other companies, while senior managers receive somewhat less. 'When profit-sharing contributions are taken into account, the shortfalls for senior managers are usually not very large. Furthermore, management jobs at MCC appear to be regarded as high-status positions in the Basque community (Malone, 2004).

What, therefore, are the lessons of the Mondragon cooperative? For adherents to a non-capitalist vision of the future of employment, the MCC is similar to other employee-owned companies such as United Airlines, United Parcel Services (UPS) and Publix Supermarkets all of whom have the majority of their stock in the hand of rank and file. But MCC goes further. First, about 80 per cent of the workers in most Mondragon companies are members and thus owners of the cooperative – a far higher percentage than in most professional service partnerships. Second, each member of a Mondragon cooperative has only one vote in company decisions; votes are not proportional to the number of shares a person owns or the size of his or her capital account. Most importantly, MCC has developed a complex hierarchical structure for organizing a large number of people and resources, with separate but interlinked representative democracies operating at many levels. When there is just one level of representative democracy (e.g., when employees collectively elect the board of directors for a whole corporation) the decision-making power of individual employees is diluted and may have little motivational effect. But when people actively participate as decision-makers in groups small enough to matter to them (most Mondragon cooperatives have fewer than 1500–2000 members), the benefits of democratic decision-making are greatly amplified.

The MCC shows that a large industrial company can be organized not primarily to maximize financial returns for its investors, but to achieve a range of financial and non-financial goals that are important to its members. For MCC, the goals include employment stability, regional economic development and social responsibility. Would such a structure work in other companies? Certainly, the Basques' distinctive history and social and cultural environment contribute to the success of the MCC. But this example does reveal that worker-owned companies can be taken to a new level of complexity with representative democracies at many different hierarchical levels.

On its website (www.mcc.es), one of the FAQs is 'Do you consider cooperatives to be an alternative to the capitalist production system?' The MCC response is 'We simply believe that we have developed a way of making companies more human and participatory. It is an approach that . . . fits in well with the latest and most advanced management models, which tend to place more value on workers themselves as the principal asset and source of competitive advantage of modern companies.' Indeed, this is perhaps the principal lesson of this example. It displays, as discussed above, that one of the so far unconsidered outcomes of the transition to post-bureaucracy is that this encourages more attention to be paid to cooperative forms of work organization. Indeed, unless this is done, then as stated earlier, it might well be the case that workers in general, and managers more particularly, might seek out these alternative forms of work organization in order to find the meaning, identity and emotional resonance with their employment that is so far proving lacking in for-profit corporations.

Financial cooperatives

Financial cooperatives include building societies (Drake and Llewellyn, 2001), credit unions (McCarthy *et al.*, 2001) and mutual insurance (Mabbett, 2001). What is so interesting about many of these financial cooperatives and other forms of financial initiative (e.g., ethical investment funds, community development finance initiatives) is that in the contemporary period their workforces are heavily populated by those who have moved out of the for-profit sector in search of greater meaning and identity in their work (see Buttle, 2005). For these workers, financial cooperatives represent a means by which they can engage in socially useful work and in a manner that provides them with meaning that was lacking in their previous careers in the private sector. One particularly prominent form of financial cooperative that has come to the fore in recent years is the credit union (see Case Study 9.2).

Case Study 9.2   Credit unions

Credit unions are cooperative financial institutions owned and controlled by their members. Their aim is to provide access to saving and affordable loans to disadvantaged communities and individuals often excluded from the conventional financial system or charged exorbitant rates for borrowing. To counter this financial exclusion and predatory lending, credit unions encourage savings among low-income households and use the income to provide affordable loans. The income generated by the interest paid is used to pay dividends to savers, and any remaining profit is shared among the members. Each credit union has a 'common bond' that determines who can join. The common bond may be based on a neighbourhood, a workplace or an association (e.g., trade union or church-based group).

The idea of credit unions emerged out of the cooperative movement in the nineteenth-century: the first credit union opened in Germany in the mid-nineteenth century and was quickly followed by similar experiments in Canada and in the US, where it became popular particularly during the Great Depression. In the UK, the first Credit Union was set up in 1964 by members of the West Indian community in Wimbledon and grew out of informal relationships between extended family groups clubbing together to save and give each other loans. Since then, credit unions have enjoyed a steady growth as a way of helping people escape poverty and improve their lives. The World Council of Credit Unions estimated that there were 123 million credit union members worldwide in 2004 and that they were growing fast in Eastern Europe, South America, Africa and the Far East (www.woccu.org).

Cooperatives, however, may catch the attention of those not only touched by post-bureaucratic work organization but disaffected and disenchanted by how this is pursued purely so as to increase profitability and competitiveness in the private sector. These disaffected workers may also turn to other non-capitalist modes of work organization at the level of communities rather than organizations.

Cooperative communities

While the cooperatives discussed above refer to individual organizations that pursue collective ownership, there is another type of cooperative organization. These seek to create entirely new communities and to significantly improve the lives of their members. They are intentional communities that pursue their aims collectively to realize some goal, and are often also referred to as communes, experimental communities and so forth. They consist of groups of people voluntarily coming together, usually in a geographical sense, to share some aspects of their lives. Beyond this, such communities take many different forms: they vary in size, structure, goals and what aspects of life are shared. It might be a household or a handful of people, or a village of hundreds or even thousands; it could be based on just sharing living accommodation (e.g., housing cooperatives), or can involve sharing economic activity or incomes. Whilst many emphasize consensus decision-making, equal participation and informal rules, others (particularly religious ones) may be governed by strong leaders and formal rules. What brings them together, moreover, may range from pragmatic considerations to shared political or religious beliefs. For example, Rigby (1976) identifies six different types of commune based on their underlying purposes: self-actualizing communes which seek to provide an environment in which individual members can feel free to explore and develop themselves and their creative potential; communes for mutual support which provide members with a sense of togetherness and a supportive environment they have not been able to find in the world 'outside'; activist communes oriented towards political critique and transformation; practical communes defined chiefly in terms of the economic and practical advantages of sharing resources; therapeutic communes orientated towards creating a social, physical or spiritual environment; and religious communes based on shared religious and spiritual beliefs.

Many such communities often reject private ownership of property, asserting that it produces an atomized social structure. Whereas private property is asserted to promote competition, they believe that collective ownership facilitates cooperation. For some of these communities, such cooperation is sufficient in itself. These communities are sometimes relatively small-scale affairs such as the Peterborough Street Community in the city of Christchurch in New Zealand (see Case Study 9.3) but can also be larger affairs and more producer-oriented as in the example of the Israeli kibbutz system (see Case Study 9.4).

Case Study 9.3 Peterborough street community, New Zealand

Located in Peterborough Street in Christchurch, New Zealand, and composed of about 12 adults plus children, the core values of this group are cooperation to tackle poverty and cooperative ownership. Peterborough Street Community was established in 1982 and occupies four adjacent houses in the city centre of Christchurch. The properties are owned by the Otakaro Land Trust, the primary objective of which is 'to relieve poverty amongst the economically disadvantaged and poor of Christchurch . . . by establishing an equitable and empowering social structure which does not create a class of poor and economically disadvantaged'. Their objectives are common ownership of land; cooperative control of profit and not-for-profit enterprises; and the creation and promotion of working examples which are locally based, democratic, sustainable and cooperative.

In the past, this community cooperative has had connections to a cooperative bakery and organic food store as well as Prometheus, New Zealand's cooperative bank. The homes are owned freehold by the Trust and members pay rent and make a labour commitment to the community. This is usually paid in regular work. Each house has a private garden as well as access to a communal garden, and buildings are at the back of the properties, including a laundry, office and a large building (formerly home to community businesses and currently used for storage). This community is relatively affluent. Members are all in paid employment (see Sargisson and Sargent, 2004).

Case Study 9.4 The Israeli 'kibbutz'

The 'kibbutz' (a Hebrew word meaning 'communal settlement') movement in Israel is an attempt to provide an alternative to capitalism without managerial authority and worker subordination and exploitation (see Avrahami, 2000; Dar,

2002; Heller *et al.*, 1998; Simons and Ingram, 2003; Warhurst, 1998; Wilson, 1999). Parker *et al.* (2006) report that 269 kibbutzim exist composed of 123,900 members. This is about 1.7 per cent of the population of Israel. The average size is less than 500 members. Membership is voluntary but subject to the approval of the community. The kibbutz movement was established at the start of the twentieth century and grew rapidly in the two decades after 1931. The pioneers wished to create an economy and society that was free, working and classless. The organizational design uses socialist principles where the community owns the means of production and all work is shared equally and rotated to give every member experience of each and every activity, including the most routine and demeaning work. In the kibbutz, members live and work communally. Nobody receives payment but all basic needs are met on an agreed basis. All members receive a small personal and equitable allowance regardless of contribution. A general assembly is the source of power and every member has equal access to it. The assembly is supplemented by committees of work branches, work allocation, culture, services, economic planning and others. The typical kibbutz has up to 30 different committees and 30–50 per cent of members annually participate in them. A general manager is elected and this is regularly rotated about every 5–7 years.

Recently, several changes are asserted to have occurred in kibbutzim. However, as Simons and Ingram (2003: 594) point out, 'only 5 to 7 percent of kibbutzim had changed so much by 1998 that they had lost the cooperative and communal character that is the basis of the official criteria for categorization as a kibbutz'. Housing and basic health provision are still provided free of charge, as well as a guaranteed education and pension, and shared ownership remains the norm. Indeed, there has also been a shift in the productive activities undertaken from agriculture to industry (the production of metals, plastics and food in the main, such that they now manufacture 9 per cent of Israel's industrial output).

Warhurst (1998) uses participant observation to provide a case study of a kibbutz. He found managers had a coordinating rather than a control function. There were no job descriptions, no direction, no monitoring, or evaluation by managers of work or workers, no records of individual workers or work group performance or attendance. Workers decided their own specific tasks and how to do them. It was the antithesis of Taylorism. Labour discipline was in part, a result of the commitment of individual members and their identification with the purposes of the kibbutz. There is a common framework of norms, values and beliefs about the organization and the importance of work to which all members, as workers, consent and conform. At least one alternative form of organization and control is possible then, Warhurst (1998) concludes, in the workplace.

Global-level non-capitalist initiatives: Focolare movement's 'economy of communion'

Until now, as Sargisson and Sergeant (2004) point out, it has often been the case when discussing 'communes' that religious communities have been left out of the equation. The shift towards the phrase 'intentional communities', however, has led to greater discussion of such organizations. It is also the case that the concentration previously has been on more locally oriented communities. Here, therefore, an example of a religious community that pursues non-capitalist production and redistribution on a global level is explored, namely the 'Focolare movement'.

'Focolare', the Italian word for 'hearth', is a symbol for 'hearth and home', the most intimate image of family, love, security and warmth. The Focolare Movement began in the 1940s, whose aim is to do unto others what you would like them to do unto you. Their intention is to promote greater unity within the human family, by transforming interpersonal relationships to promote more caring. To achieve this, the Focolare Movement in 1991 established the Economy of Communion (EOC) in Sao Paulo, Brazil, as an attempt to address the inequalities in wealth, first of all within the Focolare Movement, initially within Brazil but subsequently on a global scale (Gold, 2004; Lubich, 2001).

The distinctive vision of a 'culture of giving' was at first applied on a local scale and at the individual level in that in the early days of the Focolare the circulation of personal possessions among the various members of the community occurred based on the common bond of the shared Focolare spirituality, such as people giving away once a year all that they no longer required. In some ways, this was the first stage in the widening out of the hearth by extending it to the family and then the local community. Over time, it began to be supposed that larger spaces could also become hearths of sharing where the culture of giving might be lived out.

The Focolare Movement sought to experiment with whether the Focolare could be organized at the scale of the global economy. This is what the EOC seeks to do through the extension of the Focolare's spirituality into the realm of business. The EOC recognized that the 'communion of goods' as a strategy was insufficient as a strategy to overcome inequalities on a global scale (Bruni, 1999; Bruni and Pelligra, 2002; Gold, 2004). Although the communion of goods works as a powerful strategy of wealth redistribution at a local scale, it had obvious limitations in the context of global inequalities. What was new therefore was that enterprise, not just individuals, participated to share their profits: one-third to be given to the poor, one-third kept for reinvestment and one-third for the creation of educational structures to further promote the culture of giving. By 2002, 778 small and medium-sized businesses in 45 countries were participating in this project. Of the businesses participating, some 11 per cent were in Brazil, 33 per cent in Italy and 7 per cent in Germany, and relatively high concentrations also in Argentina (4 per cent), ex-Yugoslavia (4 per cent) and the US (5 per cent). The level of profits redistributed totals some $2 million per annum in 1996–99 (Gold, 2004).

The EOC was thus reviving the tradition of 'tithing' within modern businesses but insisting that it should become one of the chief motivations behind starting up new businesses. It was not an afterthought but an integral part of the businesses mission. How is the money distributed? It is a bottom–up process. Each individual makes a self-assessment of what they need once a year to the Focolare houses. Once the needs of each local community are totalled, every attempt is made to cover these needs first of all through making use of local resources and redistribution through the culture of giving which is the basis of Focolare spirituality. This is in many cases, especially in Western nations, sufficient to cover needs and to generate surpluses which can be shared with other communities. If the local needs cannot be met through this local communion of goods, these needs are put forward to the regional Focolare and the same process occurs. If the regional Focolare is still unable to cover these needs, the International EOC commission is contacted. Decisions on how much people need are not based on some predetermined criteria but on personal knowledge and understanding of their situation. If the total requests equal the fund available, everyone receives what they requested. In 1997, the amount of EOC funds was 80 per cent of the total requests, so each zone received 80 per cent of what they requested. The fact that the EOC makes use of existing networks and meetings means that the EOC has almost zero administration costs and charges none.

Rather than adopt a negative view that all alternative organizational forms will be co-opted by capitalism, the Focolare movement's Economy of Communion thus displays that it is wholly possible to enact and imagine how capitalist practices can themselves be co-opted by alternative economic logics in order to promote humane, just and equitable ends.

Negative visions of non-capitalist employment

Of those who discuss a vision of the future of work grounded in non-capitalist employment, or what might be termed 'a social economy' or 'third-sector vision of the future of work', relatively few adopt a negative stance. This is probably because those rejecting this vision, such as adherents to the commodification thesis, probably deem it of only minor significance and unworthy of comment due to its perceived irrelevance so far as the supposed 'realities' of work are concerned.

Of those adopting a negative stance and who do pay some attention to this vision, a common assertion is that this sphere is ineffective and unproductive compared with the for-profit sector. As shown above in the instance of consumer cooperatives, such an argument adopts the criteria for measuring success in for-profit enterprises (rather than the objectives of forms of non-capitalist employment) and then delineates non-capitalist practices as poor performers and lesser ways of organizing (e.g., Boxall and Gallagher, 1997). Such commentators never seemingly consider that if different criteria were used (e.g., their social objectives), very different outcomes might well result with for-profit enterprises being shown to be lesser mortals than their non-capitalist counterparts. This, nevertheless, is not done. Such commentators instead simply assert that this vision will not come to fruition because non-capitalist practices cannot compete with capitalist enterprise.

Another negative stance towards a future of work based on non-capitalist employment revolves around the assertion that work created in this sector is somehow poorer in quality or less stable than work provided in the private and public sectors. An example is the work of Amin *et al.* (2002a,b) on the social economy. For them, much of the work in this sector is seen as dependent on the public sector for funding and is ultimately composed of 'make-work' jobs created by the public sector in order to try to fill the jobs gap left by the public and private sectors. For them, therefore, non-capitalist employment in the social economy is not viewed as an autonomous realm but a dependent realm that represents a sphere of survival into which those marginalized and cast out by the public and private sectors are dumped in order to eke out a living and survive. It is not an alternative to the private and public spheres but a zone into which the marginalized are being off-loaded by capitalism. In this view, therefore, non-capitalist employment is seen as a servant of, and in service to, capital rather than as an alternative to capitalism.

Besides these two broad negative stances, there is also a range of what might be termed 'sympathetic critiques' by those supportive of the development of non-capitalist employment but who identify problems with how this is achieved in specific respects. One such critique is by Kasmir (1996) who expresses disappointment that the more or less democratic decisions in the Mondragon cooperative are implemented through a hierarchy of managers, experts and skilled workers. Hacker (1987) similarly claims that empirical research in workplace democracy has tended to ignore the issue of gender, with studies of Mondragon failing to note the gender issues with women clustered at the bottom of the pay and occupational hierarchies.

A final example of a negative view of this vision of the future of work is that it only considers non-capitalist employment as an alternative to the commodified realm. It fails to envisage work beyond employment as a possible alternative to capitalism. In other words, this critique highlights how this vision only seeks to substitute for-profit employment with not-for-profit employment. It does not consider whether it is possible or feasible to imagine and enact non-capitalist work practices that exist beyond the realm of formal employment, such as self-provisioning and mutual aid (e.g., Gibson-Graham, 1996, 2006; Williams, 2005a,c,d; Williams and Windebank, 2003a,b).

Evaluating the penetration of non-capitalist employment

If it is correct that some workers have had their expectations raised of what the employment-place should be delivering and find that profit-making organizations are not fulfilling their desires, then it is perhaps the case that this provides an opportunity to be seized. With such disgruntlement, a growing demand might be occurring from these employees for alternative forms of employment to which they can turn to receive the identity, self-esteem and rewards that they find missing in the soft-centred profit zone of the current employment-place. If this is the case, then non-capitalist forms of employment might fulfil this need.

Here, therefore, the degree to which non-capitalist employment has penetrated the contemporary business environment is evaluated. If such disgruntlement exists and workers are responding by seeking new opportunities outside profit-centred employment, then non-capitalist employment should be growing. This was reviewed in Chapter 4. As this showed, the evidence is that this is indeed the case. As the data from the John Hopkins Comparative Non-Profit Sector Project presented earlier reveals, this sector is not some insignificant backwater but is in fact a major 'third prong' in many countries. In the 26 countries studied, they identified that the transactions of non-profit organizations represented 4.6 per cent of GDP on average across these nations, and that there were some 31 million full-time equivalent workers (or 6.8 per cent of the non-agricultural workforce). Indeed, if the non-profit sector in the 26 nations surveyed were to be a country, its GDP of US$1.2 trillion would make it the sixth largest economy in the world, ahead of the UK, Brazil, Russia, Canada and Spain. The not-for-profit sector in consequence, is a large sphere of activity that cannot be dismissed as being of only limited or marginal importance.

Until now, however, no survey has been conducted to evaluate whether it's workers disgruntled with the for-profit sector who are shifting into this not-for-profit sector out of choice, or whether it is more those excluded from the private and public sectors who are being cast into this social economy as a last resort. Until this is evaluated, doubts will remain about whether this sphere is being used to construct positive alternatives to capitalism or whether it is more a zone into which those no longer needed by capitalism are being off-loaded, as critics suggest (e.g., Amin *et al.*, 2002a,b). This needs to be researched so as to generate greater understanding of this shift from capitalist to non-capitalist employment.

Conclusions

In sum, this chapter has reviewed a perspective towards the future of employment that is seldom put under the spotlight by those involved in business and management studies, who seemingly prefer to discuss only those visions relating to the shift towards a post-industrial/knowledge/information economy (see Chapter 6), post-Fordism (Chapter 7) and post-bureaucracy (Chapter 8). Perhaps this is because discussing the capitalist/non-capitalist employment dualism and whether a shift is/should be taking place from capitalist employment to non-capitalist employment is somehow seen as more subjective and prescriptive than discussing the shifts towards for instance post-Fordism or post-bureaucracy. Yet as has been hopefully displayed, it appears that whichever dichotomy is focused upon and ordered into a temporal sequence with one side said to be replacing the other, a strong dose of prescription is nearly always involved. Indeed, seldom do any of these visions of the future of employment allow lived practice to get in the way of their arguments about the direction of change.

Seen in this light, this perspective towards the future of employment is little different to those discussed earlier. Perhaps the only major difference is that a stronger consensus exists amongst those involved in business and management studies that the dichotomies that are the focus of the earlier perspectives and the resulting stories about how one side of the dichotomy is being replaced by the other are seen as somehow more valid, with few doubting the yarns that they spin. Quite why these should have achieved the status of facts about the future of work (as if such a thing could exist) can only be explained in terms of how these other perspectives serve the vested interests of capitalism whilst this perspective does not.

Throughout this book so far, the intention has been to first of all chart how the dualistic shifts focused upon by different visions of the future of work (e.g., informalization to formalization, Fordism to post-Fordism, bureaucracy to post-bureaucracy) are not universal trajectories but only applicable in specific contexts. By only focusing upon particular dichotomies and thus one-dimensional linear trajectories, a gross injustice is done to the complex and multiple directions of change occurring in lived practice. As has been revealed, a more accurate portrayal would be perhaps one that recognizes that there are many fragments moving in different directions in various parts of the picture. Consequently, just as some fragments are moving in the direction of post-bureaucracy and post-Fordist work practices, other fragments are moving, as this chapter has revealed, in the direction of non-capitalist employment practices. To foreground one of these fragments and obfuscate the others from view is to fail to grasp the multiple, often divergent, shifts in working practices in the contemporary economic landscape.

It is for this reason that this vision of a future of non-capitalist employment has been included. To portray such work as a primitive, traditional, stagnant, marginal, residual, weak and about to be extinguished sphere, or to put it another way as a vestige of a disappearing past, transitory or provisional, is to ignore that non-capitalist employment not only persists but is resilient and growing in the contemporary economic environment. Throughout the world, just as there are areas in which post-bureaucratic management is coming to the fore and post-Fordist work practices prevailing, there are also spheres in which non-capitalist employment practices are thriving. Unless this is recognized, then the multiple directions of change taking place will fail to be fully understood, as will the choices regarding the future of work.

Yet even when this aspect is incorporated into the picture, as above, it needs to be recognized that this still does not give anything near a complete portrait of the trajectories of work in the contemporary world. This is because all of the perspectives towards the future of work considered in Part 2 have only attempted to decipher changes in the character of employment. They do not consider work relations and forms of work organization beyond the sphere of formal employment and the employment-place. In Part 3, in consequence, attention will turn towards those perspectives that explore the future of work more widely defined.

Further reading

Birchall, J. (2001) (ed.) *The New Mutualism in Public Policy*, London: Routledge.

This edited collection offers a comprehensive review of the various factions of the co-operative movement in a variety of different nations.

Gold, L. (2004) *The Sharing Economy: Solidarity Networks Transforming Globalization*, Aldershot: Ashgate.

This provides a lucid account of a global-level non-capitalist initiative, namely the Focolare Movement's 'Economy of Communion', providing a working example of an alternative to a profit-oriented de-regulated capitalist world.

Johanisova, N. (2005) *Living in the Cracks*, Dartington: Green Books.

This book provides a detailed review of the diverse array of non-capitalist employment practices in the UK and Czech Republic.

Sargisson, L. and Sargent, L.T. (2004) *Living in Utopia: New Zealand's Intentional communities*, Aldershot: Ashgate.

This text provides a detailed analysis of the diverse array of intentional communities in New Zealand and, in doing so, demonstrates the multitude of ways in which non-capitalist employment practices are being implemented in this country.

Visions of the future of work

10

Third way visions of work organization

In Part 3, attention moves away from perspectives that focus primarily upon changes in the employment-place and towards those that expand their visions of the future of work to include work beyond employment. Indeed, it is the incorporation of such literature here that marks out this book as distinct from other business and management texts. Reflecting the emerging desire in critical management studies to rethink the meaning of work organization, Part 3 maps out how thinking about the future of work radically alters once one re-defines work to be composed of more than formal employment.

In this opening chapter of Part 3, the intention is to commence with a perspective that, although recognizing that work is more than employment, is perhaps least radical in terms of how it envisages the future of work. This is what I here term the 'third way' perspective towards the future of work. To review this vision, this chapter first of all outlines 'first way' (neo-liberal) and 'second way' (socialist) thought so as to reveal how the debates between them were/are perhaps about the best way of achieving formalization and commodification. Following this brief introduction, attention then turns towards depicting the recent 'third way' perspective and contrasts this with the conventional first and second way visions, especially in terms of how its vision for the future of work differs in terms of how it incorporates work beyond employment.

This will reveal that even though third way thought recognizes work beyond employment, a key if artificial distinction is made between its application to 'economic' and 'welfare' policy. The outcome is that it is in the sphere of welfare provision and this realm alone that third way exponents believe that not only private and public sector provision but also work beyond employment need to be harnessed (e.g., Giddens, 2000, 2002). If third way thought recognizes the role of work beyond employment as a tool for delivering welfare provision, this is not the case, however, when viewed through the lens of 'economic' policy. Here, their view of the future of work remains entrenched in an employment-centred ideology, and a largely repressive approach is adopted towards work beyond employment. This starkly contrasts with the subsequent approaches that will be outlined in Part 3 that variously envisage a future of work organization in which informal work becomes a complement or alternative to formal employment (see Chapter 11), non-capitalist economic practices an alternative to commodified work (see Chapter 12) and locally oriented work beyond employment a palliative to neo-liberal globalization (see Chapter 13).

Before reviewing how the third way envisions the future, however, it is important to briefly review conventional 'first way' (neo-liberal) and 'second way' (socialist) thought, especially in terms of how they envisage the role of work beyond employment in their visions of the future of work. As will now be shown, in theory, three contrasting approaches can be adopted towards work beyond employment when considering its future role. First of all, a repressive discourse can be adopted towards such work, which is the approach adopted by classical social democratic (second way) discourses. Secondly, a laissez-faire approach can be adopted towards such work, which is the case in neo-liberal (first way) thought and, finally, an enabling approach can be adopted that seeks to harness such work, of which the third way approach discussed here is one variant. Before discussing those perspectives that seek to harness work beyond employment both in this and the next three chapters, therefore, it is important to briefly review the visions of the future of work that seek to either eradicate or adopt a laissez-faire approach towards work beyond employment. Each is here considered in turn.

Classical social democratic discourses on work beyond employment

In classical social democratic ('second way') thought, 'free market' (de-regulated) capitalism produces many problematic effects that must be reduced or tackled by state intervention in the market sphere. The state thus has the obligation to provide public goods that markets cannot deliver or can only do so in a fractured way. A strong government presence in the economy, as well as in other realms such as welfare provision, is seen as normal and desirable. The result is that classical social democratic thought stands or falls by its capacity to deliver a society that generates greater wealth than unbridled capitalism and 'spreads that wealth in a more equitable fashion.

The strong belief inherent in this approach is thus that the state needs to pursue the objectives of full-employment and a comprehensive and universal formal welfare 'safety net' for those unable to participate in the formal labour market. As such, work beyond employment has no significant positive role to play in the future of work and welfare provision. An exemplar of this approach is the stance adopted by the ILO towards the informal economy (ILO, 2002a). For the ILO, the approach adopted in its 'decent work' campaign is that informal work should be transformed into formal employment so that fuller-employment can be achieved. No attention is paid therefore to enhancing the capacity of people to engage in informal work as a means of livelihood. Instead, the intention is not only to repress participation in such work but also to put in place the conditions by which such work can be transferred into the formal economy. For this organization, therefore, the future of work envisaged and sought is one in which all economic activity that currently takes place beyond formal employment needs to be brought into the formal realm. It is a normative stance that prescribes formalization as the route to progress and advancement.

A critical evaluation of the social democratic approach

Classical social democrats, therefore, with their repressive approach towards work beyond employment, believe that there is only one acceptable future of work and it is one in which there is a return to the 'golden age' of full-employment coupled with comprehensive formal welfare provision. This can be criticized, however, on the grounds of both its feasibility and its desirability.

So far as its feasibility is concerned, and as Chapter 3 displayed, the gap between current employment participation rates and a full-employment scenario is considerable and there is little evidence that over time it is being significantly closed. Indeed, it seems unrealistic to expect any advanced economy to achieve a state of full-employment as understood in the 1960s. To achieve this, either a return to out-dated gender divisions of labour (with men in employment and women at home) is necessary or the provision of jobs for all men and women desiring employment is required which has never so far been achieved. As the European Commission (1996a: 28) conclude, 'it is hardly likely that we will return to the full-employment of the 1960s'. It seems therefore that the old-style social democrats dream of a stable full-employment society guaranteeing incomes and participation to the vast majority of the population is receding ever further from their grasp.

If the advanced economies are not returning to the 'golden age' of full-employment, then the question that also begs an answer is whether it is any longer possible to construct a formal welfare 'safety net' to protect those households and workers excluded from employment. To evaluate this, consideration is here given to the social democratic EU rather than more neo-liberal welfare regimes such as the US. Even here, however, any review of the direction of formal welfare provision gives little cause for optimism.

The aim of the 1986 Single European Act, and the Single European Market (SEM) in particular, was to revitalize tired European economies, make industry more productive and promote faster European growth. By opening up vastly differing economies more fully to one another, the concern was that there might be a levelling down of social protection. A social dimension to the Single European Act was thus introduced in the form of the Social Charter. At the outset of discussions of a Social Charter in the EU, however, the perfunctory debate about citizens' rights was quickly transformed into a discussion of workers' rights (Culpitt, 1992; Meehan, 1993), reinforcing a trend which already existed in many Member States towards a 'bifurcated welfare model' (Abrahamson, 1992). This offers some basic protection for workers but little if any to the more marginalized populations in that a dual welfare system is fostered whereby company-based or employment-related welfare schemes take care of those in employment but neglect or exclude marginal and less privileged groups. Thus, and as Bennington *et al.* (1992) state, many were concerned that a corporatist model of welfare would evolve in the EU in which social rights were attached primarily to employment rather than to citizenship.

In the years since these fears were raised, little has occurred to dissipate such worries. The reality has been that the Social Charter has continued to focus upon workers' rights and thus exacerbated inequalities between those with and without employment. Even its attempts to introduce workers' rights, however, have met with only limited success. Pressures not only within, but also external to the EU have limited progress on this matter. For instance, competition on wage costs from countries outside the EU such as those in South East Asia, as well as the expansion of the EU to include East-Central European nations, has put great pressure on the EU member states to keep down their social costs.

Indeed, the evidence now available suggests that such constraints have resulted in cutbacks in formal welfare provision. Between 1993 and 2001, expenditure on social protection as a percentage of GDP has decreased across EU member states (see Table 10.1). This has been most pronounced in those countries where spending was amongst the highest in 1993, such as Sweden (−8.8 percentage points), Finland (−9.8 points) and the Netherlands (−12.1 points). As feared at the advent of the EU, therefore, there has been a levelling down of social protection. Those nations whose level of social protection has generally decreased most sharply are those who had the highest level of social protection in the first place. Meanwhile, and with the exceptions of Ireland and Spain, those with the lowest levels of social protection in 1993 have converged towards the norm. The result is that although there is a convergence of social protection between member states, this is happening within the context of an overall levelling down process.

Table 10.1 Expenditure on social protection as a percentage of GDP in European nations, 1993, 1998 and 2001

	1993	1998	2001	% change
Sweden	38.6	33.3	29.8	−8.8
Finland	34.6	27.2	24.8	−9.8
Netherlands	33.5	28.5	21.4	−12.1
Denmark	31.9	30.0	29.2	−2.7
France	30.9	30.5	28.5	−2.4
Belgium	29.5	27.5	24.7	−4.8
UK	29.1	26.8	21.8	−7.3
Austria	28.9	28.4	26.0	−2.9
Germany	28.4	29.3	27.4	−1.0
Italy	26.2	25.2	24.4	−1.8
Spain	24.7	21.6	19.6	−5.1
Ireland	20.5	16.1	13.8	−6.7

Sources: European Commission (2001b: 91) and Adema and Ladaque (2005: Table Annex 3)

This evidence of a levelling down should be no surprise. Even Keynes and Beveridge, the founders of the welfare state, recognized that the foundations of social welfare lie in the formal labour market. For them, full-employment, not welfare states, was the key to economic well-being. Full-employment meant low demand for social transfers and a large tax base to finance social programmes for the aged, sick and the minority of persons without jobs. Comprehensive formal welfare states were possible only so long as most people found their 'welfare' in the market most of the time (Myles, 1996). The persistently wide 'jobs gap', not to mention an ageing population, thus has profound negative implications for the future of comprehensive formal welfare provision.

If the goal of a full-employment and/or comprehensive formal welfare provision is beyond reach, the question then arises of whether it is appropriate for classical social democrats to seek the eradication of work beyond employment. In this repressive discourse towards work beyond employment where faith is put in a return to full-employment and comprehensive welfare provision, little consideration is given to the notion that this might not be achievable and that people need to be given alternative future modes of productive activity and welfare provision.

However, it is not only the problems involved in achieving full-employment and a comprehensive formal welfare state that lead one to be cautious about the classical social democratic idea of repressing work beyond employment. There is also the question of whether it is in fact possible and/or desirable to eliminate such activity. A major practical problem with seeking the eradication of civil society is that there are 'resistance cultures'. Many do not wish to reduce their civic participation and it will be difficult to persuade them to do otherwise. Such activity is deeply embedded in everyday social life, often undertaken for social as much as for economic reasons. Quite how and whether one can stop such activity is not immediately apparent. Nor arguably is the repression of such activity desirable, not least due to its impacts upon social cohesion, reciprocity, civil society and social support.

In sum, the classical social democratic view of work beyond employment as something to be repressed and eradicated is founded on a belief that it is wholly possible to return to a world of full-employment and/or comprehensive formal welfare provision. Once it is accepted that this ideal-type for the future of work and welfare is unlikely to be achieved, then a big question mark needs to be put over whether it is appropriate to continue to pursue the repression of work beyond employment which, as Chapter 3 displayed, is so central to the work organization of nations in not only the majority and transition economies but also the minority Western World.

Neo-liberal views of work beyond employment

Similar to the old-style social democrats, the neo-liberal (first way) approach again adopts the goal of full-employment as the route to 'progress'. However, the means by which this is to be achieved are very different. For neo-liberals, over-regulation of the market is to blame for many of the economic-ills befalling society (Amado and Stoffaes, 1980; Minc, 1980, 1982; Sauvy, 1984; De Soto, 1989; Stoleru, 1982). As Peck (1996: 1) summarizes, 'From this viewpoint, failure is seen to have occurred in the market, not because of the market.' The solution, in consequence, is to liberate the labour market from 'external interference' so as to give market forces free reign (Sauvy, 1984; Minc, 1980, 1982; Stoleru, 1982).

Included under the umbrella of external interference is state intervention. Antagonism to the welfare state, for example, is one of the prominent neo-liberal beliefs. The welfare state is seen as the source of all evils in much the same way as capitalism was by the left. What provides welfare if the welfare state is to be dismantled? The answer is market-led economic growth. Welfare, therefore, is understood not as the provision of state benefits but as maximizing economic progress by allowing markets to work. Despite many assuming that neo-liberals differ markedly to old-style social democrats on the welfare issue, there are some common threads. Both view the welfare state and the economy as adversaries in that one is usually seen as the root cause of problems in the other. The difference is that whilst old-style social democrats favour the welfare state and view 'free market' (unregulated) capitalism as causing poverty and inequality, neo-liberals support the free market and dislike any structure that constrains it. Old-style social democrats therefore view the welfare state as a necessary institution for the functioning of modern welfare capitalism and a prerequisite for efficiency and growth as well as individual self-realization. Neo-liberals, in contrast, view the adversarial relationship between the welfare state and the economic efficiency in the opposite manner. The welfare state is seen to interfere with individual freedoms and the ability of the market to optimize the efficient allocation of scarce resources.

Considering this view of the relationship between welfare and economy, a long-standing debate in neo-liberal thought has been the extent to which a welfare state is required. As Esping-Anderson (1994) displays, it has been with us ever since the English Poor Law reforms in the early part of the nineteenth century. Within the tradition of classical economics and libertarian thought, one extreme, exemplified by Smiles (1996), holds that virtually any socially guaranteed means of livelihood to the able-bodied would pervert work incentives and individual mobility. This, in turn, would stifle the market, freedom and prosperity. This is echoed today by those considering welfare provision to be the antithesis of social equality. As social rights are essentially claims against the income and resources of others, the welfare state is not considered a guarantor of equal status and autonomy. It is viewed as a divisive system under which a class of claimants becomes parasitic upon others' labour and property, with disastrous effects upon their morals (Gray, 1997; Murray, 1984). Others, however, such as Adam Smith, realized that society did need social provision, especially in health and education, but stressed that due to the conflicting relationship between welfare and economy, this incurs a certain price in terms of economic performance. For these neo-liberals, therefore, the issue is where to set the trade-off between equality and efficiency (Barr, 1992; Gilder, 1981; Lindbeck, 1981; Okun, 1975).

There is thus a spectrum of neo-liberal thought that ranges from those who see no need for a welfare state at one pole to those who regard the need for lesser degrees of emphasis on efficiency when moving along the continuum towards the other pole. All positions on the spectrum, however, emphasize the efficiency trade-offs of pursuing greater equality, particularly with reference to the possibly negative effect of the welfare state on savings (and hence investment), work incentives (and therefore productivity and output) and the institutional rigidities that welfare states introduce (such as in the mobility of labour).

Although such internal debates over the degree to which a welfare state should be provided are important to adherents to neo-liberalism, the fundamental fact that should not be masked is that neo-liberals are on the whole negative about how the welfare state influences economic performance. For them, competitive self-regulatory markets are superior allocation mechanisms from the viewpoint of both efficiency and justice. Government interference in distribution (aside from marginal cases of imperfections, externalities or market failure) thus risks generating crowding-out effects, maldistribution and inefficiency and the end result will be that the economy will produce less aggregate wealth than if it were left alone (Lindbeck, 1981; Okun, 1975). Some even go so far as to insist that inequalities must be accepted, and perhaps even encouraged, because their combined disciplinary and motivational effects are the backbone of effort, efficiency and productivity (Gilder, 1981).

This neo-liberal view would perhaps be harmless if it was simply an academic theorization. However, it is not. Despite being a theory that is heavily opposed to state-led change, it is ironically the state in Anglo-Saxon nations, such as the UK and the US and to a lesser extent Canada and Australia, which has been the primary vehicle for the implementation of this ideology. Indeed, this revelation is not new. Over 50 years ago, Polanyi (1944) recognized that the free market is not an organic and inevitable process but is socially constructed through continuous and controlled government interventionism.

What is the approach towards work beyond employment, therefore, in this neo-liberal view? On the whole, a positive perspective is adopted towards those who partake in such activity but there is largely seen to be no need to directly intervene in such activity in order to cultivate it. For these neo-liberals, such work is seen in two ways. Firstly, it is seen as an indicator of how the formal sphere might be organized if it were de-regulated and, secondly, it is viewed as a principal means used by the unemployed and marginalized as a means of getting-by (Matthews, 1983; Minc, 1982; Sauvy, 1984; De Soto 1989). Indeed, the only change required is that the welfare 'safety net' needs to be dismantled (e.g., Matthews 1983) so as to allow the informal realm to freely operate as a self-generating mechanism of social solidarity. The little platoons of civil society must be allowed to flourish, and will do so if unhampered by state intervention. The virtues of civil society, if left to its own devices, are asserted to include 'Good character, honesty, duty, self-sacrifice, honour, service, self-discipline, toleration, respect, justice, self-improvement, trust, civility, fortitude, courage, integrity, diligence, patriotism, consideration for others, thrift and reverence' (Green, 1993: viii). The state, it is believed, suppresses all these attributes and if they are to flourish, the state must withdraw from its interventions.

The state, particularly the welfare state, is thus seen as destructive of the civil order, particularly obligations and duties associated with the family. Informal work, meanwhile, is the people's 'spontaneous and creative response to the state's incapacity to satisfy the basic needs of the impoverished masses' (De Soto, 1989: xiv–xv). As Sauvy (1984: 274) explains, such work represents 'the oil in the wheels, the infinite adjustment mechanism' in the economy. It is the elastic in the system that allows a snug fit of supply to demand that is the aim of every economy. If left to operate unhampered by the state, then the family and civil society would be able to provide this snug fit. At present, however, this cannot happen because the state through its formal welfare provision creates a 'dependency' culture, preventing populations from taking responsibility for their own livelihoods in the informal sphere.

Critical evaluation of a neo-liberal approach

This approach is based on the idea that full-employment can and will return if market forces are allowed to operate unhindered by the state. Measured purely in terms of whether this neo-liberal approach is more effective in achieving the goal of full-employment than the classical social democratic approach, there is little doubt that this is the case. It does indeed appear that unemployment is lower in advanced economies such as the UK and the US that have pursued a neo-liberal strategy than it is in more social democratic nations of mainland Western Europe (see Chapter 2).

However, sound economic performance in terms of employment participation rates must be seen in terms of both the quality of the jobs created and the degree of social polarization that this 'success' has entailed (Conroy, 1996; Esping-Andersen, 1996; European Commission, 1996b; Fainstein, 1996; Peck, 1996). Whatever way social polarization is defined and evaluated (see Pinch, 1994; Williams and Windebank, 1995), the finding is that it is far greater in neo-liberal economies than social democratic nations. For example, the US and the UK, as the two nations that have led the race towards de-regulation, are also the nations with the highest levels of social polarization between households (see Williams and Windebank, 1995, 2003a). These nations have the highest proportion of households that have either multiple- or no-earners. We can thus only agree with Peck (1996: 2) that 'Contrary to the nostrums of neo-liberal ideology and neo-classical economics, the hidden hand of the market is not an even hand'.

A further problem is that there is little evidence that some of the fundamental tenets of this ideology will have the impact neo-liberals desire. Take, for example, the policy of stripping away the welfare state so as to encourage the population to find their welfare in formal employment. Numerous studies of the effects of reducing welfare benefits on the levels of unemployment conclude that decreasing levels of benefit (or withholding benefit) will not cause an increase in flows off the unemployment register (Atkinson and

Micklewright, 1991; Dawes, 1993; Deakin and Wilkinson, 1991/92; Dilnot, 1992; Evason and Woods, 1995; McLaughlin, 1994).

In an extensive review of the effect of benefits on (un)employment, McLaughlin (1994) concludes that the level of unemployment does have some impact on the duration of individuals' unemployment spells, but the effect is a rather small one. Following Atkinson and Micklewright (1991) and Dilnot (1992), she states that the level of unemployment benefits in the UK could not be said to contribute to an explanation of unemployment to a degree that is useful when considering policy. Moreover, extremely far-reaching cuts would be required in benefit levels to have any significant impact on the duration and level of unemployment. The effect of such cuts would be to create a regime so different from the present one from which the estimates of elasticities (of unemployment duration with respect to out-of-work benefits) are derived that their predictive usefulness would be very suspect.

Neither will taking away the cushion of the welfare state simply allow the little platoons of civil society to spring into action to allow people to get by on their own. As displayed in Chapter 3, numerous studies have detailed in depth how marginalized populations are less able to engage in informal work than more affluent populations. The result is that a *laissez-faire* approach towards informal work will merely consolidate, rather than reduce, social and spatial inequalities. Those least able to participate in informal work will remain unable to perform such activity as a coping practice. Therefore, the possibility that informal work can substitute for formal welfare provision simply by taking away the welfare safety net appears mistaken. The result is more likely to be that people will be simply left bereft of the means of survival (see, for example, Mingione, 1991; Williams, 2002b, 2004f, 2005b; Williams and Windebank, 2000a,b,c,d, 2001a,b).

Nevertheless, given the pressures being put on formal welfare provision particularly in the advanced economies, it remains obvious that something needs to be done about the way in which welfare is provided. However, the choice is not either to strive to restore full-employment and a comprehensive formal welfare 'safety net' as the old-style social democrats advocate, or to strip away the welfare safety net and de-regulate the formal labour market as a means of encouraging full-employment as the neo-liberals propose. As shown, the former is impractical and flies in the face of the direction of the advanced economies, whilst the latter, even if it were to achieve full-employment, would do so at an extremely high price in terms of the levels of absolute and relative poverty.

Given that the classical social democratic ('second way') and neo-liberal ('first way') approaches towards informal work leave marginalized populations unable to engage in alternative means of livelihood and welfare provision and thus close off the future of work, the rest of Part 3 considers other visions of the role of work beyond employment in the future. All these approaches towards informal work have one facet in common, namely they all believe that work organization in the future will see work beyond employment play a more prominent role. As will become apparent, however, there are some stark differences in terms of both why they assert this and the visions of the future of work that they promulgate. To begin to unravel these approaches, the rest of this chapter deals with the 'third way' visions of work organization, the approach which is perhaps the least radical in terms of how it envisages that the future will and/or should be different from the present.

Third way discourses on work beyond employment

Until now, it would be fair to say that there has been a good deal of confusion and debate over the approach that third way thought, especially in terms of its party political manifestations (e.g., New Labour in the UK), adopts towards work beyond employment in particular and plural economies more generally (see, for example, Jordan, 1998; Jordan and Jordan, 2000; Levitas, 1998). In order to understand third way thought on the future of work organization, it will be here argued that it is first of all necessary to recognize that a clear (if artificial) distinction is drawn between the role attached to economic activity beyond employment in the 'economic' sphere and its contribution in the realm of 'welfare' provision. In the 'economic' realm, much third way thought views work beyond employment as something to be at worst repressed and at best used as a springboard for inserting people into the formal sphere (e.g., by improving employability). In the 'social' or 'welfare' sphere, however, third way thought recognizes work beyond employment in its own right as a form of activity that can complement the private and public formal spheres as an additional means of welfare provision.

It is in the welfare sphere and this sphere alone, in consequence, that third way exponents believe that not only private and public sector provision but also a third prong of 'civil society' needs to be harnessed to meet welfare needs. As Giddens (2000: 55–6) puts it,

> The 'design options' offered by the two rival political positions were ministic – they looked either to government or to the market as the means of co-ordinating the social realm. Others have turned to the community or civil society as the ultimate sources of social cohesion. However, social order, democracy and social justice cannot be developed where one of these sets of institutions is dominant. A balance between them is required for a pluralistic society to be sustained.

In third way thought, therefore, it is a mixed economy of welfare delivery that is advocated. Transcending the public versus private provision debate, civil society is added into the equation as an additional means of welfare provision. As Giddens (2000: 81–2) continues,

> In the past, some on the left have viewed the 'third sector' (the voluntary sector) with suspicion. Government and other professional agencies should as far as possible take over from third-sector groups, which are often amateurish and dependent upon erratic charitable impulses. Developed in an effective manner, however, third-sector groups can

offer choice and responsiveness in the delivery of public services. They can also help promote local civic culture and forms of community development.

Or as the UK Prime Minister, Tony Blair (1998: 14), puts it,

> The Old Left sometimes claimed that the state should largely subsume civil society. The New Right believes that if the state retreats from social duties, civic activism will automatically fill the void. The Third Way recognizes the limits of government in the *social sphere*, but also the need for government, within those limits, to forge new partnerships with the voluntary sector . . . 'enabling' government strengthens civil society rather than weakens it, and helps families and communities improve their own performance [emphasis added].

Indeed, Rifkin (2004) has given this shift away from private/public debates to the use of three nodes – commerce, government and civil society – a geographical flavour by arguing that whilst North America remains stuck in two-sector politics, European social democracy is engaging in such three-sector politics, seeking to harness civil society. The introduction of this geographical dimension, however, perhaps obscures more than it clarifies. Such third way thought that seeks to use civil society as a third prong in the welfare delivery equation was pursued in the US under Clinton and subsequent governments as much as in Europe (Giddens, 1998).

If third way thought recognizes the role of work beyond employment as a tool for delivering welfare provision, it is necessary to reiterate, however, that this is not the case when viewed through the lens of 'economic' policy. Here, the third way approach remains entrenched in an ideology of formalization and commodification and a repressive approach is adopted towards work beyond employment in which the only rationale for cultivating such work is to provide a trampoline into the formal and commodified spheres for marginalized groups by using it to variously develop and enhance skills, as a test-bed for self-employment and means of improving employability. As Rustin (2003) puts it, post-socialists of the third way accept the advent of globalization (see Chapter 5) and seek only to mitigate and regulate somewhat the turbulences of global capitalism to which they envisage no conceivable alternative. For them, there is no alternative to an ever more commodified world in which capitalism stretches its tentacles ever wider and deeper across the globe, meaning that the only room for manoeuvre on the 'economic' front is to try to ensure that the worst excesses of this de-regulated seamless world order are mitigated by concerted state intervention in the formal economic realm.

As such, by accepting the meta-narratives of formalization, commodification and globalization, no role is accorded to work beyond employment in the economic realm. Instead, it is only in the sphere of welfare provision that such endeavour has a role in the future. In this welfare sphere, a strong sense exists that the sphere of civil society is a welfare mechanism that can complement public and private welfare provision. This third prong of civic participation represents a means of filling the 'welfare gap' left by the public and private spheres. By cultivating the civil sphere, it is believed that many welfare needs that are currently unmet by the formal public and private spheres can be fulfilled by community-based groups, voluntary work and one-to-one reciprocity.

To see how this intellectual conjuring trick is achieved whereby an artificial distinction is made between the 'economic' and the 'social/welfare' spheres and then work beyond employment categorized in the latter, consider the normative view of such endeavour by the New Labour government in the UK. Since their election in 1997, there has been a renewed emphasis on harnessing work beyond employment, which is often referred to as 'active citizenship' or 'volunteering' (e.g., Countryside Agency, 2000; DETR, 1998; DSS, 1998; Home Office, 1999; Social Exclusion Unit, 1998, 2000). Cultivating such activity is seen to bolster community spirit (e.g., Gittell and Vidal, 1998; Putnam, 2000), encourage local solutions to be sought to local problems (e.g., Cattell and Evans, 1999; Forrest and Kearns, 1999; Home Office, 1999; Silburn et al., 1999; Wood and Vamplew, 1999), promote local democratic renewal (e.g., Social Exclusion Unit, 2000) and deliver support to those in need (e.g., Portes, 1998; Williams and Windebank, 2000a,b,c,d, 2001c,d,e,f). For New Labour, however, such activity is not part of the 'economic' mode of production. Rather, it is seen as a form of welfare provision. New Labour artificially distinguishes between the 'economic' and the 'social' (or 'welfare') and, based upon this, proceeds to advocate the fostering of this 'non-economic' activity as a form of welfare provision. When depicted as an economic activity, however, a very different policy-orientation prevails. The widespread belief across the UK government is that the 'informal economy' (as it is called when seen as an economic practice) needs to be eradicated by transforming it into formal, preferably commodified, labour (e.g., Grabiner, 2000; Evans et al., 2006; Small Business Council, 2004).

Critical evaluation of the third way discourses on work beyond employment

A principal problem with viewing work beyond employment as a welfare delivery mechanism and a tool for inserting people into employment and improving employability, as both Amin et al. (2002a) and Levitas (1998) point out, is that third way thought seems solely to apply this solution to marginalized populations at present. The consequence is that it carries the inherent danger that while the majority in formal employment will pursue their livelihoods in the private and public sectors, and find their welfare in formal private and public sector welfare provision, those marginalized from employment will find themselves increasingly being inserted under a third way politics into what might be perceived as a 'second class and second rate' sphere of welfare provision. To avoid this, then the welfare provided in this sphere will need to be either of an equal status as that found in the public and private sectors, and/or such provision will need to be targeted at everybody rather than just the poor. If this is not achieved, then the inevitable end result will be a 'dual society'. A second-class form of welfare provision will arise for those marginalized from the formal sphere.

A second criticism of this approach concerns the way in which it differently views various forms of work beyond employment. While there is a desire to cultivate more organized community-based groups as vehicles for delivering welfare, micro-level informal work (e.g., child-care by parents) is viewed as ripe for formalization. 'New Labour's position assumes an individual can contribute to society through working as a paid child carer but not as an unpaid mother, though both individuals carry out the same tasks and make identical contributions' (King and Wickham-Jones, 1998: 277). This differential treatment of organized groups and micro-level informal work has been identified by many commentators (e.g., Hills, 1998; Levitas, 1998; Williams, 2003b, 2005e; Williams and Windebank, 2001b). Why formal volunteering in groups is supported and informal one-to-one aid is not is difficult to discern. One argument has been that the third way vision that hierarchically orders informal work into organized and micro-level one-to-one forms, viewing the former as a mature form of civic participation and the latter as immature, rather than viewing it as a spectrum, is a reflection of the fact that affluent populations tend to engage in organized forms of civic participation whilst marginal groups possess more informal participatory cultures (Williams, 2003b, 2005e; Williams and Windebank, 2001b).

Conclusions

This chapter has commenced the process of discussing visions of the future of work that recognize how work is more than employment. To do this, it has reviewed classical social democratic, neo-liberal and third way views on the future of work. This has revealed that the classical social democratic approach of seeking to more fully formalize work and welfare is both impractical and undesirable. It is impractical because informal work is deeply embedded in everyday life and the evidence points towards an informalization rather than formalization of work and welfare in many populations. It is undesirable because this work is often the preferred means by which people conduct many activities and a key ingredient of the social cement that binds communities together.

The neo-liberal view of work beyond employment, meanwhile, that a *laissez-faire* approach should be adopted towards it results in numerous negative consequences. The ever popular 'marginality thesis' assumes that informal work is undertaken by those marginalized from employment as a survival strategy for unadulterated economic reasons and is thus more prevalent in deprived than affluent communities. The empirical evidence of the vast majority of studies, however, is that informal work is not limited to marginal groups. Rather, they tend to conduct less informal economic activity than more affluent populations. As such, a *laissez-faire* approach towards the informal sphere merely intensifies the social inequalities resulting from formal employment.

In consequence, this chapter has turned to one of the visions that seek to harness informal work, namely third way thought. This artificially distinguishes between economic and welfare policy, viewing work beyond employment as a third prong in the welfare delivery equation that can be utilized to complement private and public sector provision. In the economic sphere, however, an employment-centred vision persists whereby the goal is to achieve full-employment as the way forward.

Of all approaches that recognize the existence of work beyond employment in their visions of the future of work, this 'third way' vision of work organization is perhaps the least radical in terms of how it envisages that the future will and/or should be different from the present. In the following chapters, other visions of the future of work will be shown to exist that also believe that work beyond employment will play a more prominent role in the future of work. As will become apparent, however, there are some stark differences in terms of both why they assert this and the visions of the future of work that they promulgate.

Further reading

Blair, T. (1998) *The Third Way: New Politics for the New Century*, London: Fabian Society.

This pamphlet by the UK Prime Minister provides a lucid account of what is meant by a third way vision of the future of work in party political discourse.

De Soto, H. (1989) *The Other Path*, London: Harper and Row.

This book by an influential Peruvian economist clearly depicts a neo-liberal vision of the future of work in which the de-regulation of the formal economy leads to formal employment resembling what is currently called 'informal work'.

Giddens, A. (1998) *The Third Way: The Renewal of Social Democracy*, Cambridge: Polity.

This seminal text by the 'guru' of the third way clearly sets out his detailed vision of the future of work and welfare.

11

Organizing work in a post-employment world

Introduction

In the last chapter, the way in which the third way approach incorporates work beyond employment into its vision of the future was discussed. This revealed that the 'third way' approach adopts an employment-centred vision of the future of work. In the realm of 'economic' policy, it views work beyond employment as something to be repressed. In the 'social' or 'welfare' sphere, however, third way thought recognizes such work in its own right as a form of activity that can complement the private and public formal spheres as an additional means of welfare provision. In this and the next two chapters, other visions are explored that move away from such employment-centred visions of the future of work. In this chapter, those who reject the formalization thesis and construct a post-employment vision of work organization are discussed, followed in the next chapter by those who reject the commodification thesis and advocate a post-capitalist future of work and then in Chapter 13 those greens who reject the globalization thesis and construct localist visions of the future of work.

Here, therefore, those rejecting the view that formalization is the route to 'progress' are considered. For adherents to the formalization thesis, a formal/informal economy binary hierarchy exists that delineates the formal economy as composed of positive attributes (and the route to 'progress') and the informal economy as composed of negative features. The post-employment commentators considered in this chapter, however, invert this binary hierarchy. For them, the formal economy is attributed with many negative features while the informal economy, which is seen to possess many positive features, is marked out as the path to 'progress' and development. In this post-employment vision of the future of work, in consequence, the desire is to reduce the centrality of employment and develop informal work as an alternative and/or complement to the formal realm (Archibugi, 2000; Aznar, 1981; Beck, 2000; Delors, 1979; Gorz, 1999; Greffe, 1981; Lalonde and Simmonet, 1978; Laville, 1995, 1996; Mayo, 1996; Rifkin, 1996; Sachs, 1984). To understand this approach, first, this chapter explores the rationales for seeking a move away from employment-centred approaches to work organization and this is then followed by an analysis of initiatives being pursued in order to enact this vision of how work should be organized in the future.

Post-employment visions of the future of work

For this group of commentators, inserting people into employment is not the only (or even the most effective) way to ensure that people are able to meet their needs and creative desires. Inserting people into formal employment so that they can earn money to pay for formal goods and services to meet their needs and desires is just one option (even if it is often viewed as the only option by many today). Another route, and one which they prescribe, is to enable people to receive goods and services through informal modes of production.

For post-employment visionaries, putting all of one's eggs into the basket of employment creation is dangerous and undesirable. Recognizing that in all countries, people still use a mixture of formal and informal work in order to meet their needs and desires; this vision of the future of work argues that rather than only look to develop the formal employment side of the equation, attention should also start to be paid to nurturing people's ability to meet their needs through informal modes of production. Put another way, these commentators envisage the future of work to be one in which there is a development of what have been variously called 'plural economies' (OECD, 1996), 'diverse economies' (Gibson-Graham, 1996), 'multi-activity' societies (Beck, 2000), 'proliferative economies' (Leyshon and Lee, 2003) or 'full-engagement' societies (Williams and Windebank, 2003a,b). Why, therefore, is such an approach advocated?

Here, the two principle rationales usually provided for developing plural economies are reviewed. These are, first, that full-employment and/or formalization is no longer seen as a feasible objective so alternative means of meeting citizens' needs and desires must be developed and, secondly, the idea that people are increasingly dissatisfied with formal employment and are seeking to achieve a better work-life balance.

Questioning the feasibility of full-employment and formalization

For many advocating a post-employment vision of the future of work, their starting point is that seeking a return to the 'golden age' of full-employment is both illogical and unrealistic (e.g., Beck, 2000; Bridges, 1995; Giddens, 1998; Gorz, 1999; Rifkin, 1996; Williams, 2004b,f,g,h, 2005f; Williams and Windebank, 2003a). It is illogical because as Chapter 3 displayed, full-employment never existed. At best, such a situation prevailed for at most three decades after the Second World War in a few advanced economies (Pahl, 1984) and even then it was only full-employment for men, not women (Gregory and Windebank, 2000). Full-employment for men and women has never existed, so it is

Table 11.1 Employment-to-working age population ratios, 1993 and 2003: a global portrait

Region	1993	2003
World	63.3	62.5
Latin America and the Caribbean	59.3	59.3
East Asia	78.1	76.6
South-East Asia	68.0	67.1
South Asia	57.0	57.0
Middle East & North Africa	45.4	46.4
Sub-Saharan Africa	65.6	66.0
Transition Economies	58.8	53.5
Industrialized Economies	55.4	56.1

Source: Derived from **ILO** (2004: Table 1.3)

illogical to envisage a future of work that seeks a return to some non-existent previous 'golden age' of full-employment.

It is also, they assert, unrealistic to seek the goal of full-employment. Table 11.1 displays the worldwide 'jobs gap' that will need to be bridged. Globally, the employment-to-population ratio for people of working age was just 62.5 per cent in 2003, meaning that for full-employment to be achieved, one job is needed for every two that currently exist; a 50 per cent increase in the number of jobs, and neither there is evidence that this gap is narrowing over time.

For Bridges (1995), therefore, those looking back at the end of the twenty-first century to the present period in history will view the current preoccupation of governments with inserting people into formal jobs as akin to trying to find deckchairs for everybody on the Titanic. Beck (2000) similarly contends that it is futile to hark back to the supposedly golden age of full-employment. Instead, he suggests that we should use the demise of a full-employment society as an opportunity to develop new ideas and models for work rather than look to previous 'golden ages' for our inspiration regarding the way forward. For these analysts, in consequence, that there are and will be insufficient jobs for everybody to be employed means that trying to achieve a full-employment society is akin to trying to allocate life belts where there are too few to go around all of the passengers.

It is not just the inability of societies to achieve full-employment that drives these commentators to reject this vision of the future of work. As revealed in Chapter 3, although it is often assumed that there is a natural and inevitable trajectory towards a formalization of work and that formal employment is now near enough the only game in town so far as the means of meeting needs and desires are concerned, the lived practice is very different throughout the world, including in the advanced economies. Not only is the informal economy about the same size as the formal economy, measured in terms of the amount of working time spent in each sphere, but no evidence exists of any universal trajectory towards formalization. As such, these post-employment commentators assert that there is a need to move beyond an employment-centred approach and to develop an approach that reflects the lived practice for the majority of the world's population. Rather than run counter to the trend in many areas of the globe, including advanced economies, by pursuing formalization, their argument is that much greater attention should be placed on developing the capabilities of citizens to engage in informal work either as a complement and/or as an alternative to formal work.

Questioning the desirability of full-employment and formalization

For post-employment visionaries, a return to the supposedly 'golden age' of full-employment and the pursuit of formalization as the route to 'progress' is not only illogical and unrealistic but also undesirable (see, for example, Beck, 2000; Gorz, 1999; Macfarlane, 1996; Williams, 2002a, 2003a; Williams and Windebank, 2001c, 2003a). This is because in their eyes, insertion into employment is often viewed as having largely negative consequences, and harnessing the ability of citizens to engage in informal work is seen to result in a saner, more humane, means of meeting citizens' needs and desires than the employment-place.

The negative consequences of insertion into employment

One reason why insertion into employment as a route to salvation is seen as undesirable relates to the growth of the working poor. As the ILO (2004) state, there are 55 million people in the world who work but still live on less than US$1 per day. These working poor represent 20 per cent of the total world employment. This, moreover, is not solely a majority world phenomenon. In the EU, some 13 per cent of households in which at least one member is in employment live below the 'poverty line', defined as earning less than 60 per cent of their country's median household income (European Commission, 2001b: 99). For a significant share of EU households in consequence, insertion into the formal labour market does not result in an escape from poverty. Oxley (1999), for example, identifies the continuously poor by defining the poverty line to be where annual incomes fall below 50 per cent of the median of household disposable income adjusted for household size, and finds that working households comprise 63.6 per cent of the continuously poor in Canada and 48.7 per cent in the US. As Beck (2000: 90) therefore puts it, 'Work and poverty, which used to be mutually exclusive, are now combined in the shape of the *working poor*.' For post-employment commentators, the shift from passive welfare policies (paying people benefits for doing nothing) to activation policies that insert the unemployed into the formal labour market has consequently merely resulted in poverty shifting from the jobless poor to the working poor. Insertion into employment, in other words, is not the wholly positive solution portrayed by adherents to full-employment and formalization.

Insertion into employment is also viewed as largely undesirable by these post-employment commentators because many formal jobs are seen as stultifying and alienating, and leave people with inadequate time to compensate for the lack of satisfaction that their job brings outside working hours (Amado and Stoffaes, 1980; Archibugi, 2000; Aznar, 1981; Gorz, 1982, 1985, 1999; Laville, 1995, 1996; Mayo, 1996). This lack of opportunity for personal growth in employment as well as the fact that the only alternative to a job is unemployment that cannot provide self-esteem, social respect, self-identity, companionship and time structure means for these analysts that employment is not perceived as positive. Aznar (1981: 39) summarizes the push towards an employment-centred society in the following manner:

> any society which proposes that its citizens spend the whole of their time, energy and empathy engaged in an activity which cannot, by its very nature, soak up this energy, is fundamentally perverse.

As Gorz (1999: 58) puts it,

> Those who continue to see work [employment]-based society as the only possible society and who can imagine no other future than the return of the past . . . do everyone the worst service imaginable by persuading us that there is no possible future, sociality, life or self-fulfilment outside employment, by persuading us that the choice is between a job and oblivion, between inclusion through employment and exclusion, between 'identity-giving socialization through work' and collapse into the 'despair' of non-being. They persuade us it is right, normal, essential that 'each of us should urgently desire' what in actual fact no longer exists and will never again lie within everyone's grasp: namely 'paid work in a permanent job', as the 'means of access to both social and personal identity', as 'a unique opportunity to define oneself and give meaning to one's life'.

The solution, as Beck (2000: 58) puts it, is that

> the idea that social identity and status depend only upon a person's occupation and career must be taken apart and abandoned, so that social esteem and security are really uncoupled from paid employment.

This is reinforced by Gorz (1999: 72) who argues that

> The imperative need for a sufficient, regular income is one thing. The need to act, to strive, to test oneself against others and be appreciated by them is quite another. Capitalism systematically links the two, conflates them, and upon that conflation establishes capital's power and its ideological hold on people's minds.

The problem for these analysts, therefore, is that employment for many workers seems to have become more rather than less central to their lives due to the way in which employment is unequally distributed across the population, whilst those excluded from such work are currently provided with no alternative means of livelihood to soak up their energies and ambitions.

It is now wellrecognized, for example, that for a large proportion of the population, employment is taking up ever more of people's time such that they have no energy left for activities outside the employment-place. As Schor (1991) argues in her 'overwork thesis', longer work hours also leads to stress, hypertension, gastric illness, heart disease, cancer, depression, broken homes, marital violence and under-socialized and antisocial children, and asserts that between 15 and 50 per cent of workers assert that they are working more hours than they wish to and are willing to trade-off income to work fewer hours. For many, however, trapped in a 'cycle of work and spend' (Schor, 1996), their only option is to work long hours or not work at all, which she contends is leading a significant minority to take the latter option and exit the formal labour market altogether by 'downshifting' and deciding to work and consume less (Schor, 2000).

For post-employment commentators, a chasm is thus often identified between government and individual attitudes towards employment. Across Western governments and well beyond, on the one hand, the desire seems to be to make employment the central focus of people's lives. Indeed, many on the Left who quite rightly used to complain about the exploitation inherent in employer–employee relationships and capitalist exchange relations are now amongst the principal advocates of inserting people precisely into this relationship. Even those feminists who were quick to highlight the dangers of patriarchal subjugation when women were confined to home seem quite happy for their sisters to enter subjugation under capitalist relations by advocating employment as the principal route to their liberation (McDowell, 2001). Few stop to consider whether advocating the greater subjugation of women by capitalist relations, especially given the low-paid nature of women's employment, is the path to liberation. Perhaps this is because they are so immersed in their own careers that they do not consider it may not be the same for others. Perhaps it is because they themselves are the employers for their sisters as cleaners and nannies. Perhaps, however, it is because they can see no feasible alternative future of work beyond a full-employment society. If the latter is indeed the case, then such academics, like their counterparts in government, it is asserted, perhaps need to start to listen to the population at large (Williams, 2005a).

At the very moment that the 'employment ethic' has moved centre-stage in both government circles and much academic theorizing, many people are starting to redefine the importance of formal employment in their lives (Cannon, 1994; Coupland, 1991; Franks, 2000; Isles, 2004; Maffesoli, 1996; Gorz, 1999; Schor, 1991; Sue, 1995; Zoll, 1989). Gorz (1999), for example, cites two surveys conducted in France for graduates of the Grandes Ecoles. A 1990 survey showed that 'what comes out way ahead of everything else is the possibility of working when it suits them, so as to be able to devote more time to personal activities'. In 1993, moreover, a survey of current and past students at the prestigious Ecole Polytechnique confirmed this disaffection regarding careers and the general preference for multi-activity and part-time working. As Gorz (1999: 62) summarizes, 'the relation to work [employment] is growing looser because life goes on elsewhere' and particularly in 'unpaid activities which are regarded as socially useful'.

Amongst Western Europeans aged between 16 and 34, 'work' or 'career' trail far behind five other priorities in the list of 'things which are really important to you personally' (Yankelovich, 1995). The five priorities are having friends (95 per cent), having enough free time (80 per cent), being in good physical shape (77 per cent), spending time with one's family (74 per cent) and having an active social life (74 per cent). Isles (2004) in the

UK similarly finds that when people are asked about what contributes to their well-being, the most widely cited factors were children (95 per cent), a partner (94 per cent), close family (81 per cent), friends (77 per cent), leisure (73 per cent) and, only then in sixth place, a job (69 per cent) just before wider family (53 per cent).

In a sample of upper-middle-class full-time employees in the US, meanwhile, Schor (1991) finds 73 per cent take the view that they would have a better quality of life if they worked less, spent less and had more time for themselves. The outcome is that some 28 per cent of those questioned had indeed chosen to 'downshift' (i.e., voluntarily earn and spend less) in order to lead a more meaningful life. In the UK, Isles (2004) also finds that 61 per cent of people wanted to work fewer hours (70 per cent of men and 52 per cent of women) and that nearly one in three in employment were either already or planning to work fewer hours, nearly one in two either already or planning to work more flexibly, nearly one in four planning to retire early and one in seven planning to give up work altogether. Most US citizens, meanwhile, feel that they would be happier if they could spend more time with their friends and family, and about a third, according to a Gallup poll, would take a 20 per cent cut in income if they or their spouses could have more free time (Durning, 1992; Motavelli, 1996).

The result, it is asserted, is that many today do not position employment at the centre of their lives. Hakim (2000), for example, explores work-lifestyle preferences amongst men and women. Table 11.2 presents her results. This divides men and women

Table 11.2 A classification of work-lifestyle preferences in the twenty-first century

Home-centred	Adaptive	Work-centred
20% of women	60% of women	20% of women
10% of men	30% of men	60% of men
Children and family life remain the main priorities throughout life	Diverse group including those who want to combine work and family, plus unplanned and unconventional careers, drifters and innovators	Main priority in life is employment or equivalent activities (e.g., politics, sport, art)
Prefer not to engage in competitive activities in the public domain	Want to work, but not totally committed to work career	Committed to employment or equivalent activities in the public domain
Qualifications obtained for intellectual value, cultural capital or as insurance policy	Qualifications obtained with the intention of working	Large investment in qualifications for employment or other activities, including extra education during adult life
Responsive to family and social policy	Very responsive to all policies	Responsive to employment policies

Source: Adapted from Hakim (2000: Tables 1.1 and 9.1)

into three broad categories: 'home-centred' people for whom family life remains their main priority throughout life; 'adaptive' people who seek to combine work and family, and 'work-centred' people whose main priority in life is their employment or similar activities. For her, a strict gender division in terms of the work-lifestyle preferences exists. While women are predominantly adaptive, men tend to be more employment-centred. Only about one-fifth of women and one in three men pursue employment-centred lifestyles. Whatever the gender divisions and proportions allocated to each category, the important finding of this table is that employment is not always centre-stage and that many are seeking a better balance between employment and family life (see also Mauthner et al., 2001).

In sum, despite the concerted attempts of Western governments to insert people into employment, it appears that for many people what they want is not the right to employment but the opportunity to choose between employment, non-employment forms of work and activity beyond work, and to combine them in ways that suit them. For post-employment commentators, therefore, there is a need to reconsider whether the 'employment ethic' should remain at the core of economic and social policy, or whether a 'work ethic' or 'care ethic' based on a broader conceptualization of economic practices is required. Just as people are recognizing and valuing activity beyond employment, there appears to be a case for economic and social policy following suit (Dean et al., 2005; Williams, 2005a; Williams and Windebank, 2001b, 2003a).

The positive attributes of participation in informal work

This employment-first mentality of Western governments is not only pushing many people to adopt employment as a central focus of their lives against their will, but also devaluing the informal sphere and its importance in meeting needs and desires. To see this, one needs to look no further than how the question 'what do you do?' is today nearly always answered by naming one's formal occupation. Those without a formal occupation often answer 'Nothing, I am just a housewife/mother.' For these post-employment commentators, this undervaluing of work outside employment is undesirable, not least due to its patriarchal overtones in the sense that it is largely women's unpaid work that is being undervalued (see Chapter 3).

It is not just the undervaluing of such work that these analysts reject as undesirable. For many, there is a perception that an employment-centred approach is also slowly destroying the informal sphere. Not only are a large number of people too tired or have too little time to even do the housework at the end of a working week, or to maintain family relationships and social capital in the wider community, but the more people enter employment, the more the capabilities to fulfil these functions reduce.

Hochschild (2003: 198) extends this argument further: 'For about a fifth of the employees I talked to at Amerco in the early 1990s and mid-1990s, family life had become like "work" and work had become more like "home".' With the shift towards high-commitment workplaces, people were viewing work as being a place for developing bonds, intimate relations, a haven and so forth, whilst home on the other hand was turning into a place of work and a commodified sphere as parents witness a 'time bind' of both employment commitments and the need to maintain the home, resulting in a work–family speed up. As Hochschild (2003: 204) puts it, 'as family life becomes de-ritualized, in certain sectors of the economy cultural engineers are busy adding ritual to work'. The result is that people are being pulled towards employment on the one hand and propelled from work beyond employment and leisure on the other.

The prolonged structural crisis of unemployment, however, is considered to provide an opportunity to re-valorize informal work. As the OECD (1996) suggests, there is a need to put the economy back into society rather than see it as an autonomous or independent element. Here, therefore, and mirroring much of the recent academic interest shown in analysts such as Polanyi (1944) and Granovetter (1973), the desire is to develop a socially embedded view of economic activity (see, for example, Lee, 1996; Verschave, 1996). The current structural crisis of unemployment for these commentators provides just such an impetus for rethinking whether all social goals should be subjugated to the economic aim of continued growth rather than a view of the 'economy' as serving the interests of society.

Based on this definition of the crisis of work, they believe that informal work has a crucial role to play. These theorists are concerned not only, or indeed, necessarily, with informal activities as they exist today, but with the possible emergence or reinforcement of a category of work which one could call 'autonomous'. Such autonomous work does not refer to a tangible empirically observable category of activity (Gorz, 1999). Instead, the notion is linked to utopian visions of what work could be in the future. Thus, autonomous work is a conceptual, as opposed to a concrete, phenomenon. It suggests that a type of work can and should come about in the future over which the producer will have a large degree of control in which creativity and conviviality will be the driving forces. In sum, autonomous work is creative, controllable and socially useful. It has a purpose for the person performing it other than earning a wage.

On the whole, the more *reformist* post-employment commentators adopt a vision of autonomous work that merges with present forms of informal work. In so doing, like Unger (1987), they view alternatives as emerging out of critical and practical engagements with the associations, personal behaviours and practices that now exist. The more *transformative* theorists, however, do not explicitly refer to types of informal work that exist today since this does not fit their aim of calling for a complete redrawing of the boundaries which divide various categories of work from one another. Instead, and as Windebank (1991) asserts following her in-depth interviews with some of these theorists, the attempt is to find new forms of autonomy and sociability in the allocation of work. What unites all these radicals is their wish to put an end to, or at least considerably reduce the domination of 'heteronomous' work, which is understood as that over which individuals have little or no control, and introduce more autonomous work which is seen as a positive move due to its satisfying nature.

Enacting a post-employment vision of the future of work

Although for some post-employment commentators the development of informal work is seen as providing an alternative to formal employment, for the majority it is in practice not argued to be an either/or choice between formal and informal work. Instead, a both/and approach is adopted. They wish to develop the informal sphere as a complement to the formal realm. Given the evidence already presented of economic plurality, some may assert that this is already the case. The problem at present, however, is twofold. First, those least able to participate in the formal sphere are also those least capable of drawing upon the informal sphere for sustenance and, secondly, policy-makers have prioritized the development of the formal sphere over the informal realm as the way forward and even in some cases sought to eradicate the informal realm in order to further develop the formal sphere.

The first step in moving from the goal of formalization to a society based on plural economies or full-engagement, therefore, is that informal work needs to be recognized and valued. As Beck (2000: 58) puts it,

> In the transition from the work [employment-centred] society to the multi-activity society, a new answer is given to the question: what is work? The concept of an 'activity society' does, it is true, include a reference to paid work, but only as one form of activity alongside others such as family work, parental work, work for oneself, voluntary work or political activity. This reminds us that people's everyday lives and work are stretched on the procrustean bed of *plural activities* – a self-evident fact that is usually obscured in the perspective of a society centred upon paid employment.

Once informal modes of production and delivery are recognized and valued, the next step is to work towards giving such work equal status. At present, this does not occur. Although there is widespread recognition in the 'social' or welfare sphere that informal work is a third prong in the welfare equation that needs to be given equal status to the formal public and private spheres, the same conceptual shift has not occurred in the so-called 'economic' sphere. Here, formal work retains its status as the only form of work of any true worth and there is strong resistance to recognizing and valuing informal modes of production as of equal value to formal work. The result is that people are currently helped in all manner of ways with 'carrots' and 'sticks' to enter the world of formal employment (see Dean et al., 2005; Peck, 2001), but little help is given to people to engage in informal modes of production.

If plural economies are to be achieved, however, then there will be a need to re-balance the priority accorded to formal work and to place as much emphasis on enabling people to engage in informal work as is given to enticing them into formal employment. If policy-making can achieve this, then post-employment commentators believe that the desires of the population at large will be reflected. As Beck (2000: 106) once again puts it, more and more people are looking both for meaningful work and opportunities for commitment outside of [formal] work. If society can upgrade and reward such commitment and put it on a level with gainful employment, it can create both individual identity and social cohesion.

The problem, however, is that whenever such a solution is raised, namely recognizing the informal sphere, this has been nearly always discussed in Western government discourses solely in relation to those marginalized from the formal sphere.

Towards a plural economy, not a dual society

At the Lisbon European Council in March 2000, EU member states set the objective of achieving a 70 per cent employment participation rate by 2010 (European Commission, 2000b: 15). Although no governments have so far explicitly discussed what is to be done with the 30 per cent of the EU population of working age (75 million people) not envisaged as being engaged in employment, it appears at present that the goal of full(er)-employment is being left in place so that the 70 per cent will find their salvation through the formal labour market while the remaining 30 per cent will be given some alternative coping mechanism. This is unlikely to be a passive welfare benefits system (where people are paid to do nothing) and it seems highly unlikely that active welfare policies will find sufficient jobs for this large segment of the population. The likelihood, therefore, is that this segment of the population will be increasingly encouraged to find their livelihood elsewhere, namely in the informal sphere. The outcome of this approach, if pursued, will be 'dual society'. The 70 per cent will continue to find their salvation through the formal labour market while the 30 per cent excluded will be left to eke out their survival in the informal sphere.

However, post-employment commentators argue that a dual society (i.e., the polarization of society into those who find their work through the formal sphere and those marginalized in the informal realm) is not the inevitable outcome of developing plural economies (i.e., a society in which both formal and informal work are recognized and valued, and households are facilitated to engage in both forms of work in order to meet their needs and wants). If the primary intention is to off-load those populations surplus to the requirements of capital onto the informal sphere, then the pursuit of economic pluralism will inevitably result in a dual society.

To avoid the advent of a dual society, therefore, it is necessary to promote economic pluralism amongst the *whole* population whereby all households and/or individuals are encouraged to engage in both formal and informal work in order to meet their needs and desires. Indeed, wherever a plural economy has been advocated, this argument is strongly upheld. Beck (2000) highlights this to be the case in Germany amongst the various liberal, green and communitarian groups pursuing a 'multi-activity' or 'dual-activity' society. It is similarly the case in France where there is a long tradition of advocating such a future of work in a way that avoids the creation of a dual society (e.g., Aznar, 1981; Delors, 1979; Gorz, 1999; Windebank, 1991). So too is such an argument prevalent in the UK (e.g., Boyle, 1999; Douthwaite, 1996; Jordan, 1998; Mayo, 1996; Williams and Windebank, 2003a) and the US (e.g., Cahn, 2000).

Conscious of the fact that both the mainstream left- and right-wing in politics might seize upon the advocacy of a plural economy so as to reduce formal welfare costs, therefore, these post-employment advocates of plural economies regard multi-activity to apply to the population as a whole rather than solely the marginalized. As Beck (2000: 60) explicitly puts it, 'Only when every man and woman has one foot in paid employment, and perhaps the other in civil labour, will it be possible to avoid a situation where the "third sector". . . becomes a ghetto of the poor.' This is the central and essential requirement if a plural economy is to avoid the creation of a dual society.

The problem, nevertheless, is that it is precisely amongst the marginalized that policy interventions are required in order to develop their capacities to engage in informal work. Indeed, unless this is the focus of policy interventions, then the informal realm will continue to consolidate, rather than reduce, socio-spatial inequalities (see Chapter 3). However, as soon as governments or the third sector adopt a policy focus on the development of informal work amongst marginalized populations, accusations will start to be raised that a dual society is being forged. There thus seems little that can be done to qualm such fears in the short run. For post-employment commentators, therefore, despite recognizing the potential for the creation of a dual society, the belief is that the focus of attention needs to be put on pursuing interventions to help the marginalized engage in informal work.

How, therefore, is this shift towards a plural economy to be achieved? Two separate but connected scenarios are proposed by these theorists. First, there is the socialist scenario in which the state would take control of heteronomous production and designate the boundaries between the autonomous and the heteronomous spheres of life. This is a state-led approach to engendering change. Second, there is a scenario that rests on the more libertarian ideal of pursuing changes in work patterns through piecemeal initiatives. Accordingly, the autonomous sphere would develop as a result of civil society nibbling away at the domains of the formal market and state.

In the first scenario, therefore, the desire is to bring about a self-managed or 'autogestionnaire' society in which the informal sphere would play a major part through state intervention. What renders this a 'socialist' scenario is that the state retains an important role in organizing the essential heteronomous work on which a society as a whole relies for the production of its staple goods (ADRET, 1977; Gorz, 1985, 1999). Gorz (1985) for example, calls for a new balance between three types of work: heteronomous work, small-scale co-operative and communal free enterprise, and autonomous household-based activity. To achieve this, the ADRET collective (1977) calls for the state to organize work so that each person would perform an average of two hours a day of 'constrained' work (which could be translated into so many days a week, months a year, and so on, according to individual tastes and circumstances). In conjunction with such work, there would be an absolute ceiling placed on the amount of goods and services produced in this manner. Such a new organization of work could not come about, they argue, without a change in the way the society and economy are organized. It cannot emerge within a productivist or growth economy fuelled by the capitalist profit motive. Thus, the role of the market economy is in some doubt in this scenario, being replaced for the most part, by the state which, it is argued, could organize heteronomous work. Given that this state-led approach is unlikely to be pursued in the current era, the focus here is upon the second approach.

The second scenario is to pursue a plural economy more through piecemeal initiatives. Accordingly, the autonomous sphere would develop as a result of civil society providing on a case-by-case and area-by-area basis alternatives to the formal market and state (e.g., Lalonde and Simmonet, 1978). The way forward here is to develop the autonomous sphere by developing civil society initiatives that replace those currently conducted by the market and the state. How, therefore, is this to be achieved?

To reduce the centrality of employment, three broad strategies are advocated by those wishing to move towards the development of plural economies. These are, first, the pursuit of employment time reduction policies so as to achieve a decline in the centrality of employment in people's lives, secondly, the advocacy of a citizen's income to break the relationship between income and employment and, finally, the adoption of various policies to enhance the capacities of people to engage in informal work in order to meet their needs and wants. Each is here considered in turn.

Employment time reduction

For many adherents to the post-employment vision of the future of work, the current public policy thrust towards reducing employment time is strongly supported (Gorz, 1999; Hayden, 1999; Lipietz, 1995; Schor, 1996). Such a strategy is seen to not only more equally distribute employment time across the population but also improve the quality of life for the employed, balance the demands of work and family, and facilitate a more equitable division of labour between women and men in the market and households.

As Table 11.3 displays, nevertheless, various approaches can be pursued to reduce time spent in employment, ranging from individual-level voluntary decisions to legislative approaches at the collective level.

Although individual-level decisions can be found throughout the world as exemplified by the decision of people to 'downshift' (Schor, 1996), the direction of change throughout the Western world appears to be away from such individual-level voluntary decisions and towards collective-level legislative approaches. One example of such an approach is Japan's 'Lifestyle superpower' five-year plan between 1992 and 1997. Seeking a reduction in average annual work-time of 2.2 per cent per annum (from 2008 to 1800 hours over the life of the plan), from 1990 to 1997 average annual hours per employee were reduced from 2064 to 1891, an 8.4 per cent decline in seven years (Hayden, 1999: 125). By far the best-known example of such an approach, however, is the EU which has introduced working-time reduction (WTR) policies. An exemplar of such an approach is to be found in France where a collective level legislative approach has been adopted (see Case Study 11.1)

Table 11.3 Level of decision regarding work-time reduction

Type of action	Individual	Collective
Voluntary	– Agreements between individual employees and employers – Individual choice of a shorter-hours job	– Collective bargaining between labour unions and employers – Tripartite consensus among government, business and labour
Legislative	– Creation of incentives to influence individual choice – Guarantees of individual rights to reduce work time – Employment standards protections for short-hours workers	– Legislated reductions of standard working week, limits on overtime, longer vacations, etc.

Source: Hayden (1999: Table 6.1)

Case Study 11.1   Working-time reduction in France

According to Hayden (1999: 133–43), the 1997 announcement of a 35-hour plan was not the first WTR initiative in France. There is a long tradition of radical thought in France about not only WTR but the future of work in general. In 1936, Leon Blum's Popular Front government cut the basic working week from 46–48 hours to 40 hours with no loss in pay and introduced two weeks paid holiday. In 1982, moreover, François Mitterand's socialist government reduced the working week from 40 to 39 hours, as well as adding a fifth week of paid vacation. After that, WTR largely disappeared from French public policy until 1993 when it re-emerged as an option to deal with rising unemployment. A small financial incentives package, introduced by the right-of-centre parliament in 1993, was expanded in the 1996 Robien law, named after the conservative parliamentarian who sponsored this legislation that provided firms which reduced working hours and increased employment by at least 10 per cent with significant reductions in payroll taxes.

Within two years, 2000 firms had taken advantage of the Robien incentives to introduce a 35- or 32-hour week (with one in four agreements leading to a 32-hour week). Some 355,000 employees had their work hours reduced, 25,000 jobs were created and a further 17,000 lay-offs avoided. The payroll tax incentives, combined with the opportunities created to reorganize production and increase productivity, made it possible for work-time to be reduced with little or no loss in pay. Of the first 1500 Robien accords, 44 per cent led to shorter hours with no loss in pay; 18 per cent maintained pay levels but with a temporary salary freeze; and 37 per cent saw a less than proportional loss in pay. In only 1 per cent of cases did shorter hours come with a proportional loss in pay.

The Robien Law created a climate of public opinion favourable to more ambitious work-time initiatives. On June 1 1997, a Socialist-led government, in coalition with the Communist Party and the Greens, came to power in France on a platform highlighting a 35-hour workweek with no loss in pay. Despite the Socialist electoral campaign slogan of '35 hours, paid 39', the resulting Aubry law did not specify wage levels. These were left to collective bargaining. Workplaces could implement 35 hours in ways best suited to their needs. It could be spread over 4 or 5 days, with alternating 4- and 5-day weeks, or it could mean 'annualized' reductions, such as additional days off and extended vacations. In June 1999, a second law was passed announcing a 'universal' 35-hour week, with various groups exempted, such as executives. Although the current media rhetoric is of the abandonment of this WTR initiative, the reality is that it is solely additional exemptions for certain groups that are being sought.

Perhaps the next step in this debate will be to argue for a life-time cap on employment. Gorz (1985), for example, projects a future scenario where people will be engaged in work-sharing with the equivalent of no more than ten years of full-time work during their life. Reducing time spent in employment, however, is not the only change being sought in order to move towards a multi-activity society.

Citizen's income

Is the formal economy the most appropriate means of distributing income? Given that less than three-quarters of the population of working age in most advanced economies have a job and that society is heavily polarized into multiple- and no-earner households (Williams and Windebank, 1995), post-employment commentators argue that income and employment need to be disentangled, and that a guaranteed minimum income should be used to distribute income. Alternatively known as a citizen's income, social wage, social dividend, social credit, guaranteed income, citizen's wage, citizenship income, existence income or universal grant, this would provide every citizen with a basic 'wage' as a social entitlement without means test or work requirement (e.g., Fitzpatrick, 1999; Jordan et al., 2000; van Parijs, 1995, 1996a,b, 2000a,b). Eligibility would be automatic for all citizens and unconditional. There would be no tests of willingness to work.

With this minimum income guarantee in hand, individuals could then choose to improve their well-being by engaging in employment so as to earn additional money in order to purchase goods and services, or they could instead choose to invest their time in self-provisioning those goods and services or helping others. The aim is to give individuals and groups increased resources for taking charge of their own lives, further power over their way of life and living conditions. If implemented, it would no longer solely be the labour market that integrated people into society but also this scheme that would offer limited material security, esteem and identity.

The origins of the idea of citizen's income have been traced to Tom Paine, Saint-Simon, Bertrand and Dora Russell, and Major CH Douglas amongst others (Van Trier, 1995). Currently, it is advocated by economists (e.g., Atkinson, 1995, 1998; Desai, 1998), political philosophers (Van Parijs, 1995, 2000a,b) and social policy commentators (Jordan, 1998). Among the main advantages claimed for such a basic income scheme are the following:

- It is neutral between paid and unpaid work, giving better incentives for low-paid employment than tax credits, but allowing choice over how to combine the two.
- It treats men and women as equals, allowing them to negotiate how to share unpaid work in households (see McKay and Vanavery, 2000).
- It combats exploitation, by allowing individuals to survive without relying on dangerous or demeaning work.
- It promotes economic efficiency, by ensuring that low-paid work is not given a special subsidy (as in tax credits) and hence labour power is not wastefully deployed.
- It promotes social justice, by treating all individuals alike, and giving extra income only to those with special care needs.

Even amongst advocates of a basic income, however, it is now accepted that a fully individualized and unconditional basic income could not be introduced in one operation, if only because of the way in which it would upset the current distribution of incomes and labour supply. Instead, and particularly for the working-age population, the growing consensus is that one should not proceed by cohorts or by categories, but start with a very modest (partial) basic income that would not be a full substitute for existing guaranteed minimum income provisions (Desai, 1998; Jordan et al., 2000; Parker and Sutherland, 1998).

Whatever the costs of a basic income scheme, this top–down solution, although necessary, is by itself insufficient if the desire is to cultivate engagement in informal work. To achieve this, such a scheme needs to be coupled with initiatives to facilitate participation in informal work. As Gough (2000: 27) argues,

> It is not enough to pay citizens a minimum income without enabling them to participate in socially significant activities, including paid and unpaid work. Similarly, the divorce of rights from duties . . . contradicts . . . the strong link between the two . . . All persons who can, should have the right – and the duty – to contribute in some way to the common wealth.

Lipietz (1992: 99) similarly argues that a universal basic allowance 'would be acceptable only if it meant that those who received it were prepared to show their solidarity with society, which is paying them'. The crucial issue confronting citizen's income, and to borrow a 'third way' phrase, is that 'there are no rights without responsibilities'. Elson (1988: 29) puts this well,

> Alongside the right to a grant should be the duty, on the part of able-bodied adults, of undertaking some unpaid household work of caring and providing for those who are unable to take care of themselves. Persons already undertaking care of a young or sick or handicapped person would be exempt.

There is thus a groundswell of opinion that a citizen's income needs to be tied to some form of active citizenship. Atkinson (1998), for example, argues for a 'participation income' and Lipietz (1995) for a new sector engaged in socially useful activity and comprised of 10 per cent of the labour force (the unemployment rate at the time he was writing). The idea, therefore, is to tie a basic income scheme to some form of participation in society. Advocates of an unconditional basic income, however, argue against such an approach (e.g., Gorz, 1999; Jordan, 1998; Jordan and Jordan, 2000). For them, the result will be new forms of compulsion akin to workfare such as compulsory work in the third sector (e.g., Elson, 1988; Offe, 1985; Rifkin, 1996).

This, however, does not necessarily follow. It is wholly possible to create what have been variously called 'passports to participation', 'participation incomes' or forms of 'community service employment' (see Williams and Windebank, 2003a) that provide basic incomes for active citizenship in a way that avoids compulsion.

Active community service

At the core of most models for security, esteem and identity is the notion of the 'working citizen'. In this post-employment approach, what is meant by 'work' is broadened to incorporate the informal sphere. At present, the promotion of security, esteem and identity is through a model that views the 'working citizen' as somebody participating in formal employment. In this view, everything is linked to a paid job, including citizenship itself as manifested by the lack of distinction drawn between citizens' rights and workers' rights.

For post-employment commentators, however, and based upon a broader definition of work that encompasses informal work, the desire is to promote an alternative model for security, esteem and identity. In this view, the 'working citizen' is integrated through not only formal but also informal work. To see how this new model of the 'working citizen' might operate, two policy options are here considered. The first seeks to extend the 'voluntary and community sector' of the New Deal programme which has been adopted in many Western nations, so as to promote integration through active citizenship (rather than formal employment alone) and the second seeks to introduce active citizens' tax credits, again being widely implemented throughout the Western world.

Civilizing New Deal. Following the lead of the US, many advanced economies have implemented workfare-type regimes as part of a general re-orientation of labour market intervention towards active policies (see Lodemel and Trickey, 2001; Peck, 2001). These workfare programmes represent a significant departure from traditional welfare systems. People are required to work in return for social assistance payments. In contrast to previous welfare and unemployment benefit programmes in which state support was passive, unconditional and entitlement-based, these new workfare regimes are conditional, work-focused and oblige participants to be active in order to receive social payments (Campbell, 2000; Robinson, 1998). The principal critique of them is that there is a compulsion element whereby people are forced to do work that they would not otherwise wish to conduct (e.g., Peck, 2001).

The intention here is to consider a modification to New Deal that would reduce the compulsion critiques that currently blight it and at the same time unleash the unemployed from the shackles that prevent them from engaging in economic practices that they might wish to undertake but are currently prevented from carrying out. The proposal is that the 'voluntary and community' sector of the New Deal programme could be extended to allowing the unemployed to define the 'social contribution' that they wish to make. This would not only negate the workfare critiques aimed at this programme but also release the unemployed to take greater responsibility for the nature of their integration into the world of work.

Individuals could be empowered to stake a claim under the 'voluntary and community sector' of New Deal concerning their contribution to society. The precise scope of work that might be acceptable and the problems involved in deciding on the breadth of such activity are dealt with below but would certainly include caring activities and organizing community groups. Hence, somebody who was the principal carer of a young pre-school child or an elderly dependent person would have this essential work recognized under the 'community and voluntary sector' of New Deal and they would be paid an activity benefit for doing this work. Similarly, those organizing and running community groups such as LETS, time banks and credit unions would again receive an activity benefit paid at a higher rate than the zero-activity benefit level in recognition of their contribution.

An example of a similar initiative is to be found in Australia. Here, there has been some recognition that various activities are socially legitimate for those who are claiming out-of-work benefits. It has been understood, for example, that care work should be accredited. Both lone parents, and one parent in a couple, can claim a 'parenting allowance'. This is income-tested on one's own and one's partner's income, and is payable to parents with children aged up to 16 (Hirsch, 1999).

Although this policy proposal would start to conquer the workfare critiques associated with active labour market policies such as the New Deals, a key problem that this proposal fails to modify is the meaning of a 'working citizen' amongst those who are not eligible for New Deal. The likely outcome is that it would introduce a 'dual society'. Those eligible to choose the contribution that they wish to make to their communities are only those who are unemployed. The likelihood, therefore, is that the new forms of work undertaken would be seen as a second-rate and second-class 'economy' for those excluded from the formal labour market. Below, therefore, a more comprehensive proposal for facilitating a multi-activity society is explored that is more inclusive in terms of the groups who could be mobilized to renegotiate their contribution to society.

Active citizens' credits (ACC). The conventional contract between the state and out-of-work households offers income in exchange for a duty to search for employment if one is able. Only a few groups are exempted from this obligation. Engaging in parenting, for example, has not been considered acceptable. Here, however, a scheme is proposed that could not only recognize such informal work but also reward those individuals who engage in such endeavour, and thus promote a multi-activity society. This scheme is based on the notion of accrediting active citizenship. Drawing upon the ideas for citizens' service (Briscoe, 1995; Hirsch, 1999; McCormick, 1994) and a participation income (Atkinson, 1998), the intention of 'active citizens' credits' (ACC) is to record, store and reward participation in caring and other work conducted for the good of their community (Williams and Windebank, 2003a). Under this non-compulsory scheme, individuals would engage in a self-designed portfolio of work of their choosing for which they would be reimbursed.

This would be non-compulsory in that individuals could freely choose whether or not to participate. It would also allow the individuals participating in this scheme to themselves decide the portfolio of economic practices that they wish to undertake. The goals behind such a proposal are to recompense and value work which currently goes unrecognized and unvalued; to encourage active citizenship without recourse to compulsion; to harness informal work; to create a 'full-engagement' society by enabling people who wish to make a particular 'social contribution' to do so; to incorporate the multi-dimensionality of social inclusion and exclusion into policy-making; and to tackle poverty through means other than mere insertion into the formal work.

The idea that such a scheme should be developed to encourage individuals to engage in freely chosen work to benefit their community is perhaps uncontroversial. The major controversy is over how to reward people. One option is to embed this proposal within the tax credit approach that is emerging in many advanced economies (e.g., Liebman, 1998; Meadows, 1997; Millar and Hole, 1998). Just as there exist 'employment tax credits' for those working as a full-time employee, pensioner tax credits, disability and sickness tax credits, Williams and Windebank (2003a) propose 'active citizens tax credits' for those participating in caring activities and other work for the good of their community, subdivided into three further types of tax credit: parents tax credits, carers tax credits and community worker tax credits.

If adopted, a multi-activity society would be engendered by recording, storing and rewarding engagement in informal work. The result would be the creation of a society founded upon the principle of multi-activity without a radical policy overhaul.

Besides these top–down initiatives to create the conditions for participation in informal work and create a multi-activity society, adherents to this approach also advocate a whole host of bottom–up or grassroots initiatives to encourage people to engage in informal work. Many of these initiatives, such as local exchange trading schemes, time banks, hours and so forth will be discussed in some detail in Chapters 12 and 13. The details of these initiatives, therefore, are not repeated here. Instead, and for the sake of brevity, just one example not included elsewhere is here provided. This is the idea of creating what are called 'employee mutuals' to encourage people to engage in collective self-help for the good of their community (see Case Study 11.2).

Case Study 11.2   Employee mutuals

Still on the drawing board, Employee Mutuals are a new local organization that the unemployed, employed and firms can voluntarily join through the payment of a weekly subscription fee (Bentley and Mulgan, 1996; Leadbeater and Martin, 1997). Members earn points on a smartcard from work that they conduct for members of the Mutual and they can then buy goods and services from other Mutual members. As such, they are envisioned as 'new institutions for collective self-help' that match local demand for work with local supply. Their intention is, first, to allow people to undertake the many one-off jobs that need doing but that they are unable to afford to do formally and, secondly, to help employers fill vacancies and to bring together workers and businesses to meet shared needs for training.

The proponents of Employee Mutuals have argued from the outset for special welfare benefit rules to be applied to members of the Mutual. These would make it easier for members to combine income from part-time or temporary work on the Mutual with welfare benefits so as to reduce the barrier whereby people are deterred from engaging in such organizations and making the transition from welfare to work because if they do such jobs they will lose their entitlement to benefit. In return for such preferential treatment regarding their ability to work whilst claiming benefits, jobless members of a Mutual would make a token weekly contribution but would contribute at least 15 hours per week of services in kind. In return, the mutual would provide not only work but also training and childcare facilities, job searches and a job placement service, as well as job accreditation and a social life, where necessary.

The current proposal in the UK is that central government should set up a National Council for Employee Mutuals to establish a legal and regulatory framework for the new movement. Having done this, benefit rules would need to be modified for the Employee Mutual members to allow easier transfer from

---

welfare into work via part-time or temporary jobs, and tax incentives should be given to encourage individuals and organizations to join such organizations. A series of pilot schemes would be then set up to test how different variations on the Employee Mutual model would work under different circumstances, and the aim would be to create a national movement of at least 250 Employee Mutuals with half a million members. These, therefore, would be new local 'labour exchanges' for employers and employees.

Conclusions

In this chapter, those rejecting the view that formalization is the route to 'progress' have been considered. The formalization thesis is permeated by a formal/informal economy binary hierarchy that delineates the formal economy as composed of positive attributes (and the route to progress) and the informal economy as composed of negative features. The post-employment commentators considered here invert this binary hierarchy. For them, the formal economy is attributed with many negative features while the informal economy, which is seen to possess many positive features, is marked out as the route to 'progress' and development. In this post-employment vision of the future of work, in consequence, the desire is to reduce the centrality of employment and develop informal work as an alternative and/or complement to the formal realm.

What is perhaps so valuable about this perspective, therefore, is the way in which it directly refutes the formalization thesis which asserts that there is a natural and inevitable shift towards an employment-centred society. By providing a counter-narrative, it holds up a mirror that displays how the formalization thesis is just as much a prescriptive ideology about what should be the future of work as this post-employment vision. Until now, the formalization thesis has been usually taken to be descriptive of the direction of work rather than a prescriptive ideology about where it should be heading. This post-employment perspective, however, uncovers how this is far from the case and provides a lens through which the formalization thesis can be re-read as a prescriptive narrative.

It is perhaps timely, however, for those advocating the post-employment vision to be subjected to a similar type of critical evaluation. So far, this has seldom been the case. Their perception that informal economies are necessarily a better alternative to formal employment, for example, suggests a certain 'romantic aesthetic' (Leyshon, 2005) about the informal sphere. As Samers (2005) argues, however, what is perhaps required is a de-romanticization of informal work. The notions used by post-employment commentators thus need to be subjected to the same critical investigation that is currently the case with adherents to formalization. This is a major gap in the literature on the future of work. Although some case studies point to how deprived populations engage in informal work out of necessity and it is mostly routine monotonous work that is conducted, while it is only in affluent populations that such work is freely chosen, enjoyable and rewarding (see Williams, 2005a,b,c), the romanticism of informal work is seldom subject to critical investigation. It would be useful therefore if in future a more critical approach to this post-employment vision of the future of work is adopted.

For the moment, however, this must be left aside until such time as a more critical literature develops. Instead, attention here turns to those commentators who counter the second dominant narrative so far as the future of work is concerned, namely that we are living in an ever more commodified world, by positing alternative post-capitalist visions of the future of work organization.

Further reading

Beck, U. (2000) *The Brave New World of Work*, Cambridge: Polity.

This book by a prominent social scientist is a good example of the arguments used by adherents to a post-employment vision of the future of work.

Gorz, A. (1999) *Reclaiming Work: Beyond the Wage-Based Society*, Cambridge: Polity.

This is one of the seminal texts of the post-employment vision of the future of work that provides a lucid account of the rationales for such an approach.

Latouche, S. (1993) *In the Wake of Affluent Society: An Exploration of Post-Development*, London: Zed.

This book argues that 'development' is universally viewed as a process of Westernization, displays its impossibility as a global ideal and offers the reader an alternative model of society grounded in an informalization of society.

OECD (1996) (ed.) *Reconciling Economy and Society: Towards a Plural Economy*, Paris: OECD.

This edited collection provides a well-rounded range of commentaries that each depict various facets of a post-employment vision of the future of work and, in total, add up to a persuasive call for the implementation of plural economies.

12

Work organization in a post-capitalist world

Introduction

This chapter explores those perspectives towards the future of work that contest the narrative that the world is/should be pursuing a path of commodification. Unlike adherents to the commodification thesis who believe that 'there is no alternative to capitalism' (see Chapter 2), these post-capitalist visionaries seek to both imagine and enact a future of work beyond a commodified world. As Callinicos (2003: 27) puts it,

> one of the most powerful motivating forces behind the anti-capitalist movement is a rebellion against the process of commodification that has been accelerating since the neo-liberal hegemony was established . . . Informing it is a moral revulsion against the debasement produced by the reduction of everything to a commodity to be bought and sold. 'Le Monde n'est pas une marchandise!' (the world is not for sale) is one of the main slogans of the movement.

These post-capitalists therefore seek to create a multiplicity of alternative economic spaces as demonstrative acts that another future is possible beyond a commodified world.

For those adhering to the commodification thesis, these post-capitalist commentators are often perceived as 'dreamers' and 'utopians'. As shown in Chapter 4, nevertheless, discussing the inevitable and natural advent of a commodified world is just as much prescribing the future (rather than describing lived practice). There is no difference. It is just as erroneous to extrapolate from specific instances of commodification that capitalist hegemony is the inevitable future of work as it is to derive from the advent of specific non-capitalist practices that the future of work will be inevitably and immutably post-capitalist. The reality is that the future of work is not already chosen. This chapter, similar to the others in this book, therefore reports those seeking to enact a particular vision of the future of work. In this sense, post-capitalists are no different to any other commentators discussed in this book. The only difference is that whilst these post-capitalists are nearly always viewed as making normative statements, some of the other

241

visions have been so far erroneously perceived as descriptions rather than prescriptions about the future of work.

Post-capitalist visions for work organization

Although all post-capitalist visions share a desire to imagine and enact a future of work beyond a commodified world, there are many different strands of post-capitalist thought (see Callinicos, 2003; Parker et al., 2006). Here, for the sake of brevity, two broad but nevertheless overlapping streams of post-capitalist thought regarding the future of work organization are identified, namely 'anti-capitalism' and 'anarchism'.

Anti-capitalist visions of the future of work

Until now, few business and management studies texts on work organization have deemed the 'anti-capitalist movement' and their ideas worthy of consideration. Yet any review of the contrasting perspectives towards the future of work would be incomplete without discussing this large and growing global movement. Indeed, given that the anti-capitalist movement is at present probably the most prominent movement calling for a radical revision to work organization, it cannot be omitted (for reviews, see Bircham and Charlton, 2001; Brecher et al., 2000; Callinicos, 2003; Notes from Nowhere, 2004; Smith, 2001; Starr, 2001).

Although there have long been anti-capitalist visions of the future of work, what distinguishes the contemporary perspectives from earlier versions is that they no longer always seek an alternative grand narrative to replace capitalism, such as communism or socialism. Indeed, in part, this is due to the discrediting, whether rightly or wrongly, of these alternative ideologies with the collapse of the socialist bloc. Although it is highly debateable whether the 'socialist bloc' was 'state socialist', or whether it was 'state capitalism' in the sense of being a bureaucratized centrally planned type of market-orientated industrial-military capitalism, this discrediting of such alternative meta-ideologies is captured by Giddens (2002: 11) when he asserts that 'to pretend or imply that there is a known alternative to the market economy is a delusion'. Present-day anti-capitalist commentators fully agree. This is not to say, however, that there is no alternative.

Contrasting anti-capitalism perspectives

Callinicos (2003) differentiates the various forms of anti-capitalism into the following types:

> *Reactionary anti-capitalism* – this rejects the social system in the name of some earlier state of affairs;

Bourgeois anti-capitalism – seeks all the advantages of modern social conditions without the struggle and dangers that necessarily result. Argues that capitalism has become too powerful and needs to be reformed, but not overthrown;

Reformist anti-capitalism – advocates the return to a more regulated capitalism and stresses the role of the nation state as an agent of desirable social transformation. The focus is on the national and international levels as the main fields of action, rather than the local level, promoting measures such as the Tobin tax;

Localist anti-capitalism – advocates a reformed and decentralized economy to remedy the ills of contemporary capitalism;

Autonomist anti-capitalism – rejects centralized power and advocates a decentralized coalition of coalitions à la Hardt and Negri (2000).

Socialist anti-capitalism – views socialism as the alternative to capitalism, as discussed in Chapter 10 under the heading of 'classical social democratic thought' as well as in Part I when exploring those who adopt a negative stance towards a commodified world and a de-regulated global economy.

Akin to most lists of perspectives, whatever the subject under enquiry, Callinicos (2003), similar to nearly all other commentators, ends with the approach that he favours, namely socialist anti-capitalism.

What is important about such a list, however, is not which perspective is right or wrong, or best or worst, but that it highlights the diversity of perspectives that constitute this movement. As Tormey (2004) puts it, this is a 'movement of movements' comprised of a multiplicity of factions joined together only by the fact that they have a 'common enemy' (Starr, 2001). The anti-capitalism movement, therefore, is not a singular entity but a loose and decentralized network of groups, movements and organizations possessing many different views about what political tactics should be used to challenge global capitalism, as well as what should replace it.

Indeed, and as highlighted above in the list of anti-capitalist perspectives offered by Callinicos (2003), the opposition to capitalism and degree of change sought varies considerably. At one end of the spectrum are the *reformist* anti-capitalists who challenge capitalism as it currently operates. They tend to be against de-regulated global capitalism, but believe that there are ways in which capitalism can be regulated to operate in the interests of society and the environment rather than merely of big business. This often involves advocating the type of regulated capitalism found in social democratic thought that seeks to harness the productive energies of capitalism but ensure that its benefits are more equally distributed. Amongst such reformists, or what Callinicos (2003) calls the bourgeois and reformist anti-capitalist visions, one often witnesses the advocacy of proposals for legal and political frameworks that could regulate capitalism, make it more caring and more responsible (Held, 2000). Examples include those who desire the transformation of the World Bank, the International Monetary Fund (IMF) and the World Trade Organization (WTO) into institutions of global democratic governance that would guarantee minimum rights, standards of living and environmental protection globally, or those who seek to introduce fiscal policies to redistribute wealth from rich to poor countries such as the Tobin tax (see Case study 12.1) or pursue 'fair trade' initiatives.

Case Study 12.1 Association for a Taxation of Financial Transactions and for the Aid of Citizens (ATTAC)

Association for a Taxation of Financial Transactions and for the Aid of Citizens began in France in the summer of 1998 and was launched as an international movement in December 1998. By 2005, it had over 80,000 members worldwide in nearly 40 countries (see www.attac.org). Arising out of a concern that financial globalization was destroying the sovereignty of nation states and citizens' power to determine their own destiny, ATTAC promotes measures such as a taxation of international financial transactions (named the Tobin Tax, after the American economist who proposed it in 1972), sanctions on tax havens, the abolition of pension funds and their replacement by state pensions. ATTAC argues that even a Tobin Tax of 0.1 per cent would raise some £100 billion per annum, mostly from Western nations, which could be redistributed to the majority world to tackle poverty and inequality as well as promote food security and sustainable development (www.attac.org). ATTAC believes that government will not promote such changes and encourages citizens to take direct action 'to take back, together, the future of our world'. Not affiliated to any political party, ATTAC is a loose non-hierarchical network bringing together people who identify with its objectives.

Continuing along the spectrum of anti-capitalist thought and midway between these reformists and more radical perspectives discussed below are commentators such as Albert (2003) with his vision of a participatory economics, or what he calls 'parecon' for short. This envisages a future of work organization that is non-capitalist and based on solidarity, equity, diversity, and people democratically controlling their own lives, but which utilizes existing institutions. Its central institutional and organizational principles are social rather than private ownership; nested worker and consumer councils and balanced job complexes rather than corporate workplace organization; remuneration for effort and sacrifice rather than for property and power, or output; participatory planning rather than markets or central planning; and participatory self-management rather than class rule.

As one progresses along the spectrum towards the other end, however, more *radical* anti-capitalists become prominent that seek to overthrow capitalism. These visions are what Callinicos (2003) calls the 'localist' and 'autonomist' anti-capitalist perspectives. The localist anti-capitalist perspective and its vision of the future of work will be dealt with in the next chapter since this vision has positioned itself as a counter-narrative to 'globalization' (de-regulated global capitalism) even though its advocates are generally opposed to all forms of capitalism. Here, therefore, attention will be paid to the 'autonomist' anti-capitalist movement (see Case Study 12.2). Popularized in recent years by the work of Hardt and Negri (2000) in their *Empire*, the programme they promote for achieving a post-capitalist world requires, first, a new 'abstract internationalism' based on the demand for 'global citizenship', secondly, the right to a social wage and a guaranteed minimum income for everybody and, thirdly, the right to 're-appropriation' which is a diverse concept covering not only languages, communication and knowledge but also machines, and covering issues from bio-politics to the conscience.

Case Study 12.2   Autonomia

Autonomia emerged in Italy during the 1970s inspiring a new left-wing politics, namely 'autonomist Marxism'. Developing out of a critique of the reformist politics and hierarchical character of the Italian Communist Party (PCI) and trade unions, its first expression was in *operaismo* ('workerism') in the late 1960s which rather than aim to improve work conditions, believed that the 'refusal of work' was the main way of pursuing workers' independence from capital. During the 1970s, autonomia operaia ('workers' autonomy') shifted its politics away from the factory to a broader terrain that led to various, often illegal, practices, from collective 'free shopping' to the self-reduction of charges for bus fares or rents, or the squatting of Centri Social or 'social centres' (see below). The refusal of work extended into a generalized rejection of work-orientated and organized society, and the search for alternative economic spaces, that operated autonomously from the state and the capitalist political economy. For some, this meant taking politics into the cultural domain, and part of the movement centred on the development of creative or cultural projects, such as free radio stations, artists' collectives, or small independent publishers.

Whilst the use of illegal practices such as free shopping or squatting was considered a legitimate rejection of capitalist order, the Autonomist movement generally condemned violence. However, in the late 1970s, the Italian state became increasingly repressive following the kidnapping and murder of Aldo Moro (leader of the Christian Democratic Party) by the Red Brigades, and associated Autonomia with such armed groups. In 1979, therefore, Toni Negri, one of Autonomia's most famous proponents, and hundreds of other participants in Autonomia were arrested on charges of involvement with the Red Brigades. With such persecution, Autonomia was marginalized in 1980s. However, from the 1990s, there was a resurgence of this movement, aided by the publication of *Empire* (2000) by Toni Negri and Michael Hardt.

Autonomists insist on workers' autonomy from capital. Rather than seeing capitalist development as being governed by the logic of capital accumulation, in the vein of orthodox Marxism, autonomism emphasizes the role of working class struggle in shaping development. Thus, the working class is not seen as having to wait for capitalism to follow its logic towards its own eventual downfall, but is a potential agent of change that can overturn capitalism through its actions, such as the refusal of work. Autonomia also redefines the composition of the 'working class' (see Wright, 2002). According to Negri, the rise of post-Fordism and its increasing reliance on 'immaterial labour' (e.g., emotional or intellectual labour) has broadened the working class from the 'mass worker' typical of Fordist production to the 'multitude', a broad category that includes all whose labour is directly or indirectly exploited by and subjected to capitalist norms of production and reproduction. For Autonomists, in post-Fordism, capitalism relies on an increasing encroachment upon the subjectivity and lives of the multitude, and this represents its weakness for, coming back to the theme of workers' autonomy, it exposes the dependent, parasitic nature of capitalism. The more capitalism encroaches upon the lives and subjectivities of the multitude, the more dependent it becomes on the multitude, and the more possibility for resistance it opens up.

Source: Parker *et al.* (2006)

The anti-capitalism movement, therefore, is composed of a diverse range of visions ranging from those seeking to reform capitalism by seeking greater regulation of capitalist production to those seeking its overthrow and replacement. This movement of movements is united only in the sense that they have a common enemy of de-regulated capitalism. Although some believe that this movement of movements should become more united, the majority see in its disparate nature its strength, first, because it makes the movement more difficult for anyone to control, contain or attack and, secondly, because it creates the conditions in which people can decide themselves what alternative world they want to construct.

Anarchist visions of the future of work

Running parallel to (or perhaps within) the above anti-capitalist movement and existing alongside radical greens (considered in Chapter 13) are anarchist visions of the future of work. Derived from the Greek word meaning 'without rulers', anarchism views authority, especially state authority, as oppressive and socially dysfunctional, and instead pursues the principles of individual autonomy and voluntary cooperation. It is both a social philosophy and a political movement (Marshall, 1993, May, 1994; Reedy, 2002; Ward, 2004). However, and similar to the anti-capitalist movement, with whom it shares both the rejection of capitalism and the direct action tactics, there are diverse (overlapping) streams of anarchist thought (see Case Study 12.3).

Case Study 12.3   Types of anarchism

Individualist anarchism. With its origins in the work of Max Stirner who argued that the only principled form of political action was the pursuit of individual self-interest and self-realization, all institutions, authorities, organizations and belief systems are seen as oppressive because they limit individual autonomy. This individualist tradition in anarchism is expressed frequently in libertarian and right-wing anarchism.

Libertarian and right anarchism. Primarily existing in the US, and rejected as a form of anarchism by many, commentators such as Robert Nozick, Murray Rothbard and Lew Rockwell combine anti-statist liberalism (or 'minarchism') and the individualist tradition so as to reject collectivist approaches to social organization in favour of private property held by autonomous individuals who are free to exchange their property and labour through free markets. All aspects of society can be organized it is held, through individual contracting. Here, and in stark contrast to other variants of anarchism, there is no commitment to equity or worker's control of labour and production. Some might view this school as a utopian neo-liberal vision of the future of work.

Anarcho-communism. With its roots in Mikhail Bakunin, Peter Kropotkin and Emma Goldman, this popular form of anarchism seeks to abolish private property and profit-motivated monetary exchange. It envisages a future of work in which work is under the direct control of producers, and goods and services are directly exchanged or given according to desire and need. Production and society are organized through self-directed communities and organization is based on the principles of free association and individual affinity. Complex social structures derive from networks based on voluntary federation by smaller units. Modern forms of production and information technology are popularly claimed to make such federal structures and autonomous communities a viable means of organizing.

Anarcho-syndicalism. This type of anarchism seeks large-scale political change through industrial action, particularly the general strike, so as to defend the universal interests of workers and to aid the overthrow of capitalism. Inherent in this view is the idea that labour organizations based on self-governing structures represent the green-shoots out of which will emerge the direct control of production by workers.

Anarcho-feminism. With its origins in the work of Emma Goldman, this branch of radical feminism views patriarchy to be the form of oppressive authority out of which develops all others forms of oppression.

Anarcho-primitivism and green anarchism. Based on the belief that technology, urbanization, the division of labour and so forth are inherently alienating and destructive, anarcho-primitivists, such as John Zerzan, view the future as a return to the past, advocating a return to a pre-industrial (sometimes even a pre-agricultural) existence. Only small-scale non-hierarchical communities will enable human beings to live freely and ethically. Green anarchists, such as Murray Bookchin, similarly advocate smaller-scale localized communities as the only feasible way to live in harmony with the natural world (see also 'radical greens' in Chapter 13).

Religious Anarchism. Religious beliefs often lead to forms of social radicalism. Leo Tolstoy's Christian Anarchism was partly inspired by the 'communism' of the Apostolic Church and the rejection of all forms of authority other than the divine. Mahatma Gandhi was strongly influenced by Tolstoy's ideas particularly the opposition to secular authorities through non-violent mass protest.

Post-structuralist anarchism. This theoretical development seeks to take classical anarchist theory beyond its humanistic assumptions of a belief in the 'natural' goodness of humanity. Michel Foucault, Gilles Deleuze and Felix Guattari, for example, call for a diverse multiplicity of beliefs and practices, viewing any overarching system as potentially oppressive. One outcome is a shift away from traditional forms of left-wing mass action to a more local and individualistic micro-politics aimed at personal emancipation.

Source: Parker *et al.* (2006)

Having outlined these various post-capitalist visions of the future of work grounded in the interrelated anti-capitalist and anarchist movements, attention now turns towards how these visionaries seek to enact a post-capitalist society.

Enacting post-capitalist futures of work organization

For *reformist* post-capitalists, the desire is to reform the capitalist system in order to take greater account of the social and environmental costs of capitalism. In other words, the belief is that these costs should be moved onto the balance sheet. Opposed to de-regulated global capitalism, and believing that capitalism can be regulated to operate in the interests of society and the environment rather than merely big business, interventions are pursued to create a regulated capitalism by designing legal and political frameworks at both the national and the international levels to try to make it more caring and responsible to people and the environment (see, for example, the arguments by Giddens, 1998; Held, 2000).

For reformists, therefore, the intention is not to overthrow capitalism. It is to humanize or improve it. Today, multiple examples exist of such reformism. These range from campaigns to introduce regulatory controls to prevent climate change, reduce global inequalities and regulate financial markets through campaigns to intervene in animal exploitation (factory-farming, live animal exports), unfair trade (sweated labour usage in developing countries) and harmful environmental practices (loss of natural resources, pollution and climate change). For instance, reformists call for unfair trade practices to be countered with 'fair trade'. They do not call for a transcendence of over-consumption. Reflecting this, there have been a multitude of recent books such as *Fair Trade: Market-Driven Ethical Consumption* (Nicholls and Opal, 2005), displaying precisely this lack of opposition to consumer-driven society and an intent solely to reform it. In the same vein are a multitude of books on the 'ethical consumer' (see for example, Harrison *et al.*, 2005) that seek merely to reform consumption rather than question materialist over-consumption itself.

For more *radical* anti-capitalists, however, the intention is not to reform capitalism but to replace it. The objective, unlike in the past, is seldom today about replacing it with some new meta-ideology from above such as communism or socialism. Rather, very different strategies and tactics are now being pursued. To see this, first, its strategies for re-imagining the future of work will be reviewed here followed by its tactics for enacting a different future of work.

Strategies for re-imagining the future of work

For many post-capitalists, engagement in mapping the advent of an ever more hegemonic capitalism helps create what is then seen since it leads people to believe that there is no alternative or room for manoeuvre. For these commentators, therefore, there is a need to recognize, value and create non-capitalist economic practices that are already here and emerging so as to shine a light on the demonstrable construction of alternative possibilities and futures (e.g., Byrne *et al.*, 2001; Escobar, 1995; Community Economies Collective, 2001; Gibson-Graham 1995, 1996, 2003, 2006; Gibson-Graham and Ruccio, 2001; Williams, 2005a). For such post-capitalists, therefore, a discursive analysis of the commodification thesis is required coupled with the articulation of alternative regimes of representation and practice in order to imagine and enact alternative futures of work.

To deconstruct commodification or capitalist hegemony as a natural and inevitable future, two principal strategies are pursued. On the one hand, and using discourse analysis (see Derrida, 1967), this is achieved by questioning, first, the Western idea that there are objects/identities that are stable, bounded and constituted via negation and, secondly, the hierarchical nature of this binary mode of thinking whereby the first term is endowed with positivity at the expense of the other. To do this, at least three approaches are employed. One approach is to revalue the subordinate term, namely 'non-commodified practices', as witnessed in attempts to attach a value to unpaid forms of work or to seek to attach higher monetary values to such work. The problem, however, as Derrida points out, is that revaluing the subordinate term in a binary hierarchy is difficult since it also tends to be closely associated with the subordinate terms in other dualisms (e.g., non-commodified work is associated with reproduction, emotion, subjectivity, woman and the non-economic, and commodification with production, reason, objectivity, men and the economic).

Another strategy is thus to blur the boundaries between the terms, highlighting similarities on both sides of the dualism so as to undermine the solidity and fixity of identity/presence, showing how the excluded other is so embedded within the primary identity that its distinctiveness is ultimately unsustainable. For example, the household is represented as also a site of production – of various goods and services – and the factory also as a place of reproduction (see Gibson-Graham, 2003). A third and final approach is to recognize the inter-dependencies between the two sides of the dualism (commodified and non-commodified work) and how they shape and are shaped by each other in a process of mutual iteration. This is clearly shown by the fact that non-commodified work is larger and of a more creative, rewarding and non-routine character in relatively commodified households and that the existence of such non-commodified work is not only a by-product of engagement in the commodified sphere but also how participation in the commodified sphere is in part also a by-product of such engagement in the non-commodified realm (e.g., where a model railway enthusiast sets up a self-employed business). Pursuing any of these three strategies can thus challenge the hierarchical binaries that pervade contemporary thought and have until now stifled recognition of the 'other' that is non-commodified work and the recognition of alternative futures of work.

On the other hand, and alongside this Derridean challenge, post-capitalist theorists have also followed in the path of Foucault (1991) and sought to deconstruct commodification through, first, a critical analysis of the violences and injustices perpetrated by a theory or system of meaning (what it excludes, prohibits and denies); and, secondly, a genealogical analysis of the processes, continuities and discontinuities by which a discourse comes to be formed. Escobar (1995) exemplifies this approach when discussing 'development' in a Third World context. His work traces the historical production of the 'Third World' – that collection of countries whose populations came to be represented as poor, illiterate, malnourished, underemployed, requiring aid, and in need of Western models of development. The Third World was the problem for which 'development' was the solution – through the establishment of a range of institutions, practices and experts that were empowered to exercise domination in the name of the scientifically justified development project. Escobar's close reading reveals how the practice of identifying barriers to growth and prescribing development pathways has in effect violently 'subjected' individuals, regions and entire countries to the powers and agencies of the development apparatus. The subjects produced within and by this discourse are ill equipped to think outside this presumed order and truth of the economic development story and to reject a vision of the 'good society' emanating from the West. Escobar's Foucauldian approach to development discourse has opened the way towards 'unmaking' the Third World, by highlighting its constructedness and the possibility of alternative constructions. Importantly, his work points the way towards a repositioning of subjects outside a discourse that produces subservience, victimhood and economic impotence (Gibson-Graham and Ruccio, 2001). As Sachs (1992: 3) puts it, 'it is not the failure of development which has to be feared, but its success'. Indeed, for Esteva (2001: 7) the majority world has been

> transmogrified into an inverted mirror of others' reality: a mirror that belittles them and sends them off to the end of the queue, a mirror that defines their identity, which is really that of a heterogeneous and diverse majority, simply in terms of a homogenizing and narrow minority.

Similar to Escobar, Gibson-Graham (1996, 2006) also attempt to re-read economic development but in relation to Western economies. For her/them (i.e., they are two authors writing as one) and, adopting a similar Foucauldian approach, the commodification thesis is seen to produce a regime of representation that constructs identities and which symbolizes, manages and creates the place of people and nations. To cartographically represent commodification is thus to locate and chart the configurations of power in the world. With Western commodification, both the referent and the context, the plural economies of other nations have been deemed to have a problem of backwardness that needs to be resolved. Using commodification as a benchmark of 'development' and 'progress' and measuring countries against it, a linear and uni-dimensional trajectory of economic development is imposed that represents non-Western nations as backward and traditional, and positions those at the front with a closed future of ever greater commodification (see Massey, 2005). This, for them, is a representation of reality and discursive construction that reflects the power, and serves the interests, of capital. By representing the future as a natural and inevitable shift towards commodification, one is engaged in the active constitution of economic possibility, shaping and constraining the actions of economic agents and policy-makers. As Byrne et al. (2001: 3) put it,

> To re-read a landscape we have always read as capitalist, to read it as a landscape of difference, populated by various capitalist and noncapitalist economic practices and institutions – that is a difficult task. It requires us to contend not only with our colonized imaginations, but with our beliefs about politics, understandings of power, conceptions of economy, and structures of desire.

By re-visioning the economic landscape of the minority world Western countries as composed of a plurality of economic practices – both commodified and non-commodified – the implications are twofold. First, it suggests that out there in the world are other economic practices besides the commodified realm. Secondly, by locating non-commodified practices as existing in the here and now, one is engaged in the demonstrable construction and practice of alternatives to capitalism. Unlike some on the left who still seek a complete system that could overthrow capitalism and provide a replacement, here, what is being considered by these theorists are the multiplicity of ways of leaving, abandoning the market or becoming and practising non-capitalist activities. By representing non-capitalist economic activities as existing and emerging and as therefore possible, the act of making such activities visible enables the constitution of alternatives to capitalism. This re-reading of Western economies is not simply about bringing minority practices to light. It is about opening up the Western economies to re-signification.

For some, nevertheless, it might be asserted that pinpointing such alternative economic practices only reveals a series of disjointed and dispersed economic practices that represent no real challenge to capitalism. How, for example, can the presence of mundane and routine subsistence work possibly represent a challenge to the grandeur of capitalism? Byrne *et al.* (2001: 16), however, do not feel that this is the case:

> We can view the household as hopelessly local, atomized, a set of disarticulated and isolated units, entwined and ensnared in capitalism's global order, incapable of serving as a site of class politics and radical social transformation. Or we can avoid conflating the micro logical with the merely local and recognize that the household is everywhere; and while it is related in various ways to capitalist exploitation, it is not simply consumed or negated by it. Understanding the household as a site of economic activity, one in which people negotiate and change their relations of exploitation and distribution in response to a wide variety of influences, may help to free us from the gloom that descends when a vision of socialist innovation is consigned to the wholesale transformation of the 'capitalist' totality.

To view the market in this light is to de-centre capitalism from its position at the heart of the Western world and to bring to the fore the possibility of alternative economic practices and futures beyond the hegemony of the commodified realm. The intention here, therefore, is to destabilize the market as a presumed or inherently hegemonic system, questioning its naturalized dominance by representing it as one of many forms of economic practice.

For many commentators, recognizing non-capitalist economic practices was simply the first step in the process. Their view, perhaps somewhat naively, is that this is something that has been already achieved, not least by the feminist movement. Based on this, the emphasis has been on trying to move forward the discussion by constructing alternative means of livelihood through which these non-capitalist economic practices might be cultivated (rather than merely recognized). The importance of this contemporary post-capitalist perspective, grounded in post-structuralism, is that it perhaps explains the reasons for the lack of success in gaining acceptance of a perspective of economic plurality and initiatives to foster non-commodified work. It reveals how revaluing non-commodified work and envisaging futures beyond commodification directly challenges not simply core beliefs about the contemporary mode of economic organization and the future of work but also capitalism itself.

Tactics for enacting post-capitalism

The contemporary post-capitalism movement differs from previous similar movements not only in terms of how it re-envisions capitalism but also in terms of the type of politics it practices. Official oppositional politics is replaced by 'unofficial' movements and groups, operating mainly outside the mainstream political process of parties, elections and parliaments, who pursue direct involvement and actions such as mass protests, sit-ins, disruptions, the creation of alternative medias and various forms of grass-roots action. It is, to repeat, a movement of movements, apparently disorganized but with a capacity to coordinate the voices and activities of a myriad of different groups into a global dialogue, meaning that many small marginal groups become not only visible but also linked. To take just one example, the Zapatistas' demands for Mayan rights to access common land (De Angelis, 2000) have resonated with the struggles of many other oppressed groups throughout the world.

Here, therefore, rather than use the terms 'anti-capitalist', anti-globalization' or 'anti-corporate', which all seek only to define this movement by what it is against and obfuscate the more positive and constructive visions that this movement has regarding the future of work organization, the term 'post-capitalist' has been employed. As others have put it (e.g., Bircham and Charlton, 2001; Brecher *et al.*, 2000; Callinicos, 2003; Notes from Nowhere, 2004; Smith, 2001; Starr, 2001), this movement that gives itself no name, has no leaders but whose leaders lead by obeying, no blueprint but only dreams of possible futures, no common ideology but a desire for change can be fairly well defined in terms of its tactics and how they have evolved (see Case Study 12.4). If it became widely accepted that free market capitalism was the 'only game in town' with the dismantling of the Berlin Wall on 9 November 1989, it took barely ten years for a new type of opposition to it to become visible, marked by the 'anti-capitalist' demonstration in Seattle on 30 November 1999 when the World Trade Organization (WTO) gathered to launch a new round of trade talks. The 'Battle of Seattle' represented a significant turning point. The consensus since the collapse of the Berlin Wall, namely that capitalism had won and was the only feasible and possible future, was for the first time in the post-socialist era opposed. Further protests quickly followed in Washington (16 April 2000 and 20 January 2001), Millau (30 June 2000), Melbourne (11 September 2000), Prague (26 September 2000), Seoul (10 October 2000), Nice (6–7 December 2000), Quebec City (20–21 April 2001), Gothenburg (14–16 June 2001) followed by Genoa (20–21 July 2001).

Case Study 12.4   The evolution of the anti-globalization movement

'Mahatma Gandhi offers us some signposts for our journey in his summary of the Indian independence struggle: "First, they ignore you. Then they laugh at you.

Then they fight you. Then you win." We can follow the path of the anti-capitalist struggle using these signposts from 1994 to the present.

First they ignore you. Between 1994 and 1999 we were largely invisible. As far as the powerful were concerned, there was no opposition to capitalism, no alternative to the "free" market. . . .

Then they laugh at you. 1999 was the summer of corporate love, when the dot-com bubble was at its height and business forecasters, with stunning hubris, were predicting that from here on the stockmarket would simply continue to go up – forever. Not coincidentally, this was the summer the anti-capitalist movement emerged as a global event, when an earthy, rambunctious carnival against capital interrupted trading in the City of London. The contagion spread with the Seattle WTO shutdown later that year . . . "A Noah's ark of flat-earth advocates, protectionist trade unions, and yuppies looking for their 1960s fix" jibed Thomas Friedman . . . The *Wall Street Journal* jeered at the "Global Village idiots . . . bringing their bibs and bottles".

By the time of the World Bank protests in Prague in September 2000, the laughing was sounding forced. *The Economist's* editorial was shrill, making its "case for globalization" with the picture of a poor African child – purportedly a future beneficiary of globalization – on its front cover. They were sounding less sure of themselves as they insisted that economic globalization is the "best of many possible futures for the world economy".

Then they fight you. The confrontations got worse . . . Genoa saw the most brutal suppression of the movement in the global north to date, when they shot Carlo Giuliani dead . . .

. . . Six weeks after the Genoa protests, the first of a five-part series of full-page articles appeared in the UK edition of the *Financial Times* under the title "Capitalism Under Siege: Globalization's Children Strike Back". It claimed: "Just over a decade after the fall of the Berlin wall . . . there is a growing sense that global capitalism is once again fighting to win its argument". Hours after the paper hit the newsstands, Islamist terrorists attacked New York and Washington . . . Pundits who were five years late in noticing our emergence were now eager to be the first to proclaim us dead. The editor of *The Guardian* wrote "Since September 11, there is no appetite for anti-capitalism, no interest, and the issues that were all-consuming a few months ago seem irrelevant now". The FT series was pulled.

. . . rumours of the movement's death were greatly exaggerated. Even in New York City itself, a few months after 11 September, 20,000 protested against the World Economic Forum . . . Simultaneously in Porto Alegre, Brazil, over 60,000 – six times more than the previous year – met for the World social forum under the optimistic slogan "Another World is Possible". . . . That March in Barcelona, half a million people taking part in protests against the European Union summit showed they understood the new reality they faced after Genoa.

What Genoa and 11 September marked, in fact, was the end of the first, emergent stage of the movement. . . .

Then you win. . . . The second stage of the movement will be harder than the first. It's a stage of working closer to home, a stage where mass action on the streets is balanced (but not entirely replaced) with creating alternatives to capitalism in our neighbourhoods, our towns and cities.

. . . yet returning to our neighbourhoods, we must not fetishize the local, retreat into sub-cultural ghettos, nor forget that we are the world's first grass-roots-led global political project. We must not undo the global ties that bind us together in a world-wide network.

. . . The anti-capitalist movement is the most sustained recent attempt to reinvent the notion of revolution into a constantly evolving process rather than the triumph of an ideology . . . We are not creating a new ideology to impose from above, to "replace" capitalism . . . Rather than seeking a map to tomorrow, we are developing our own journeys, individually and collectively, as we travel.

. . . What is needed is not for more people to become activists, but for the everyday fabric of society to become engaged . . . We are everywhere? We're not . . . but we could be. And if we're going to be, then we have to acknowledge what a scary thought that really is: for once "we" are everywhere, then there will be nothing to define ourselves against, and so "we" will be nowhere. If we really want to make the world a better place then that's what we have to want . . . For when "we" are truly everywhere, we will be nowhere – for we will be everyone.'

Source: Notes from Nowhere, 2004: 499–511

This, therefore, is not a revolution in the traditional sense of an overthrow but rather a revolution of a thousand cuts whereby each initiative does its own little bit to undermine the solidity and presence of capitalism as an overarching force and to display that there are alternative non-capitalist practices available to deliver goods and services. It is a 'war of the swarm' that has no central leadership or command structure, is multi-headed and thus impossible to decapitate. Although some post-capitalist socialists such as Callinicos (2003) liken this to 'desertion' in the sense that it does nothing to address the enormous concentration of productive resources in the hands of capitalism and states allied to them and argues that such initiatives are always 'subject to the permanent danger of incorporation' (Callinicos, 2003: 94), today, localized action represents the tidal force underpinning post-capitalist tactics (see Gibson-Graham, 2006).

Here, therefore, just a few of the multitude of different ways of seeking a release from capitalism, or at least developing complementary alternative means of livelihood, are briefly reviewed. All of these initiatives seek to create 'not-for-profit zones' of economic practice. A first example is the social centres initiative in Italy, currently popular amongst autonomous anti-capitalists as a means of providing an alternative to capitalism (see Case Study 12.5).

Case Study 12.5 Italian *centri sociali* ('social centres')

In the 1970s in Italy, traditional public spaces and meeting places such as open squares, workplaces, party offices or the premises of groups involved in the anti-capitalist movement were disappearing. In the 1980s and 1990s, groups began to organize on a non-hierarchical basis the renovation of private- and public-owned empty properties to turn them into spaces open to the general public in the form of self-managed Social Centres (i.e., squatted properties which became the venue for social and political events). To do this, collective action in the form of cooperative working is used.

Regarded as laboratories of cultural innovation and political subversion, centri sociali ('social centres') spread across Italian urban areas during the 1990s, attracting many young people seeking to escape from both traditional employment and the Italian nuclear family to live collectively, by squatting in abandoned buildings such as warehouses, factories or schools, and surviving on precarious jobs, the 'expropriation' of food from supermarkets and restaurants, and the self-reduction of bus fares, concert or cinema tickets. In sum, these social centres provide self-managed alternative economic spaces, autonomous from the state and market, for social, cultural, political and economic experimentation.

Besides these social centres, many others types of alternative economic space are being established as complements and/or alternatives to capitalism (for a review, see Leyshon *et al.*, 2003; Parker *et al.*, 2006). Here, and to display the type of initiatives being pursued, attention focuses on just one of the more popular non-capitalist economic experiments taking place in not only Western but also transition and Third World nations over the past decade or so, namely the development of local currencies.

Towards non-capitalist work practices: the local currency experiments

The local currency movement and its experiments with creating alternative currencies is what Starr (2001) terms a 'relocalization' movement or what Leyshon and Lee (2003: 16) view as 'day-to-day experiments in performing the economy otherwise'. The creation of local money occurs when people in a locality decide to form a local association and to create a medium of exchange through which goods and services can be provided. The perception is often that there are many people in an area with needs and many who wish to provide goods and services, but what prevents this demand and supply coming together is a lack of money. They thus decide to create their own local currency in order that people can trade goods and services with each other and meet local needs.

Unlike conventional bartering (in which two actors trade directly with one another), local currencies connect a wider network of people together. Some local currency schemes have printed money whereas others operate through virtual currency that exists only in computerized accounts. Local currency systems also differ according to whether they are based on the labour time required to produce such services or goods, or whether they are based on the value of the services or goods provided. Whatever form they take, however, local currencies represent tools for rebuilding local economies because they keep wealth within the community rather than allow it to flow out (Bowring, 1998; Meeker-Lowry, 1996). By creating closed economies in that the local currency cannot be used outside the area, they prevent money from leaking out of the local area (Williams, 1996a). They also promote the trading of goods and services whereas national money often restricts exchange because of its scarcity. Ideologically, local currencies promote principles of egalitarianism, ecology and sustenance through independence from the capitalist economy (Lee, 1996; Solomon, 1996), decreasing the environmental externalities of long-distance transportation and trade (Hawken, 1994; Milani, 2000).

Three principle types of local currency experiment currently exist, namely Local Exchange and Trading Schemes (LETS), time banks and hours. Here, each is briefly considered in turn.

Local Exchange and Trading Schemes (LETS). This is the most popular and widespread form of local currency experiment. A LETS occurs where a group of people form an association and create a local unit of exchange. Members then list their offers of, and requests for, goods and services in a directory that they exchange-priced in a local unit of currency. Individuals decide what they want to trade, who they want to trade with, and how much trade they wish to engage in. The price is agreed between the buyer and the seller. The association keeps a record of the transactions by means of a system of cheques written in the local LETS units. Every time a transaction is made, these cheques are sent to the treasurer who works in a similar manner to a bank sending out regular statements of account to the members. No actual cash is issued since all transactions are by cheque and no interest is charged or paid. The level of LETS units exchanged is thus entirely dependent upon the extent of trading undertaken. Neither does one need to earn money before one can spend it. Credit is freely available and interest-free.

The first LETS was established in 1983 in the Comox Valley in British Columbia by Michael Linton, an unemployed computer programmer. This initiative came to prominence when he ran a workshop at The Other Economic Summit (TOES) in England in the mid-1980s. Participants in this workshop then took back the idea to their own countries where they implemented schemes and the idea diffused. By 2000, there were over 2000 communities in Europe, Canada, Australia, New Zealand, Asia and Africa that had established LETS (Cohen-Mitchell, 2000). An online LETS directory contains information on 1500 LETS in 29 countries (Taris, 2004). Although in some countries such as the UK, the popularity of LETS probably peaked at the turn of the millennium, in many other countries the development of LETS is still catching on and rapidly growing.

Research conducted on LETS includes case studies of individual LETS in the UK (Caldwell, 2000; North, 1998, 2005; O'Doherty *et al.*, 1999; Pacione, 1997; Seyfang, 1997; Williams, 1996a,b,d,e,f), Australia (Jackson, 1997), Germany (Schroeder, 2002, 2006) and Mexico (Lopezllera-Mendez and DeMeulenaere 2000). Case studies of multiple operations in the UK (Lee, 1996; Thorne, 1996; Williams *et al.*, 2001a,b), Australia (Ingleby, 1998), New Zealand (Williams, 1996c) and Norway (Gran, 1998) have also been conducted. In 1995, Williams (1996a,c) administered a postal survey to coordinators of all UK LETS as well as Australian and New Zealand schemes (Williams, 1997). In 1999, Williams *et al.* (2001a,b) repeated this survey of coordinators as well as conducting a survey of participants in the UK. The finding was that in the UK in 1999, the 303 LETS had some 22,000 members and an average turnover equivalent to £4664. LETS members are predominantly aged 30–49, women, from relatively low-income groups and either not employed or self-employed. Just 2 per cent join explicitly to gain access to formal employment and these are all people seeking to promote or gain business so as to become self-employed. The rest join either for ideological reasons such as to promote alternatives to capitalism (23 per cent) or to seek alternative or complementary means of livelihood for themselves (75 per cent).

Time banks. The Time Dollar network started in Miami, Florida, in 1983 by law professor Edgar Cahn (Cahn, 2000; Cahn and Rowe, 1996; Jacobson *et al.*, 2000). The idea is that everybody has talents and can contribute their time to become 'co-producers' rather than mere consumers of social welfare initiatives. Some time dollar schemes are very much welfare initiatives run by voluntary associations. Others have the appearance of LETS or hours schemes in that they are very much alternative economies favoured by alternative people (counter-cultural greens and anti-capitalists). They are egalitarian in their design in that each hour of service earns the same credits as any other, regardless of the skills involved. Computerized accounts keep track of member credits and debits. The Time Dollar Network's online directory lists 53 time dollar operations in the US (Time Dollar Institute, 2005; see also www.timedollar.org). Cahn inspired the founding of time banks in the UK in 1998, and the US version has recently been also renamed 'Time Banks US'. Time Banks UK in 2005 had 70 active time banks and 70 in development (Time Banks UK, 2005). Studies of the UK have been provided (Seyfang, 2002; Seyfang and Smith, 2002) and display that time banks have overtaken LETS as the fastest growing type of local currency scheme, at least in the UK. In part, this may be due to their more egalitarian pricing of services. In other part, however, it is due to support from the UK government for such schemes. While LETS participants were often vehemently opposed to such schemes being co-opted by the state and their institutionalization such as for active welfare purposes, and they deliberately marketed themselves as alternative 'economic' systems, time banks have positioned themselves as 'welfare' rather than 'economic' vehicles and there has been greater willingness amongst their founders to present themselves as third sector welfare mechanisms that provide a civil society complement to private and public sector welfare provision.

Hours systems. The success and growth of LETS in the late 1980s inspired community activist Paul Glover to establish a printed local currency in Ithaca, New York, in 1991 (see Glover, 2000; www.ithacahours.org). Ithaca hours, unlike LETS and time banks, is a paper currency whose value is linked to the US dollar. Each 'one hour' Ithaca bill is equivalent to $10 because this was the approximate average hourly wage in the area at the time the system started. The notes come in six denominations ranging from one-tenth Hour ($1) to two hours ($20) to facilitate a variety of transaction types. Participants perceive the value in terms of dollars rather than labour time expended. Since its foundation, over $105,000 (10,500 hours) have been issued and thousands of participants (including 4000 businesses) have exchanged the currency. The directory ('Hour Town') has over 1000 listings of available and sought-after goods and services. Jacob *et al.* (2004a,b) find that the average user is well educated, has a preference for green politics and experience in social activism. Many are self-employed and the average user has only a modest income (60.5 per cent of respondents earned less than $30,000 per annum). The average participant spends 35 hours ($350) and spends 30 hours ($300) per year.

Collom (2005) identifies 82 similar hour systems in the US. These are mostly located in populations with lower household incomes, higher poverty and unemployment rates, and larger self-employment sectors, as well as in areas with younger populations, higher educational attainment and fewer married people and less residential stability.

Today, these local currency activists are networked into a global movement through Internet discussion groups (see, for example, www.le.ac.uk/ulmc/ijccr). Although there is a widespread consensus within the local currency movement that these schemes are 'alternatives to capitalism', and many participants would align themselves with the anti-capitalist movement (perhaps with the exception of some members of time banks), these vehicles are also of appeal to many others from a variety of political backgrounds not necessarily adhering to post-capitalism. As such, there has been some conflict about opening up these alternative monetary spaces to a wider range of participants. Although these demonstrative experiments have a transformative aspect for those engaged in them in that they reveal to participants that exchange does not always have to be profit-motivated, many instigating these schemes have a well-founded fear about expanding them in case they are both co-opted by the state and watered down in terms of their anti-capitalist objectives.

Conclusions

It is often assumed by adherents to the commodification thesis that they are being pragmatic, while others telling alternative stories about the future of work are mere 'dreamers' and 'utopians'. However, once it is realized that narratives of a natural and inevitable trajectory towards a commodified world are just as much prescribing a future, rather than describing lived practice, as those arguing that the world is not becoming more commodified, then discourses that display how another world is possible move more centre-stage to become possibilities rather than fairy tales. As was clearly displayed in Chapter 4, no clear evidence exists that capitalism is penetrating deeper and wider across the globe. Rather, different processes appear to be taking place in varying populations. Therefore, to extrapolate from those crevices of economic life where there is a growing hegemony of capitalism and to intimate this as the future of work is just as narrow minded as extrapolating from the advent of non-capitalist practices that the future of work will be inevitably and immutably post-capitalist. The reality is that the future of work organization is multiple and divergent in different places. It is more open than these narratives suggest. It is not already chosen.

This chapter has thus reviewed just some of the post-capitalist visions for work organization of those who reject the commodification thesis. Although in the past this rejection was based on an understanding of the largely negative consequences of a commodified world, recent decades have seen a positive stance taken by those asserting post-capitalist visions in recognizing that this is itself a liberatory project that opens up the future to the enactment and imaging of alternatives. Here, therefore, the contrasting visions of post-capitalist futures for work by both anti-capitalist and anarchist thinkers have been reviewed along with the prominent contemporary strategies and tactics being employed in order to implement this vision of the future of work. It is not just the opposition to capitalism, however, that has resulted in this enacting and imagining of alternative futures for work beyond a commodified world.

Further reading

Callinicos, A. (2003) *An Anti-Capitalist Manifesto*, Cambridge: Polity Press.

This reviews the development of the anti-capitalist movement, distinguishes the various factions within it and explores the strategic dilemmas facing it.

Escobar, A. (1995) *Encountering Development: The Making and Unmaking of the Third World*, Princeton, NJ: Princeton University Press.

This seminal text deconstructs the discourse of 'development' in the majority (Third) world by highlighting its constructedness and in doing so raises the possibility of alternative futures of work beyond this dominant 'development' discourse.

Gibson-Graham, J.K. (2006) *Post-Capitalist Politics*, Minneapolis: University of Minnesota Press.

This book seeks to re-imagine capitalist society by bringing to the fore the host of alternatives in the present so as to demonstrate that there is an alternative to a hegemonic capitalism.

Notes from Nowhere (2003) *We are Everywhere: The Irresistible Rise of Global Anticapitalism*, London: Verso (www.WeAreEverywhere.org).

This book provides the reader with a wealth of case studies of the anti-globalization movement so as to display the multitude of ways in which this movement is enacting a post-capitalist future of work and organization.

13

Green visions of work organization

Introduction

In previous chapters, those visions of the future of work have been explored that contest the dominant narratives of formalization and commodification with counter-narratives which argue that the world is not, or should not be, pursuing the paths of formalization and/or commodification. In this chapter, 'green' or 'environmentalist' visions of the future of work are reviewed. The stronger versions of these green perspectives on the future of work represent one of the main perspectives contesting the meta-narrative of globalization. Others also contesting this globalization narrative include, first, the so-called 'anti-globalization movement' explored in the last chapter since this movement is more correctly seen as opposed to capitalism in its totality rather than purely neo-liberal globalization and, secondly, those social democratic visions considered in Chapter 5 which argue how there is/should be greater state intervention to limit neo-liberal globalization. When taken together, these cover the major streams of thought that contest the view that the future is inevitably one of globalization.

In order to detail those green perspectives that contest the narrative of globalization, this chapter will reveal that it is important to distinguish radical from reformist green visions of the future of work. Until now, in much of the business and management studies literature when discussing 'green' visions of the future of work, it has been reformist ('environmental-lite') perspectives, or what others call 'shallow environmentalism' or 'weak sustainability', that have predominated. Discussions have tended to revolve around how capitalism needs to be reformed, such as by seeking greater corporate responsibility with regard to environmental matters. The outcome is that the future of work is envisaged largely as business-as-usual, with a little tinkering at the margins to include environmental costs on the balance sheet.

This whole raft of promoting environmental corporate responsibility in the business and management literature, however, is grounded in a particular view of what I here call the 'environmental paradox'. For nearly all green commentators, that is, there is an inconsistency between what is demanded of the earth and what the earth is capable of supplying (see Cahill, 2001; Cahill and Fitzpatrick, 2001; Fitzpatrick and Cahill, 2002; Goodin, 1992; Williams and Millington, 2004). For those recognizing this and thus devoting themselves to considering how 'sustainable development' can be achieved, either a reduction in human demands on the earth is required or an increase in resources so that this gap can be bridged. Indeed, it is this process of gradually conjoining demands and resources – the infinite and finite aspects of human life – that variously defines what is meant by the process of sustainable development.

How, therefore, can demands and resources be made to conjoin? It is this question, or more precisely the answers given, that produce the contrasting green visions of the future of work (and views of sustainable development). This is because the question of how to conjoin demands and resources can be answered in several ways. The first broad way (sometimes known as 'weak sustainability' or 'shallow environmentalism') is to argue that humankind needs to expand the stock of resources. This can be done by developing renewable resources, creating substitutes for non-renewable resources, making more effective use of existing resources and/or by searching for technological solutions to environmental problems such as resource depletion and pollution.

A second way of answering the question (known as 'strong sustainability' or 'deep ecology') is to argue that the demands humankind make on the earth need to be revised so that, for instance, we consume less. In this view, in consequence, rather than adapt the earth to suit ourselves, we adapt ourselves to meet the finitude of nature. A third way ('moderate sustainability') combines elements of these two core approaches. It seeks to both expand the stock of resources and reduce demands on this stock in order to conjoin resources and demands. It is apparent, therefore, that a continuum of environmental thought exists with, at the one end, reformist commentators seeking to alter the resource side of the equation and, at the other end, radical greens focusing upon changing the demand-side. Here, and for the sake of simplicity, these two core schools of green thought are reviewed, always recognizing that this is in reality a spectrum of thought rather than an either/or dualism.

Reformist green visions of the future of work

For green reformists, sometimes termed 'weak sustainability' or 'shallow environmentalism', there is no need to transform either the predominant Western narrative on nature or the existing dominant discourse concerning what constitutes economic 'progress' and 'development'. Nature is predominantly seen as a resource to which we have a right of dominion and there is a belief that economic growth is a valid measure of 'progress' and objective to pursue in the future (O'Riordan, 1996).

Reformist greens, that is, adopt an anthropocentric (human-centred) discourse on the relationship between people and nature. This is composed of three strands: the perception that people are separate from nature; the idea that nature is a 'resource' to be used for people's benefit and the view that humankind has the right to dominate nature. Taken together, these three strands represent what might be considered a Judaeo-Christian conceptualization of the connection between people and nature. As Genesis (chapter 1, verse 28) states, 'be fruitful and multiply and replenish the earth and subdue it; and have dominion over the fish of the sea, and over the fowl of the air and over every living thing that moveth upon the earth'. Although of course this is open to various interpretations, the dominant Judaeo-Christian reading has been that human beings are separate from nature and that nature is a resource to be exploited by and for people. It reads humankind as the sole source of value and nature merely as a raw material to be manipulated for our purposes. Reformist greens do not contest this dominant set of beliefs about the relationship between humankind and nature. Instead, the intention is to understand nature so that it can be manipulated, controlled and managed for the benefit of humankind.

At the heart of this reformist green vision of the future of work, moreover, is an implicit optimism. There is a confidence that people will be able to find a solution to environmental problems. They will be able to enhance the stock of 'resources'. Technological progress, it is assumed, will enable people to manipulate the earth to meet the insatiable demands of humankind. Any problems will thus be solved through technological development (e.g., Thurow, 2000). There is an acceptance, therefore, that the trajectory of economic development and people's demands do not need to change and an optimism about the aptitude of humankind to solve resource depletion problems. Faith is placed in scientific and technological expertise. The scientists in their white lab coats will solve the environmental paradox by manipulating the resource stock to meet our demands (e.g., Naisbitt et al., 2001).

As stated above, however, green thought is a spectrum of ideas, not an either/or dualism. In practice, therefore, there is a gradation of thought amongst reformist greens. Although all reformist greens believe that there is no need to rethink what is meant by progress and economic development, a spectrum of stances prevail that to differing degrees seek concessions towards environmental protection. Although some merely seek to clear up the ill-effects of undiluted capitalism using our creativity, for others the logic of prevention rather than cure is adopted. Initiatives advocated include the provision of environmental management agencies, more efficient use of resources, better project appraisal techniques to assess the environmental impacts of proposals and economic adjustments to take into account environmental costs. All such reformist green initiatives, however, are embedded in a belief that economic growth and resource exploitation can continue, but that what is required is a better accommodation of environmental issues, with the extent to which they are accommodated varying to different degrees depending on where they are on the continuum of reformist green thought.

Indeed, two increasingly popular green reformist stances are, first, that it is possible to improve the efficiency of economic growth so that it uses fewer natural resources and, secondly, that economic growth can continue but there is a need to redistribute the costs and benefits in a more equitable manner. The first idea is sometimes referred to as 'ecological modernization' (e.g., Christoff, 1996; Dryzek, 1997; Hajer, 1995; Mol,

1999; Mol and Sommerfield, 2000; Roberts, 2005). As Banerjee (2003: 170) summarizes, 'the scientific rationality of ecological modernization constructs a global discourse of environmental problems to which the only solution is for society to "modernise itself out of the environmental crisis" by increased investments in new "environmentally friendly" technologies'. The second stance that economic growth can continue but there is a need to redistribute the costs and benefits more equally on either an intra- or an inter-generational level has become known as 'environmental justice' in the US and 'just sustainability' in the UK (Ageyman and Evans, 2004).

Common to all these popular reformist green visions, nevertheless, are the core tenets of weak sustainability. A human-centred worldview is adopted, there is an emphasis on a growth-oriented approach to economic development, a relative lack of consideration is given to the need for radical change in people's demands on the earth and inherent in such a vision is a view of nature as merely a collection of natural resources that can be subdued by humans.

A further example of such a reformist green vision regarding the future of work is found in the current Corporate Social Responsibility (CSR) approach towards environmental matters (e.g., Hopkins, 2003; Monbiot, 2002; Waddock and Bodwell, 2002). Here, discussions revolve around how capitalism needs to be reformed by business moving environmental costs onto the balance sheet. On the whole, this CSR approach is based on the notion that companies can regulate their own behaviour and in doing so hope to persuade governments that there is no need for compulsory measures of regulatory control (Newton and Harte, 1997; Monbiot, 2002).

Another instance of a reformist green approach is 'green consumerism' which intimates that environmental problems can be resolved if individuals change their shopping habits and buy environmentally sound products, rather than consume less. As Plant and Plant (1991: 7) assert, however, green consuming does not deal with issues such as economic growth on a finite planet, the power of TNCs or the structure of society,

> because the commodity spectacle is so all-engaging, 'light' green business tends to merely perpetuate the colonization of the mind, sapping our visions of an alternative and giving the idea that our salvation can be gained through shopping rather than through social struggle and transformation. In this respect, green business at worst is a danger and a trap.

'Fair trade' represents yet another example. This is the idea that consumers in the minority world of the Western nations should organize to promote more equitable trade relationships with producers in the majority world (see James, 2000). Fair trade, however, seeks not system transformation but rather changes in the development of fair micro-relationships among a series of market actors starting with the immediate producers through an alternative distribution system to the socially aware consumer. As Banerjee (2003: 165) points out, however, 'Arguments that question the sustainability of current economic systems are rarely found in the literature'.

Although there are doubtless some in the business world who honestly and faithfully adhere to the values of green reformism and seek to construct a future of work organization that pays some attention to the need for conservation of natural resources, a stream of literature in recent years has begun to highlight how many apparent advocates of shallow environmentalism are not always concerned environmentalists (Beder, 2000, 2002; Lubbers, 2002). As Case Study 13.1 highlights, there has emerged an accusation that many business interests are engaged in what is called 'greenwashing'.

Case Study 13.1   Greenwashing

'Greenwash', according to the 10th edition of the Concise Oxford Dictionary published in 1999, is a noun meaning 'disinformation disseminated by an organization so as to present an environmentally responsible public image' (cited in Rowell, 2002: 19). As Rowell (2002) argues, however, its meaning has now expanded. Rather than solely image making, it now also involves more comprehensive manoeuvring to co-opt the environmental movement.

In the edited collection entitled *Battling Big Business: Countering Greenwash, Infiltration and Other Forms of Corporate Bullying*, Lubbers (2002: 11) shows 'the counter-strategies which . . . industries are using against their critics: rebranding themselves as environmentally friendly; co-opting their critics; forming front groups which masquerade as citizens' organizations, lobbying behind the scenes of governments and international agencies; suing their critics for libel; and employing private security firms to spy on, even infiltrate, the opposition'. Beder (2002), similarly, in her book *Global Spin: The Corporate Assault on Environmentalism*, details the many ways in which a corporation wishing to oppose environmental regulations, or support an environmentally damaging development, do so. Besides openly doing so in its own name, Beder (2002) argues that they often adopt more effective means by having a group of citizens or experts (and sometimes a coalition of such groups) promoting the outcomes desired by the corporation whilst claiming to represent the public interests. When such groups do not already exist, she argues that corporations often pay a public relations firm to create such 'front groups'.

According to Beder (2002), this use of front groups to represent industry interests in the name of concerned citizens is a relatively recent phenomenon. She cites, for example, the Global Climate Coalition, a coalition of 50 US trade associations and private companies representing oil, gas, coal, automobile and chemical interests, who fight restrictions on greenhouse gas emissions; the Information Council on the Environment, which is a coal industry front group who publish information that global warming will not happen; the Alliance for Responsible CFC Policy, representing chemical companies, who argue that the substitution of hydrochlorofluourocarbons (HCFCs) for chloroflourocarbons (CFCs) is not in the public interest because of the costs; the Coalition for Sensible Regulation, a coalition of developers and corporate farmers in the West; and the Alliance for Sensible

Environmental Reform, which represents polluting industries. These alleged front groups all portray themselves as moderate and representing the middle ground, using words like 'reasonable', 'sensible' and 'sound', which implicitly positions environmental groups as extremists.

Besides this engagement of corporate interests in 'greenwashing', such as by using front groups to portray themselves as coinciding with a greater public interest, it is important to recognize how public relations firms also help businesses gain support to facilitate business-as-usual for their clients. As the Institute of Propaganda Analysis identifies, rather than engage in debate, two basic propaganda techniques are often used, 'name-calling' and 'glittering generalities' to belittle more radical green visions (Delwich, 1995; Fleming, 1995; Lee and Lee, 1995). 'Name-calling' involves labelling an idea or group of people so that others reject them or treat them negatively, without putting forward evidence in support. For example, labelling radical greens as 'eco-terrorists' or using negatively charged words such as 'coercion', 'waste' or 'radical' to describe their ideas all aim to win support for reformist visions. A classic name-calling device used is to call people NIMBY's – Not in My Back Yard – thereby labelling them as self-interested, or to describe them as 'Going BANANA' – Build Absolutely Nothing Anywhere Near Anything (see Gismondi et al., 1996). Such labels seek to harm the reputation and therefore effectiveness of those not adhering to the reformist stance. 'Glittering generalities', meanwhile, involve the use of vague, abstract, positive terms such as 'common sense', 'commitment', 'democracy' and 'scientific' to win approval for something without recourse to evidence. It is the reverse of name-calling. For example, it might identify the market with 'freedom of choice' and polluting activities with 'job creation', and the right to build a polluting industry with 'democracy'.

Reformist green visions seeking 'business-as-usual', therefore, do not on the whole contest globalization. Indeed, they are often supportive of constructing a de-regulated world in which businesses can seamlessly move across borders without recourse to regulation. To find green views that contest the globalization thesis, therefore, one has to turn to the more radical green visions regarding the future of work.

Radical green visions of the future of work

Unlike commentators on the 'weaker' side of the spectrum of green thought who focus on the resource-side of the equation when seeking to conjoin resources and demands, those on the 'stronger' side emphasize how the demand-side needs to change. These radical green visions view the earth as finite and assert that no habitable future is possible unless humankind rethinks, first, its attitude towards nature and, secondly, its conceptualization of economic 'progress' and 'development' (e.g., Capra and Spretnak, 1985; Dobson, 1993; Ekins and Max-Neef, 1992; Fodor, 1999; Goldsmith et al., 1995; Henderson, 1999; Hoogendijk, 1993; Mander and Goldsmith, 1996; McBurney, 1990;

Robertson, 1998; Roseland, 1998; Trainer, 1996; Warburton, 1998; Wright, 1997). For these analysts, the 'weaker' versions of sustainable development are much more about 'sustaining development' rather than sustaining nature.

Here, in consequence, a very different view of the relationship between people and nature is adopted. The objective is to again protect natural ecosystems but not simply for the pleasure of people as is so often the case in anthropocentrism. Instead, the argument is that nature has biotic rights (e.g., Capra and Spretnak, 1985; Devall, 1990; Devall and Sessions, 1985; Naess, 1986, 1989; Skolimowski, 1981). Nature is seen to have a right to remain unmolested that does not require justification in human terms. Just as there are inalienable 'human rights' that require no justification, these theorists assert that nature has similar rights that do not need to be justified in terms of their benefits to humankind. The problem for these radical greens, or 'ecocentrists' (O'Riordan, 1996), is that these biotic rights are not currently being respected. Writers such as Zimmerman (1987: 22) thus call for 'the elimination of the anthropocentric world view that portrays humanity itself as the source of all value and that depicts nature solely as raw material for human purposes'. Anthropocentrism, in other words, is replaced by bio-centric egalitarianism, by which is meant inter-species equity that recognizes non-human or biotic rights (Eckersley, 1992).

Grounded in this ecocentric philosophy, a very different view is adopted of what is meant by economic 'progress' and 'development'. For these radical greens, the passing of socialism is not to be mourned. The old quarrels between neo-liberals and socialists were simply over the best way of boosting productivism and realizing greater materialism for the majority of people. The advent of New Labour's third way (see Chapter 10) is argued to continue in the same vein, merely introducing a further alternative to de-regulated capitalism now that socialism is dead. For these greens, the differences between these approaches are differences that make no difference. They disagree with both of these objectives and thus place themselves outside this left-to-right spectrum of political thought.

For them, the pursuit of greater materialism and enhanced productivism displays how what were originally means to an end have become ends in themselves (e.g., Capra and Spretnak, 1985; Dobson, 1993; Mander and Goldsmith, 1996; Robertson, 1991). For example, the acquisition of material goods was originally a means to achieving the end of well-being. Today, they argue, such a means has become an end in itself (e.g., Dobson, 1993; Mander and Goldsmith, 1996; Robertson, 1981, 1985, 1991). For them, there is a need to redefine 'wealth' as 'well-being' rather than the acquisition of material goods. In so doing, they mirror Aristotle's critique of moneymaking (chrematistics). Aristotle viewed the point of economic activity as enabling people to live well, which involved having sufficient time to develop friendships, pursue the arts and participate in political deliberation. For this to be achieved, production was to be directed towards use-values, and it was necessary to have some notion of sufficiency with regard to material consumption. He saw economic activity directed towards moneymaking as pathological, as mistaking for the ends (see Sayer, 2001). Aristotle, of course, could not have envisaged that what for him was an aberration was to become a system imperative.

In order to achieve such 'well-being' for humans and non-humans, these radical greens thus assert that there is a need to reconsider, first, the relationship between people and nature and, secondly, flowing from this, the direction of economy and society (e.g., Devall, 1990; Eckersley, 1992; Goodin, 1992). For them, the common strategy advocated is a small-scale decentralized way of life based upon greater self-reliance so as to create a social and economic system less destructive towards nature (e.g., Douthwaite, 1996; Ekins and Max-Neef, 1992; Gass, 1996; Goldsmith *et al.*, 1995; Henderson, 1999; Lipietz, 1995; Mander and Goldsmith, 1996; McBurney, 1990; Morehouse, 1997; Robertson, 1985; Roseland, 1998; Trainer, 1996). To achieve this, the now established concept of 'thinking globally and acting locally' is the key. Global problems such as the destruction of nature can only be overcome by acting in a local manner (e.g., Hines, 2000; Mander and Goldsmith, 1996). Take, for example, their view of the economy and economic progress. Rather than pursue the end of economic growth through outward-looking strategies that seeks to meet the needs and desires of others living outside their area, their vision of the future of work organization is to pursue inward-looking approaches focused upon meeting local basic needs (rather than external desires) through the pursuit of self-reliance (e.g., Ekins and Max-Neef, 1992; Robertson, 1985, 1991; Morehouse, 1997).

From the viewpoint of this perspective, formal employment has a tendency to promote open economies. Informal economic activities, meanwhile, are seen to be more in keeping with their desire for inward-looking strategies and their objective of sustainable development (e.g., Henderson, 1999; Mander and Goldsmith, 1996; Warburton, 1998). Therefore, the development of informal work resonates with their desire for a more localized self-reliant form of economic development. As Robertson (1981) puts it, developing informal work is essential to the creation of a 'saner, more humane and ecological' (SHE) future rather than a 'hyper-expansionist' (HE) future. For radical greens, the development of informal work is thus a means of bringing about more self-reliant sustainable economies (e.g., Henderson, 1999; Mander and Goldsmith, 1996; Warburton, 1998). There is consequently a large body of green political thought that seeks to recognize and foster economic pluralism in order to achieve sustainable economic development (e.g., Brown, 2001; Dobson, 1993; Ekins and Max-Neef, 1992; Fodor, 1999; Goldsmith *et al.*, 1995; Hawken, 1994; Henderson, 1978, 1999; Hoogendijk, 1993; Mander and Goldsmith, 1996; McBurney, 1990; Robertson, 1991; Roseland, 1998; Trainer, 1996; Warburton, 1998; Wright, 1997).

This is often interpreted outside of this approach as a desire to return to some pre-industrial past based on self-sufficiency. Importantly, however, these ecologists do not seek for everything to be produced locally, nor do they seek an end to trade. They simply seek to forge a better balance between producing for local, regional, national and international markets (Douthwaite, 1996; Porritt, 1996). They also seek to gain greater control over what is produced, where, when and how, so localities are less dependent upon the foibles of the global economic system for their future well-being. In other words, they seek self-reliance, not self-sufficiency. Far from reducing living standards, moreover, it is argued to make economic sense for a locality to increase its net income and thus wealth, environmental sense to reduce unnecessary degradation and resource consumption, and social and political sense to consider more directly meeting the needs and wants of citizens. For them, the promotion of informal work is central and essential to achieving such goals.

From this viewpoint, finding a formal job in order to earn money so as to pay somebody else on a formal basis to provide a good or service is not the only way of meeting needs and desires. There are also more direct routes. A new balance between employment on the one hand, and informal activities on the other, is thus sought in the form of a 'mixed economy'. However, this mixed or plural economy is not advocated solely in the realm of welfare provision as in the third way approach that calls for 'mixed economies of welfare' (see Chapter 10). Instead, it is also applied to the organization of working time. For these analysts, there is a need to develop a more pluralistic mixed economy in the form of the public (state), private (market) and informal (non-market work) economic spheres that it believes can live harmoniously together.

Until now, as stated, few business and management studies curricula move beyond the light-green CSR approach when considering environmental issues to consider such radical green visions of the future of work. However, Valerie Fournier in a contribution to the edited volume, *Manifestos for the Business School of Tomorrow*, has begun to think through some of the implications of introducing deeper green ideas into the Business School curriculum (see Case Study 13.2). What this brings to light is that even if one rejects such a radical green vision of the future of work organization, introducing such an approach to Business School students remains important because it allows them to realize the common assumptions being made in mainstream approaches.

Case Study 13.2   Introducing deep green thought into Business School curricula: some implications

'The idea of degrowth or "decroissance" could be useful to denounce the tyranny of growth, and provoke debate about alternatives. Despite the social and environmental damage that growth causes, no political or economic leader is prepared to abandon the holy grail of permanent economic growth; and Business Schools have not been any more imaginative or forthcoming in their search for alternatives. "Sustainable growth" is about as radical as it gets: growth all the same, but with a social and environmental conscience, so a bit of "Business Ethics" and maybe "Green management" thrown into MBA curricula. Rather than unquestioningly carrying on taking growth as the obvious end of it all, Business Schools could use the notion of degrowth to engage in debates about the consequences, costs, value of growth, and about viable alternatives. Instead of researching and teaching "growth strategies", Business Schools could explore strategies for "degrowth": what would be the impact of producing less? How would/should the impact of degrowth be distributed? What could we produce less of? If people's livelihood can no longer (only) rely on producing and selling more McDonalds, cars or cheap holidays, how else can societies, communities, individuals provide for themselves? Exploring strategies for degrowth may encourage rethinking economic relations outside "the market" or at least the commodity market. For example, this may involve looking at unwaged work. Whilst the only form of work in sight in the organization and HRM literature is "waged employment", feminist critiques, among others, have shown that there is a whole sector of the economy that functions on unwaged labour; this includes not only domestic work but also self-employment, cooperative membership, free family labour, and the various help and exchange networks people have created in their communities. Shouldn't Business Schools have something to say about these other forms of work? Shouldn't they open students' imagination of work beyond the unlikely prospect of a lucrative career in the city, or the more likely prospect of a job in a call centre? Coupled with degrowth would also have to be explorations into non-consumption, non-buying behaviour, non-market exchange, or at least non-monetary market exchange'.

(Fournier, 2005: 202)

Before turning to how this radical green vision of the future of work seeks to enact localization, it is important to state that different variants of this approach exist. One prominent sub-school of thought that has received some attention in recent years is 'eco-feminism' (see Case Study 13.3). Although many further sub-schools could be distinguished such as social ecologists, socialist ecologists and spiritual ecologists to name but a few, for the purpose of this chapter, which is to explore different visions of the future of work, it is unnecessary. All such sub-schools adopt broadly the same perspective towards the future of work, seeking localization and greater self-reliance.

Case Study 13.3 Eco-feminist visions

Rooted in the core values of deep ecology, eco-feminism perhaps goes deeper than deep ecology in arguing that it is not human-centredness (anthropocentrism) that causes environmental problems but rather male-centredness (androcentrism). For eco-feminists, in other words, a link is made between men's domination of nature and men's domination of women, arguing that the master–slave role that marks man's association with nature is reiterated in man's relationship with women (Daly, 1979; Easlie, 1981; King, 1983; Merchant, 1980, 1996). Merchant (1996: 76) sums up ecofeminism in the following manner:

The ancient identity of nature as nurturing mother, who provides for the needs of mankind in an ordered, planned universe, links women's history with the history of the environment and ecological change . . . but another opposing image of nature as female was also prevalent: wild and uncontrollable nature that could render violence, storms, droughts and general chaos. Both were identified with the female sex and were projections of human perceptions onto the external world. The metaphor of the earth as nurturing mother gradually vanished as a dominant image as the scientific revolution proceeded to mechanize and to rationalize the world view. The second image, nature as disorder, called forth an important modern idea, that of power over nature.

Primavesi (2000), similarly, grounds her ecofeminism in a binary hierarchical ordering of the world that validates certain violent interactions between men and women and between them and their material environments. As she argues, 'One of the strongest most enduring hierarchical distinctions made by men has been that between them and women/nature. This has been paralleled by an identification of women with Nature, which has led historically to a personification of "nature" as female, and to images of it as maternal, nurturing, fruitful, passive and virginal, images bolstered by metaphorical clusters around seed, womb, fertility and barreness which imply an active partner, man' (Primavesi, 2000: 131). For Primavesi (2000: 133), therefore, there is 'a perception of nature/earth, women/body as material, irrational, passive, dependent and immanent, needing to be subordinated to and dominated by culture, man, reason and spirit which are rational, active, independent and transcendent'.

Enacting radical green visions of the future of work

Given the evidence in Chapter 5 that globalization is by no means a natural and inevitable tendency, but is a direction of development promoted by those with a powerful vested interest in a de-regulated global economic order, it is perhaps interesting to reflect how those seeking globalization are nevertheless often viewed as describing an organic and immutable future of work (rather than prescribing the future that they wish to see) whilst those advocating localization are frequently cast as dreamers and utopians. This reflects the current dominance of the neo-liberal ideology in which globalization provides the framework for their dream of a de-regulated global order. Localization, meanwhile, is more often than not cast in a negative manner as a form of primitivism that is seeking to return citizens to some previous pre-capitalist golden age. As Seabrook (2003: 117) caricatures it,

> In a globalizing world self-reliance has become an object of scorn. Any country or region which considers disengagement from globalization is accused of being backward-looking,

yearning for a vanished past. Self-reliance leads to "autarchy". You cannot cut yourself off from the world. At best inefficient and bureaucratic, it leads in the end to the genocidal madness of Pol Pot or the ideological tomb of North Korea. Starvation and misery are the fate of those on whom it is practised, regimes which know what the people want better than the people themselves.

However, and as Hines (2000: x) states, localization 'is not trying to put the clock back . . . It is not against trade, it just wants trade where possible to be local. The shorter the gap between producer and consumer, the better the chance for the latter to control the former'. This is similarly reinforced by Pettifor and Greenhill (2003: 214) when they assert that 'localization' means 'keeping production and consumption within an appropriate area, such as a country or sub-region; or it could mean promoting trade and investment within and between regions, in order to ensure fairer competition and reduce transport costs while maintaining some of the advantages of scale'.

If those neo-liberals advocating globalization pursue their goal of a seamless and borderless de-regulated world economy by seeking to strip away regulations and state intervention wherever it is to be found so as to achieve their nirvana, what do these radical greens advocate in order to achieve their localist vision of the future of work organization? One key starting point for all of these commentators is that a sufficiency (rather than efficiency) perspective should be adopted and that initiatives that facilitate localization (rather than globalization) should be pursued. As Hines (2000: viii) puts it,

> Everything that could be produced within a nation or region should be. Long-distance trade is then reduced to supplying what could not come from within one country or geographical grouping of countries. This would allow an increase in local control of the economy and the potential for it being shared out more fairly, locally. Technology and information would be encouraged to flow, when and where they could strengthen local economies. Under these circumstances, beggar-thy-neighbour globalization gives way to the potentially more cooperative better-your-neighbour localization.

What initiatives are pursued, therefore, in order for this to be achieved? Here, just a few of the many different policy initiatives that seek to imagine and enact localization are reviewed. There are many more than can be covered here. Nevertheless, the initiatives that follow at least give a taste of the wide range of different types of measure being used by these radical greens in order to enact a green vision of the future of work organization. As will now be shown, these initiatives range from the creation of whole communities in order to implement a localist vision of the future of work to piecemeal initiatives that focus upon localizing some particular aspect of economic production.

To commence, an exemplar of a whole community being established to pursue a green localist vision of the future of work is provided. Often drawn upon in radical green thought to depict what is possible, the Auroville community in southern India seeks to develop a self-reliant sustainable economy as a demonstration of the feasibility of localization (see Case Study 13.4).

Case Study 13.4   Auroville, Southern India

Auroville, founded in 1968 in the South of India, is an emergent community whose purpose is to 'realise human unity' and promote sustainable development (www.auroville.org). In 2005, it had some 1800 residents from 35 countries. Based on the vision of Sri Aurobindo and Mirra Alfassa to create a community where people of all countries can live in peace and harmony, Auroville represents a place of spiritual realization, not bound by any religious dogma. It aims to be a place where spiritual needs have precedence over the pursuit of material enjoyments; where work becomes a means of expressing oneself and serving the community rather than a way of gaining one's livelihood; where the community provides for every resident's subsistence; where human relations are based on co-operation and solidarity rather than competition.

Auroville is designed for 50,000 citizens, a number that would enable the production of all goods and services to meet the needs of the community. Its architectural design is based on different zones for different activities: a green belt designed for agricultural and leisure activities; an industrial zone including small arts, crafts and manufacturing businesses meant to cover the needs of the city; a residential zone; a cultural zone providing arts and science education and research (e.g., Auroville has a Research Centre in Appropriate Technology); an international zone with houses for each nation acting as embassies of different cultures; and finally the Matrimandir, a 100-foot high elliptical sphere with surrounding gardens and walkways representing the physical and spiritual centre of Auroville.

Auroville is both a vision of an ideal place and a living experiment in which residents actively try to create the social, economic and organizational conditions for spiritual development and 'human unity'.

Auroville, however, is not the only example of whole communities being formed to implement a localist vision of the future of work. Indeed, Auroville is one community in a network of communities termed the Global Ecovillage Network (GEN) that seeks to promote the idea of ecovillages (see Case Study 13.5).

Case Study 13.5   Ecovillages

Ecovillages are human-scale settlements in which human activities are integrated into the natural world in a way that is supportive of healthy human development and can be successfully continued into the indefinite future (http://gen.ecovillage.org). Although many alternative definitions exist, all make at least reference to three central dimensions underpinning ecovillages:

- a social dimension: ecovillages are seen as communities in which people feel supported by and responsible to those around them. To this end, they should be small enough to enable members to know each other and to fully participate in community life decisions;
- an ecological dimension that involves creating lifestyles that have a low impact on the environment. In practice, this often points towards community self-reliance in food and energy; and
- a spiritual and cultural dimension. Whilst not all ecovillages have an explicit spiritual dimension, they are supportive of spiritual practices and diversity, and they encourage cultural enrichment and artistic expression.

Ecovillages are based on a critique and rejection of global capitalism and its pursuit of economic growth. As such, ecovillages view themselves quite clearly as part of the anti-globalization movement and move towards localization. Indeed, they are represented in the European and World Social Forum. They provide, it is contended, a living example of a sustainable alternative to global capitalism. Indeed, in 1998, ecovillages were named among the United Nations' list of 100 best practices for sustainable living.

The ecovillage movement, nevertheless, is still in its nascent stages and only began to become more organized from 1991 onwards when various sustainable communities met and created the Global Ecovillage Network (GEN). The network includes a wide variety of settlements, from well-established communities, such as Findhorn in Scotland, Crystal Waters in Australia, eco-towns like Auroville in South India, urban rejuvenation projects like Christiania in Copenhagen, to many smaller communities. In practice, ecovillages vary enormously in terms of size, location, composition and activities. Most include between 50 and 500 members (Jackson, 2004) and are experimenting with a variety of social and ecological practices such as consensus decision-making, inter-generational care, alternative economic models, ecological building techniques, permaculture, renewable energy systems and alternative modes of education and social welfare.

To communities in the global South, the idea of ecovillages offers an alternative developmental path to neo-liberal 'structural adjustment' policies promoted by the IMF and the World Bank. For example, the Senegalese government has embraced the ecovillage idea as a key part of its strategic development policy (Jackson, 2004). Finally, whilst the word 'ecovillage' may suggest a rural setting, ecovillages have also developed in cities where they have focused, for example, on ecological 'retrofitting of buildings', energy saving, the creation of social networks or the establishment of Community Supported Agriculture projects with local farmers (Jackson, 2004).

Besides these experiments to create whole communities in order to pursue localization, there are a host of much smaller-scale communities that attempt to also implement such visions. Given that radical greens adhere to the 'small is beautiful' (Schumacher, 1973) paradigm, it is important here to also highlight some of the smaller-scale communities also pursuing a localist vision of the future of work organization so as not to fall into the trap of 'big is beautiful'. Case Study 13.6 describes the Karuna Falls community on North Island in New Zealand whilst Case Study 13.7 provides a brief overview of the Cricklegrass communal organic farm this time on South Island again in New Zealand.

Case Study 13.6   Karuna Falls, New Zealand

Established as a rural commune at the head of a valley on the Coromandel Peninsula at Waikawau Bay on North Island in New Zealand in 1976, the Karuna Falls community describes itself as an ecovillage. Food is grown organically and the community expresses a commitment to permaculture (see Case Study 13.8). It is composed of some 20 adults who live in their own homes and share ownership of the valley. It is now a national centre for the dissemination of permaculture. Its 20 members are long-standing residents.

The aim is to integrate low impact horticulture, agriculture and lifestyle, and members are committed to conserve the land whilst gaining sustenance from it. Some 700 acres of the land is a dedicated reserve and the remaining 50 acres support the community with homes, nut and fruit orchards, gardens and paddocks and they grow much of their own food. Membership involves a NZ$3000 fee, which buys the right to build a house. It is possible to 'sell' one's house to another member but not at a market price and this has only happened twice in 25 years. Communal buildings include a central community building and workshops (see Sargisson and Sergent 2004: 123).

Case Study 13.7   Cricklegrass communal organic farm, New Zealand

Founded in 1973, in Oxford on South Island, New Zealand, there are five adults living on this farm, which is owned by Heartwood Trust. Their aim is to pursue an ecologically sustainable organic communal lifestyle. On this rural farm of 40 acres, there are high levels of communal commitment and energy. The farm generates a small income that is reinvested. Current members are all aged in their twenties and in 2001 none had been a member for more than three years. The farmland is mixed arable and pastoral. Buildings include a range of sheds, grain stores and pigsties, complete with pigs. Gardens include vegetable plots, herb gardens and a nursery. Members live together communally in the large farmhouse with courtyard garden. Each has their own bedroom within the house but share other space, including the kitchen, office, living room, bathrooms and television room. Day-to-day life is interactive and collective. They live communally, eat together and work together on the farm. Members pay a low cash rent and also a 'sweat rent', which involves a commitment to work for four hours a week on the property. Most exceed this commitment. Commitment and energy are high and members work hard for the community. Income from the farm generates their rent and small income, most of which is re-invested back into the farm (Sargisson and Sergeant, 2004).

Not all localization initiatives, however, are purely related to the development of sustainable communities. Localization is also pursued via a whole host of additional initiatives that range from projects to improve local multiplier effects by pursuing strategies to prevent the leakage of money out of local economies such as campaigns to 'buy local', encourage local ownership and pursue import substitution (Shuman, 1998; Williams, 1997), through initiatives to encourage local production and consumption such as community supported agriculture, box schemes, permaculture (see Case Study 13.8) and local currencies (see Chapter 12), to individual-level initiatives such as the pursuit of 'voluntary simplicity' (Elgin, 1993).

Case Study 13.8   Permaculture

Permaculture, a contraction of *perma*nent and agri*culture*, and a phrase coined by Bill Mollison (Mollison, 1979, 1991, 1992), is a holistic approach to organic farming involving the careful design of living space and relationships (see www.permaculture.org.uk; www.permaculture.co.uk). It offers a practical blueprint for food production, building design and economic and social relationships as well as an implicit ethical code. It is about designing sustainable ecological human habitats and food production systems that are self-sustaining. Permaculture privileges household and community self-reliance in food, but recognizes that this can only be achieved by considering the economic and social systems within which production takes place: 'Self-reliance in food is meaningless unless people have access to land, information, and financial resources. So in recent years it has come to encompass appropriate legal and financial strategies, including strategies for land access, business structures, and regional self-financing. This way it is a whole human system' (Mollison, 1991: vii).

Permaculture has a strong ethical foundation articulated in terms of three principles: care of the earth, meaning that humankind has no more right to survive than any other species; care of people, meaning that everybody should have access to the resources necessary to their existence; and fair share, meaning only those natural resources necessary to cover basic needs are used. This involves setting limits to consumption to preserve ecosystems and not deprive others (including future generations) of necessary resources, as well as redistributing surpluses to those under-supplied (Whitefield, 2000: 6).

In practice, permaculture has been associated with the localization of production and consumption as this limits transport and the use of fossil fuel, as well as providing the necessary conditions for the conservation of nature and minimizing the impact of human actions (see Bell, 1992).

For radical greens, therefore, there is a shared vision of the good life and by enacting these initiatives they are attempting to demonstrate that this is realizable now. Indeed, for some such as Seabrook (2004: 236–7), 'In the culture of globalism, every act of humanity, every effort to answer need locally, every shared gesture, every pooling of resources, every act of giving out of the generosity of the unsubdued spirit is a form of resistance.' Although this imagining and enacting of a more localized world is primarily pursued through bottom–up initiatives, as discussed above, there is also sometimes a focus on top–down initiatives to construct this more localized organization of work.

There is some interest displayed, that is, in both the construction of an alternative system of global governance and the de-globalization of national economies by re-orientating them from an outward- to an inward-looking orientation (Bello, 2004; Hines, 2000). This is mostly manifested in the provision of support to broader campaigns that will facilitate the implementation of this vision of a localized world. Throughout the green movement, for example, there is widespread support for the 'work-time reduction' (WTR) policies discussed in Chapter 11. As Hayden (1999: 32) explains,

> the links between work time and an environmental agenda are not all that obvious to many people. In general terms WTR can be a key component in enabling people to 'live more lightly on the earth' by working less, consuming less, and living more. More specifically, WTR connects to an ecological vision in four principal ways. First, it is a central element in an ecologically sound response to unemployment. Second, shorter work hours can form the core of a new, non-material vision of progress by providing a green way to benefit from economic and technological advances. Third, WTR can provide people with the time necessary to participate in the creation of an ecologically sustainable and more equitable society. Finally, an enhanced ability to choose shorter work hours would open up new opportunities for a more 'simple' or 'frugal' way of living, based on a lower quantity of consumption and a higher quality of life – and such choice would contribute over time to the subversion of consumer society.

From this viewpoint, therefore, the pursuit of WTR reduces unemployment and redistributes the employment available opening the way to a more ecologically sustainable lifestyle. It also facilitates a shift in the balance between formal and informal work, the latter being seen as more in keeping with the development of a localized sustainable economy due to its resonance with self-reliance. As Torgerson (2001: 475) puts it, 'there is no questioning of the way the formal economy has become dis-embedded, populated by abstract, anonymous actors. To focus on the informal economy, in contrast, means throwing into question dramatically the prevailing horizon of possibility and promoting more concrete and personal forms of human interaction' which is seen to be more in keeping with the development of sustainable economies.

Conclusions

Having explored in the previous two chapters visions of the future of work that contest the dominant narratives of formalization and commodification with counter-narratives that extol post-employment and post-capitalist visions of the future of work, this chapter has presented one of the main bodies of literature contesting the meta-narrative of globalization, namely green visions of the future of work. The other perspectives contesting globalization have been elsewhere discussed, with the so-called 'anti-globalization movement' explored in the last chapter as part of the post-capitalist literature since they are more correctly seen as opposed to capitalism as a whole rather than purely neo-liberal globalization, and the social democratic vision of the future of work that argues how there is/should be greater state intervention to limit neo-liberal globalization considered in Chapter 5. Taken together, these cover the major streams of thought that contest globalization.

When examining whether and how green perspectives towards the future of work contest globalization, this chapter has highlighted that it is important to distinguish between its reformist and radical variants. Until now, in much of the business and management studies literature, the incorporation of green thought has tended to be largely limited to what I have here called 'environmental-lite' literature, or what others have called shallow environmentalism or weak sustainability, in that discussions have tended to revolve around reforming capitalism, such as by asserting that there is a need for corporate responsibility with regard to environmental matters. As such, the future of work organization is largely business-as-usual, albeit with a little tinkering at the margins to partially include environmental costs on the balance sheet.

As shown, however, this environmental-lite approach is grounded in a particular view of the 'environmental paradox'. For green commentators, that is, there is an inconsistency between what is demanded of the earth and what the earth is capable of supplying. For those recognizing this, either a reduction in human demands on the earth is required or an increase in the resources so that this gap can be bridged.

These environmental-lite commentators believe that demands and resources can be conjoined through an expansion of the stock of resources by developing renewable resources, creating substitutes for non-renewable ones, making more effective use of existing resources and/or by searching for technological solutions to problems such as resource depletion and pollution.

Another way of responding to this environmental paradox, however, argued by radical greens, or what have elsewhere been called deep ecology, ecocentric or strong sustainability commentators, is to assert that the demands made on the earth need to be reduced, such as by consuming less. In this view, in consequence, rather than adapt the earth to suit humankind, humankind adapts to meet the finitude of nature. A third way ('moderate sustainability') combines elements of these two core approaches. In this chapter, particular attention has been paid to radical green thought that has not so far had much of an airing in the business and management studies literature. This reveals how this approach pursues localization, and initiatives supported that imagine and enact such a vision of the future of work organization.

In consequence, just as neo-liberals advocate the pursuit of globalization to achieve their goal of a seamless and borderless de-regulated world economy by seeking to strip away regulations and state intervention wherever they are found so as to achieve their nirvana, these deep greens advocate the pursuit of localization in order to achieve their goal of a vision of work organization that is more in tune with ecologically sustainable development. Akin to many other perspectives towards the future of work discussed in this book, therefore, this approach again sets out a dualism (in this case the globalization/localization dichotomy) and here inverts the conventional binary hierarchy that in this case endows globalization with positive attributes and localization with negative connotations. For these analysts, it is localization that is full of positive attributes and globalization packed full of largely negative features. Its consequent argument, which directly contests the dominant narrative, is that there is a need to move from globalization to localization if 'progress' is to be achieved. As such, and as outlined at the very start of this chapter, this radical green vision of the future of work is a direct counter-narrative to the globalization thesis that so dominates discourse in the present day.

What is so valuable about this perspective, therefore, is that it directly refutes the globalization thesis, which asserts that there is a natural and inevitable shift towards a de-regulated and seamless world economy. By providing a counter-narrative, it not only holds up a mirror that displays how the globalization thesis is just as much a prescriptive ideology as this localization thesis, but also reveals that what one figures as the trajectory of development depends on where one looks. Just as there are examples that can be drawn upon as evidence of a process of globalization, there are similarly just as many examples of localization. It just depends on how one looks and where one looks (and why one looks). Although in some populations, places, sectors and occupations, there might be a trajectory towards de-regulated globalization, there are many instances of other populations, places, sectors and occupations in which the trajectory is towards localization.

Until now, however, these alternatives have been defined as small-scale, marginal, peripheral, even superfluous initiatives of minor consequence. Yet as Chapter 5 displayed, the apparently omnipresent and universal shift towards a de-regulated global economy is far from ubiquitous or even evident. It appears, in consequence, that the future is not already chosen. There are choices available and the future of work is far more open than so far considered. This applies not just to formalization and commodification but also to the notion of globalization.

Further reading

Douthwaite, R. (1996) *Short Circuit: Strengthening Local Economies for Security in an Unstable World*, Dartington: Green Books.

This sets out the justifications for pursuing localized economies as an alternative to a global economy along with an in-depth analysis of various methods, including local currencies, for implementing localization.

Hines, C. (2000) *Localization: A Global Manifesto*, London: Earthscan.

This book is one of the most comprehensive expositions of a localization perspective towards work that sets out both the rationales and the strategies to be pursued.

Henderson, H. (1999) *Beyond Globalisation: Shaping a Sustainable Global Economy*, London: Kumarian Press.

This text provides a classic exposition of the localization perspective towards work and a critique of the globalization approach.

Mander, J. and Goldsmith, E. (1996) (eds) *The Case Against the Global Economy: And for a Turn Toward the Local*, San Francisco: Sierra Club.

This edited collection provides the reader with the environmental case for replacing globalization with a localized approach to economic development.

14

Conclusions: futures of work

This final chapter synthesizes the previous chapters to draw together the arguments of the book. Throughout this book, it has been revealed that despite there being many diverse perspectives towards the future of work, a similar storyline is often adopted. First, a narrative is constructed in which most, if not all, economic activity is marshalled into one side or the other of some dichotomy which is deemed crucial for understanding the future of work (e.g., Fordist and post-Fordist work practices, bureaucratic and post-bureaucratic work organizations; informal and formal work; non-commodified and commodified work). Secondly, and having crammed economic life into this dualism, the two sides are then ordered into a temporal sequence whereby one dualistic opposite is depicted as universally replacing the other. The resultant portrait is nearly always that a one-dimensional linear trajectory is portrayed towards some '-ation' (e.g., formalization, globalization, commodification), '-ism' (e.g., post-industrialism, informationalism) or 'post-something-or-other' (e.g., post-capitalism, post-Fordism, post-bureaucracy). As shown throughout this book, however, such a storyline fails to do justice to lived practice by obfuscating the multiple and divergent trajectories, ignoring the many other dimensions along which transitions are taking place.

In this final chapter, therefore, the intention is to begin to move closer to an approach towards the future of work more appreciative of the multiple and divergent trajectories in working life in the contemporary world. Here, a more kaleidoscopic view of the future of work will be advocated in which there are no universal linear processes but instead many fragments moving in different directions in various parts of the picture. This re-visioning of the future of work has major implications for thought and practice that will be addressed. Before doing so, however, the findings of the preceding chapters need to be synthesized.

Dominant narratives about the direction of work

In the first part of this book, the dominant narratives about the direction of work were analysed. Here, it was highlighted how a number of visions which pinpoint some dichotomy and order the two sides into a temporal sequence in which one immutably, inevitably and universally replaces the other over time have attained the status of 'facts' about the future of work (as if such a thing could exist), namely the discourses of formalization, commodification and globalization. Rather than pay homage to these tales of universal one-dimensional linear trajectories, as has been the case in so many books written on the future of work, a more critical approach was adopted. Evaluating critically each of these narratives in turn, the intention has been to reveal that these are not universal but particularistic trends that are only valid if one looks in a specific manner in particular places.

To display this, Chapter 2 introduced these three narratives that dominate how the future of work is envisaged at the present juncture in history. Depicting three modes of delivering goods and services, namely the 'market' (private sector), the 'state' (public sector) and 'informal or community sector', this chapter revealed how the current widespread consensus is that most nations are witnessing a common trajectory of economic development (where the future is seen as a linear extrapolation of a perceived past trajectory rather than in cyclical or dialectical terms). First, it was shown that the future of work has been all too often viewed as involving an ongoing 'formalization' of work in the sense that goods and services are increasingly produced and delivered through the formal (market and state) sphere under the social relations of formal employment rather than through the informal sphere (here termed the 'formalization' thesis). Secondly, it was revealed that this formal production and delivery of goods and services has been portrayed as increasingly occurring through the market sector rather than by the state or informal sphere (the commodification thesis) and, finally, this formalization and commodification of work has been depicted as increasingly taking place with an open (de-regulated) world economy (i.e., the globalization thesis).

Given the widespread belief in all of these narratives regarding the direction of work, and how they are often treated as objective facts rather than visions of the future of work, the next three chapters set about evaluating critically each of these oft-told tales in turn and recasting them as just as much ideological prescriptions as any other perspective towards the future of work. The widely recited storyline of a linear and universal demise of the informal economy and concomitant growth of the formal economy (the formalization thesis) was the subject matter of Chapter 3. Until now, this narrative has been so strongly held that the degree of formalization has been used as a measuring rod to define Third World countries as 'developing' and the First World as 'advanced', with informal work consequently viewed as a manifestation of 'backwardness' that will disappear with economic 'advancement' and 'modernization'. Here, therefore, the future of work has been cast in stone; a one-dimensional linear trajectory has been envisaged and it is one in which there is a natural and inevitable process of formalization. Reviewing evidence from the Western 'advanced' economies, transition economies and the majority (Third) world, however, little evidence was found of any universal linear progression towards formalization. Instead, heterogeneous development paths were identified not only across these different regions of the world but also within them. The outcome was to cast strong doubts over this meta-narrative often portrayed as an immutable fact about the trajectory of work that closes off the future to anything other than formalization.

Chapter 4 then turned its attention to another widely held narrative that similarly curtails what is considered feasible so far as the future of work is concerned. This is the discourse of commodification in which capitalism is viewed as having become an ever more powerful, expansive and totalizing force that is penetrating deeper into each and every corner of economic life as its tentacles stretch wider across the globe to colonize those areas previously left untouched. Again, this has been widely accepted as a somewhat indisputable and irrefutable fact, not only amongst neo-liberals who celebrate this future but also amongst a wide array of commentators heavily opposed to its encroachment but who adopt a fatalistic despondence about its inevitability. Analysing whether capitalist firms rather than the state and community increasingly produce and distribute goods and services, however, Chapter 4 revealed that this is far from a universal process. Again reviewing the evidence from the advanced, transition and majority world, different trajectories were identified both within and across the populations of these regions, intimating that the future is far more open than often assumed.

In Chapter 5, the third pillar that has acted to close off the future of work was critically evaluated, namely the story of the shift towards an ever more open world economy (i.e., the globalization thesis) and how people, organizations and governments have no choice to bow to the power of this inevitable force. Scrutinizing evidence of the degree of economic, financial, cultural and political globalization, this chapter unravelled that the imagined economies of globalization are very much a product of a particular way of looking at the world and a result of only looking in particular narrow confined spaces, and that once one interrogates this phenomenon, a very different picture emerges of the shallow and uneven contours of globalization.

Futures for employment

Having displayed the fallacy of these dominant narratives about universal linear directions of work organization and revealed the multiple trajectories in lived practice, Part II turned its attention to the principal visions that are portrayed regarding the future of employment. Once again, these similarly delineate some dualism (e.g., industrial/post-industrial society, Fordism/post-Fordism, bureaucratic/post-bureaucratic management) and then depict a linear progression from one side of the binary to the other over time. Chapter 6 reviewed those commentaries that represent the future of work primarily in terms of a shift from an industrial society to a post-industrial, information or knowledge economy, Chapter 7 those portraying the future of work in terms of a shift from Fordist to post-Fordist practices, Chapter 8 those depicting a shift from bureaucratic to post-bureaucratic work organization and Chapter 9 the somewhat less popular vision that capitalist employment practices are being replaced by not-for-profit employment practices.

All of these visions were displayed to be far from as clear-cut as is sometimes intimated and less all-embracing. Indeed, rather than a temporal streamlined evolution from one to the other, these dichotomies were revealed to conflate present-day differences across space, sectors and occupations into a temporal sequence, in which one side of the coin (e.g., industrialism, Fordism, bureaucracy, capitalist employment) is supplanted by the other side of the coin (e.g., post-industrial, post-Fordism, post-bureaucracy, non-capitalist employment). For all of these visions of the future of employment, therefore, the lived practice was revealed to be that many organizations include elements of both sides of these dichotomies and that the boundaries between the two are much fuzzier than often intimated. For recent commentators considering some of these perspectives (e.g., the post-Fordist and post-bureaucratic literature), this is sometimes taken as evidence that 'hybrid' forms are emerging. What is much more likely, however, it was argued, is that there have been organizations which have always displayed elements of both sides of the dichotomy and that such dualistic thought was never capable of delineating the lived practices.

This, however, is not to suggest that there is far greater continuity than so far supposed, as some commentators suggest (e.g., Thompson and McHugh, 2002). Rather, it is an argument that such linear one-dimensional visions of the trajectory of work organization are too simple to capture the multiple and divergent trajectories taking place in the employment-place. As argued, a more accurate portrayal would be perhaps the recognition that there are many fragments moving in different directions in various parts of the picture. Consequently, just as some fragments are moving in the direction of post-bureaucracy and post-Fordist work practices, other fragments are moving, as Part II revealed, in the direction of Fordism and bureaucracy. To foreground one of these fragments and obfuscate the others from view is to fail to grasp the diverse, often contradictory, shifts in working practices in the contemporary business world. For a fuller understanding of the future of work, therefore, it is no use focusing upon one dualism or fragment.

Indeed, it is for precisely this reason that the vision of a future of non-capitalist employment was here included. To portray such work as a primitive, traditional, stagnant, marginal, residual, weak and about to be extinguished sphere or, to put it another way, as a vestige of a disappearing past, transitory or provisional ignores that non-capitalist employment not only persists but is resilient and growing in parts of the contemporary economic landscape. Throughout the world, just as there are areas in which post-bureaucratic management is coming to the fore and post-Fordist work practices prevailing, there are also spheres in which non-capitalist employment practices are thriving. Unless this is recognized, then the multiple and divergent directions of change taking place will fail to be fully understood.

Indeed, in the final part of the book, a number of cosy assumptions shared by all those visions focusing upon changes in formal employment when depicting visions of the future of work were unravelled. For many commentators who have escaped the contemporary tendency to view formal employment as the only form of work, the changes in the nature of employment depicted in Part II are unimportant. For them, all these visions of the future of employment ultimately fail to shake off the core assumptions of employment-centred society, namely that employment is the sole source of work, that employment should remain seen as the dominant form of work and that there is no need to challenge the employment-centred view of work and the obfuscation of other forms of work. In Part III, in consequence, attention turned towards those perspectives that explore the future of work more widely defined.

Visions of the future of work

In Part III, those visions of the future of work often ignored in conventional management and business studies texts were considered. These are the visions that reject either descriptively or prescriptively the meta-narratives of formalization, commodification and globalization and depict alternative futures for work organization.

In Chapter 10, the 'third way' vision of the future of work was reviewed. While 'first way' (neo-liberal) and 'second way' (socialist) thought was shown to be ultimately about whether private or public sector provision is the best way of achieving formalization and commodification, third way thought was revealed to incorporate civil society as a third prong into such discussions, albeit only when considering the future of welfare provision. In the realm of economic policy, however, third way thought was shown to remain an employment-centred ideology grounded in a prescription of formalization, commodification and globalization.

This starkly contrasts with the other visions of work discussed in Part III that contest on descriptive and/or normative grounds either the meta-narrative of formalization by expounding post-employment visions of the future of work (Chapter 11), commodification by propagating post-capitalist visions (Chapter 12) or globalization by promoting localization (Chapter 13).

In all of these counter-narratives to the dominant discourses, it was revealed that a common call is made to cease mapping an ever more formalized, commodified and/or globalized world, not least because this creates what is then seen. Instead, and for these analysts, there is a need to recognize, value and create informal, non-capitalist and/or localist practices that are here and emerging so as to shine a light on the demonstrable construction of alternative possibilities and futures (e.g., Byrne et al., 2001; Escobar, 1995; Community Economies Collective, 2001; Gibson-Graham, 1995, 1996, 2006; Gibson-Graham and Ruccio, 2001; Williams, 2005a).

What is so valuable about these post-employment, post-capitalist and localist counter-narratives of the future of work is thus that they open up possible futures for work beyond formalization, commodification and globalization as well as alternative economic sites to re-signification. Perhaps less convincing, however, is that these commentators often simply invert the normative judgements of the formalization, commodification and globalization theses. Rather than attach positive attributes to formalization, commodification and globalization, and negative attributes to informalization, de-commodification and localization, they simply do the reverse. The result is that just as the dominant narratives over-romanticize formalization and so forth, these visionaries do the same with informalization, de-commodification and localization. Ultimately, therefore, such commentators perhaps do little more than simply continue with the same mode of thought as the dominant narratives by constructing a dichotomy which envisages or prescribes an either/or choice and then concocts this in a temporal manner as a one-dimensional linear transformation from some 'old' to 'new' form of work organization.

Conclusions

Until now, those highlighting either the limited degree to which specific visions of the future of work actually reflect lived practice, or the shortcomings of using only one dichotomy to portray the complex and multiple directions of change, have tended to argue that there is far greater continuity with the past than normally intimated in the visions of the future of work reviewed in this book (e.g., Nolan and Wood, 2003; Noon and Blyton, 2002; Ransome, 1999; Thompson and McHugh, 2002; Warhurst and Thompson, 1998; White et al., 2004). As Thompson and McHugh (2002: 189) put it, 'Continuity in organizational structure, work and employment might not be as exciting a message, but it is often a more accurate one.'

At first glance, it might be assumed that this volume reinforces such a stance. For example, its finding that informal and non-commodified work persists and that formalization and commodification is far from hegemonic, as well as that post-Fordist and post-bureaucratic practices are far from all-pervasive, seems to support this argument for recognizing the continuity between the present-day and the past. Here in this concluding section, however, it is necessary to reflect on whether this is indeed the case. Although this book has displayed that there is relatively more continuity with the past than many futurologists explicate, it has not denied the possibility for change. Indeed, quite the opposite is the case. It has argued, similar to many others, that there is both continuity and change occurring (Blyton and Turnbull, 1994; Jacques, 1998; Legge, 1995; Ransome, 2005). The changes asserted to be taking place, however, are not configured in some one-dimensional linear manner as being towards some singular -ism, -ation, or post-something- or- other. Instead, what this book has revealed is that there are multiple changes taking place that vary across space, sectors, occupations and populations. The outcome is that rather than a process of convergence, a divergence of trajectories is revealed and a picture of the future painted that is much more variable, diverse and open than usually considered in one-dimensional portraits.

Although in some nations, sectors, occupations or population groups, shifts towards formalization, commodification, globalization, information society, post-Fordism, post-bureaucracy and non-capitalist employment practices can be identified, once the lens is widened and other nations, sectors, occupations or population groups examined, shifts in the opposite direction can be marked out, namely informalization, de-commodification, localization, industrialism, Fordism, bureaucracy and capitalist practices. In other words, there are multiple, often contradictory, trajectories being pursued in different sites. Although this notion that there is no one evident future but various futures of work depending on where one looks might not seem so radical and clear-cut as what some management gurus convey in their usually one-dimensional linear stories, it is, as shown, more reflective of the lived practices. Importantly, it also opens up the future. There are no linear trajectories, no unstoppable forces, no inevitable tendencies, but instead heterogeneous paths with various fragments in the picture moving in different directions.

None of the individual perspectives towards the future of work considered in this book, therefore, wholly capture and reflect these heterogeneous directions in which work organization is moving in the contemporary world. For the future of work to be more fully understood, it is not only the continuity with the past but also the diverse and inconsistent trajectories that need to be recognized. It is only in so doing that the many possibilities for the future of work organization start to become apparent along with the degree to which the future of work is open.

Yet even if this book concludes that the future of work is not so closed as usually intimated in most of the visions reviewed here, and therefore the future organization of work more in our hands than frequently assumed, it would be a misnomer to end this book leaving readers assuming that the future is what we wish to make it. Not only are some narratives of the future, such as formalization, commodification and globalization, supported by some very powerful vested interests, whose interests are helping mould the world of work into the image they desire, but for most individuals today, the future is anything but in their hands. For most people, the range of alternative possibilities open to them is very limited. Although affluent households and individuals in Western economies, for example, might be able to sometimes choose the type of work that they engage in and use to get tasks completed, for the vast majority this is not the case. Similarly, although there are some able to downshift to simpler lives, for others this is not a possibility. Although divergent trajectories and a mass of possibilities for the direction of change thus exist on a global level, this is not the case for all individuals and populations in their everyday lives. Some are confined to Fordist employment practices or formal employment, others largely confined to informal practices. The task ahead, therefore, is surely to work towards ensuring that people have greater choice about the type of work in which they want to engage. If this book in displaying that the future is not cast in stone, and that it is wholly possible to imagine all manner of alternative futures of work, helps to stimulate greater discussion of how to open up the future more for those who currently have little choice, then it will have fulfilled its objective.

References

Abrahamson, P. (1992) 'Welfare pluralism: Towards a new consensus for a European social policy?', in L. Hantrais, M. O'Brien and S. Mangen (eds) *The Mixed Economy of Welfare*, Loughborough: Cross-National Research Paper no. 6, European Research Centre, Loughborough University.

Adema, W. and Ladaque, M. (2005) *Net Social Expenditure 2005 Edition*, Paris: OECD.

Adler, P. (1997) *Hybridization of HRM: Two Toyota Transplants Compared*, Working Paper, University of Southern California.

Adler, P. (1998) 'Teamworking today – social implications', in J.-P. Durand, J. Castillo and P. Stewart (eds) *Teamwork in the Auto Industry: New Horizon or Passing Fashion?*, Paris: La Decouverte.

ADRET (1977) *Travailler Deux Heures par Jour*, Paris: Seuil.

Ageyman, J. and Evans, B. (2004) 'Just sustainability': The emerging discourse of environmental justice in Britain?', *Geographical Journal*, 170, 2: 155–64.

Aglietta, M. (1979) *A Theory of Capitalist Regulation: The US Experience*, London: Verso.

Ahearne, A., Griever, D. and Warnock, F. (2004) 'Information costs and home bias an analysis of US holdings of foreign equities', *Journal of International Economics*, 62: 313–36.

Albert, M. (1993) *Capitalism against Capitalism*, New York: Four Walls Eight Windows.

Albert, M. (2003) *Parecon: Life after Capitalism*, London: Verso.

Allen, S. and Wolkowitz, C. (1987) *Homeworking: Myths and Realities*, London: Macmillan.

Altvater, E. and Mahnkopf, B. (1997) 'The world market unbound', *Review of International Political Economy*, 4: 448–71.

Alvesson, M. and Willmott, H. (1996) *Making Sense of Management: A Critical Introduction*, London: Sage.

Amado, J. and Stoffaes, C. (1980) 'Vers une socio-economie duale', in A. Danzin, A. Boublil and J. Lagarde (eds) *La Societe Francaise et la Technologie*, Paris: Documentation Francaise.

Amin, A. and Thrift, N. (2004) 'Introduction', in A. Amin and N. Thrift (eds) *The Blackwell Cultural Economy Reader*, Oxford: Blackwell.

Amin, A., Cameron, A. and Hudson, R. (2002a) *Placing the Social Economy*, London: Routledge.

Amin, A., Cameron, A. and Hudson, R. (2002b) 'The UK social economy: Panacea or problem?', in I. Bartle and D. Castiglione (eds) *Social Capital in the Economy*, Colchester: Russell Papers Civic Series 2002/04, University of Essex.

Anderson, B. (2001a) 'Why madam has so many bathrobes: Demand for migrant domestic workers in the EU', *Tijdschrift voor Economische en Sociale Geografie*, 92, 1: 18–26.

Anderson, B. (2001b) 'Different roots in common ground: Trans-nationalism and migrant domestic workers in London', *Journal of Ethnic and Migration Studies*, 27, 4: 673–83.

Anderson, P. (2000) 'Renewals', *New Left Review*, II, 1: 1–22.

Anheier, H.K. (1992) 'Economic environments and differentiation: A comparative study of informal sector economies in Nigeria', *World Development*, 20, 11: 1573–85.

Appadurai, A. (1990) 'Disjuncture and difference in the global cultural economy', *Public Culture*, 2, 2: 1–24.

Appelbaum, E. and Batt, R. (1994) *The New American Workplace: Transforming Work Systems in the United States*, Ithaca, NY: Cornell University Press.

Archibugi, F. (2000) *The Associative Economy: Insights beyond the Welfare State and into Post-capitalism*, London: Macmillan.

Armenakis, A.A. and Bedeian, A.G. (1999) 'Organisational change: A review of theory and research in the 1990s', *Journal of Management*, 25: 291–335.

Arnstberg, K. and Boren, T. (eds) (2003) *Everyday Economy in Russia, Poland and Latvia*, Stockholm: Almqvist and Wiksell International.

Aronowitz, S. and Cutler, J. (eds) (1998) *Post-Work: The Wages of Cybernation*, London: Routledge.

Atkinson, A. and Micklewright, J. (1991) 'Unemployment compensation and labour market transitions: A critical review', *Journal of Economic Literature*, 29: 1679–727.

Atkinson, A.B. (1995) *Public Economics in Action: The Basic Income/Flat Tax Proposal*, Oxford: Oxford University Press.

Atkinson, A.B. (1998) *Poverty in Europe*, Oxford: Blackwell.

Atkinson, J. (1985) 'Flexibility: Planning for an Uncertain Future', *Manpower Policy and Practice*, 1: 25–50.

Atkinson, J. (1987) 'Flexibility or Fragmentation? The UK Labour Market in the Eighties', *Labour and Society*, 12: 87–105.

Avrahami, E. (2000) *The Changing Kibbutz: An Examination of Values and Structure*, Ramat Efal, Israel: Yad Tabenkin.

Aznar, G. (1981) *Tous a Mi-temps, ou le Scenario Bleu*, Paris: Seuil.

Azurmendi, J. (1991) *El Hombre Cooperativo: Pensiamento do Arizmendiarrieta*, Mondragon: Otalora Institute.

Babson, S. (ed.) (1995) *Lean Work*, Detroit: Wayne State University Press.

Bacon, N., Ackers, P., Storey, J. and Coates, D. (1998) 'It's a small world: Managing human resources in small businesses', in C. Mabey, G. Salaman and J. Storey (eds) *Strategic Human Resource Management: A Reader*, London: Sage.

Banerjee, S.B. (2003) 'Who sustains whose development? Sustainable development and the reinvention of nature', *Organisation Studies*, 24, 1: 143–80.

Bangassa, K. (1999) 'Performance of UK Investment Trusts: 1980–1994', *Journal of Business Finance and Accounting*, 26, 9: 1141–68.

Barker, J.R. (1993) 'Tightening the iron cage: Coercive control in self managing teams', *Administrative Science Quarterly*, 38: 408–37.

Barlett, D.L. and Steele, J.B. (2002) *The Great American Tax Dodge: How Spiralling Fraud and Avoidance are Killing Fairness, Destroying the Income Tax, and Costing You*, Los Angeles: University of California Press.

Barley, S. (1996) *The New World of Work*, London: British–North American Committee.

Barley, S. and Kunda, G. (1992) 'Design and devotion: Surges of rational and normative ideologies of control in managerial discourse', *Administrative Sciences Quarterly*, 37: 363–99.

Barnard, C.I. (1938) *The Functions of the Executive*, Cambridge, MA: Harvard University Press.

Barr, N. (1992) 'Economic theory and the welfare state: A survey and interpretation', *Journal of Economic Literature*, 30: 741–803.

Barrientos, A. and Ware Barrientos, S. (2003) 'Social protection for informal workers in the horticulture industry', in F. Lund and J. Nicholson (eds) *Chains of Production, Ladders of Protection: Social Protection for Workers in the Informal Economy*, Durban: University of Natal School of Development Studies.

Barthe, M.A. (1985) 'Chomage, travail au noir et entraide familial', *Consommation*, 3: 23–42.

Barthe, M.A. (1988) *L'Economie Cachée*, Paris: Syros Alternatives.

Baruch, Y. (2000) 'Teleworking: benefits and pitfalls as perceived by professionals and managers', *New Technology, Work and Employment*, 15, 1: 34–49.

Beck, U. (2000) *The Brave New World of Work*, Cambridge: Polity.

Becker, F. and Steele, F. (1995) *Workplace by Design*, San Francisco: Jossey-Bass.

Beder, S. (2000) *Selling the Work Ethic: From Puritan Pulpit to Corporate PR*, London: Zed.

Beder, S. (2002) *Global Spin: The Corporate Assault on Environmentalism*, Dartington: Green Books.

Bell, D. (1960) *The End of Ideology*, London: Collier Macmillan.

Bell, D. (1973) *The Coming of Post-Industrial Society*, New York: Basic Books.

Bell, D. (1976) *The Cultural Contradictions of Capitalism*, London: Heinemann.

Bell, D. (1980) 'The social framework of the information society', in T. Forrester (ed.) *The Microelectronics Revolution*, Oxford: Basil Blackwell.

Bell, G. (1992) *The Permaculture Way*, London: Thornsons.

Bello, W. (2004) *Deglobalization: Ideas for a New World Economy*, London: Zed.

Bender, D.E. (2004) *Sweated Work, Weak Bodies: Anti-sweatshop Campaigns and Languages of Labor*, New Brunswick: Rutgers University Press.

Bennholdt-Thomsen, V. and Mies, M. (1999) *The Subsistence Perspective: Beyond the Globalized Economy*, London: Zed.

Bennholdt-Thomsen, V., Faraclas, N. and von Werlhof, C. (2001) 'Introduction', in V. Bennholdt-Thomsen, N. Faraclas and C. von Werlhof (eds) *There is an Alternative: Subsistence and Worldwide Resistance to Corporate Globalization*, London: Zed.

Bennington, J., Baine, S. and Russell, J. (1992) 'The impact of the Single European Market on regional and local economic development and the voluntary and community sectors', in L. Hantrais, M. O'Brien and S. Mangen (eds) *The Mixed Economy of Welfare*, Loughborough: Cross-National Research Paper no. 6, European Research Centre, University of Loughborough.

Bentley, T. and Mulgan, G. (1996) *Employee Mutuals: The 21st Century Trade Union?*, London: Demos.

Benton, L. (1990) *Invisible Factories: The Informal Economy and Industrial Development in Spain*, New York: State University of New York Press.

Berger, S. and Dore, R. (eds) (1996) *National Diversity and Global Capitalism*, Ithaca, NY: Cornell University Press.

Berking, H. (1999) *Sociology of Giving*, London: Sage.

Beveridge, W. (1944) *Full-Employment in a Free Society*, London: George Allen and Unwin.

Beveridge, W. (1948) *Voluntary Action: A Report of Methods of Social Advance*, London: George Allen and Unwin.

Beynon, H. (1992) 'The end of the industrial worker?', in N. Abercrombie and A. Warde (eds) *Social Change in Contemporary Britain*, Cambridge: Polity.

Biggart, N.W. (1989) *Charismatic Capitalism: Direct Selling Organisations in America*, London: University of Chicago Press.

Birchall, J. (2001a) 'Introduction', in Birchall, J. (ed.) *The New Mutualism in Public Policy*, London: Routledge.

Birchall, J. (2001b) 'Consumer co-operatives in retrospect and prospect', in J. Birchall (ed.) *The New Mutualism in Public Policy*, London: Routledge.

Bircham, E. and Charlton, J. (eds) (2001) *Anti-Capitalism: A Guide to the Movement*, London: Bookmarks.

Blackler, F. (1995) 'Knowledge, knowledge work and organizations: An overview and interpretation', *Organisation Studies*, 16, 6: 1021–46.

Blair, T. (1998) *The Third Way: New Politics for the New Century*, London: Fabian Society.

Blau, P. (1955) *Exchange and Power in Social Life*, New York: Wiley.

Blau, P. and Scott, W.R. (1963) *Formal Organisations: A Comparative Approach*, London: Routledge and Kegan Paul.

Blauner, R. (1964) *Alienation and Freedom*, Chicago: University of Chicago Press.

Bloch, M. and Parry, J. (1989) 'Introduction', in J. Parry and M. Bloch (eds) *Money and the Morality of Exchange*, Cambridge: Cambridge University Press.

Block, F. (1994) 'The roles of the state in the economy', in N.J. Smelser and R. Swedbert (eds) *The Handbook of Economic Sociology*, Princeton, NJ: Princeton University Press.

Block, F. (2002) 'Rethinking capitalism', in N.W. Biggart (ed.) *Readings in Economic Sociology*, Oxford: Blackwell.

Blommestein, H. (ed.) (1999) 'Impact of institutional investors on financial market', in OECD *Institutional Investors in the New Financial Landscape*, Paris: OECD.

Blyton, P. and Turnbull, P. (1994) *The Dynamics of Employee Relations*, London: Macmillan.

Bogle, J.C. (1999) *Common Sense on Mutual Funds: New Imperatives for the Intelligent Investor*, New York: Wiley.

Boren, T. (2003) 'What are friends for? Rationales of informal exchange in Russian everyday life', in K. Arnstberg and T. Boren (eds) *Everyday Economy in Russia, Poland and Latvia*, Stockholm: Almqvist and Wiksell International.

Boron, A.A. (2005) *Empire and Imperialism: A Critical Reading of Michael Hardt and Antonio Negri*, London: Zed.

Boswell, J. (1990) *Community and the Economy*, London: Routledge.

Bowring, F. (1998) 'LETS: An eco-socialist alternative', *New Left Review*, 232: 91–111.

Boxall, A. and Gallagher, N. (1997) 'Mutuality at the crossroads', *Financial Stability Review*, October.

Boyle, D. (1999) *Funny Money: In Search of Alternative Cash*, London: Harper Collins.

Braverman, H. (1974) *Labor and Monopoly Capital: The Deregulation of Work in the Twentieth Century*, New York: Monthly Review Press.

Brecher, J., Costello, T. and Smith, B. (2000) *Globalisation from Below: The Power of Solidarity*, Boston, MA: South End Press.

Bridges, W. (1995) *Jobshift: How to Prosper in a Workplace without Jobs*, London: Nicholas Brealey.

Briscoe, I. (1995) *In Whose Service? Making Community Service Work for the Unemployed*, London: Demos.

Bromley, R. and Gerry, C. (1979) *Casual Work and Poverty in Third World Cities*, Chichester: Wiley.

Brown, A. and Keep, E. (1999) *Review of Vocational Education and Training Research in the United Kingdom*, University of Warwick: SKOPE.

Brown, L. (2001) *Eco-Economy: Building a New Economy for the Environmental Age*, London: Norton.

Bruni, L. (ed.) (1999) *Economia di Comunione: per una nuova dimensione nell'economia*, Rome: Citté Nuova.

Bruni, L. and Pelligra, V. (eds) (2002) *Economia Come Impegno Civile: relazionalitá, ben-essere ed Economia di Comunione*, Rome: Citté Nuova.

Bryman, A. (2004) *The Disneyization of Society*, London: Sage.

Bryson, J., Daniels, P., Henry, N. and Pollard, J. (eds) (2001) *Knowledge, Space, Economy*, London: Routledge.

Buchanan, D.A. and Boddy, D. (1983) *Organisations in the Computer Age: Technological Imperatives and Strategic Choice*, London: Prentice Hall.

Buchanen, D. (1993) 'Principles and practices of work design', in K. Sisson (ed.) *Personnel Management in Britain*, Oxford: Blackwell.

Buchanen, D. (1994) 'Cellular manufacture and the role of teams', in J. Storey (ed.) *New Wave Manufacturing Strategies*, Liverpool: Paul Chapman.

Bunting, M. (2004) *Willing Slaves: How the Overwork Culture is Ruling Our Lives*, London: Harper Collins.

Burawoy, M. and Verdery, K. (eds) (1999) *Uncertain Transition: Ethnographies of Change in the Postsocialist World*, Lanham MD: Rowman and Littlefield, Lanham.

Burch, S. (1991) *Teleworking: A Glimpse of the Future*, Martlesham: BT.

Burns, D., Williams, C.C. and Windebank, J. (2004) *Community Self-Help*, Basingstoke: Palgrave Macmillan.

Burrell, G. (1997) *Pandemonium: Towards a Retro-Organisational Theory*, London: Sage.

Buttle, M. (2005) 'The social investment sector and post-structural economic geography', PhD thesis, School of Geography, University of Birmingham, Birmingham.

Button, K. (1984) 'Regional variations in the irregular economy: A study of possible trends', *Regional Studies*, 18: 385–92.

Byrne, K., Forest, R., Gibson-Graham, J.K., Healy, S. and Horvath, G. (2001) *Imagining and Enacting Non-Capitalist Futures*, Rethinking Economy Project Working Paper no. 1 (http//:www.arts.monash.edu.au/projects/cep/knowledges/byrne.html).

Cahill, M. (2001) *Social Policy and the Environment*, Brighton: The Gildredge Press.

Cahill, M. and Fitzpatrick, T. (2001) (eds) *Environmental Issues and Social Welfare*, Oxford: Blackwell.

Cahn, E. (2000) *No More Throw-Away People: The Co-production Imperative*, Washington, DC: Essential Books.

Cahn, E. and Rowe, J. (1992) *Time Dollars: The New Currency that Enables Americans to Turn Their Hidden Resource – Time – into Personal Security and Community Renewal*, Chicago: Family Resource Coalition of America.

Caldwell, C. (2000) 'Why do people join local exchange and trading systems?', *International Journal of Community Currency Research*, 4 (http://www.le.ac.uk/ulmc/ijccr)

Callinicos, A. (2003) *An Anti-Capitalist Manifesto*, Cambridge: Polity Press.

Cameron, A. and Palan, R. (2004) *The Imagined Economies of Globalization*, London: Sage.

Camilleri, J. and Falk, J. (1992) *The End of Sovereignty? The Politics of a Shrinking and Fragmenting World*, Aldershot: Edward Elgar.

Campbell, M. (2000) 'Reconnecting the long-term unemployed to labour market opportunity: The case for a local active labour market policy', *Regional Studies*, 34, 7: 655–68.

Cannon, D. (1994) *Generation X and the New Work Ethic*, London: Demos.

Caplow, T. (1982) 'Christian gifts and kin networks', *American Sociological Review*, 47: 383–92.

Cappechi, V. (1989) 'The informal economy and the development of flexible specialisation in Emilia Romagna', in A. Portes, M. Castells and L.A. Benton (eds) *The Informal Economy: Studies in Advanced and Less Developing Countries*, Baltimore: The John Hopkins University Press.

Capra, F. and Spretnak, C. (1985) *Green Politics*, London: Hutchinson.

Carr, F. (1994) 'Introducing teamworking: a motor industry case study', *Industrial Relations Journal*, 25, 3: 199–209.

Carrier, J.G. (1998) 'Introduction', in J.G. Carrier and D. Miller (eds) *Virtualism: A New Political Economy*, Oxford: Berg.

Carruthers, B.G. and Babb, S.L. (2000) *Economy/Society: Markets, Meanings and Social Structure*, Thousand Oaks, CA: Pine Oaks.

Carruthers, B.G. and Espeland, W.N. (2001) 'Money, meaning and morality', in N.W. Biggart (ed.) *Readings in Economic Sociology*, Oxford: Blackwell.

Casey, C. (1995) *Work, Self and Society: After Industrialism*, London: Routledge.

Castells, M. (1989) *The Informational City: Information Technology, Economic Restructuring and the Urban Regional Process*, Oxford: Basil Blackwell.

Castells, M. (1996) *The Rise of the Network Society*, Oxford: Blackwell.

Castells, M. (1998) *End of the Millennium, Volume 3 of The Information Age: Economy, Society and Culture*, Oxford: Blackwell.

Castells, M. (2000) 'Materials for an exploratory theory of the networked society', *British Journal of Sociology*, 51: 5–24.

Castells, M. and Portes, A. (1989) 'World underneath: The origins, dynamics and effects of the informal economy', in A. Portes, M. Castells and L.A. Benton (eds) *The Informal Economy: Studies in Advanced and Less Developing Countries*, Baltimore: John Hopkins University Press.

Castillo, J.J. (1999) 'Which way forward for the sociology of work? An introduction', *Current Sociology*, 47: 1–4.

Castree, N., Coe, N.M., Ward, K. and Samers, M. (2004) *Spaces of Work: Global Capitalism and the Geographies of Labour*, London: Sage.

Cattell, V. and Evans, M. (1999) *Neighbourhood Images in East London: Social Capital and Social Networks on Two East London Estates*, York: York Publishing Services.

Chadeau, A. and Fouquet, A.-M. (1981) 'Peut-on mesurer le travail domestique?', *Economie et Statistique*, 136: 29–42.

Cheal, D. (1988) *The Gift Economy*, London: Verso.

Cheng, L.L. and Gereffi, G. (1994) 'The informal economy in East Asian development', *International Journal of Urban and Regional Research*, 18, 2: 194–219.

Child, J. and McGrath, R.G. (2001) 'Organisations unfettered: Organization forms in an information-intensive economy', *Academy of Management Journal*, 44: 1135–48.

Chordia, T. (1996) 'The structure of mutual fund charges', *Journal of Financial Economics*, 41, 1: 3–39.

Christensen, K. (1989) 'Home based clerical work: No simple truth, no simple reality', in E. Boris and C. Daniels (eds) *Homework: Historical and Contemporary Perspectives on Paid Labour at Home*, Chicago: University of Illinois Press.

Christoff, P. (1996) 'Ecological modernization, ecological modernities', *Environmental Politics*, 5: 476–500.

Ciscel, D.H. and Heath, J.A. (2001) 'To market, to market: Imperial capitalism's destruction of social capital and the family', *Review of Radical Political Economics*, 33, 4: 401–14.

Ciulla, J. (2000) *The Working Life: The Promise and Betrayal of Modern Work*, London: Random House.

Clamp, C. (2000) 'The internationalisation of Mondragon', *Annals of Public and Cooperative Economics*, 71: 557–77.

Clark, G. (2000) *Pension Fund Capitalism*. Oxford: Oxford University Press.

Clark, G.L. and Root, A. (1999) 'Infrastructure shortfall in the UK: The private finance initiative and government policy', *Political Geography*, 18: 341–65.

Clarke, S. (1990) 'New utopia's for old: Fordist dreams and post-Fordist fantasies', *Capital and Class*, 42: 131–55.

Clegg, S. (1990) *Modern Organizations: Organization Studies in the Postmodern World*, London: Sage.

Clegg, S.R. and Hardy, C. (1996) 'Organizations, organization and organizing', in S. Clegg, C. Hardy and W.R. Nord (eds) *Handbook of Organization Studies*, London: Sage.

Coates, D. (ed.) (2002a) *Capitalist Models: Divergence and Convergence*, Aldershot: Edward Elgar.

Coates, D. (ed.) (2002b) *Capitalist Models Under Challenge*, Aldershot: Edward Elgar.

Coates, D. (ed.) (2002c) *The Ascendancy of Liberal Capitalism*, Aldershot: Edward Elgar.

Cochrane, A. and Pain, K. (2000) 'A globalising society?', in D. Held (ed.) *A Globalising World? Culture, Economics and Politics*, London: Routledge.

Cohen-Mitchell, T. (2000) 'Community currencies at a cross-roads: New ways forward', *New Village Journal*, 2 (http://www.ratical.org/many.worlds/cc/cc@xRoads.html).

Cole, R. (1989) *Strategies for Learning: Small Group Activities in the Post-modern World*, Berkeley, CA: University of California Press.

Collins, D. (1997) 'Knowledge work or working knowledge? Ambiguity and confusion in the analysis of the "knowledge age"', *Employee Relations*, 19, 1: 38–50.

Collinson, D.L., Edwards, M. and Rees, C. (1997) *Involving Employees in Total Quality Management*, London: DTI.

Collom, E. (2005) 'Community currency in the United States: The social environments in which it emerges and survives', *Environment and Planning A*, 37: 1565–87.

Comeliau, C. (2002) *The Impasse of Modernity; Debating the Future of the Global Market Economy*, London: Zed.

Community Economies Collective (2001) 'Imagining and enacting noncapitalist futures', *Socialist Review*, 28: 93–135.

Connolly, P. (1985) 'The politics of the informal sector: A critique', in N. Redclift and E. Mingione (eds) *Beyond Employment: Household, Gender and Subsistence*, Oxford: Blackwell.

Conroy, P. (1996) *Equal Opportunities For All*, Brussels: European Social Policy Forum Working Paper I, DG V, European Commission.

Cooke, P. (2002) *Knowledge Economies: Clusters, Learning and Cooperative Advantage*, London: Routledge.

Corbridge, S., Thrift, N.J. and Martin, R. (1996) *Money, Power and Space*, Oxford: Blackwell.

Cornforth, C., Thomas, A., Lewis, J. and Spear, R. (1988) *Developing Successful Worker Cooperatives*, London: Sage.

Cornuel, D. and Duriez, B. (1985) 'Local exchange and state intervention', in N. Redclift and E. Mingione (eds) *Beyond Employment: Household, Gender and Subsistence*, Oxford: Basil Blackwell.

Cortada, J. (ed.) (1998) *The Rise of the Knowledge Worker*, Boston: Butterworth-Heinnemann.

Countryside Agency (2000) *The State of the Countryside 2000*, London: Countryside Agency.

Coupland, D. (1991) *Generation X: Tales for an Accelerated Culture*, New York: St. Martin's Press.

Courpasson, D. (2000) 'Managerial strategies of domination: Power in soft bureaucracies', *Organization Studies*, 21, 1: 141–61.

Crook, S., Paklulski, J. and Waters, M. (1992) *Postmodernization: Change in Advanced Societies*, London: Sage.

Cross, R. and Smith, J. (1995) *Customer Bonding*, Lincolnwood, IL: NTC Business Books.

Crouch, C. (1999) 'The skills creation triangle out of balance', *Renewal*, 7, 4: 60–71.

Crouch, C. and Streek, W. (eds) (1997) *Political Economy of Modern Capitalism: Mapping Convergence and Diversity*, Thousand Oaks, CA: Sage.

Culpitt, I. (1992) *Welfare and Citizenship*, London: Sage.

Daly, H.E. (2003) 'Globalization and its inconsistencies', in A. Pettifor (ed.) *Real World Economic Outlook: The Legacy of Globalization: Debt and Deflation*, Basingstoke: Palgrave Macmillan.

Daly, M. (1979) *Gyn/Ecology: The Metaethics of Radical Feminism*, London: Women's Press.

Dandeker, C. (1990) *Surveillance, Power and Modernity*, Cambridge: Polity.

Danford, A. (1998) 'Teamworking and labour relations in the autocomponents industry', *Work, Employment and Society*, 12, 3: 409–31.

Dar, Y. (2002) 'Communality, rationalization and distributive justice: Changing evaluation of work in the Israeli kibbutz', *International Sociology*, 17, 1: 91–111.

Dasgupta, N. (1992) *Petty Trading in the Third World: The Case of Calcutta*, Aldershot: Avebury.

Davis, P. (2004) *Human Resource Management in Cooperatives: Theory, Process and Practice*, Geneva: International Labour Office.

Dawes, L. (1993) *Long-term Unemployment and Labour Market Flexibility*, Leicester: Centre for Labour Market Studies, University of Leicester.

Dawson, G. (2000) 'Work: From certainty to flexibility?', in G. Hughes and R. Ferguson (eds) *Ordering Lives: Family, Work and Welfare*, London: Routledge.

De Angelis, M. (2000) 'Globalization, new internationalism and the Zapatistas', *Capital and Class*, 70: 9–35.

De Geus, A. (1999) *The Living Company: Growth, Learning and Longevity in Business*, London: Nicholas Brealey.

De Pardo, M.L., Castano, G.M. and Soto, A.T. (1989) 'The articulation of formal and informal sectors in the economy of Bogota, Colombia', in A. Portes, M. Castells and L. Benton (eds) *The Informal Economy: Studies in Advanced and Less Developed Countries*, Baltimore: John Hopkins University.

De Soto, H. (1989) *The Other Path*, London: Harper and Row.

De Soto, H. (2001) *The Mystery of Capital: Why Capitalism Triumphs in the West and Fails Everywhere Else*, London: Black Swan.

De Witte, M. and Steijn, B. (2000) 'Automation, job content and underemployment', *Work, Employment and Society*, 14, 2: 245–64.

Deakin, S. and Wilkinson, F. (1991/92) 'Social policy and economic efficiency: The deregulation of labour markets in Britain', *Critical Social Policy*, 33: 40–51.

Deal, T.E. and Kennedy, A.A. (1982) *Corporate Cultures: The Rites and Rituals of Corporate Life*, Reading, MA: Addison-Wesley.

Dean, H., Bonvin, J.-M., Vielle, P. and Farvaque, N. (2005) 'Developing capabilities and rights in welfare-to-work policies', *European Societies*, 7, 1: 3–26.

DEGW and BRE (1996) *New Environments for Working*, London: DEGW International.

Dekker, P. and van den Broek, A. (1998) 'Civil society in comparative perspective: Involvement in voluntary associations in North America and Western Europe', *Voluntas*, 9, 1: 11–38.

Delbridge, R., Turbull, P. and Wilkinson, B. (1992) 'Pushing back the frontiers: Management control and work intensification under JIT/TQM regimes', *New Technology, Work and Employment*, 7, 2: 97–106.

Delors, J. (1979) 'Le troisieme secteur: le travail au-dela de l'emploi', *Autrement*, 20: 147–52.

Delwich, A. (1995) *Propaganda Techniques*, Washington DC: Institute for Propaganda Analysis (http://www.carmen.artsci.washington.edu/propaganda/home.htm).

Derrida, J. (1967) *Of Grammatology*, Baltimore: John Hopkins University Press.

Desai, M. (1998) *A Basic Income Proposal*, London: Social Market Foundation.

Despres, C. and Hiltrop, J.-M. (1995) 'Human resource management in the knowledge age: Current practice and perspectives in the future', *Employee Relations*, 17, 1: 9–23.

DETR (1998) *Community-based Regeneration Initiatives: A Working Paper*, London: HM DETR.

Devall, B. (1990) *Simple in Means, Rich in Ends: Practising Deep Ecology*, London: Green Print.

Devall, B. and Sessions, G. (1985) *Deep Ecology: Living as if Nature Mattered*, Salt Lake City: Peregrine Smith Books.

Dicken, P. (2003) *Global Shift: Reshaping the Global Economic Map in the 21st Century* (4th edn), London: Sage.

Dilnot, A. (1992) 'Social security and labour market policy', in I.E. McLaughlin (ed.) *Understanding Employment*, London: Routledge.

Doane, D., Srikajon, D. and Ofrenco, R. (2003) 'Social protection for informal workers in the garment industry', in F. Lund and J. Nicholson (eds) *Chains of Production, Ladders of Protection: Social Protection for Workers in the Informal Economy*, Durban: School of Development Studies, University of Natal.

Dobson, R.V.G. (1993) *Bringing the Economy Home from the Market*, New York: Black Rose Books.

Donzelot, J. (1991) 'Pleasure in work', in G. Burchell, C. Gordon and P. Miller (eds) *The Foucault Effect: Studies in Governmentality*, Hemel Hempstead: Harvester Wheatsheaf.

Douthwaite, R. (1996) *Short Circuit: Strengthening Local Economies for Security in an Unstable World*, Dartington: Green Books.

Drake, L. and Llewellyn, D.T. (2001) 'The economics of mutuality: A perspective on UK building societies', in J. Birchall (ed.) *The New Mutualism in Public Policy*, London: Routledge.

Drucker, P. (1969) *The Age of Discontinuity*, London: Heinemann.

Drucker P. (1988) 'The coming of the new organization', *Harvard Business Review*, 88: 45–53.

Drucker, P. (1993) *Postcapitalist Society*, Oxford: Butterworth-Heinnemann.

Drucker, P. (1998) 'The future that has already happened', *The Futurist*, 32, 8: 16–18.

Drucker, P. (2002) *Managing in the Next Society*, Oxford: Butterworth-Heinnemann.

Dryzek, J. (1997) *The Politics of the Earth*, Oxford: Oxford University Press.

DSS (1998) *A New Contract for Welfare*, London: HMSO.

Du Gay, P. (1991) 'Enterprise culture and the ideology of excellence', *New Formations*, 13: 45–61.

Du Gay, P. (2000) *In Praise of Bureaucracy*, London: Sage.

Du Gay, P. (2005) 'The values of bureaucracy: An introduction', in P. du Gay (ed.) *The Values of Bureaucracy*, Oxford: Oxford University Press.

Duffy, F. (1997) *The 'New Office'*, London: Conran Octopus.

Dumazedier, J. (1967) *Toward a Society of Leisure*, London: Collier-Macmillan.

Dumontier, F. and Pan Ke Shon, J.-L. (1999) *En 13 ans, moins de temps contraints et plus de loisirs*, Paris: INSEE Premiere 675.

Durning, A. (1992) *How Much is Enough? The Consumer Society and the Future of the Earth*, London: Earthscan.

Earle, J. (1986) *The Italian Co-operative Movement*, London: Allen and Unwin.

Easlie, B. (1981) *Science and Sexual Oppression: Patriarchy's Confrontation with Women and Nature*, London: Weidenfeld and Nicholson.

Eckersley, R. (1992) *Environmentalism and Political Theory: Towards an Ecocentric Approach*, London: UCL Press.

Economist Intelligence Unit (1982) *Coping with Unemployment: The Effects on the Unemployed Themselves*, London: Economist Intelligence Unit.

Edison, H. and Warnock, F. (2003) 'A simple measure of the intensity of capital controls', *Journal of Empirical Finance*, 10: 81–103.

Edwards, R.C. (1979) *Contested Terrain: The Transformation of the Workplace in the Twentieth Century*, New York: Basic Books.

Ehrenreich, R.C. and Edelstein, J.D. (1983) 'Consumers and organizational democracy: American new wave cooperatives', in C. Crouch and F. Heller (eds) *Organizational Democracy and Political Processes*, New York: Wiley.

Ekins, P. and Max-Neef, M. (1992*) Real-Life Economics: Understanding Wealth Creation*, London: Routledge.

Elgin, D. (1993) *Voluntary Simplicity*, New York: William Morrow.

Elson, D. (1988) 'Market socialism or socialization of the market?', *New Left Review*, 172, 11–29.

Escobar, A. (1995) *Encountering Development: The Making and Unmaking of the Third World*, Princeton, NJ: Princeton University Press.

Espenshade, J. (2004) *Monitoring Sweatshops: Workers, Consumers and the Global Apparel Industry*, Philadelphia: Temple University Press.

Esping-Andersen, G. (1994) 'Welfare states and the economy', in N.J. Smelser and R. Swedberg (eds) *The Handbook of Economic Sociology*, Princeton: Princeton University Press.

Esping-Andersen, G. (1996) 'After the golden age? Welfare state dilemmas in a global economy', in G. Esping-Anderson (ed.) *Welfare States in Transition: National Adaptations in Global Economies*, London: Sage.

Esteva, G. (2001) 'Mexico: Creating your own path at the grassroots', in V. Bennholdt-Thomsen, N. Faraclas and C. von Werlhof (eds) *There is an Alternative: Subsistence and Worldwide Resistance to Corporate Globalization*, London: Zed.

Etzioni, A. (1961) *A Comparative Analysis of Complex Organisations*, New York: Free Press.

European Commission (1996a) *Employment in Europe 1996*, Luxembourg: European Commission DG for Employment, Industrial Relations and Social Affairs.

European Commission (1996b) *For a Europe of Civic and Social Rights: Report by the Comite des Sages*, Luxembourg: European Commission DG for Employment, Industrial Relations and Social Affairs.

European Commission (2000a) *The Social Situation in the European Union 2000*, Brussels: European Commission.

European Commission (2000b) *Employment in Europe 2000*, Brussels: European Commission.

European Commission (2001a) *EU Employment and Social Policy, 1999–2001: Job, Cohesion, Productivity*, Luxembourg: Office for Official Publications of the European Communities.

European Commission (2001b) *The Social Situation in the European Union 2001*, Brussels: Commission of the European Communities.

Eurostat (2005) *Total Employment Rate*, http://epp.eurostat.cec.eu.int/portal/page?_pageid=1996,39140985@_dad=portal&_schem

Evans, M., Syrett, S. and Williams, C.C. (2006) *The Informal Economy and Deprived Neighbourhoods: A Systematic Review*, London: Office of the Deputy Prime Minister.

Evason, E. and Woods, R. (1995) 'Poverty, deregulation of the labour market and benefit fraud', *Social Policy and Administration*, 29, 1: 40–55.

Fainstein, N. (1996) 'A note on interpreting American poverty', in E. Mingione (ed.) *Urban Poverty and the Underclass*, Oxford: Basil Blackwell.

Faraclas, N.G. (2001) 'Melanesia, the banks, and the BINGOs: Real alternatives are everywhere (except in the consultants' briefcases)', in V. Bennholdt-Thomsen, N. Faraclas and C. von Werlhof (eds) *There is an Alternative: Subsistence and Worldwide Resistance to Corporate Globalization*, London: Zed.

Fayol, H. (1916) *General and Industrial Management*, London: Pitnam.

Featherstone, M. (1995) *Undoing Culture: Globalization, Postmodernism and Identity*, London: Sage.

Felstead, A., Jewson, N. and Walters, S. (2005) *Changing Places of Work*, Basingstoke: Palgrave Macmillan.

Fitzpatrick, T. (1999) *Freedom and Security: An Introduction to the Basic Income Debate*, London: Macmillan.

Fitzpatrick, T. and Cahill, M. (eds) (2002) *Greening the Welfare State*, London: Palgrave.

Fleming, C.A. (1995) 'Understanding propaganda from a general semantics perspective'. *Etc.*, 52, 1: 2–12.

Florida, R. (2002) *The Rise of the Creative Class and How It's Transforming Work, Leisure, Community and Everyday Life*, New York: Basic Books.

Fodor, E. (1999) *Better not Bigger: How to Take Control of Urban Growth and Improve Your Community*, Stony Creek, NJ: New Society.

Ford, R.C. and McLaughlin, F. (1995) 'Questions and answers about telecommuting', *Business Horizons*, 38, 2: 66–72.

Forrest, R. and Kearns, A. (1999) *Joined-up Places? Social Cohesion and Neighbourhood Regeneration*, York: York Publishing Services.

Fortin, B., Garneau, G., Lacroix, G., Lemieux, T. and Montmarquette, C. (1996) *L'Economie Souterraine au Quebec: mythes et realites*, Laval: Presses de l'Universite Laval.

Foucault, M. (1977) *Discipline and Punish: The Birth of the Prison*, London: Penguin.

Foucault, M. (1991) 'Governmentality', *Ideology and Consciousness*, 6: 5–21.

Foudi, R., Stankiewicz, F. and Vanecloo, N. (1982) 'Chomeurs et economie informelle', *Cahiers de l'observation du changement social et culturel*, no. 17, Paris: CNRS.

Fournier, V. (2005) 'Yes', in C. Jones and D. O'Doherty (eds) *Manifestos for the Business School of Tomorrow*, Finland: Dvalin Books.

Franks, S. (2000) *Having None of It: Women, Men and the Future of Work*, London: Granta.

Frenkel, S., Korczynski, M., Donohue, L. and Shire, K. (1995) 'Re-constituting work', *Work, Employment and Society*, 9, 4: 773–96.

Friedman, T. (1999) *The Lexus and the Olive Tree*, New York: Harper Collins.

Gallie, D. (1991) 'Patterns of skill change: Upskilling, deskilling or the polarization of skills', *Work, Employment and Society*, 5, 3: 319–51.

Gallin, D. (2001) 'Propositions on trade unions and informal employment in time of globalisation', *Antipode*, 19: 531–49.

Galpin, S. and Sims, D. (1999) 'Narrative and identity: Inflexible working and teleworking', in P. Jackson (ed.) *Virtual Working*, London: Routledge.

Gamble, J., Morris, J. and Wilkinson, B. (2004) 'Mass production is alive and well: The future of work organization in East Asia', *International Journal of Human Resource Management*, 15, 2: 397–409.

Gardiner, J. (1997) *Gender, Care and Economics*, Basingstoke: Macmillan.

Garrahan, P. and Stewart, P. (1992) *The Nissan Enigma: Flexibility at Work in a Local Economy*, London: Mansell.

Gass, R. (1996) 'The next stage of structural change: Towards a decentralised economy and an active society', in OECD (ed.) *Reconciling Economy and Society: Towards a Plural Economy*, Paris: OECD.

Geary, J.F. and Dobbins, A. (2001) 'Teamworking: A new dynamic in the pursuit of management control', *Human Resource Management Journal*, 11: 3–23.

Geertz, C. (1963) *Old Societies and New States: The Quest for Modernity in Asia and Africa*, Glencoe, IL: Free Press.

Gershuny, J. (1978) *After Industrial society? The Emerging Self-service Economy*, London: Macmillan.

Gershuny, J. (2000) *Changing Times: Work and Leisure in Post-industrial Society*. Oxford: Oxford University Press.

Gershuny, J. and Jones, S. (1987) 'The changing work/leisure balance in Britain 1961–84', *Sociological Review Monograph*, 33: 9–50.

Gershuny, J. and Miles, I. (1983) *The New Service Economy: The Transformation of Employment in Industrial Societies*, London: Frances Pinter.

Gershuny, J., Godwin, M. and Jones, S. (1994) 'The domestic labour revolution: A process of lagged adaptation', in M. Anderson, F. Bechhofer and S. Kendrick (eds) *The Social and Political Economy of the Household*, Oxford: Oxford University Press.

Gertler, M. (2003) 'Tacit knowledge and the economic geography of context', *Journal of Economic Geography*, 3: 75–99.

Gibson-Graham, J.K. (1995) 'Identity and economic plurality: Rethinking capitalism and 'capitalist hegemony', *Environment and Planning D*, 13: 275–82.

Gibson-Graham, J.K. (1996) *The End of Capitalism as We Knew It?: A Feminist Critique of Political Economy*, Oxford: Blackwell.

Gibson-Graham, J.K. (2003) 'Poststructural interventions', in E. Sheppard and T.J. Barnes (eds) *A Companion to Economic Geography*, Oxford: Blackwell.

Gibson-Graham, J.K. (2006) *Post-Capitalist Politics*, Minneapolis: University of Minnesota Press.

Gibson-Graham, J.K. and Ruccio, D. (2001) ' "After" development: Re-imagining economy and class', in J.K. Gibson-Graham, S. Resnick and R. Wolff (eds) *Re/presenting Class: Essays in Post-modern Marxism*, London: Duke University Press.

Giddens, A. (1998) *The Third Way: The Renewal of Social Democracy*, Cambridge: Polity.

Giddens, A. (2000) *The Third Way and Its Critics*, Cambridge: Polity.

Giddens, A. (2002) *Where Now for New Labour?*, Cambridge: Polity.

Gilder, G. (1981) *Wealth and Poverty*, New York: Basic Books.

Gismondi, M., Sherman, J., Richardson, J. and Richardson, M. (1996) 'Goldfish, horse logging, jock talk, and star wars: Debunking industry's green PR', *Alternatives Journal*, Fall.

Gittell, R. and Vidal, A. (1998) *Community Organizing: Building Social Capital as a Development Strategy*, London: Sage.

Glatzer, W. and Berger, R. (1988) 'Household composition, social networks and household production in Germany', in R.E. Pahl (ed.) *On Work: Historical, Comparative and Theoretical Approaches*, Oxford: Basil Blackwell.

Glover, P. (2000) *A History of Ithaca Hours*, http://www.ithacahours.com/archive/0001.html

Glyn, A. and Sutcliffe, B. (1992) 'Global but leaderless? The new capitalist order', in R. Miliband and L. Panitch (eds) *New World Order: The Socialist Register*, London: Merlin Press.

Gold, L. (2004) *The Sharing Economy: Solidarity Networks Transforming Globalisation*, Aldershot: Ashgate.

Goldschmidt-Clermond, L. (1982) *Unpaid Work in the Household: A Review of Economic Evaluation Methods*, Geneva: ILO.

Goldschmidt-Clermont, L. (1993) *Monetary Valuation of Unpaid Work: Arguing for an Output Measurement*, Geneva: Bulletin of Labour Statistics, no. 3, International Labour Office.

Goldschmidt-Clermont, L. (1998) *Measuring and Valuing Non-SNA Activities, Handbook of National Accounting, Household Accounting: Experiences in the Use of Concepts and Their Compilation – Household Satellite Extensions*, New York: United Nations.

Goldschmidt-Clermont, L. (2000) *Household Production and Income: Some Preliminary Issues*, Geneva: Bureau of Statistics, International Labour Office.

Goldsmith, E., Khor, M., Norberg-Hodge, H. and Shiva, V. (eds) (1995) *The Future of Progress: Reflections on Environment and Development*, Dartington: Green Books.

Goodin, R. (1992) *Green Political Theory*, Cambridge: Polity.

Gordon, D. (1996) *Fat and Mean: The Corporate Squeeze of Working Americans and the Myth of Managerial 'Downsizing'*, New York: Free Press.

Gorz, A. (1982) *Farewell to the Working Class: An Essay on Post-industrial Socialism*, London: Pluto.

Gorz, A. (1985) *Paths to Paradise*, London: Pluto.

Gorz, A. (1999) *Reclaiming Work: Beyond the Wage-based Society*, Cambridge: Polity.

Gottdiener, M. (2001) *The Theming of America: Dreams, Visions and Commercial Spaces*, Boulder, CO: Westview.

Gough, I. (2000) *Global Capital, Human Needs and Social Policies*, Basingstoke: Palgrave.

Grabiner, Lord (2000) *The Informal Economy*, London: HM Treasury.

Gran, E. (1998) 'Green domination in Norwegian LETSsystems: Catalyst for growth or constraint on development?', *International Journal of Community Currency Research*, 4 (http://www.le.ac.uk/ulmc/ijccr).

Granovetter, M. (1973) 'The strength of weak ties', *American Journal of Sociology*, 78, 6: 1360–80.

Graves, W. (1998) 'The geography of mutual fund assets', *The Professional Geographer*, 50, 2: 243–55.

Gray, J. (1997) *Enlightenment's Wake*, London: Routledge.

Green, D. (1993) *Reinventing Civil Society: The Rediscovery of Welfare Without Politics*, London: Institute for Economic Affairs.

Greffe, X. (1981) 'L'economie non-officielle', *Consommation*, 3: 5–16.

Gregg, P. and Wadsworth, J. (1996) *It Takes Two: Employment Polarisation in the OECD*, Discussion Paper no. 304, London: Centre for Economic Performance, London School of Economics.

Gregory, A. and Windebank, J. (2000) *Women and Work in France and Britain: Theory, Practice and Policy*, Basingstoke: Macmillan.

Gregory, C.A. (1982) *Gifts and Commodities*, London: Academic Press.

Grey, C. (2005) *A Very Short, Fairly Interesting and Reasonably Cheap Book About Studying Organizations*, London: Sage.

Grey, C. and Mitev, N. (1995) 'Reengineering organizations: A critical appraisal', *Personnel Review*, 24, 1: 6–18.

Groonroos, C. (1984) *Strategic Management and Marketing in the Service Sector*, London: Chartwell-Bratt.

Gudeman, S. (2001) *The Anthropology of Economy*, Oxford: Blackwell.

Guest, D. (1987) 'Human resource management and industrial relations', *Journal of Management Studies*, 27, 4: 377–97.

Guisinger, S. and Irfan, M. (1980) 'Pakistan's informal sector', *Journal of Development Studies*, 16, 4: 412–26.

Gulick, L. and Urwick, L. (1937) *Papers on the Science of Administration*, New York: Columbia University Press.

Hacker, S. (1987) 'Women workers and the Mondragon System of Industrial cooperatives', *Gender and Society*, 1: 358–79.

Hajer, C. (1995) *The Politics of Environmental Discourse*, Oxford: Clarendon Press.

Hakim, C. (2000) *Work-Lifestyle Choices in the 21st Century*, Oxford: Oxford University Press.

Hall, P. (1996) 'The global city', *International Social Science Journal*, 147: 15–24.

Hall, S. and Jacques, M. (1989) *New Times: The Changing Face of Politics in the 1990s*, London: Lawrence and Wishart.

Hamel, G. and Prahalad, C.K. (1996) 'Competing in the new economy: Managing out of bounds', *Strategic Management Journal*, 17: 237–42.

Hammer, M. and Champy, J. (1993) *Reengineering the Corporation*, London: Nicholas Brealey.

Hancock, P. and Tyler, M. (2001) *Work, Postmodernism and Organization: A Critical Introduction*, London: Sage.

Hancock. P.G. (1997) 'Citizenship or vassalage? Organisational membership in the age of unreason', *Organisation*, 4, 1: 93–111.

Handy, C. (1984) *The Future of Work: A Guide to a Changing Society*, Oxford: Blackwell.

Handy, C. (1989) *The Age of Unreason*, London: Arrow.

Handy, C. (1995) *The Empty Raincoat: Making Sense of the Future*, London: Arrow.

Handy, C. (2002) *The Hungry Spirit*, London: Arrow.

Hannerz, U. (1990) 'Cosmopolitans and locals in world culture', *Theory, Culture and Society*, 7, 2: 237–51.

Hapke, L. (2004) *Sweatshop: The History of an American Idea*, New Brunswick: Rutgers University Press.

Harding, R. and Cowell, F. (2004) *Social Entrepreneurship Monitor United Kingdom 2004*, London: London Business School (www.gemconsortium.org).

Hardt, M. and Negri, A. (2000) *Empire*, Cambridge, MA: Harvard University Press.

Harris, J. (1996) *Getting Employees to Fall in Love with Your Company*, New York: Amacom.

Harrison, R., Newholm, T. and Shaw, D. (eds) (2005) *The Ethical Consumer*, London: Sage.

Harvey, D. (1982) *The Limits to Capital*, Oxford: Blackwell.

Harvey, D. (1989) *The Condition of Post-Modernity: An Enquiry into the Origins of Cultural Change*, Oxford: Blackwell.

Harvey, D. (2000) *Spaces of Hope*, Edinburgh: Edinburgh University Press.

Harwood, T. (1996) 'Work and its future', *Left Business Observer*, 72.

Hawken, P. (1994) *The Ecology of Commerce*, London: Harper Collins.

Hayden, A. (1999) *Sharing the Work, Sparing the Planet: Work Time, Consumption and Ecology*, London: Zed.

Heckscher, C. (1995) *White Collar Blues: Management Loyalties in an Age of Corporate Restructuring*, New York: Basic Books.

Heckscher, C. and Donnellon, A. (1994) *The Post Bureaucratic Organisation: New Perspectives on Organisational Change*, London: Sage.

Heelas, P. (1991a) 'Cults for capitalism: Self-religions, magic and the empowerment of business', in P. Gee and J. Futo (eds) *Religion and Power: Decline and Growth*, London: British Sociological Association.

Heelas, P. (1991b) 'Reforming the self: Enterprise and the character of Thatcherism', in R. Keat and N.Abercrombie (eds) *Enterprise Culture*, London: Routledge.

Heelas, P. (1992) 'The sacralisation of the self, and New Age capitalism', in N. Abercrombie and A. Warde (eds) *Social Change in Contemporary Britain*, Cambridge: Polity.

Heelas, P. (1996) *The New Age Movement: The Celebration of the Self and the Sacralisation of Modernity*, Oxford; Blackwell.

Held, D. (2000) 'Introduction', in D. Held (ed.) *A Globalising World? Culture, Economics and Politics*, London: Routledge.

Held, D. (2005) 'Globalization: The dangers and the answers', in A. Barnett, D. Held and C. Henderson (eds) *Debating Globalization*, Cambridge: Polity.

Held, D., McGrew, A., Goldblatt, D. and Perraton, J. (1999) *Global Transformations: Politics, Economics and Culture*, Cambridge: Polity.

Hellberger, C. and Schwarze, J. (1986) *Umfang und struktur der nebenerwerbstatigkeit in der Bundesrepublik Deutschland*, Berlin: Mitteilungen aus der Arbeits-market-und Berufsforschung.

Heller, F., Pusic, E., Strauss, G. and Wilpert, B. (1998) *Organisational Participation: Myth and Reality*, Oxford: Oxford University Press.

Henderson, H. (1978) *Creating Alternative Futures*, New York: Putnam and Sons.

Henderson, H. (1999) *Beyond Globalisation: Shaping a Sustainable Global Economy*, London: Kumarian Press.

Henwood, D. (1996) 'Work and its future', *Left Business Observer*, 72.

Heydebrand, W.V. (1989) 'New organisational forms', *Work and Occupations*, 16, 3: 323–57.

Hill, C. (1991) *The World Turned Upside Down*, London: Penguin.

Hill, S., Martin, R. and Harris, M. (2000) 'Decentralization, integration and the post-bureaucratic organization: The case of R & D', *Journal of Management Studies*, 37, 4: 563–85.

Hills, J. (1998) *Thatcherism, New Labour and the Welfare State*, London: Centre for Analysis of Social Exclusion Paper 13, London School of Economics.

Himmelweit, S. (ed.) (2000) *Inside the Household: From Labour to Care*, Basingstoke: Macmillan.

Himmelweit, S. and Simonetti, R. (2000) 'Nature for sale', in S. Hinchlife and K. Woodward (eds) *The Natural and the Social: Uncertainty, Risk and Change*, London: Routledge/Open University.

Hines, C. (2000) *Localization: A Global Manifesto*, London: Earthscan.

Hirsch, D. (1999) *Welfare beyond Work: Active Participation in a New Welfare State*, York: York Publishing Services.

Hirst, P. and Thompson, G. (1992) 'The problem of "globalisation": International economic relations, national economic management and the formation of trading blocs', *Economy and Society*, 21: 357–96.

Hochschild, A.R. (1979) 'Emotion work, feeling rules and social structure', *American Journal of Sociology*, 85, 3: 551–75.

Hochschild, A.R. (1983) *The Managed Heart: Commercialisation of Human Feeling*, Berkeley, CA: University of California Press.

Hochschild, A.R. (1993) 'Preface', in S. Fineman (ed.) *Emotion in Organisations*, London: Sage.

Hochschild, A.R. (1998) *The Time Bind: When Work Becomes Home and Home Becomes Work*, New York: Metropolitan Books.

Hochschild, A.R. (2003) *The Commercialization of Intimate Life: Notes from Home and Work*, Berkeley, CA: University of California Press.

Hollingsworth, J. and Bayer, R. (eds) (1997) *Contemporary Capitalism: The Embeddedness of Institutions*, Cambridge: Cambridge University Press.

Home Office (1999) *Community Self-Help – Policy Action Team no. 9*, London: Home Office.

Hoogendijk, W. (1993) *The Economic Revolution: Towards a Sustainable Future by Freeing the Economy from Money-Making*, Utrecht: International Books.

Hopkins, M. (2003) *The Planetary Bargain: Corporate Social Responsibility Matters*, London; Earthscan.

Horgen, T.H., Joroff, M.L., Porter, W.L. and Schon, D.A. (1999) *Excellence by Design: Transforming Workplace and Work Practice*, New York: John Wiley.

Howcroft, J. (1998) 'Customer satisfaction in retail banking', *The Service Industries Journal*, 11, 1: 11–17.

Howe, L. (1990) *Being Unemployed in Northern Ireland: An Ethnographic Study*, Cambridge: Cambridge University Press.

Huczynski, A. (1993) *Management Gurus: What Makes Them and How to Become One*, London: Routledge.

Hudson, R. (2005) *Economic Geographies: Circuits, Flows and Spaces*, London: Sage.

Hutchins, D. (1988) *Just in Time*, Aldershot: Gower.

Hutton, W. (1995) *The State We're In*, London: Jonathan Cape.

Huws, U., Jagger, N. and O'Regan, S. (1999) *Teleworking and Globalisation*, Brighton: Institute for Employment Studies.

Huws, U., Korte, V. and Robinson, S. (1990) *Telework: Towards the Elusive Office*, Chichester: Wiley.

ILO (1996) *World Employment 1996/97: National Policies in a Global Context*, Geneva: International Labour Organization.

ILO (1997) *World Employment 1997–98*, Geneva: International Labour Organization.

ILO (2001) *World Employment Report 2001: Life at Work in the Information Economy*, Geneva: International Labour Organization.

ILO (2002a) *Decent Work and the Informal Economy*, Geneva: International Labour Organization.

ILO (2002b) *Women and Men in the Informal Economy: A Statistical Picture*, Geneva: International Labour Organization.

ILO (2004) *World Employment Report 2004–05: Employment, Productivity and Poverty Reduction*, Geneva: International Labour Organization.

ILO (2005) *Global Employment Trends Brief*, Geneva: International Labour Organization.

Ingleby, J. (1998) 'Local exchange and trading systems (LETS) in Australia: A new tool for community development', *International Journal of Community Currency Research*, 2 (http://www.le.ac.uk/ulmc/ijccr).

Ironmonger, D. (1996) 'Counting outputs, capital inputs and caring labor: Estimating gross household product', *Feminist Economics* 2, 3: 37–64.

Ironmonger, D. (2000) 'Measuring volunteering in economic terms', in J. Warburton and M. Oppenheimer (eds) *Volunteers and Volunteering*, Sydney: Federation Press.

Ironmonger, D. (2002) *Valuing Volunteering: The Economic Value of Volunteering in South Australia*, Melbourne: Government of South Australia.

Isles, N. (2004) *The Joy of Work?*, London: The Work Foundation.

Jackson, M. (1997) 'The problem of over-accumulation: Examining and theorising the structural form of LETS', *International Journal of Community Currency Research*, 4 (http://www.le.ac.uk/ulmc/ijccr).

Jackson, R. (2004) 'The Ecovillage Movement', *Permaculture Magazine*, 40, Summer: 1–11.

Jacob, J. (2003) 'Alternative lifestyle spaces', in A. Leyshon, R. Lee and C.C. Williams (eds) *Alternative Economic Spaces*, London: Sage.

Jacob, J., Brinkeroff, M., Jovic, E. and Wheatley, G. (2004a) 'HOUR town: Paul glover and the genesis and evolution of Ithaca HOURS', *International Journal of Community Currency Research*, 8: 29–41 (http://www.le.ac.uk/ulmc/ijccr).

Jacob, J., Brinkeroff, M., Jovic, E. and Wheatley, G. (2004b) 'The social and cultural capital of community currency: An Ithaca HOURS case study survey', *International Journal of Community Currency Research*, 8: 42–56 (http://www.le.ac.uk/ulmc/ijccr).

Jacobson, W., MacMaster, P., Thonnings, T. and Cahn, E. (2000) *Family Support and Time Dollars: How to Build Community Using Social Capital*, Chicago, IL: Family Support America.

Jacques, R. (1996) *Manufacturing the Employee*, London: Sage.

Jacques, R. (1998) 'Managing for the next century – or the last?', in C. Mabey, G. Salaman and J. Storey (eds), *Strategic Human Resource Management: A Reader*, London: Sage.

James, D. (2000) 'Fair trade, not free trade', in K. Danaher and R. Burbach (eds) *Globalize This!*, Monroe, ME: Common Courage Press.

Jensen, L., Cornwell, G.T. and Findeis, J.L. (1995) 'Informal work in nonmetropolitan Pennsylvania, *Rural Sociology*, 60: 91–107.

Jessop, B. (2002) *The Future of the Capitalist State*, Cambridge: Polity.

Johanisova, N. (2005) *Living in the Cracks*, Dartington: Green Books.

Jones, B. (1997) *Forcing the Factory of the Future: Cybernation and Societal Institutions*, Cambridge: Cambridge University Press.

Jordan, B. (1998) *The New Politics of Welfare: Social Justice in a Global Context*, London: Sage.

Jordan, B. and Jordan, C. (2000) *Social Work and the Third Way: Tough Love as Social Policy*, London: Sage.

Jordan, B., Agulnik, P., Burbridge, D. and Duffin, S. (2000) *Stumbling Towards Basic Income: The Prospects for Tax-Benefit Integration*, London: Citizen's Income Study Centre.

Juster, T.F. and Stafford, F.P. (1991) 'The allocation of time: Empirical findings, behavioural models and problems of measurement', *Journal of Economic Literature*, 29, 2: 471–522.

Kalleberg, A. (2001) 'Organising flexibility: The flexible firm in a new century', *British Journal of Industrial Relations*, 39: 479–504.

Kaminsky, G. and Schmuckler, S. (2002) *Short-run Pain, Long-run Gain: The Effects of Financial Liberalization*, unpublished working paper, Washington, DC: International Monetary Fund.

Kanter, R. (1977) *Men and Women of the Corporation*, New York: Basic Books.

Kanter, R. (1989) *When Giants Learn to Dance*, London: Simon and Schuster.

Karoly, L.A. and Panis, C.W.A. (2004) *The 21st Century at Work: Forces Shaping the Future Workforce and Workplace in the United States*, Santa Monica, CA: Rand.

Karolyi, A. and Stulz, R. (2003) 'Are assets priced locally or globally?', in G. Constantinides, M. Harris and R. Stulz (eds) *The Handbook of the Economics of Finance*, New York: North-Holland Publishers.

Kasmir, S. (1996) *The Myth of Mondragon: Cooperatives, Politics and Working Class Life in a Basque Town*, New York: State University of New York Press.

Kerr, C., Dunlop, J., Harbison, F. and Meyers, C. (1973) *Industrialism and Industrial Man*, Harmondsworth: Penguin.

Kerr, D. (1998) 'The private finance initiative and the changing governance of the built environment', *Urban Studies*, 35: 277–301.

Kindelberger, C.P. (1969) *American Business Abroad*, New Haven, CT: Yale University Press.

King, D. and Wickham-Jones, M. (1998) 'Bridging the Atlantic: The Democratic (Party) origins of welfare to work', in M. Powell (ed.) *New Labour, New Welfare State? The 'Third Way' in British Social Policy*, Bristol: The Policy Press.

King, Y. (1983) 'Toward an ecological feminism and a feminist ecology', in J. Rothschild (ed.) *Machina ex dea: Feminist Perspectives on Technology*, Oxford: Pergamon.

Knights, D. and McCabe, D. (1994) 'Total quality management and organisational "grey" matter', paper presented at Work, Employment and Society conference, Canterbury, Kent, September.

Kobrin, S.J. (1997) 'Electronic cash and the end of national markets', *Foreign Policy*, Summer, 65–77.

Kochan, T. and Osterman, P. (1998) 'The mutual gains enterprise', in C. Mabey, G. Salaman and J. Storey (eds) *Strategic Human Resource Management: A Reader*, London: Sage.

Kochan, T., Katz, H. and McKersie, R. (1986) *The Transformation of American Industrial Relations*, New York: Basic Books.

Koopmans, C.C. (1989) *Informele Arbeid: vraag, aanbod, participanten, prijzen*, Amsterdam: Proefschrift Universitiet van Amsterdam.

Kostera, M. (1995) 'The modern crusade: The missionaries of management come to eastern Europe', *Management Learning*, 26: 331–52.

Kovel, J. (2002) *The Enemy of Nature: The End of Capitalism or the End of the World?* London: Zed.

Kumar, K. (1995) *From Post-Industrial to Post-Modern Society: New Theories of the Contemporary World*, Oxford: Blackwell.

Kunda, G. (1992) *Engineering Culture: Control and Commitment in a High-Tech Corporation*, Philadelphia: Temple University Press.

Lagos, R.A. (1995) 'Formalising the informal sector: Barriers and costs', *Development and Change*, 26: 110–31.

Laing, A., Duffy, F., Jaunzens, D. and Willis, S. (1998) *New Environments for Working*, London: BRE and DEGW.

Lalonde, B. and Simmonet, D. (1978) *Quand Vous Voudrez*, Paris: Pauvert.

Latouche, S. (1993) *In the Wake of Affluent Society: An Exploration of Post-development*, London: Zed.

Latour, B. (1993) *We Have Never Been Modern*, Hemel Hempstead: Harvester Wheatsheaf.

Latour, B. (1995) 'The manager as network', *Organizational Studies*, 6: 13–24.

Lautier, B. (1994) *L'Economie Informelle dans le Tiers Monde*, Paris: La Decouverte.

Lave, J. and Wenger, E. (1991) *Situated Learning: Legitimate Peripheral Participation*, Cambridge: Cambridge University Press.

Laville, J.-L. (1995) 'La crise de la condition salariale: emploi, activite et nouvelle question sociale', *Esprit*, 12: 32–54.

Laville, J.-L. (1996) 'Economy and solidarity: Exploring the issues', in OECD (ed.) *Reconciling Economy and Society: Towards a Plural Economy*, Paris: OECD.

Law, A. (1999) *Creative Compnay: How St. Lukes Became the Ad Agency to End All Ad Agencies*, London: John Wiley.

Law, A. (2001) *Open Minds; 21st Century Business Lessons and Innovations from St Lukes*, New York: Texere.

Lazreg, M. (2002) 'Development: Feminist theory's cul-de-sac', in K. Saunders (ed.) *Feminist Post-Development Thought: Rethinking Modernity, Post-colonialism and Representation*, London: Zed.

Leadbeater, C. (1999) *Living on Thin Air: The New Economy*, Harmondsworth: Penguin.

Leadbeater, C. and Martin, S. (1997) *The Employee Mutual: Combining Flexibility with Security in the New World of Work*, London: Demos.

Leadbetter, C. (1997) *The Rise of the Social Entrepreneur*, London: Demos.

Lee, A. and Lee, E.B. (1995) 'The iconography of propoaganda analysis', *Etc.*, 52, 1: 13–17.

Lee, R. (1996) 'Moral money? LETS and the social construction of economic geographies in south east England', *Environment and Planning A*, 28: 1377–94.

Lee, R. (1999) 'Production', in P. Cloke, P. Crang and M. Goodwin (eds) *Introducing Human Geographies*, London: Arnold.

Lee, R. (2000a) 'Informal sector', in R.J. Johnston, D. Gregory, G. Pratt and M. Watts (eds) *The Dictionary of Human Geography*, Oxford: Blackwell.

Lee, R. (2000b) 'Shelter from the storm? Geographies of regard in the worlds of horticultural consumption and production', *Geoforum*, 31: 137–57.

Legge, K. (1989) 'Human resource managemnt: A critical analysis', in J. Storey (ed.) *New Perspectives in Human Resource Management*, London: Routledge.

Legge, K. (1995) *Human Resource Management: Rhetorics and Realities*, Basingstoke: Macmillan.

Lemieux, T., Fortin, B. and Frechette, P. (1994) 'The effect of taxes on labor supply in the underground economy', *American Economic Review*, 84, 1: 231–54.

Lesser, E.L. and Storck, J. (2001) 'Communities of practice and organisational performance', *IBM Systems Journal*, 40, 4 (http://www.research.ibm.com/journal/sj/404/lesser.html).

Levitas, R. (1998) *The Inclusive Society? Social Exclusion and New Labour*, Basingstoke: Macmillan.

Lewchuck, W. and Robertson, D. (1996) 'Working conditions under lean production: A worker-based bench marking survey', in P. Stewart (ed.) *Beyond Japanese Management: The End of Modern Times?*, London: Routledge.

Lewis, A. (1959) *The Theory of Economic Growth*, London: Allen and Unwin.

Lewis, B.R. (1988) 'Customer care in service orgaisations', *International Journal of Operations and Production Management*, 8: 3.

Lewis, K.K. (1999) 'Trying to explain the home bias in equities and consumption', *Journal of Economic Literature*, 37: 571–608.

Leyshon, A. (1995) 'Geographies of money and finance I', *Progress in Human Geography*, 19: 531–43.

Leyshon, A. (1997) 'Geographies of money and finance II', *Progress in Human Geography*, 21, 3: 381–92.

Leyshon, A. (1998) 'Geographies of money and finance III', *Progress in Human Geography*, 22, 3: 433–46.

Leyshon, A. (2005) 'Introduction: Diverse economies', *Antipode*, 37, 5: 856–62.

Leyshon, A. and Lee, R. (2003) 'Introduction: alternative economic geographies', in A. Leyshon, R. Lee and C.C. Williams (eds) *Alternative Economic Spaces*, London: Sage.

Leyshon, A. and Thrift, N.J. (1997) *Money/Space: Geographies of Monetary Transformation*, London: Routledge.

Leyshon, A., Lee, R. and Williams, C.C. (eds) (2003) *Alternative Economic Spaces*, London: Sage.

Lichtenstein, P.M. (1986) 'The concept of the form in the economic theory of alternative organisations', in S. Jansson and A.B. Hellmark (eds) *Labour-Owned Firms and Workers' Cooperatives*, London: Gower.

Liebman, J. (1998) *Lessons about Tax-Benefit Integration from the US Earned Income Tax Credit Experience*, York: York Publishing Services.

Lindbeck, A. (1981) *Work Disincentives in the Welfare State*, Stockholm: Institute for International Economic Studies, University of Stockholm.

Lipietz, A. (1992) *Towards a New Economic Order: Post-Fordism, Ecology and Democracy*, Cambridge: Polity.

Lipietz, A. (1995) *Green Hopes: The Future of Political Ecology*, Cambridge: Polity.

Littler, C.R. (1982) *The Development of the Labour Process in Capitalist Societies*, Aldershot: Gower.

Lobo, F.M. (1990a) 'Irregular work in Spain', in *Underground Economy and Irregular Forms of Employment, Final Synthesis Report*, Brussels: Office for Official Publications of the European Communities.

Lobo, F.M. (1990b) 'Irregular work in Portugal', in *Underground Economy and Irregular Forms of Employment, Final Synthesis Report*, Brussels: Office for Official Publications of the European Communities.

Lodemel, I. and Trickey, H. (2001) *An Offer You Can't Refuse: Workfare in International Perspective*, Bristol: The Policy Press.

Lopezllera-Mendez, L. and DeMeulenaere, S. (2000) 'Towards an economy in the hands of the people: The Tianguis Tlaloc local currency system', *International Journal of Community Currency Research*, 4 (http://www.le.ac.uk/ulmc/ijccr).

Lozano, B. (1989) *The Invisible Workforce: Transforming American Business with Outside and Home-based Workers*, New York: The Free Press.

Lubbers, E. (ed.) (2002) *Battling Big Business: Countering Greenwash, Infiltration and Other Forms of Corporate Bullying*, Dartington: Green Books.

Lubell, H. (1991) *The Informal Sector in the 1980s and 1990s*, Paris: Organisation for Economic Co-operation and Development.

Lubich, C. (2001) *L'Economia di Comunione: storia e profezia*, Rome: Citté Nuova.

Lund, F. (2003) 'Introduction: A new approach to social protection', in F. Lund and J. Nicholson (eds) *Chains of Production, Ladders of Protection: Social Protection for Workers in the Informal Economy*, Durban: School of Development Studies, University of Natal.

Lutz, M. (1999) *Economics for the Common Good: Two Centuries of Social Economic Thought in the Humanistic Tradition*, London: Routledge.

Luxton, M. (1997) 'The UN, women and household labour: Measuring and valuing unpaid work', *Women's Studies International Forum*, 20: 431–9.

Lyon, D. (1993) 'An electronic panopticon: A sociological critique of surveillance theory', *Sociological Review*, 41, 4: 653–78.

Mabbett, D. (2001) 'Mutuality in insurance and social security: Retrospect and prospect', in J. Birchall (ed.) *The New Mutualism in Public Policy*, London: Routledge.

Macfarlane, R. (1996) *Unshackling the Poor: A Complementary Approach to Local Economic Development*, York: Joseph Rowntree Foundation.

MacLeod, G. (1997) *From Mondragon to America: Experiments in Community Economic Development*, Sidney, Nova Scotia: University of Cape Breton Press.

Maffesoli, M. (1996) *The Time of the Tribes: The Decline of Individualism in Mass Society*, London: Sage.

Maldonado, C. (1995) 'The informal sector: Legalization or laissez-faire?', *International Labour Review*, 134, 6: 705–28.

Malone, T.W. (2004) *The Future of Work: How the New Order of Business will Shape Your Organization, Your Management Style and Your Life*, Boston, MA: Harvard Business School Press.

Mander, J. and Goldsmith, E. (eds) (1996) *The Case Against the Global Economy: And for a Turn Toward the Local*, San Francisco: Sierra Club.

Marshall, P. (1993) *Demanding the Impossible: A History of Anarchism*, London: Fontana Books.

Martin, C.J. (1996) 'Economic strategies and moral principles in the survival of poor households in Mexico', *Bulletin of Latin American Research*, 15, 2: 193–210.

Martin, R. and Sunley, P. (2001) 'Rethinking the "economic" in economic geography: Broadening our vision or losing our focus?', *Antipode*, 33: 148–61.

Martin, R.L. (1999a) 'The new economic geography of money', in R. Martin (ed.) *Money and the Space Economy*, London: Wiley.

Martin, R.L. (1999b) 'Selling off the state: Privatisation, the equity market and the geographies of shareholder capitalism', in R. Martin (ed.) *Money and the Space Economy*, London: Wiley.

Massey, D. (2000) 'The geography of power', in B. Gunnell and D. Timms (eds) *After Seattle: Globalization and Its Discontents*, London: Catalyst.

Massey, D. (2005) *For Space*, London: Sage.

Mathews, R. (1999) *Jobs of Their Own: Building a Stakeholder Society*, London: Pluto.

Mathews, R. (2001) 'Mutuals in regional economic development: Mondragon and Desjardins', in J. Birchall (ed.) *The New Mutualism in Public Policy*, London: Routledge.

Mattera, P. (1980) 'Small is not beautiful: Decentralised production and the underground economy in Italy', *Radical America*, 14, 5: 67–76.

Matthews, K. (1983) 'National income and the black economy', *Journal of Economic Affairs*, 3, 4: 261–7.

Mauthner, N., McKee, L. and Strell, M. (2001) *Work and Family Life in Rural Communities*, York: York Publishing Services.

Maxwell, T. (2000) 'All change at securities trust', *Martin Currie Investment Trusts Communique*, 5: 3.

May, T. (1994) *The Political Philosophy of Poststructuralist Anarchism*, Pennsylvania: Pennsylvania State University Press.

Mayo, E. (1933) *The Human Problems of Industral Civilisation*, New York: Macmillan.

Mayo, E. (1996) 'Dreaming of work', in P. Meadows (ed.) *Work Out or Work In? Contributions to the Debate on the Future of Work*, York: Joseph Rowntree Foundation.

McBurney, S. (1990) *Ecology into Economics Won't Go: Or Life Is Not a Concept*, Dartington: Green Books.

McCabe, D., Knights, D. and Wilkinson, A. (1994) *Quality Initiatives in Financial Services*, Research report, Manchester: Financial Services Research Centre, Manchester School of Management, UMIST.

McCarthy, O., Briscoe, R. and Ward, M. (2001) 'Mutuality through credit unions: A cross-national approach', in J. Birchall (ed.) *The New Mutualism in Public Policy*, London: Routledge.

McCormick, J. (1994) *Citizens' Service*, London: Institute for Public Policy Research.

McDowell, L. (2001) 'Father and Ford revisited: Gender, class and employment change in the new millennium', *Transactions of the Institute of British Geographers*, NS 26, 4: 448–64.

McEwan, C. (2001) 'Geography, culture and global change', in P. Daniels, M. Bradshaw, D. Shaw and J. Sidaway (eds) *Human Geography: Issues for the 21st Century*, London: Prentice Hall.

McKay, A. and Vanavery, J. (2000) 'Gender, family and income maintenance: A feminist case for citizen's basic income', *Social Politics*, 7, 2: 266–84.

McKinlay, A. and Taylor, P. (1996) 'Power, surveillance and resistance', in P. Ackers, C. Smith and P. Smith (eds) *The New Workplace and Trade Unionism*, London: Routledge.

McKinlay, A. and Taylor, P. (1997) 'Foucault and the politics of production', in A. McKinlay and K. Starkey (eds) *Foucault, Management and Organisation*, London: Sage.

McLaughlin, E. (1994) *Flexibility in Work and Benefits*, London: Institute of Public Policy Research.

Meadows, P. (1997) *The Integration of Taxes and Benefits for Working Families with Children: Issues Raised to Date*, York: York Publishing Services.

Meagher, K. (1995) 'Crises, informalization and the urban informal sector in sub-Saharan Africa', *Development and Change*, 26, 2: 259–84.

Meehan, E. (1993) *Citizenship and the European Community*, London: Sage.

Meeker-Lowry, S. (1996) 'Community money: The potential of local currency', in J. Mander and E. Goldsmith (eds) *The Case Against Globalization*, San Francisco: Sierra Club Books.

Meiksins Wood, E. (2003) 'A manifesto for global capital?', in G. Balakrishnan (ed.) *Debating Empire*, London: Verso.

Mellor, M., Hannah, J. and Stirling J. (1988) *Worker Co-operatives in Theory and Practice*, Milton Keynes: Open University Press.

Merchant, C. (1980) *The Death of Nature: Women, Ecology and the Scientific Revolution*, Oxford: Pergamon.

Merchant, C. (1996) *Earthcare*, London: Routledge.

Merton, R. (1949) *Social Theory and Social Structure*, New York: Collier Macmillan.

Mĕstrović, S. (1997) *Post-Emotional Society*, London: Sage.

Meurs, M. (2002) 'Economic strategies of surviving post-socialism: Changing household economies and gender divisions of labour in the Bulgarian transition', in A. Rainnie, A. Smith and A. Swain (eds) *Work, Employment and Transition: Restructuring Livelihoods in Post-communism*, London: Routledge.

Milani, B. (2000) *Designing the Green Economy: The Post-industrial Alternative to Corporate Globalisation*, Lanham, MD: Rowman and Littlefield.

Milkman, R. (1997) *Farewell to the Factory: Auto Workers in the Late Twentieth Century*, Berkeley: University of California Press.

Milkman, R. (1998) 'The new American workplace: high road or low road?', in P. Thompson and C. Warhurst (eds) *Workplaces of the Future*, Basingstoke: Palgrave.

Millar, J. and Hole, D. (1998) *Integrated Family Benefits in Australia and Options for the UK Tax Return System*, York: York Publishing Services.

Miller, D. (ed.) (2001) *Home Possessions: Material Culture Behind Closed Doors*, Oxford: Berg.

Miller, P. and Rose, N. (1990) 'Governing economic life', *Economy and Society*, 19: 1–31.

Minc, A. (1980) 'Le chomage et l'economie souterraine', *Le Debat* 2: 3–14.

Minc, A. (1982) *L'Apres-Crise a Commence*, Paris: Gallimard.

Mingione, E. (1991) *Fragmented Societies: A Sociology of Economic Life beyond the Market Paradigm*, Oxford: Basil Blackwell.

Mingione, E. and Morlicchio, E. (1993) 'New forms of urban poverty in Italy: Risk path models in the North and South', *International Journal of Urban and Regional Research* 17, 3: 413–27.

Mitchell, K., Marston, S.A. and Katz, C. (2004) 'Life's work: An introduction, review and critique', in K. Mitchell, S.A. Marston and C. Katz (eds) *Life's Work: Geographies of Social Reproduction*, Oxford: Blackwell.

Mol, A.P.J. (1999) 'Ecological modernisation and the environmental transition of Europe', *Journal of Environmental Policy and Planning*, 1, 167–81.

Mol, A.P.J. and Sommerfield, D.A. (eds) (2000) *Ecological Modernisation Around the World*, London: Cass.

Mollison, B. (1979) *Permaculture: Practical Design for Town and Country in Permanent Agriculture*, Stanley, Tasmania: Tagari Books.

Mollison, B. (1991) *Introduction to Permaculture*, Stanley, Tasmania: Tagari Publications.

Mollison, B. (1992) *Permaculture: A Designer's Manual*, Stanley, Tasmania: Tagari Books.

Monbiot, G. (2002) 'The greens get eaten', in E. Lubbers (ed.) *Battling Big Business: Countering Greenwash, Infiltration and Other Forms of Corporate Bullying*, Dartington: Green Books.

Mooney, J.D. and Riley, A.C. (1931) *Onward Industry*, New York: Harper.

Morehouse, W. (1997) (ed.) *Building Sustainable Communities: Tools and Concepts for Self-reliant Economic Change*, Charlbury: Jon Carpenter.

Morel, C. (2003) *Corporate Support of the Arts in France*, Sheffield: PhD thesis, Department of French Studies, University of Sheffield.

Morris, L. (1994) 'Informal aspects of social divisions', *International Journal of Urban and Regional Research*, 18: 112–26.

Motavelli, J. (1996) 'Enough!', *E: The Environmental Magazine*, 7, 2: 28–35.

Mueller, F. (1994) 'Teams between hierarchy and commitment: Change strategies and the "internal environment" ', *Journal of Management Studies*, 31: 383–404.

Murgatroyd, L. and Neuburger, H. (1997) 'A household satellite account for the UK', *Economic Trends*, 527: 63–71.

Murray, C. (1984) *Losing Ground: American Social Policy, 1950–1980*, New York: Basic Books.

Myles, J. (1996) 'When markets fail: Social welfare in Canada and the US', in G. Esping-Anderson (ed.) *Welfare States in Transition: National Adaptations in Global Economies*, London: Sage.

Myreson, J. and Ross, P. (1999) *The Creative Office*, London: Lawrence King.

Naess, A. (1986) 'The deep ecology movement: Some philosophical aspects', *Philosophical Inquiry* III, 1/2: 10–31.

Naess, A. (1989) *Ecology, Community and Lifestyle: Outline of an Ecosophy*, Cambridge: Cambridge University Press.

Naisbitt, J. (1984) *Megtrends: Ten New Directions Transforming Our Lives*, New York: Warner Brothers.

Naisbitt, J., Naisbitt, N. and Phillips, D. (2001) *High Tech/High Touch: Technology and Our Search for Meaning*, London: Nicholas Brealey.

Neef, R. (2002) 'Observations of the concept and forms of the informal economy in eastern Europe', in R. Neef and M. Stanculescu (eds) *The Social Impact of Informal Economies in Eastern Europe*, Aldershot: Ashgate.

Newton, T. and Harte, G. (1997) 'Green business: Technicist kitsch?', *Journal of Management Studies*, 34/1: 75–98.

Nicholls, A. and Opal, C. (2005) *Fair trade: Market-driven ethical consumption*, London: Sage.

Nilsson, J. (2001) 'Farmer co-operatives: Organisational models and their business environment', in J. Birchall (ed.) *The New Mutualism in Public Policy*, London: Routledge.

Nohria, N. (1992) 'Is a network perspective a useful way of studying organizations?', in N. Nohria and R.G. Eccles (eds) *Networks and Organizations*, Boston, MA: Harvard Business School Press.

Nolan, P. and Slater, G. (2003) 'The labour market: History, structure and prospects', in P.K. Edwards (ed.) *Industrial Relations: Theory and Practice*, Oxford: Blackwell.

Nolan, P. and Wood, S. (2003) 'Mapping the future of work', *British Journal of Industrial Relations*, 41, 2: 165–74.

Nonaka, I. (1991) 'The knowledge-creating company', *Harvard Business Review*, November–December: 96–104.

Nonaka, I. and Takeuchi, H. (1995) *The Knowledge-Creating Company: How Japanese Companies Create the Dynamics of Innovation*, Oxford: Oxford University Press.

Nonaka, I., Toyama, R. and Konno, U. (2001) 'SECI, Ba and leadership: A unified model of dynamic knowledge creation', in I. Nonaka and D. Teece (eds) *Managing Industrial Knowledge: Creation, Transfer, Utilization*, London: Sage.

Noon, M. and Blyton, P. (2002) *The Realities of Work*, Basingstoke: Palgrave.

Norberg-Hodge, H. (2001) 'Local lifeline: Rejecting globalization-embracing localization', in V. Bennholdt-Thomsen, N. Faraclas and C. von Werlhof (eds) *There is an Alternative: Subsistence and Worldwide Resistance to Corporate Globalization*, London: Zed.

North, P. (1998) 'Exploring the politics of social movements through "sociological intervention": A case study of Local Exchange Trading Schemes', *The Sociological Review*, 46, 3: 564–82.

North, P. (2005) *Alternative Currency Movements as a Challenge to Globalisation? A Case Study of Manchester's Local Currency Networks*, Aldershot: Ashgate.

Notes from Nowhere (2003) *We are Everywhere: The Irresistible Rise of Global Anticapitalism*, London: Verso (www.WeAreEverywhere.org).

O'Brien, R. (1992) *Global Financial Integration: The End of Geography*, London: Royal Institute of International Affairs.

O'Doherty, R.K., Durrschmidt, J., Jowers, P. and Purdue, D.A. (1999) 'Local exchange and trading schemes: A useful strand of community development?', *Environment and Planning A*, 31: 1639–53.

O'Neill, P. and Gibson-Graham, J.K. (1999) 'Enterprise discourse and executive talk: Stories that destabilize the company', *Transactions of the Institute of British Geographers*, 24: 11–22.

O'Neill, P.M. (1997) 'Bringing the qualitative state into economic geography', in R. Lee and J. Wills (eds) *Geographies of Economies*, London: Arnold.

O'Riordan, T. (1996) 'Environmentalism on the move', in I. Douglas, R. Huggett and M. Robinson (eds) *Companion Encyclopaedia of Geography*, London: Routledge.

Obstfeld, M. and Rogoff, K. (2000) 'New directions for stochastic open economy models', *Journal of International Economics*, 50, 1: 117–53.

OECD (ed.) (1996) *Reconciling Economy and Society: Towards a Plural Economy*, Paris: OECD.

OECD (1997) *Framework for the Measurement of Unrecorded Economic Activities in Transition Economies* (OCDE/GDE (97), 177), Paris: OECD.

OECD (2002) *Measuring the Non-Observed Economy*, Paris: OECD.

Offe, C. (1985) *Disorganised Capitalism: Contemporary Transformations of Work and Politics*, Cambridge: Polity.

Ohmae, K. (1990) *The Borderless World: Power and Strategy in the Interlinked Economy*, London: Harper Collins.

Ohmae, K. (1995a) *The Evolving Global Economy*, Cambridge, MA: Harvard Business Review Books.

Ohmae, K. (1995b) *The End of the Nation-State: The Rise of Regional Economies*, London: Harper Collins.

Okun, A.M. (1975) *Equality and Efficiency: The Big Trade-off*, Washington, DC: Brookings Institute.

Olson, M. (1989) 'Organisational barriers to professional telework', in E. Boris and C. Daniels (eds) *Homework: Historical and Contemporary Perspectives on Paid Labour at Home*, Chicago: University of Illinois Press.

Olson, M.H. and Primps, S.B. (1984) 'Working at home with computers: Work and non-work issues', *Journal of Social Issues*, Fall: 97–112.

Orru, M., Biggart, N.W. and Hamilton, G.G. (1997) *The Economic Organisation of East Asian Capitalism*, Thousand Oaks, CA: Sage.

Oxley, H. (1999) 'Income dynamics: Inter-generational evidence', in Centre for Analysis of Social Exclusion (ed.) *Persistent Poverty and Lifetime Inequality: The Evidence*, London: CASE Report 5, London School of Economics.

Pacione, M. (1997) 'Local Exchange Trading Systems as a response to the globalisation of capitalism', *Urban Studies*, 34: 1179–99.

Pahl, R.E. (1984) *Divisions of Labour*, Oxford: Blackwell.

Pahl, R.E. (1995) *After Success*, Cambridge: Polity.

Painter, J. (2003) 'State and governance', in E. Sheppard and T.J. Barnes (eds) *A Companion to Economic Geography*, Oxford: Blackwell.

Palmer, B. (1979) 'Class, conception and conflict', *Review of Radical Political Economics*, 7, 2: 31–49.

Parker, H. and Sutherland, H. (1998) 'How to get rid of the poverty trap: Basic income plus national wage', *Citizens Income Bulletin*, 25: 11–14.

Parker, M. (1993) 'Life after Jean-Francois', in J. Hassard and M. Parker (eds) *Postmodernism and Organisations*, London: Sage.

Parker, M. (1997) 'Organizations and citizenship', *Organisation*, 4, 1: 75–92.

Parker, M. (2000) *Organizational Culture and Identity: Unity and Divison at Work*, London: Sage.

Parker, M. (2002a) 'Utopia and the organizational imagination', in M. Parker (ed.) *Utopia and Organization*, Oxford: Blackwell.

Parker, M. (2002b) 'Utopia and the organizational imagination: Eutopia', in M. Parker (ed.) *Utopia and Organization*, Oxford: Blackwell.

Parker, M. (2002c) *Against Management*, Cambridge: Polity.

Parker, M., Fournier, V. and Reedy, P. (2006) *Dictionary of Utopia and Alternatives*, London: Zed.

Parry, J.M. (1994) 'Mondragon pushed to the peak of success', *The European*, 28 October.

Pavlovskaya, M. (2004) 'Other transitions: Multiple economies of Moscow households in the 1990s', *Annals of the Association of American Geographers*, 94: 329–51.

Peattie, L.R. (1980) 'Anthropological perspectives on the concepts of dualism, the informal sector and marginality in developing urban economies', *International Regional Science Review*, 5, 1: 1–31.

Peck, J. (1996) *Work-Place: The Social Regulation of Labour Markets*, London: Guildford Press.

Peck, J. (2001) *Workfare States*, London: Guildford Press.

Peppard, J. and Rowland, P. (1995) *The Essence of Business Process Re-engineering*, London: Prentice Hall.

Perrow, C. (1992) 'Small firm networks', in N. Nohria and R.G. Eccles (eds) *Networks and Organisations*, Boston: Harvard University Business School Press.

Peters, T. (1987) *Thriving on Chaos: Handbook for a Management Revolution*, London: Harper and Row.

Peters, T. (1992) *Liberation Management*, London: Macmillan.

Peters, T. (1994) *The Tom Peters Seminar: Crazy Times Call for Crazy Organisations*, London: Macmillan.

Peters, T. and Waterman, R. (1982) *In Search of Excellence*, New York: Warner Communications.

Pettifor, A. (2003a) 'Executive summary', in A. Pettifor (ed.) *Real World Economic Outlook: The Legacy of Globalization: Debt and Deflation*, Basingstoke: Palgrave Macmillan.

Pettifor, A. (2003b) 'Introduction', in A. Pettifor (ed.) *Real World Economic Outlook: The Legacy of Globalization: Debt and Deflation*, Basingstoke: Palgrave Macmillan.

Pettifor, A. and Greenhill, R. (2003) 'Framework for economic justice and sustainability', in A. Pettifor (ed.) *Real World Economic Outlook: The Legacy of Globalization: Debt and Deflation*, Basingstoke: Palgrave Macmillan.

Piirainen, T. (1997) *Towards a New Social Order in Russia: Transforming Structures and Everyday Life*, Aldershot: Dartmouth.

Pils, F. and Macduffie, J.P. (1997) 'Japanese and local influences: Human resource practices and policies of north American transplants in north America', in P. Stewart (ed.) *Employee Relations: Continuity and Innovation*, Acts du Gerspia, 21, Oxford: Oxford University Press.

Pinch, S. (1994) 'Social polarization: A comparison of evidence from Britain and the United States', *Environment and Planning A* 25, 6: 779–95.

Piore, M. and Sabel, C. (1984) *The Second Industrial Divide: Possibilities for Prosperity*, New York: Basic Books.

Plant, C. and Plant, J. (1991) *Green Business: Hope or Hoax*, Bidefored: Green Books.

Polanyi, K. (1944) *The Great Transformation*, Boston: Beacon Press.

Polanyi, M. (1967) *The Tacit Dimension*, London: Routledge and Kegan Paul.

Pollert, A. (1988a) 'Dismantling flexibility', *Capital and Class*, 34: 42–75.

Pollert, A. (1988b) 'The flexible firm: Fixation or fact?', *Work, Employment and Society*, 2, 3: 281–316.

Pollert, A. (1996) ' "Teamwork" on the assembly line', in P. Ackers, C. Smith and P. Smith (eds) *The New Workplace and Trade Unionism*, London: Routledge.

Porritt, J. (1996) 'Local jobs depend on local initiative', *Finance North*, September/October: 88.

Porteous, D.J. (1995) *The Geography of Finance: Spatial Dimensions of Intermediary Behaviour*, Aldershot: Avebury.

Porter, M.E. (1990) *The Competitive Advantage of Nations*, London: Macmillan.

Portes, A. (1994) 'The informal economy and its paradoxes', in N.J. Smelser and R. Swedberg (eds) *The Handbook of Economic Sociology*, Princeton: Princeton University Press.

Portes, A. (1998) 'Social capital: Its origins and applications in modern sociology', *Annual Review of Sociology*, 24, 1: 1–24.

Portes, A., Blitzer, S. and Curtis, J. (1986) 'The urban informal sector in Uruguay: Its internal structure, characteristics and effects', *World Development*, 14, 6: 727–41.

Powell, J. (2002) 'Petty capitalism, perfecting capitalism or post-capitalism? Lessons from the Argentinean barter network', *Review of International Political Economy*, 9, 4: 224–36.

Powell, W. (1990) 'Neither market nor hierarchy: Network forms of organisation', in G. Thompson, J. Frances, R. Lavacic and J. Mitchell (eds) *Markets, Hierarchies and Networks*, London: Sage.

Poynter, G. (2002) *Restructuring in the Service Industries: Management Reform and Workplace Reform and Workplace Relations in the UK Service Sector*, London: Mansell.

Prethus, R. (1962) *The Organisational Society*, London: Macmillan.

Primavesi, A. (2000) *Sacred Gaia: Holistic Theology and Earth System Science*, London: Routledge.

Prime, D., Zimmeck, M. and Zurawan, A. (2002) *Active Communities: Initial Findings from the 2001 Home Office Citizenship Survey*, London: Home Office.

Pringle, R. (1989) *Secretaries Talk: Sexuality, Power and Work*, London: Verso.

Procter, S.J. and Mueller, F. (eds) (2000) *Teamworking*, Basingstoke: Macmillan.

Putnam, R. (2000) *Bowling Alone: The Collapse and Revival of American Community*, London: Simon and Schuster.

Putterman, L. (1990) *Division of Labor and Welfare: An Introduction to Economic Systems*, Oxford: Oxford University Press.

Quijano, A. (2001) 'The growing significance of reciprocity from below: Marginality and informality under debate', in F. Tabak and M.A. Crichlow (eds) *Informalization: Process and Structure*, Baltimore: John Hopkins University Press.

Quinn, D. (1997) 'The correlates of change in international financial regulation', *American Political Science Review*, 91: 531–51.

Rakowski, C.A. (1994) 'Convergence and divergence in the informal sector debate: A focus on Latin America, 1984–92', *World Development*, 22, 4: 501–16.

Ram, M., Edwards, P. and Jones, T. (2002) *Employers and Illegal Migrant Workers in the Clothing and Restaurant Sectors*, London: DTI Central Unit Research.

Ramsay, H. (1992) 'Swedish and Japanese work methods: Comparisons and contrasts', *European Participation Monitor*, 3: 37–40.

Ransome, P. (1999) *Sociology and the Future of Work: Contemporary Discourses and Debates*, Aldershot: Ashgate.

Ransome, P. (2005) *Work, Consumption and Culture: Affluence and Social Change in the Twenty-First Century*, London: Sage.

Raymond, S. and Cunliffe, R. (1997) *Tomorrow's Office: Creating Effective and Humane Interiors*, London: E and F Spon.

Reed, M. (1992) *The Sociology of Organisations: Themes, Perspectives and Prospects*, Hemel Hempstead: Harvester Wheatsheaf.

Reed, M. (1996) 'Expert power and control in late modernity: An empricial review and theoretical synthesis', *Organisation Studies*, 17, 4: 573–97.

Reed, M. (2005) 'Beyond the iron cage? Bureaucracy and democracy in the knowledge economy and society', in P. du Gay (ed.) *The Values of Bureaucracy*, Oxford: Oxford University Press.

Reedy, P. (2002) 'Keeping the black flag flying: Anarchy, utopia and the politics of nostalgia', in M. Parker (ed.) *Utopia and Organization*, Oxford: Blackwell.

Reich, R. (1991) 'Who is them?', *Harvard Business Review*, March–April.

Reich, R. (1993) *The Work of Nations*, London: Simon and Schuster.

Reich, R. (2002) *The Future of Success*, London: Vintage.

Reid, M. (1934) *Economics of Household Production*, New York: John Wiley.

Rice, R.E. and Katz, J.E. (2003) 'Comparing internet and mobile phone usage: Digital divides of usage, adoption and dropouts', *Telecommunications Policy*, 27, 8–9: 597–623.

Rifkin, J. (1990) *The Myth of the Market: Promises and Illusions*, Dartington: Green Books.

Rifkin, J. (1996) *The End of Work: The Decline of the Global Labor Force and the Dawn of a Post-market Era*, New York: G.P. Putnam.

Rifkin, J. (2000) *The Age of Access: How the Shift from Ownership to Access is Transforming Modern Life*, Harmondsworth: Penguin.

Rifkin, J. (2004) *The European Dream: How Europe's Vision of the Future is quietly Eclipsing the American Dream*, Cambridge: Polity.

Rigby, A. (1976) *Communes in Britain*, London: Routledge.

Ritzer, G. (1993) *The McDonaldization of Society: An Investigation into the Changing Character of Contemporary Social Life*, London: Sage.

Ritzer, G. (1995) *Expressing America: A Critique of the Global Credit Card Society*, Thousand Oaks, CA: Pine Forge Press.

Ritzer, G. (1998) *The McDonaldization Thesis: Explorations and Extensions*, London: Sage.

Ritzer, G. (1999) 'Assessing the resistance', in B. Smart (ed.) *Resisting McDonaldization*, London: Sage.

Roberts, B. (1989) 'Employment structure, life cycle and life chances: Formal and informal sectors in Guadalajara', in A. Portes, M. Castells and L. Benton (eds) *The Informal Economy: Comparative Studies in Advanced and Third World Countries*, Baltimore: John Hopkins Press.

Roberts, B. (1990) 'The informal sector in comparative perspective', in M. Estellie Smith (ed.) *Perspectives on the Informal Economy*, New York: University Press of America.

Roberts, P. (2005) 'Wealth from waste: Local and regional economic development and the environment', *Geographical Journal*, 170, 2: 126–34.

Robertson, J. (1981) 'The future of work: Some thoughts about the roles of men and women in the transition to a SHE future', *Women's Studies International Quarterly*, 4: 83–94.

Robertson, J. (1985) *Future Work: Jobs, Self-employment and Leisure After the Industrial Age*, Aldershot: Gower/Temple Smith.

Robertson, J. (1991) *Future Wealth: A New Economics for the 21st Century*, London: Cassells.

Robertson, J. (1998) *Beyond the Dependency Culture: People, Power and Responsibility*, London: Adamantine.

Robinson, J. and Godbey, G. (1997) *Time for Life: The Surprising Ways Americans Use Their Time*, Pennsylvania: Pennsylvania State University Press.

Robinson, P. (1998) 'Employment and social inclusion', in C. Oppenheim (ed.) *An Inclusive Society: Strategies for Tackling Poverty*, London: IPPR.

Rodgers, D. (2001) 'Housing co-operatives and social exclusion', in J. Birchall (ed.) *The New Mutualism in Public Policy*, London: Routledge.

Roethlisberger, F.J. and Dickson, W.J. (1939) *Management and the Worker*, Cambridge, MA: Harvard University Press.

Rosanvallon, P. (1980) 'Le developpement de l'economie souterraine et l'avenir des societe industrielles', *Le Debat*, 2: 8–23.

Rose, M. (1991) *The Post-Modern and the Post-Industrial*, Cambridge: Cambridge University Press.

Rose, N. (1990) *Governing the Soul: The Shaping of the Private Self*, London: Routledge.

Rose, N. (1999) *Powers of Freedom: Reframing Political Thought*, Cambridge: Cambridge University Press.

Rose, R. and Haerpfer, C.W. (1992) *Between State and Market*, Strathclyde: Centre for the Study of Public Policy, University of Strathclyde.

Roseland, M. (ed.) (1998) *Towards Sustainable Communities: Resources for Citizens and Their Governments*, Stony Creek, CT: New Society Publishers.

Ross, A. (2004) *Low Pay High Profile: The Global Push for Fair Labor*, London: The New Press.

Ross, R.J.S. (2004) *Slaves to Fashion: Poverty and Abuse in the New Sweatshops*, Ann Arbor: University of Michigan Press.

Rostow, W.J. (1960) *The Stages of Economic Growth: A Non-communist Manifesto*, Cambridge: Cambridge University Press.

Rowell, A. (2002) 'The spread of greenwash', in Lubbers, E. (ed.) *Battling Big Business: Countering Greenwash, Infiltration and Other Forms of Corporate Bullying*, Dartington: Green Books.

Roy, C. (1991) 'Les emplois du temps dans quelques pays occidentaux', *Donnes Sociales*, 2: 223–5.

Rupert, G. (1992) 'Employing the New Age: Training seminars', in J. Lewis and J.J.G. Melton (eds) *Perspectives on the New Age*, Albany, NY: State University of New York Press.

Rustin, M. (1989) 'The politics of post-Fordism: or, the trouble with "New Times"', *New Left Review*, 175: 54–77.

Rustin, M. (2003) 'Empire: A postmodern theory of revolution', in G. Balakrishnan (ed.) *Debating Empire*, London: Verso.

Ruston, D. (2003) *Volunteers, Helpers and Socialisers: Social Capital and Time Use*, London: Office of National Statistics.

Sabel, C. (1982) *Work and Politics: The Division of Labour in Industry*, Cambridge: Cambridge University Press.

Sabel, C. (1994) 'Flexible specialisation and the re-emeregnce of regional economies', in A, Amin (ed.) *Post-fordism: A Reader*, Oxford: Blackwell.

Sachs, I. (1984) *Development and Planning*, Cambridge: Cambridge University Press.

Sachs, W. (1992) 'Introduction', in W. Sachs (ed.) *The Development Dictionary*, London: Zed.

Salamon, L.M. and Anheier, H.K. (1999) *The Emerging Sector Revisited: A Summary, Revised Estimates*, Baltimore, MD: Center for Civil Society Studies.

Salamon, L.M., Anheier, H.K., List, R., Toepler, S. and Wojcieck Sokolowoski, S. (1999) *Global Civil Society: Dimensions of the Nonprofit Sector*, Baltimore: Center for Civil Society Studies.

Samers, M. (2005) 'The myopia of "diverse economies", or a critique of the "informal economy"', *Antipode*, 37, 5: 875–86.

Sargisson, L. and Sargent, L.T. (2004) *Living in Utopia: New Zealand's Intentional Communities*, Aldershot: Ashgate.

Sassen, S. (1989) 'New York City's informal economy', in A. Portes, M. Castells and L.A. Benton (eds) *The Informal Economy: Studies in Advanced and Less Developing Countries*, Baltimore: John Hopkins University Press.

Sassen, S. (1991) *The Global City: New York, London, Tokyo*, Princeton: Princeton University Press.

Sassen, S. (1997) *Informalisation in Advanced Market Economies*, Issues in Development Discussion Paper 20, Geneva: International Labour Office.

Sauvy, A. (1984) *Le Travail Noir et l'Economie de Demain*, Paris: Calmann-Levy.

Sayer, A. (2001) 'For a critical cultural economy', *Antipode* 33, 4: 687–708.

Scharmer, C.O. (2001) 'Self-transcending knowledge: Organising around emerging realities', in I. Nonaka and D. Teece (eds) *Managing Industrial Knowledge: Creation, Transfer and Utilization*, London: Sage.

Schoenberger, E. (1998) 'Discourse and practice in human geography', *Progress in Human Geography*, 22: 1–14.

Schor, J. (1991) *The Overworked American: The Unexpected Decline of Leisure*, New York: Basic Books.

Schor, J. (1996) 'Work, time and leisure in the USA', in C. Gratton (ed.) *Work, Leisure and the Quality of Life: A Global Perspetive*, Sheffield: Leisure Industries Research Centre.

Schor, J. (2000) 'A new politics of consumption', in I. Cohen and J. Rogers (eds) *Do Americans Shop Too Much?* Boston: Beacon Press.

Schroeder, R.F.H. (2002) 'Talente Tauschring Hannover (TTH): Experiences of a Greman LETS and the relevance of theoretical reflections', *International Journal of Community Currency Research*, 6 (http://www.le.ac.uk/ulmc/ijccr).

Schroeder, R.F.H. (2006) 'Community currencies in Germany', *International Journal of Community Currency Research*, 10 (http://www.le.ac.uk/ulmc/ijccr).

Schumacher, E.F. (1973) *Small is Beautiful*, London: Blond and Briggs.

Scott, A.J. (2001) 'Capitalism, cities and the production of symbolic forms', *Transactions of the Institute of British Geographers*, NS 26: 11–23.

Seabrook, J. (2003) *The No-Nonsense Guide to World Poverty*, London: Verso.

Seabrook, J. (2004) *Consuming Cultures: Globalization and Local Lives*, Oxford: New Internationalist Publications.

Semler, R. (2003) *The Seven-Day Weekend: A Better Way to Work in the 21st century*, London: Arrow Books.

Senge, P.M. (1999) *The Fifth Discipline: The Age and Practice of the Learning Organization*, London: Century Business.

Sewell, G. (1998) 'The discipline of teams: The control of team-based industrial work through electronic and peer suveillance', *Administrative Science Quarterly*, 43: 397–428.

Sewell, G. and Wilkinson, B. (1992) ' "Someone to watch over me": surveillance, discipline and the just-in-time labour process', *Sociology* 26, 2: 271–89.

Seyfang, G. (1997) 'Examining local currency systems: A social audit approach', *International Journal of Community Currency Research*, 1 (http://www.le.ac.uk/ulmc/ijccr).

Seyfang, G. (2002) 'Tackling social exclusion with community currencies: From LETS to time banks', *International Journal of Community Currency Research*, 6 (http://www.le.ac.uk/ulmc/ijccr).

Seyfang, G. and Smith, K. (2002) *The Time of Our Lives: Using Time Banking for Neighbourhood Renewal and Community Capacity Building*, London: New Economics Foundation.

Sharpe, B. (1988) 'Informal work and development in the west', *Progress in Human Geography*, 12, 3: 315–36.

Shipman, A. (2002) *The Globalization Myth*, London: Icon.

Shiva, V. (2001) 'Globalization and Poverty', in V. Bennholdt-Thomsen, N. Faraclas and C. von Werlhof (eds) *There is an Alternative: Subsistence and Worldwide Resistance to Corporate Globalization*, London: Zed.

Shuman, M.A. (1998) *Going Local: Creating Self-reliant Communities in a Global Age*, New York: Free Press.

Shurmar-Smith, P. and Hannam, K. (1994) *Worlds of Desire, Realms of Power: A Cultural Geography*, London: Arnold.

Sik, E. (1993) 'From the second economy to the informal economy', *Journal of Public Policy*, 12, 2: 153–75.

Sik, E. (1994) 'From the multicoloured to the black and white economy: The Hungarian second economy and the transformation', *Urban Studies*, 31, 1: 47–70.

Silburn, R., Lucas, D., Page, R. and Hanna, L. (1999) *Neighbourhood Images in Nottingham: Social Cohesion and Neighbourhood Change*, York: York Publishing Services.

Silver, J. (1987) 'The ideology of excellence: Mangement and neo-conservatism', *Studies in Political Economy*, 24: 105–29.

Simons, T. and Ingram, P. (2003) 'Enemies of the state: The interdependence of institutional forms and the ecology of the kibbutz, 1910–1997', *Administrative Science Quarterly*, 48: 592–621.

Simpson, L. (1999) *Working from the Heart: A Practical Guide to Loving What You Do for a Living*, London: Vermillion.

Singh, K. (2000) *Taming Global Financial Flows: Challenges and Alternatives in the Era of Financial Globalization – A Citizen's Guide*, London: Zed.

Skolimowski, H. (1981) *Eco-Philosophy: Designing New Tactics for Living*, London: Marion Boyars.

Slater, D. and Tonkiss, F. (2001) *Market Society: Markets and Modern Social Theory*, Cambridge: Polity.

Small Business Council (2004) *Small Businesses in the Informal Economy*, London: Small Business Council.

Small Business Service (2005) *A Survey of Social Entreprises across the UK*, London: SBS (www.sbs.gov.uk).

Smart, B. (1999) (ed.) *Resisting McDonaldization*, London: Sage.

Smiles, S. (1996) *Self-Help: With Illustrations of Conduct and Perseverance*, London: Institute of Economic Affairs.

Smith, A. (2002a) 'Culture/economy and spaces of economic practice: Positioning households in post-communism', *Transactions of the Institute of British Geographers*, 27, 2: 232–50.

Smith, A. (2002b) 'Rethinking "survival" in austerity: Economic practices and household economies in Slovakia', in A. Rainnie, A. Smith and A. Swain (eds) *Work, Employment and Transition: Restructuring Livelihoods in Post-communism*, London: Routledge.

Smith, D.M. (2000) 'Marxian economics', in R.J. Johnston, D. Gregory, G. Pratt and M. Watts (eds) *The Dictionary of Human Geography*, Oxford: Blackwell.

Smith, J. (2001) 'Globalizing resistance: The battle of Seattle and the future of social movements', *Mobilization: An International Journal*, 6, 1: 1–20.

Smith, M.K. (2003) 'Communities of practice'. *Encyclopaedia of Informal Education* (www.infed.org/biblio/communities_of_practice.htm).

Smith, P. and Kearney, L. (1994) *Creating Workplaces Where People Can Think*, San Francisco: Jossey-Bass.

Social Exclusion Unit (1998) *Bringing Britain Together: A National Strategy for Neighbourhood Renewal*, Cm4045, London: HMSO.

Social Exclusion Unit (2000) *National Strategy for Neighbourhood Renewal: A Framework for Consultation*, London: The Stationary Office.

Solomon, L.D. (1996) *Rethinking our Centralized Monetary System: The Case for a System of Local Currencies*, Westport, CT: Praeger.

Sorge, A., Hartmann, G., Warner, M. and Nicholas, I. (1983) *Microelectronics and Manpower in Manufacturing*, Aldershot: Gower.

Stanworth, C. (1997) 'Telework and the information age', *New Technology, Work and Employment*, 13, 1: 51–62.

Starr, A. (2001) *Naming the Enemy: Anti-corporate Movements Confront Globalization*, London: Zed.

Steijn, B. (2004) 'ICT, organisations and labour in the information society', in P. Littlewood, I. Glorieux, and I. Jönsson (eds) *The Future of Work in Europe*, Aldershot: Ashgate.

Steingard, D.S. and Fitzgibbons, D.E. (1993) 'A postmodern deconstruction of total quality management (TQM)', *Journal of Organisational Change Management*, 6, 5: 27–42.

Stephenson, C. (1996) 'The different experiences of trade unionism in two Japanese plants', in P. Ackers, C. Smith and P. Smith (eds) *The New Workplace and Trade Unionism*, London: Routldge.

Stewart, T.A. (2003) *The Wealth of Knowledge: Intellectual Capital and the Twenty-first Century Organization*, London: Nicholas Brealey.

Stoleru, L. (1982) *La France a Deux Vitesses*, Paris: Flammarion.

Stonier, T. (1983) *The Wealth of Information: A Profile of the Post-industrial Economy*, London: Methuen.

Stulz, R.M. (1999) 'International portfolio flows and security markets', in M. Feldstein (ed.) *International Capital Flows*, Chicago, IL: University of Chicago Press.

Stulz, R.M. (2005) 'The limits of financial globalization', *Journal of Finance*, LX, 4: 1595–638.

Sue, R. (1995) *Temps et Ordre Social*, Paris: PUF.

Taris, J. (2004) *LETS Groups around the World*, http://www.lets-linkup.com.

Taylor, F.W. (1911a) *The Principles of Scientific Management*, New York: Harper.

Taylor, F.W. (1911b) *Shop Management*, New York: Harper.

Taylor, P. and Bain, P. (1998) 'An assembly line in the head: The call centre labour process', *Industrial Relations Journal*, 30, 2: 101–7.

Taylor, R. (2002a) *Britain's World of Work: Myths and Realities*, Leeds: ESRC Future of Work Programme, Leeds University.

Taylor, R. (2002b) *The Future of Work-Life Balance*, Leeds: ESRC Future of Work Research Programme, Leeds University.

Thackray, J. (1993) 'Fads, fixes and fictions', *Management Today*, June.

Thompson, G. (2000) 'Economic globalisation?', in D. Held (ed.) *A Globalising World? Culture, Economics and Politics*, London: Routledge.

Thompson, G., Frances, J., Lavacic, R. and Mitchell, J. (eds) (1991) *Markets, Hierarchies and Networks*, London: Sage.

Thompson, P. (1993) 'Fatal distraction: Postmodernism and organization theory', in J. Hassard and M. Parker (eds) *Postmodernism and Organizations*, London: Sage.

Thompson, P. and Alvesson, M. (2005) 'Bureacracy at work: Misunderstandings and mixed blessings', in P. du Gay (ed.) *The Values of Bureaucracy*, Oxford: Oxford University Press.

Thompson, P. and Findlay, T. (1999) 'Changing the people: Social engineering in the contemporary workplace', in A. Sayer and L. Ray (eds) *Culture and Economy after the Cultural Turn*, London: Sage.

Thompson, P. and McHugh, P. (2002) *Work Organisations: A Critical Introduction* (3rd edn), Basingstoke: Palgrave Macmillan.

Thompson, P. and Warhurst, C. (1998) (eds) *Workplaces of the Future*, Basingstoke: Macmillan.

Thorne, L. (1996) 'Local exchange trading systems in the United Kingdom: A case of re-embedding?', *Environment and Planning A*, 28: 1361–76.

Thrift, N.J. (2000) 'Commodities', in R.J. Johnston, D. Gregory, G. Pratt and M. Watts (eds) *The Dictionary of Human Geography*, Oxford: Blackwell.

Thrift, N.J. (2005) *Knowing Capitalism*, London: Sage.

Thurow, L. (2000) *Creating Wealth: The New Rules for Individuals, Companies and Countries in a Knowledge-based Economy*, London: Nicholas Brealey.

Tickell, A. (2001) 'Progress in the geography of services II: Services, the state and the rearticulation of capitalism', *Progress in Human Geography*, 25, 2: 283–92.

Tievant, S. (1982) 'Vivre autrement: echanges et sociabilite en ville nouvelle', *Cahiers de l'OCS*, Vol. 6, Paris: CNRS.

Time Banks UK (2005) '*Welcome to TBUK*', http://www.timebanks.co.uk.

Time Dollar Institute (2005) '*Time dollar directory*', http://www.timedollar.org/r_td_directory.htm.

Toffler, A. (1970) *Future Shock*, New York: Random House.

Toffler, A. (1981) *The Third Wave*, London: Bantam.

Tokman, V.E. (1978) 'An exploration into the nature of informal–formal sector relationships: The case of Santiago', *World Development*, 6: 1065–75.

Tokman, V.E. (1986) 'Adjustment and employment in Latin America: The current challenges', *International Labour Review*, 125, 5: 533–43.

Tomaney, J. (1990) 'The reality of workplace flexibility', *Capital and Class*, 40: 29–60.

Tomaney, J. (1994) 'A new paradigm of work organisation and technology', in A. Amin (ed.) *Post-Fordism: A Reader*, Oxford: Blackwell.

Torgerson, D. (2001) 'Rethinking politics for a green economy: A political approach to radical reform', *Social Policy and Administration*, 35, 5: 472–89.

Tormey, S. (2004) *Anti-Capitalism: A Beginner's Guide*, Oxford: Oneworld Publications.

Touraine, A. (1974) *The Post-Industrial Society*, London: Wildwood House.

Townley, B. (1993) 'Foucault, power/knowledge and its relevance for human resource management', *The Academy of Management Review*, 18, 3: 518–45.

Townley, B. (1994) *Reframing Human Resource Management*, London: Sage.

Townsend, A.R. (1997) *Making a Living in Europe: Human Geographies of Economic Change*, London: Routledge.

Trainer, T. (1996) *Towards a Sustainable Economy: The Need for Fundamental Change*, Oxford: Jon Carpenter.

Tsoukas, H. and Cummings, S. (1997) 'Marginalisation and recovery: The emergence of Aristotelian themes in organisation studies', *Organization Studies*, 18, 4: 655–83.

Turner, G. and Myerson, J. (1998) *New Workspace, New Culture*, London: Design Council/Gower.

Unger, R. (1987) *Social Theory: Its Situation and Its Task*, Cambridge: Cambridge University Press.

Van Eck, R. and Kazemeier, B. (1985) *Swarte Inkomsten uit Arbeid: resultaten van in 1983 gehouden experimentele*, Den Haag: CBS-Statistische Katernen nr 3, Central Bureau of Statistics.

Van Geuns, R., Mevissen, J. and Renooy, P.H. (1987) 'The spatial and sectoral diversity of the informal economy', *Tijdschrift voor Economische en Sociale Geografie*, 78, 5: 389–98.

Van Maanen, J. (1991) 'The smile factory: Work at Disneyland', in P.J. Frost, L.F. Moore, M.R. Louis, C.C. Lundberg and J. Martin (eds) *Reframing Organisational Culture*, London: Sage.

Van Maanen, J. and Kunda, G. (1989) ' "Real feelings": Emotional expressions and organisational culture', in L.L. Cummings and B.N. Straw (eds) *Research in Organisational Behaviour*, Vol. 11, Greenwich, CT: JAI Press.

Van Parijis, P. (1995) *Real Freedom for All: What (if anything) is Wrong with Capitalism?*, Oxford: Oxford University Press.

Van Parijis, P. (1996a) 'Basic income and the two dilemmas of the welfare state', *The Political Quarterly*, 67, 1: 57–8.

Van Parijis, P. (1996b) 'L'allocation universelle contre le chomage: de la trappe au sociale', *Revue Francaise des Affaires Sociales*, 50, 1: 111–25.

Van Parijis, P. (2000a) *Basic Income: Guaranteed Income for the XXIst Century?*, Barcelona: Fundació Rafael Campalans.

Van Parijis, P. (2000b) 'Basic income and the two dilemmas of the welfare state', in C. Pierson and F.G. Castles (eds) *The Welfare State: A Reader*, Cambridge: Polity.

Van Trier, W. (1995) *Every One a King*, PhD dissertation, Leuven: University of Leuven, Department of Sociology.

Vann, K. and Bowker, G.C. (2004) 'Instrumentalizing the truth of practice', in A. Amin and N. Thrift (eds) *The Blackwell Cultural Economy Reader*, Oxford: Blackwell.

Verschave, F.-X. (1996) 'The House that Braudel built: Rethinking the architecture of society', in OECD (ed.) *Reconciling Economy and Society: Towards a Plural Economy*, Paris: OECD.

Waddington, J. and Whitston, C. (1996) 'Empowerment versus intensification: Union perspectives of change in the workplace', in P. Ackers, C. Smith and P. Smith (eds) *The New Workplace and Trade Unionism*, London: Routledge.

Waddock, S. and Bodwell, C. (2002) 'From TQM to TRM: Total responsbility management approaches', *Journal of Corporate Citizenship*, 7: 113–26.

Wade, R. (1996) 'Globalization and its limits: Reports of the death of the national economy are greatly exaggerated', in S. Berger and R. Dore (eds) *National Diversity and Global Capitalism*, Ithaca, NY: Cornell University Press.

Wallace, C. and Haerpfer, C. (2002) 'Patterns of participation in the informal economy in East-Central Europe', in R. Neef and M. Stanculescu (eds) *The Social Impact of Informal Economies in Eastern Europe*, Aldershot: Ashgate.

Wallace, C., Haerpfer, C. and Latcheva, R. (2004) *The Informal Economy in East-Central Europe 1991–1998*, Vienna: Institute for Advanced Studies.

Warburton, D. (1998) *Community and Sustainable Development: Participation in the Future*, London: Earthscan.

Warburton, P. (1999) *Debt and Delusion*, Harmondsworth: Penguin.

Ward, C. (2004) *Anarchism: A Very Short Introduction*, Oxford: Oxford University Press.

Warde, A. (1990) 'Household work strategies and forms of labour: Conceptual and empirical issues', *Work, Employment and Society*, 4, 4: 495–515.

Warf, B. (1999) 'The hypermobility of capital and the collapse of the Keynesian state', in R. Martin (ed.) *Money and the Space Economy*, London: Wiley.

Warhurst, C. (1998) 'Recognizing the possible: The organization and control of a socialist labour process', *Administrative Science Quarterly*, 43: 470–97.

Warhurst, C. and Thompson, P. (1998) 'Hands, hearts and minds: Changing work and workers at the end of the century', in P. Thompson and C. Warhurst (eds) *Workplaces of the Future*, Basingstoke: Palgrave.

Warren, M.R. (1994) 'Exploitation or co-operation? The political basis of regional variation in the Italian informal economy', *Politics and Society*, 22, 1: 89–115.

Watson, T.J. (2001) *In Search of Management: Culture, Chaos and Control in Managerial Work*, Harlow: Prentice Hall.

Watson, T.J. (2003) *Sociology, Work and Industry* (4th edn), London: Routledge.

Watts, M. (1999) 'Commodities', in P. Cloke, P. Crang and M. Goodwin (eds) *Introducing Human Geographies*, London: Arnold.

Weber, M. (1978) *Economy and Society: An Outline of Interpretive Sociology*, Berkeley, CA: University of California Press.

Webster, F. (1995) *Theories of the Information Society*, London: Routledge.

Webster, F. and Robbins, K. (1993) ' "I'll be watching you": Comment on Sewell and Wilkinson', *Sociology*, 27: 243–52.

Weiss, J.M. (1994) 'Telecommuting boosts employee output', *HR Magazine*, 39, 2: 51–4.

Wenger, E. (1998) *Communities of Practice: Learning, Meaning and Identity*, Cambridge: Cambridge University Press.

Wenger, E., McDermott, R. and Snyder, O. (2002) *Cultivating Communities of Practice*, Boston: Harvard Business School Press.

Wheen, F. (2004) *How Mumbo-Jumbo Conquered the World*, London: Harper Perennial.

Whitaker, A. (1992) 'The transformation in work: Post-Fordism revisited', in M. Reed and M. Hughes (eds) *Rethinking Organisation: New Directions in Organisational Theory and Analysis*, London: Sage.

White, M., Hill, S., Mills, C. and Smeaton, D. (2004) *Managing to Change? British Workplaces and the Future of Work*, Basingstoke: Palgrave Macmillan.

Whitefield, P. (2000) *Permaculture in a Nutshell* (3rd edn), East Meon, Hampshire: Permanent Publications.

Whitley, R. (ed.) (2002) *Competing Capitalisms: Institutions and Economies*, Aldershot: Edward Elgar.

Whyte, W.F. and Whyte, K.K. (1991) *Making Mondragon: The Growth and Dynamics of the Worker Co-operative Complex* (revised 2nd edn), Ithaca, NY: ILR Press.

Whyte, W.H. (1956) *The Organisation Man*, New York: Simon and Schuster.

Wilkinson, A. (1992) 'The other side of quality: Soft issues and the human resource dimension', *Total Quality Management*, 3, 3: 323–9.

Wilkinson, A. and Willmott, H. (1994) 'Introduction', in A. Wilkinson and H. Wilmott (eds) *Making Quality Critical: New Perspectices on Organisational Change*, London: Routledge and Kegan Paul.

Willcocks, L. and Grint, K. (1997) 'Re-inventing the organization? Towards a critique of business proecess re-engineering', in I. McLoughlin and M. Harris (eds) *Innovation, Organisational Change and Technology*, London: International Thomson Business Press.

Williams, C.C. (1996a) 'An appraisal of Local Exchange and Trading Systems (LETS) in the United Kingdom', *Local Economy*, 11, 3: 275–82.

Williams, C.C. (1996b) 'Informal sector responses to unemployment: An evaluation of the potential of Local Exchange and Trading Systems (LETS)', *Work, Employment and Society*, 10, 2: 341–59.

Williams, C.C. (1996c) 'Local currencies and community development: An evaluation of green dollar exchanges in New Zealand', *Community Development Journal*, 31, 4: 319–29.

Williams, C.C. (1996d) 'Local Exchange and Trading Systems (LETS): A new source of work and credit for the poor and unemployed?', *Environment and Planning A*, 28, 8: 1395–415.

Williams, C.C. (1996e) 'Local purchasing and rural development: An evaluation of Local Exchange and Trading Systems (LETS)', *Journal of Rural Studies*, 12, 3: 231–44.

Williams, C.C. (1996f) 'The new barter economy: An appraisal of Local Exchange and Trading Systems (LETS)', *Journal of Public Policy*, 16, 1: 55–71.

Williams, C.C. (1997) 'Local Exchange and Trading Systems (LETS) in Australia: A new tool for community development?', *International Journal of Community Currencies Research*, 1 (www.le.ac.uk/ulmc/ijccr).

Williams, C.C. (2002a) 'A critical evaluation of the commodification thesis', *The Sociological Review*, 50, 4: 525–42.

Williams, C.C. (2002b) 'Beyond the commodity economy: The persistence of informal economic activity in rural England', *Geografiska Annaler B*, 83, 4: 221–33.

Williams, C.C. (2003a) 'Evaluating the penetration of the commodity economy', *Futures*, 35: 857–68.

Williams, C.C. (2003b) 'Developing community involvement: Contrasting local and regional participatory cultures in Britain and their implications for policy', *Regional Studies*, 37, 5: 531–41.

Williams, C.C. (2004a) *Cash-in-hand work: The underground sector and hidden economy of favours*, Basingstoke: Palgrave Macmillan.

Williams, C.C. (2004b) 'Towards a commodified world? Re-reading economic development in western economies', *International Journal of Economic Development*, 6, 1: 1–21.

Williams, C.C. (2004c) 'Rethinking the "economy" and uneven development: Spatial disparities in household coping capabilities in contemporary England', *Regional Studies*, 38, 5: 507–18.

Williams, C.C. (2004d) 'A borderless world of hypermobile and homeless capital? An evaluation of financial flows in the mutual fund industry', *The Industrial Geographer*, 2, 2: 1–13.

Williams, C.C. (2004e) 'Geographical variations in the nature of undeclared work', *Geografiska Annaler B*, 86, 3: 187–200.

Williams, C.C. (2004f) 'The myth of marketization: An evaluation of the persistence of non-market activities in advanced economies', *International Sociology*, 19, 4: 437–49.

Williams, C.C. (2004g) 'Beyond commodification: Re-reading the future of work', *Foresight*, 6, 6: 329–37.

Williams, C.C. (2004h) 'Contesting the marketization thesis: Some evidence from western economies', *Futures Research Quarterly*, 20, 4: 41–58.

Williams, C.C. (2005a) *A Commodified World? Mapping the Limits of Capitalism*, London: Zed.

Williams, C.C. (2005b) 'Market delusions: Rethinking the trajectories of post-socialist societies', *Foresight*, 7, 3: 48–60.

Williams, C.C. (2005c) 'Work organization in post-socialist societies', *Futures*, 37, 10: 1145–57.

Williams, C.C. (2005d) 'The market illusion: Re-reading work in advanced economies', *International Journal of Sociology and Social Policy*, 25, 10/11: 106–18.

Williams, C.C. (2005e) 'A critical evaluation of hierarchical representations of community involvement: Some lessons from the UK', *Community Development Journal*, 40, 1: 30–8.

Williams, C.C. (2005f) 'Surviving post-socialism: Coping practices in East-Central Europe', *International Journal of Sociology and Social Policy*, 25, 9: 64–76.

Williams, C.C. and Millington, A. (2004) 'The diverse and contested meanings of sustainable development', *Geographical Journal*, 170, 2: 99–104.

Williams, C.C. and Windebank, J. (1995) 'Social polarisation of households in contemporary Britain: A "whole economy" perspective', *Regional Studies*, 29, 8: 723–32.

Williams, C.C. and Windebank, J. (1998) *Informal Employment in the Advanced Economies: Implications for Work and Welfare*, London: Routledge.

Williams, C.C. and Windebank, J. (2000a) 'Self-help and mutual aid in deprived urban neighbourhoods: Some lessons from Southampton', *Urban Studies*, 37: 127–47.

Williams, C.C. and Windebank, J. (2000b) 'Paid informal work in deprived neighborhoods', *Cities*, 17, 4: 285–91.

Williams, C.C. and Windebank, J. (2000c) 'Helping each other out? Community exchange in deprived neighbourhoods', *Community Development Journal*, 35, 2: 146–56.

Williams, C.C. and Windebank, J. (2000d) 'Helping people to help themselves: Some policy lessons from deprived urban neighbourhoods in Southampton', *Journal of Social Policy*, 29, 3: 355–73.

Williams, C.C. and Windebank, J. (2001a) *Revitalising Deprived Urban Neighbourhoods: An Assisted Self-Help Approach*, Aldershot: Ashgate.

Williams, C.C. and Windebank, J. (2001b) 'Beyond social inclusion through employment: Harnessing mutual aid as a complementary social inclusion policy', *Policy and Politics*, 29, 1: 15–28.

Williams, C.C. and Windebank, J. (2001c) 'A critical evaluation of the formalisation of work thesis: Some evidence from France', *SAIS Review*, XXI, 1: 117–22.

Williams, C.C. and Windebank, J. (2001d) 'Beyond profit-motivated exchange: Some lessons from the study of paid informal work', *European Urban and Regional Studies*, 8, 1: 49–61.

Williams, C.C. and Windebank, J. (2001e) 'Paid informal work in deprived urban neighbourhoods: Exploitative employment or co-operative self-help?', *Growth and Change*, 32, 4: 562–71.

Williams, C.C. and Windebank, J. (2001f) 'Paid informal work: A barrier to social inclusion?', *Transfer: Journal of the European Trade Union Institute*, 7, 1: 25–40.

Williams, C.C. and Windebank, J. (2001g) 'Reconceptualising paid informal exchange: Some lessons from English cities', *Environment and Planning A*, 33, 1: 121–40.

Williams, C.C. and Windebank, J. (2001h) 'Acquiring goods and services in lower-income populations: An evaluation of consumer behaviour and preferences', *The International Journal of Retail and Distribution Management*, 29, 1: 16–24.

Williams, C.C. and Windebank, J. (2003a) *Poverty and the Third Way*, London: Routledge.

Williams, C.C. and Windebank, J. (2003b) 'The slow advance and uneven penetration of commodification', *International Journal of Urban and Regional Research*, 27, 2: 250–64.

Williams, C.C., Aldridge, T., Lee, R., Leyshon, A., Thrift, N. and Tooke, J. (2001a) *Bridges into Work? An Evaluation of Local Exchange and Trading Schemes (LETS)*, Bristol: Policy Press.

Williams, C.C., Aldridge, T., Lee, R., Leyshon, A., Thrift, N. and Tooke, J. (2001b) 'Local Exchange and Trading Schemes (LETS): A tool for community renewal?', *Community, Work and Family*, 4, 3: 355–61.

Williams, K., Cutler, T., Williams, J. and Haslam, C. (1997) 'The end of mass production', *Economy and Society*, 16: 405–39.

Williams, K., Haslam, C. and Williams, J. (1992a) 'Ford versus Fordism: The beginning of mass production?', *Work, Employment and Society*, 6, 4: 517–55.

Williams, K., Haslam, C., Williams, J., Cutler, T., Adcroft, A. and Juhal, S. (1992b) 'Against lean production', *Economy and Society*, 21, 3: 321–54.

Willmott, H. (1993) 'Strength is ignorance, slavery is freedom: Managing culture in modern organisations', *Journal of Management Studies*, 30, 4: 515–52.

Willmott, H. (1995) 'What has been happening in organisation theory and does it matter?', *Personnel Review*, 24, 8: 33–53.

Wilson, F.M. (1999) *Organisational Behaviour: A Critical Introduction*, Oxford: Oxford University Press.

Windebank, J. (1991) *The Informal Economy in France*, Aldershot: Avebury.

Winslow, C.D. and Bramer, W.L. (1994) *Future Work: Putting Knowledge to Work in the Knowledge Economy*, New York: Free Press.

Wolff, A. (1989) *Whose Keeper?*, Berkeley: University of California Press.

Wood, M. and Vamplew, C. (1999) *Neighbourhood Images in Teeside: Regeneration or Decline?*, York: York Publishing Services.

Worthington, I. (1997) *Reinventing the Workplace*, Boston: Architectural.

Wright, C. (1997) *The Sufficient Community: Putting People First*, Dartington: Green Books.

Wright, S. (2002) *Storming Heaven: Class Composition and Struggle in Italian Autonomist Marxism*, London: Pluto Press.

WTO (1995) *Annual report, 1996*, Geneva: World Trade Organization.

Wuthnow, R. (1992) *Acts of Compassion: Caring for Others and Helping Ourselves*, Princeton, NJ: Princeton University Press.

Yankelovich, D. (1995) *Young Adult Europe*, Paris: Yankelovich Monitor.

Zafirovski, M. (1999) 'Probing into the social layers of entrepreneurship: Outlines of the sociology of enterprise', *Entrepreneurship and Regional Development*, 11: 351–71.

Zelinsky, M. (1997) *New Workplaces for New Workstyles*, New York: McGraw-Hill.

Zelinsky, M. (2002) *The Inspired Workplace: Designs for Creativity and Productivity*, Gloucester, MA: Rockport.

Zelizer, V.A. (1994) *The Social Meaning of Money*, New York: Basic Books.

Zimmerman, M.E. (1987) 'Feminism, deep ecology and environmental ethics', *Environmental Ethics*, 9: 21–44.

Zohar, D. and Marshall, I. (2001) *Spiritual Intelligence: The Ultimate Intelligence*, London: Bloomsbury.

Zohar, D. and Marshall, I. (2005) *Spiritual Capital: Wealth We Can Live By*, London: Bloomsbury.

Zoll, R. (1989) *Nicht So Wie Unsere Eltern*, Oplandan: Westdeutscher Verlag.

Zuboff, S. (1988) *In the Age of the Smart Machine: The Future of Work and Power*, Oxford: Heinemann.

Index

Business process re-engineering (BPR), 160, 163, 165, 167
Business schools, 182–3, 270–1

Cadbury-Schweppes, 94
Call centres, 171
Cameroon, 55
Canada
    Americanization of, 108
    credit unions in, 192
    local exchange trading schemes in, 257–8
    neo-liberalism, 211
    time allocation, 41–2
    transnational corporations in, 93–4
    Winnebago-Itasca travellers club, 23
Canon, 94
Capitalism (*see also* Commodification)
    varieties of, 25–6
Caribbean, 108, 221
Carrefour, 95
Cash-in-hand work, *see* Informal employment
CCTV, 124
Cemex, 95
Chad, 55
Charitable contributions, 76
Chevron, 95
Chile, 57–8
China, 21, 60–1, 107, 187
Citizen's income, 122, 233–7
Civil society, *see* Informalization
Coalition for Sensible Regulation, 266
Coca Cola, 94, 105
Colombia, 58
Commercialism (*see also* Commodification)
    language of, 27
Commercialization, *see* Commodification
Commitment, 7
Commodification
    in advanced economies, 66–80
    definition of, 2–6, 19–24
    evidence of, 26–31
    gender disparities, 77–80
    majority world, 84–7
    in post-socialist societies, 80–4
    views of, 24–6, 168, 215, 241–61, 282, 287–8
Commodity frontiers, 28–9
Communes, 193–5, 274–7

Communities of interest, 22–3
Communities of practice, 164–5
Community supported agriculture, 275
Compart Spa, 94
Consumer cooperatives, 184–5
Control methods, 7, 158–60, 169–70, 172–7
Conviction capitalism, 160
Cooperative communities, 193–5, 274–7
Cooperative organizations, 184–93
Corporate culture, 163–4, 166, 168
Corporate social responsibility, 265, 270
Costa Rica, 58
Cote d'Ivoire, 55, 108
Credit card industry, 147, 171
Credit unions, 184–5, 188–9, 192–3
Cricklegrass organic farm, 276–7
Croatia, 47, 48, 50, 51
Crown Cork and Seal, 94
Cultural globalization, *see* Globalization
Culture, economization of, 25, 105–9
Customer-oriented bureaucracies, 177
Customer-supplier relationships, 22–3, 137
Cybernated economy, 122
Czech Republic, 47, 48, 50, 51, 107

Daimler-Chrysler, 95
Danon Group, 94
De-commodification, 3, 8, 241–61, 287
Deconstruction, 250
Democracy attitudes towards, 106–9
Denmark
    Christiana, 275
    employment participation rates, 39–40
    social protection, 208–9
    time allocation, 41–2
De-skilling thesis, 133–4, 138, 148, 159
Developing countries, *see* Majority world
Diageo, 94
Digital divide, 122–3
Discourse analysis, 249–50
Disney, 143
Disneyization, 143–4
Domestic outsourcing, 43–6
Domestic servants, 30, 79
Domestic work, *see* Self-provisioning
Dow Chemical, 95
Downshifting, 67, 184, 222–6, 231

Du Pont, 95
Dual economy thesis, 16
Dual society, 216, 229–31, 236

East Asia
  Americanization of, 107–8
  employment-to-population ratio, 221
  mass production, 147
  trade flows, 96–7
East-Central Europe, *see* Post-socialist
  societies
Ecocentrism, 268
Eco-feminism, 271–2
Ecological modernization, 264–5
Ecological visions, 262–81
Economic globalization, *see* Ecovillages;
  globalization
Ecovillages, 274–7
Ecuador, 58
Edison International, 96
Egypt, 108
E-lancers, 121
Electrolux, 94
Elf Aquitaine, 95
Emotional labour, 144, 162–3, 246
Employee mutuals, 238–9
Employee representation, 165
Employment
  centred ideology, 219–20, 224, 228
  flexibility of, 149–50
  participation rates, 39–41, 78, 221, 229
  quality of, 123–4
ENI Group, 95
Environmental justice, 265
Environmentalism, *see* Ecological
  visions
Ericsson, 94
Ethical consumption, 249, 265
Ethical investment funds, 192
Ethiopia, formalization, 53–4
European Union
  Americanization of, 108
  attitudes towards employment, 224
  employment participation rates, 39–40,
    207–8, 229
  not-for-profit sector, 73–4
  trade flows, 96–7
  volunteering, 70
  working poor, 222

Experimental communities, 193–5
Exxon/Mobil, 94

Fair trade, 244, 249, 265
Family-friendly working, 138, 141–2
Fiat, 95
Financial cooperatives, 192–3
Financial globalization, *see* Globalization
Financial markets, 25, 98–104
Finland
  not-for-profit sector in, 75
  social protection in, 208–9
  time allocation in, 41–2
  transnational corporations in, 94–6
First World, *see* Minority world
Flexible specialization, 131, 135
Flexible work, 131–52
Focolare movement, 196–7
Ford, 95, 148, 151
Fordism, 131–5, 145–51, 284–5, 288
Foreign Direct Investment, 93, 97–8
Formal economy, *see* Formalization
Formalization
  in advanced economies, 39–46, 215
  definition of, 12–19
  in East-Central Europe, 46–53
  in majority world, 53–65
  views of, 219–40, 283, 287
France
  Americanization of, 107
  attitudes towards employment in, 224
  distribution of informal work, 42–3
  employment participation rates in, 40
  financial markets in, 100–4
  international trade, 92
  not-for-profit sector in, 73–5
  social protection in, 208–9
  time allocation in, 41–2
  transnational corporations in, 94–6
  working-time reduction in, 232–3
Fujitsu, 95
Full-employment, 39–41, 139–40, 206–9,
  220–6
Functional flexibility, 136–7, 153

Gender disparities in work, 77–80, 198, 207,
  220–1, 225–6
Gender progress, 79
General Electric, 93–5

Total quality management, 153, 160, 162–3, 165, 166
TotalFina, 94
Toyota, 93–5, 136, 142
Trade unions, 148, 238–9
Transition economies, *see* Post-socialist societies
Transnational corporations, 93–6
Tunisia, 55
Turkey, 54, 107

Uganda, 108
Ukraine, 47, 48, 50, 51, 107
Underground economy, *see* Informal employment
Unilever, 94
United Airlines, 191
United Kingdom
  Americanization of, 107
  attitudes towards employment in, 224, 225
  credit unions in, 192
  distribution of informal work, 42, 43–6
  employee mutuals, 238–9
  employment participation rates in, 40, 78
  financial markets in, 99–104
  flexible work practices in, 149–50
  ICT in, 126–7
  international trade, 92
  neo-liberalism, 211
  New Deal in, 236–7
  New Labour, 214–16
  not-for-profit sector, 73–5
  organizational commitment in, 176–7
  organizational cultures in, 174–5
  self-provisioning in, 68
  social entrepreneurship in, 184
  time allocation in, 41–2
  time banks in, 258–9
  transnational corporations in, 93–6
  volunteering in, 70
  worker co-operatives in, 185
United Parcel Services, 191
Unpaid exchange
  advanced economies 69, 70, 71
  definition of, 15
  in England, 43, 44, 45, 46
  in post-socialist societies, 46–52, 81–4
Upskilling thesis, 121, 148

USA
  attitudes towards employment, 225
  back-to-the-land, 67
  bureaucratic management in, 171
  credit unions in, 192
  cultural globalization, 105–9
  distribution of informal work, 43
  employment participation rates in, 40
  financial markets in, 99–104
  flexible work in, 149–50
  Focolare movement, 196, 197
  hours schemes, 259, 260
  international trade, 92
  knowledge workers in, 124, 128
  neo-liberalism, 211
  New Deal, 236–7
  not-for-profit sector in, 73, 74, 75
  recreational vehicle industry in, 23
  skill polarization in, 148
  theming consumption in, 143
  time allocation in, 41, 42
  time dollars in, 258, 259
  trade flows, 96, 97
  transnational corporations, 94, 95, 96
  volunteering, 69
  Winnebago-Itasca travellers club, 23
Usinor, 95
Uzbekistan, 107

Vassalage, 141–2
Veba Group, 95
Venezuela, Americanization of, 108
Viag, 95
Vietnam, 107
Virtualism, 17
Vivendi, 95
Volkswagen Group, 93, 94, 95
Voluntary simplicity, 277
Volunteering, 15, 69, 70, 71, 214, 215
Volvo, 94

Wal-Mart, 96
Washington consensus, 31
Weber, Max, 154–5
Western world, *see* Minority world
Westernization, 105–9
Willing slaves, 158, 179
Winnebago-Itasca travellers club, 23
Work, definition of, 14